The Family Structure in Islam

Hammūdah 'Abd al 'Āṭī

The Family Structure in Islam

Hammūdah 'Abd al 'Atī

PREFACE

Since this study largely relies on the classical, original sources, it makes constant reference to Arabic works not available in English. To translate the titles of these sources would be of little use to most readers. Similarly, adherence to any standard system of citation would be equally unhelpful, because of the complicated, often ambiguous forms of titles, publishers, places of publication, and other bibliographical data. I have therefore adopted a method of footnoting and transliteration that should be both adequate for the use of scholars familiar with Arabic and intelligible to the non-specialist. A separate section at the end of the text contains expanded comments and specific citations of the sources which are fully listed in the concluding Bibliography. When two or more works by the same author or editor are included, each is given a number (1, 2, 3, etc.). References in the notes will include only the author's name, the number of the work, the volume (if multiple), and page numbers. It is hoped that this abbreviated form will facilitate identification of relevant documentation.

The transliteration has presented another type of difficulty. Islamic concepts, Arabic names, and book titles are given different English spellings by different authors. This is confusing enough, but the difficulty is aggravated when there are direct quotations from these sources. Nothing can be done about what is already in print; when reproduced here, such passages will appear as they are printed in the original. In all other cases, however, I have adopted a standardized system of transliteration. For the Arabic letters and sounds which have no exact equivalents in the English alphabet, the approximations outlined below will be used as closely as possible.

1. The macron will indicate long vowels:
 ā = long *a*, as in *sand* and *hall;*
 ī = long *i*, as *ee* in *feel;*
 ū = long *u*, as *oo* in *tooth.*

i

2. The dot is used under certain "emphatic" letters pronounced with the tongue raised toward the palate:

d = roughly as d in mud;

s = as s in *sun;*

t = as t in *lot;*

z = a strong emphatic sound with no English
    equivalent;

h = a guttural h slightly stronger than h.

hamza = a glottal stop, as in the cockney *li'l bo'ls;*

'ain = a guttural sound, with no English equivalent;

dh = as *th* in *this;*

gh = a strong guttural g;

Kh = as *ch* in Scottish *loch;*

q = a guttural k, pronounced far back in the throat;

sh = as in *ship;*

th = as *th* in *think.*

For a fuller description of the transliteration system, see,
for example, Bernard Lewis, *The Arabs in History*, p. 8. Also
consult "Rules for Transliteration from Arabic to English",
adopted by the Association of Muslim Social Scientists.

ACKNOWLEDGMENTS

This study is only the first part of a projected analytical survey of the development of Islamic institutions. It lays the historical and conceptual foundations for more systematic studies in contemporary Muslim life. Whether one wishes to examine the differences between the Muslim scene now and in the classical formative period, or the discrepancy between the ideal conception of Islamic law and its application, or the comparisons and contrasts among various regions of the Muslim world, one can find a point of departure in this volume.

Acknowledgments here are more than a decorative ritual. The completion of this work was made possible in the first place by the generous aid of Princeton University and the Rockefeller Foundation. Professor Morroe Berger of the Sociology Department and Chairman of the Council on International and Regional Studies at Princeton has been helpful in many capacities. Professor Eugene Nassar of the English Department at Utica College of Syracuse University has been kind enough to read the manuscript and to make constructive suggestions. Other editorial revisions were contributed by Professor A. Leland Jamison of the Department of Religion, Syracuse University. To these scholars and institutions I am indebted, a debt which one acknowledges with both delight and pride.

Hammūdah 'Abd al 'Atī, Utica College

*****

The American Trust Publications acknowledges the help of Imam Muḥammad bin Saud University, Riyadh, Saudi Arabia, which placed a pre-publication order for this book.

Proofreading was done by Dr. Kaukab Siddique, Dr. Erdogan Gurmen, Dr. Eugene Paul Nassar and the author himself. In fact one of the last acts of Dr. Hammūdah 'Abd al 'Ati, before he died on September 19, 1976, was the completion of proofreading of this book over which he took great pains. May God fill his grave with light.

CONTENTS

Preface

Foreword by Prof. Morroe Berger

Foreword

The scholarly world is fortunate to have this cogent study by Dr. Hammūdah 'Abd al 'Aṭī, and I am happy to have this opportunity to introduce it and to point out some of its special virtues. In doing so, however, I will be doing the reader only a small service before he proceeds to delve into the study, for its many virtues are evident merely in the reading.

Dr. 'Abd al 'Aṭī deals with a wide array of topics touching on religion, set roles and the family, law, and social change. These are basic, sensitive issues in the structure of social life; they arouse the strongest feelings among people. The author approaches these disputed questions with very high qualifications: a deep, personal familiarity with Islām and a scholar's knowledge of it as well as of modern social science. He is thus able to combine sympathy and objectivity to produce understanding.

After an education in the school system of al Azhar, the world's center of Islāmic learning in Cairo, Dr. 'Abd al 'Aṭī pursued his studies in Canada and the United States. He thus added to the rigorous training of a venerable religious system, a thorough grounding in Western Orientalist and social science approaches.

This book is a departure from recent emphases on economic development and Arab nationalism. Dr. 'Abd al 'Aṭī goes deeper into the history and social institutions of the Islāmic world by considering how religious inspiration, law and social conditions during the first four centuries of Islām together shaped ideas about what the family system of Muslims should become. He deals with formative institutions in the time of their own formation. He shows that social conditions outside the religious system did not fix the ideas of Muslims about the family, though these conditions did set certain boundaries within which those ideas developed. If the author had stayed within religious conceptions, there would be nothing to add to the subject except a further treatment of divine precepts and Muslims' interpretation of them. Believing, however, that divine law does not eliminate human choice, he relates this law to the mode of life of the time. Dr. 'Abd al 'Aṭī might also have asked how far the Muslim prescription for family institutions was followed in reality; that question he regards as legitimate but rather difficult to illuminate in the present state of our knowledge.

Within the limits of his enquiry, the author squarely confronts the most difficult issues of scholarship and morals concerning Islām. These are, in terms of Western studies and attitudes, plural marriage, modes of divorce, social equality in mating, and "sensuousness." He not only sheds light on these old questions but asks us to contemplate why they continually arise. "Polygyny in Islām," he observes in passing, "is a subject to which every observer seems to project his own particular mind and age."

From his vast amount of research into the social order in which Islām arose, one of Dr. 'Abd al 'Aṭī's important conclusions is the diversity of morals and behavior. This view is an antidote to the easy generalizations (deteriorating into stereotypes) we have grown accustomed to in this domain. He shows, on several occasions, that certain combinations of traits attributed to certain groups are incompatible with one another. He points out that in seeking to understand ideas and events in the distant past an explanation of their origins is not necessarily an explanation of their persistence. He relates Islāmic law and Muslims' behavior to rules and conduct in other societies while still appreciating, as in the case of social equality in mating, that each society is special in relation to others (as well as diverse within itself). He follows contemporary social science, yet sees value in the work of older scholars who have raised and illuminated important questions, contributions that have not been outdated by later studies or even taken into full account by them.

Dr. 'Abd al 'Aṭī's methods, therefore, are rigorous and per-

suasive. Although his work does not settle issues, it clears away
a lot of deadwood (the result of ignorance, prejudice and inadequate scholarship) that has obstructed the path to their
settlement. With regard to dowry, for example, he shows the
weakness of several hoary explanations (including some advanced by Muslim jurists) and then offers hypotheses leading
to further inquiry that are much more promising.

At a time when the possibility and even the desirability of
objectivity in the social sciences are challenged, this book
shows its value in quality of mind and in research procedure.
Dr. 'Abd al 'Aṭī points out that Muslim apologists have compared the Islāmic ideal with Western practice, while Western
apologists (often called scholars) compare Islāmic practice
with the Western ideal. He shows that these fatuous comparisons do not proceed from scholarly motives, and his work de-
prives them of their long-standing excuses and justifications.
For that, and for his demonstration of the explanatory value
of alternative approaches based on solid social research and
clear thinking, we are in his debt.

Morroe Berger

1   INTRODUCTION

A. Presuppositions and Methodology

From the earliest periods of human history, as S. R. Reiber has remarked, "religion and the family have been intimately related. Each has an influence upon the other . . . . Neither can be fully understood apart from the other."[1] This interconnection may explain the apparent gap in conventional studies of the Muslim family structure between two unbalanced approaches: the clearly "normative-moralistic" approach, and the nonnormative, sometimes called the sociological or anthropological approach. Since the Muslim family system is based on religious principles and norms, most writers have dealt with the subject from a religious, normative point of view almost exclusively. But this approach has almost always been polaristic. There are those Muslim writers who seem disposed only to applaud the Islāmic family system, viewing it from an idealistic standpoint and mistaking what should be for what actually has been. Others seem disposed to condemn the system, as if they saw in it an aberration from some abstract universal standard of morality. Neither normative standpoint makes useful distinctions between what have been called the "ideological" and the "behavioral" components of the sociocultural world, or the "existential" and the "normative" imperative ideas. In other words, the *ideal*, the *ought-to-be* realm is confused with the *actual*, the *is* realm.[2] Implicit in both is a tinge of ethnocentrism, of self-righteousness, of determinism.

The nonnormative approach, on the other hand, too often has paid insufficient attention to the underlying religious-moral principles. As a result, to call such an approach sociological or anthropological may be an overstatement.

Each of these two approaches, the normative and the nonnormative, seems to be inadequate by itself and at times even polemical, if not openly biased. The two deserve to be inte-

1

grated in a complementary fashion. To that end, among other things, this study is oriented.

If we consider the Muslim family as both a religious-normative *and* a social-behavioral system, it will be possible to treat the family norms as a variable dependent upon, independent of, or interdependent with the variable of actual family behavior. This analysis is not committed to any kind of determinism. It is interested only in seeking for the most probable explanations. It would seem reasonable, therefore, to assume that the respective positions of the religious-normative and the social-behavioral components of the family system are in certain methodological ways interchangeable.

Without assuming, then, the primacy of either the religious-normative elements or the social-behavioral counterparts, we can feel free to approach the problem from either direction, since both can in principle provide acceptable starting points, other things being equal. But a choice must be made, and it may be more practical to begin the analysis of the family system with the religious-normative elements and then explore their interrelations with their social-behavioral counterparts. This choice is based on the fact that the former elements, as presented in the law sources, are better known to us and hence more reliable than the latter. Yet, as Parsons has pointed out, this does not mean that ideas, especially normative, imperative ideas, "must arise through some process of 'immaculate conception' unsullied by social and economic forces or that they influence action by some automatic mysterious process of self-realization or 'emanation' without relation to the other elements of the social system." [3]

Our analysis will attempt to discuss the family structure in Islām as Muslims have actually seen it, as they know it, and as they might see it. These perspectives have long been a battleground of polemics, apologetics, and partisanship. I have no particular interest in this fascinating but largely unproductive pursuit, nor do I wish in this particular context to join the combatants. An explanation or interpretation need not represent one's own personal views nor imply approval or condemnation. In the following pages, I hope to limit myself to an exploratory analysis of the Muslim mind with a view to gaining an insight into its unspoken values. In short, this study will strive for the perspectives of "cultural relativism".

The cultural relativist tries only to see the culture of a people as they themselves would view it. To authenticate his own presentation, he may "take" their role and exercise some empathy, but that does not preclude objectivity. On the other hand, cultural universals are limited in number, and moralistic universalism borders on ethnocentrism, which has proven to be a dead end. This makes cultural relativism a useful frame of reference.[4]

In this type of study one must try to be objective. But to be such, one must be "appreciative", which means being able to see the bright and the dark, the attractive and the repulsive. Yet, here lies an acute dilemma, for neither the bright nor the dark is always so viewed by all observers. What appears to some scholars as an enlightened spirit of scientific criticism may look to others like a destructive, malicious assault. What is well rounded and objective to some scholars may appear to others polemical, apologetic, and defensive. In Islāmic studies, this dilemma is the bitter legacy of centuries of mutual misunderstanding and prejudice. The point is made as a reminder lest we become drawn into the controversies or lose sight of our main objective. There may be occasions for criticism and countercriticism, but the chief purpose of this study is to describe, explain, and interpret the family system in Islām according to the most likely reading of the Muslim mind. If anything else is imputed to the discussion, it is neither the desired nor the desirable goal of the writer.

With these intentions, then, we will examine the family structure in the context of Islāmic law, religion, and classical Muslim society, focusing on the basic laws and dimensions of marriage, kinship roles, legitimacy, divorce and inheritance.

The methodological procedure will center around three points: the normative (both proscriptive and prescriptive) provisions relating to the family; the "ideal" and societal sources of these provisions; and the relationship between these and the general sociocultural environment. The norms will be descriptively stated and, whenever tenable, sociologically explained with occasional recourse to "interpretations" from a phenomenological, cultural-relativist standpoint. The study will also utilize comparative analysis drawn from pre-Islāmic and other societies.

The sociological perspective will be used, though not exclusively. Sometimes that perspective is the only way to explain otherwise inexplicable positions. It is most helpful in objectively assessing oversimplistic views of the Muslim family; much of the traditional suspicion, prejudice, and misunderstanding in this area can be brought to light and attributed to misdirected analogies between one system's ideal elements and another's behavioral manifestations.

Our general context is Islāmic law, religion, and society. Our temporal context will be confined to the formative period of Islāmic law, that is, to the first four centuries or so of Islāmic history (roughly from the seventh to the eleventh century). This period is particularly significant because it was the time during which Islāmic law developed and Muslim society reached its full growth. The end of that period marked the culmination of a religious-legal process to which nothing of major moment has been added.[5] Moreover, because little of the basic Muslim family structure had changed, until recently, it would seem reasonable to take this period as fairly representative of the general outlook of Islām and the founders of Muslim society. However, this historical demarcation will not exclude the use of sources and material of later generations. In fact, there are cases where the ideas of the formative period are made available only through later works. The spatial range of the study has had to be limited. We cannot attempt to deal with the concrete family structures of the different Muslim societies of the period. The analysis will not be concerned exclusively with any particular society of any given time; only some societies will be considered, and only insofar as their social conditions were relevant to the family law.

The historical period covered by this study witnessed some unusual combinations of rapid social change, political rivalry, military action, intellectual dynamism, material affluence, and character transformation.[6] It will be interesting to examine the Muslim family structure under these changing conditions to see how far and in what way the family system interacted with the total situation.

B. *Arabian Society Before Islām*

Although the quest for the origins of social institutions is a fascinating and controversial one, no such quest will be attempted here. Much of the history of pre-Islāmic Arabia is obscured by myth and legend. Romantic notions have been confounded with factual elements. Even some of the most elementary postulates and assumed "facts" have been critically questioned.[7] But one fact that seems to stand out as perhaps the most striking characteristic of Arabian society is its diversity. In southern Arabia, the language was different from that of the north and was written in a different alphabet. The southerners were sedentary people who subsisted largely by agriculture, which may have reached a high degree of development. Their political organization was at first monarchic, but the king's authority was limited by councils of notables and at a later date by a kind of feudalism.[8] On the other hand, the northern population was itself diverse. The introduction of Hellenistic influence into central and northern Arabia produced a series of semi-civilized border states. Though Arab in origin these states were strongly under the influence of Hellenized culture, and generally used the Aramaic language. Their dominant mode of life was Bedouin tribalism. In addition, there were such important exceptions

as that of the oasis and of those more advanced towns established here and there by settled nomads, the most important
being Makkah. But even in Makkah, as Lewis has observed,
the population was diverse: "the central and ruling element
. . . consisted of a kind of merchant aristocracy. After them
came a population of smaller traders of more recent settlement
and humbler status, and finally a 'proletariat' of foreigners
and Bedouins." [10]

The structure of Arabian society was also diverse with
regard to the nature of the social bond or the basis of social
solidarity. In southern Arabia, the principle of solidarity
appears to have been at first the kind that usually obtains
between king and subject, and at a later time to have taken
on some traits of feudalistic fealty. Among the central and
northern nomads, god and cult were the bond of tribal identity
and the symbolic expression of tribal cohesion. At Makkah,
"the real basis of unity remained the class solidarity of the
merchants." [11]

Diversity is probably most obvious in the religious realm.
Different forms of pagan idolatry, Judaism, Christianity, Zo-
roastrianism, and Hanīfism (a general form of monotheism)
were all embraced by various elements of the population.
Arberry has succinctly described the situation thus:

> In the spreading wastes and thronging townships of Arabia
> at the turn of the sixth century A.D. many voices were
> heard . . . expressive of many divergent points of view. Jew
> and Christian were not uncommon. . . . Echoes of Zoroastrian
> doctrines clashed with a vague and rather mysterious mono-
> theism attributed to people known as Hanīfs.[12]

Diversity may also be seen in the various degrees of contact between the different parts of Arabia and the surrounding
world. One significant index of this diversity is that Persian
and Byzantine culture permeated Arabia through several
channels, among them the foreign colonies in the peninsula.
Jewish and Christian settlements in various parts of Arabia
helped to spread Aramaic and Hellenistic culture.[13] What
led these foreigners to settle among the Arabs, where rugged

nomadism, booty, plunder and violence are believed to have reigned supreme? How did they manage to survive, let alone be culturally or socially influential, in an environment that is generally characterized as hostile, lawless, unprincipled, and unpredictable? Perhaps these colonies and their supposed cultural influence were not what they are said to have been in a society whose purpose "is to unite men for offense and defense" and whose whole law "really resolves itself into a law of war".[14] Or perhaps both sides of the picture are overdrawn.

In what sense, then, can one speak of an Arabian society? Certainly the Arabs were not politically integrated. It is generally held that the Arabs "used to be very defective in organizing power and incapable of combined action".[15] Moreover, they took pride in feeling no need for rulers, considering it degrading to be coerced or to pay taxes.[16] Nor can the identifying principle of Arabian society be the economic system, the religious ideology, or the general mode of life; we have already seen how heterogeneous these were. Perhaps the only alternative is the kinship system, but here again one must not lose sight of time, space, mode of life and other variables.[17]

Diversity of the Arabian social system did not, nevertheless, mean chaos.[18] No social system can be regarded as viable if it fails to satisfy a minimum of requisites through certain mechanisms.[19] One way to identify these mechanisms is to look for the smallest social unit through which the requisites are satisfied and the mechanisms developed. In the case of Arabia, the first unit to come to mind is the tribe. Admittedly, there is a certain degree of arbitrariness in this choice, for the Arabs had apparently experienced types of social organization both larger and smaller than the tribe.[20]

The Arabian tribe was held together as a social unit "by a traditional sentiment of unity . . . of blood, and by the recognition and exercise of certain mutual obligations and social duties and rights. . . . According to the theory of the

Arab genealogists, the groups were all patriarchal tribes, formed, by subdivision of an original stock, on the system of kinship through male descents." [21] At the time of Muḥammad, the tribal bond was conceived as one of kinship; tribesmen *regarded* themselves as of one blood.[22]

Yet, as Smith points out, the tribal system "was being broken up from within by the growth of the idea of family as opposed to stock ties and of private as distinct from stock rights." [23] At Makkah this dissolution of the tribal solidarity was accompanied by a growing individualism and by the emergence of a new sense of unity based on common economic intrests. Even there tribal unity still dominated the attitudes of the elite.[24]

A primary effect of these various bonds and placement mechanisms was the enlargement of the kinship unit, in which pure-blood tribesmen formed the core. In addition to these, the group generally included a number of slaves and clients. The latter were of two kinds: "freedmen, and free Arabs of other kins living under the protection of the tribe or of its chief or some influential man." [25] The pure-blood tribesmen consisted of the chief and his family and of the group of families who acknowledged him. At Makkah the situation was somewhat different. The real functional units were not clans or kinship groups as such, but rather small groups of merchants with their families and dependents, including mercenaries, caravan personnel, middlemen, debtors who were unable to pay their debts, wage workers and the clients or *mawālī*.[27]

Crucial as they were, blood ties and custom were not the only social forces in the ongoing social life of the tribe. There was also, for example, the ideal of *murū'ah or murūwah,*— that is, manliness,—a quality that has been described as "bravery in battle, patience in misfortune, persistence in revenge, protection of the weak, defiance of the strong." The strength of a man's *murūwah* in large part determined the degree of respect and authority he commanded.[28] To some extent, honor took the place of law and of the moral idea of right and wrong. Loyalty, fidelity, and mutual consultation in decision-making were other important norms of Arabian society.[29]

In a summary statement, Patai singles out five basic characteristics as unique to the Biblical and Middle Eastern family "in every epoch from the most ancient time down to the present: Such a family is (1) endogamous, practicing marriage within one's own social group (2) patrilineal, tracing descent through the father and the male line, (3) patriarchal, empowering the father with formal and final authority in the family (4) extended, including three or more generations in the same household and (5) polygynous, practicing plurality of wives." He concludes that, "the full cluster of these traits is found nowhere outside the Middle East."[30]

Although useful heuristically, such generalizations are rather risky; many exceptions and variants have been pointed out among the patterns that have been dominant in Arabia at one time or another. Similarly, there are unresolved issues concerning lineage, the precise boundaries of endogamy, the limits of the extended family, and so on. Other questions can be raised as to whether these traits would be consistent with one another and with the total Arabian setting.[31] In view of what has been noted about the tribal structure and the living conditions of pre-Islāmic Arabia, the following propositions may be suggested for consideration. Endogamy is not likely to prevail where polygyny does. Strict patriarchality and the extended family can hardly endure in a kinship system, such as the Arabian, where the patriarch had no more than moral authority. Endogamy and patriarchality are unlikely to be found in a population generally characterized by frequent roaming, physical mobility, change of lineage, and freedom of affiliation. Contemporaneous, as distinct from successive, polygyny is not likely to coexist with free divorce or repudiation by which the Arabian system has been characterized. Neither is free divorce compatible with endogamy and the extended family, nor are these correlative with the way women are believed to have been treated or rather mistreated. Perhaps

other propositions can be derived from this list of traits and
perhaps, too, the list itself can be extended. This would seem
to support the point of departure in this part of the discussion,
that is, the diversity of the Arabian social system and of the
views of those who have attempted to analyze it.

One of the few established facts about Arabia before Islām
is the existence there of some Jewish and Christian communities. Beyond this general fact, nothing much can be
ascertained. Scholars hold different opinions regarding the
racial and social origins, the size, locale, level of development, and cultural significance of these groups. It will not
serve our purpose to examine these opinions in any detail;
a few general remarks may be helpful.

For the events of what Goitein calls the "three most decisive decades of oriental history (about 615-645 A.D.) not
a single contemporary account has come from Jewish sources.
Beyond that crucial period, the first two hundred and fifty
years after the rise of Islām are the most obscure in Jewish
history." He disputes a common assumption that "Arabia
was the common homeland of the Semites and that Israel was
nothing but an Arab tribe. . . . [This] is nothing but a series
of misconceptions. The people of Israel, as soon as we can
recognize it from concrete historical accounts—say from the
time of the Judges onwards [about 1200 *B. C.*]—is an entirely
agricultural people." [32] Nevertheless, this observation may be
more omissive than inclusive. Life in Arabia had its "unavoidable requirements," and the Arabian Jews had become
Arab tribesmen, at least externally.[33] Until the racial-social
origins of the Arabian Jews and the extent of their contact
with the outside world of Jewry can be satisfactorily demonstrated, their relations with the native Arabs will remain obscure and so will their supposed influence on Islām.[34]

Christianity, too, penetrated into Arabia quite early, but
little is known about its growth or influence, except in the
most northern areas. Because Christianity involved no requirements of ethnic exclusivity, the racial and social composition of Arabian Christians was more diverse than that of

the Jews.[35] Christian churches were established only where there were citizens of mixed Arab, Greek and Roman population. Contrary to some recent suggestions, there is no evidence that Christianity "had any deep hold upon the inhabitants of the Arabian Peninsula proper." [36] Yet in spite of ideological and behavioral differences, Christian missionaries were free to preach at public rallies. Moreover, whatever the internal divisions within the Christian groups and whatever their doctrinal disputes with the Jews at the time, it seems that the native Arabs were neither much involved nor concerned with such controversies. Their relations with the Christians and the Jews seem to have remained unaffected by disputes within those groups.[37]

C. *The Rise of Islām*

Arabia's religious diversity has prompted a variety of speculations. Before Islām, Arabian religion was nominal, or formal, or superstitious. Arab paganism "had been losing its grip during the sixth century *A. D.* . . . . People found themselves frightened and conscious of their evil deeds." [38] Or, in another view, tribal religion was crucial to communal life, where god and cult were the badge of identity and apostasy was equated with treason. Whatever the interpretation, one thing seems clear: religion apparently played a major part in that environment.[39]

A related question is whether Islām simply represented the Bedouin mind projected into the realm of religion or was a religion that developed in an urban environment and took on urban characteristics. Modern research, however, has shown what Gibb and others call the untenability of the common assumption of the Bedouin origin of Islām.[40] The development of the first Islāmic century, according to Gibb, "confirmed the character of Islām as a strong, self-confident, conquering faith."

From this has come its unyielding and even hostile attitude to everything that lay outside itself, but also its record of broad tolerance of diversity within its own community, refusal to persecute those of other communities, and the dignity with which it endured moments of eclipse. But still more astonishing than the speed of conquests was their orderly character.[41]

It is noteworthy, and perhaps curious, that the military undertakings of the Arab Muslims accompanied the immediate release of their intellectual energies, that neither of these concomitants hindered the other, and that both were stimulated by the religious sentiment created by Islām. As Gibb has observed, "the transformation is amazing when one looks back to the intellectual poverty of Medina a bare hundred years before, still more when it is remembered that it was in the main the work of Arabs themselves, building upon the foundations laid by Mohammad, self-evolved with none but the most meagre external influences." [42]

During the ninth and tenth centuries, Islāmic civilization reached its climax of interaction between the material and spiritual elements. Yet, as it happened, the penetration of Greek thought provoked a conflict which grew in bitterness as the years went by.[43] Nevertheless, the conflict did not result in intellectual stagnation, but in rechanneling the flow of intellectual energies. The religious culture and scholarship embraced other forms of activity and by some minor accommodations converted them into their own instruments. It was held that the religious culture intrinsically provided sufficient opportunity and stimulus to intellectual creativity. Such creativity produceu several new sciences and considerably improved the old ones. But the master science of the Muslims was law.[44]

Islāmic law was crucial to the development of Muslim society, not only because of its intellectual pre-eminence but, first and foremost, because of its social, moral, and political role in the drama of Islāmic history:

> Islāmic law was the most far-reaching and effective agent in moulding the social order and the community life of the Muslim peoples . . . . Moreover, Islāmic law gave practical expression to the characteristic Muslim

quest for unity .... [And] however seriously the political and military strength of the vast Empire might be weakened, the moral authority of the law was but the more enhanced and held the social fabric of Islām compact and secure through all the fluctuations of political fortune.[45]

By the end of the tenth century, a "great" civilization had been built up, "brilliant," "wealthy" and "enterprising." The whole was a "visible embodiment" of the spiritual, intellectual, and temporal "might of Islām." From that time on, the state gradually diverged more and more from the path of earlier generations; the result was political disintegration and internal strife. But the decline of Muslim political power did not mean a corresponding decline of the forces of Islāmic society. In fact, it would almost seem that the decline of the former injected a new vitality into the latter.[46]

D. *Islāmic Law*

The nature of law in Islām has been variously conceived: is it divinely revealed, or socially grounded? positive, or supernatural? immutable or adaptive? Disagreements seem to stem from uncritical use of two equivocal concepts, *sharī'ah* and *fiqh*. *Sharīah* is usually defined by Muslim scholars as the body of "those institutions which Allah has ordained in full or in essence to guide the individual in his relationship to God, his fellow Muslims, his fellowmen, and the rest of the universe." [47] It may be compared in certain respects to some denotations of the Western concept of "natural law." According to the classical view, it is the basis for the moral judgement of actions as good or bad, and thus it can come only from God.[48]

The term *fiqh* literally denotes intelligence or knowledge. Technically, however, it is the name given to jurisprudence in Islām. It does not designate the principal Islāmic laws that are to regulate all aspects of public and private life; rather, it is a subsidiary science of those laws. In older theological language, the word "is applied to the independent exercise of the intelligence, the decision of legal points by one's own judgment in the absence or ignorance of traditions bearing on the case in question." [49]

Although *fiqh* is the science of *sharī'ah* and can often be used synonymously,[50] the two concepts suggest to the Muslim mind analytically different but actually related things. Muslims speak freely of different schools or *madhahib* of *fiqh*, but they do not refer to *sharī'ah* in the same way. To them, *sharī'ah* is one comprehensive system of law that is divine in origin, religious in essence, and moral in scope. It does not exclude *fiqh*, but it is not identical with it. In contrast, *fiqh* is a human product, the intellectual systematic endeavor to interpret and apply the principles of *sharī'ah*. At any rate, the referents of the two concepts are readily distinguishable at least analytically. The confusion arises when the term *sharī'ah* is used uncritically to designate not only the divine law in its pure principal form, but also its human subsidiary sciences including *fiqh*. It is apparently in this wide sense that the term *sharī'ah* is usually translated as "Islāmic Law," meaning both the pure principal provisions of the law and its applied subsidiary sciences. Consequently, those who subscribe to the divine origin and the unchangeable essence of Islāmic law seem to mistake the general for the variant, that is, to view the whole legal system of Islām as identical with *sharī'ah* in its strict pure sense. Similarly those who subscribe to the social basis and the human character of Islāmic law seem to view the whole system as identical with one part thereof, that is, *fiqh* which, strictly speaking, is human and socially grounded.

Much of this confusion can probably be avoided if the analytical distinction between *sharī'ah* and *fiqh* is borne in mind and if it is realized that Islāmic law is held by Muslims to encompass two basic elements: the divine, which is unequivocally commanded by God or His Messenger and is designated as *sharī'ah* in the strict sense of the word; and the human, which is based upon and aimed at the interpretation

INTRODUCTION

and/or application of *sharī'ah* and is designated as *fiqh* or applied *sharī'ah*.[51]

E. *The General Characteristics of Islāmic Law*

Islāmic law is "evolutionary" in that its full growth took centuries and passed through various phases. It began with general principles stated in the basic sources of Islām, namely, the Qur'ān and the Traditions of the Prophet. At first, it dealt with simple, practical problems of everday life, but as time went on it grew complex and inclusive. Its sources encompassed a wide range of *basic, supplementary* and *rational* roots, as the following simplified outline shows.[52]

Basic Sources

The Qur'ān, the revealed word of Allah.

The Sunnah of the Prophet, his deeds, words and indirect authorization or Sunnah *taqrīriyyah*.

Supplementary Sources

Revelations of Allah before the Prophet, to previous prophets and peoples

Consensus of the Prophet's Companions or qualified jurists

The enlightened judgment of a qualified Companion

'*Urf*, i.e., customs, precedents, mores, etc.

Rational Sources

Analogy (*Qiyās*)

Preference (*Istiḥsān*)

Public interest (*Maṣlaḥah*)

The "Means" or Instrumentalities (*Daharā'ī'*)

Presumption of continuity (*Istiṣḥāb*)

Independent disciplined reasoning (*Ijtihād*)

Whatever the implications of the controversy over the religious versus the social origins of law and the relationship between Islāmic and other legal systems, certain characteristic features of Islāmic law are unmistakable. In Islām, religion and law, in Gibbs words:

are indivisible. . . . Law is the external concept of religion. . . . From this follow two important consequences as distinguishing features of law in Islām. . . . The first

is the width of the field it covers. . . . The second is the
spirit by which its judgments are made. . . . In framing
its definitions, therefore, the ethical aspect is paramount;
and in no case may the legal judgment conflict with it.[53]

The system as a whole "is, in Maine's sense, a system of
equity. . . . Like other systems of equity, it is addressed to the
individual conscience and acts *personam*. . . . It differs from
other systems of equity in that it is not content to exist alongside the original law it supersedes, but rather abrogates or
absorbs it." In accordance with the strict legal element,
justice remains, but in accordance with Islām, "religion demands that it shall be tempered with mercy or even, in the
relation between man and man, replaced by mercy." [54]

Moreover, one fundamental rule in Islāmic law is the
principle of "liberty" or "permissibility" *(ibāḥah),* that is,
everything is in essence lawful unless explicitly designated
otherwise. Islāmic law, like other systems of law, recognizes
that social life would be unthinkable without some specific
rules. But, and probably unlike them, it extends its appli-
cations to overt and covert behavior, to the manifest acts and
the innermost feelings and thoughts of man. It is true that
such covert aspects of behavior may not fall within the
realms of formal law; but this is probably where the moral-
religious precepts become most meaningful. An act is not
only legal or illegal, formally ethical or unethical, behavioral-
ly physical or mental; it is, above all else, a total involvement
that is highly consequential and judiciously weighed by a very
sensitive scale. Thus, any action can be classified in Islāmic
law under one of five basic categories: obligatory; voluntary
but meritorious and commendable; neutral, permissible, or
unlawful; reprehensible; and forbidden.

There are, of course, finer classifications and grades and
intermediate grades in between.[55] On the basis of this outlook, human action is highly consequential in the direct legal,
moral and religious sense. Action in Islāmic law is rewarded
or punishable in the here and now if it is judicially detectable,
and in the hereafter if it is not so. This is part of the actor's

definition of the situation, a definition which takes the conception of Allah as a basic element of the entire situation of action. It is also part of the definition of the situation that the norms provided by Islāmic law are for the welfare of man here as well as hereafter.[56]

What empowered this complex and multidimensional system was probably the combination of five factors. One is the belief in the absolute sovereignty of Allah and the brotherhood of Muslims. The second is the characteristic effort to hold fast to old and well-tried ways and assimilate to them the new situations—fixity, tempered with flexibility. Third is the application of the law to the committed only, namely to the Muslim in whose conception all is from Allah, and all shall return to Him. Fourth is the independence of the jurists in their formulations and decisions. Finally, there is the conception of the law as a comprehensive, unified and unifying force.[57]

To understand and explain the system, it is necessary to realize the complementary nature of its religious, moral, and legal elements. Considering Islāmic law from the strictly legal, moral, or religious point of view alone is probably more misleading than helpful. Even taking legalism and morality into consideration, but disregarding religion, is more omissive than inclusive and may be just as misleading. What seems lacking in the views of most critics is adequate appreciation of the religious component, whose purpose is to integrate and reinvigorate the ethical and legal elements, and whose appeal to or impact upon the actor may be greater than that of formal codes of law and ethics.[58]

At any rate, the most characteristic feature of Islāmic law may be stated in the following proposition: while Islāmic law attempts to "moralize" legal action and formalities by placing them in the context of religion and morality, it tends to discourage the formalization or "ritualization" of the religious and moral precepts. This may be correlated with the designation of social control as ultimately moral.

The fact that Islāmic law holds the religious, moral, and

legal elements as indivisible may suggest that in the Islāmic conception of society the mechanisms of social control are likewise indivisible. Human behavior is so complex that to control it in a comprehensive way there must be an integrative synthesis of religion, morality and law. This tendency of Islām may also suggest that the legal system of a society is determined by, and in turn determines, the ends of that society. Because of both the worldly involvement and the otherworldly concern of Muslim society, Islāmic law was formulated with a view to incorporating in one system a religious spirit, a moral fabric, and a mundane practicality.

In short, Islāmic law is distinguished by the variety of its sources, by the wide areas of "behavior" it covers as well as the range of the religious, moral, and legal principles of action it contains. It assigns to man a greater responsibility and to action more consequences than are perhaps found in comparable systems of law or behavior. It sets before man ends beyond his immediate sense of time and space, conceiving God as an integral part of any action situation.

2 THE FOUNDATIONS AND BOUNDARIES
OF THE FAMILY

A. Definition and Bases of the Family

The observation was made more than two decades ago and is still true that, when used alone, the term family is ambiguous. The layman and even the social scientist applies it indiscriminately to several social groups which, despite functional similarities, exhibit important points of difference.[1] Many classifications and typologies have been suggested to clarify the term. Yet they have produced, in some instances at least, more confusion than clarity.[2] Part of the problem, it seems, is the inevitable overlapping of kinship and family boundaries and the inherent difficulty of setting a universally accepted line of demarcation.

To avoid this confusion, we suggest an operational definition of the family as the term will be used in the Islāmic context. Operationally defined, the term family will be used to designate a special kind of structure whose principles are related to one another through blood ties and/or marital[3] relationships, and whose relatedness is of such a nature as to entail "mutual expectations" that are prescribed by religion, reinforced by law, and internalized by the individual.[4]

Clearly this definition is posited on the mutual expectations that follow from membership in such a structure. The membership may be ascribed as a result of natural blood ties, or acquired through marriage, or be both ascribed and acquired if the membership unit includes, as it may, more than a married pair. Familial rights and obligations are not determined solely by either blood ties or marital relationship alone; the two criteria are neither mutually exclusive nor necessarily complementary. Our point of departure is not, therefore, which of the two kinds of relationship excludes or supercedes the other but rather which kind of relationship

19

involves which rights and obligations. We must analyze the religio-social implications of given degrees of relationship since not every relationship is consequential in these terms and since the consequential relationships are not necessarily the same in all respects.

B. *Forms of the Family in Islām*

Our definition of family makes no reference to the residential factor because the family members may or may not occupy the same residential unit. As far as their mutual expectations are concerned, it makes no fundamental difference how or where they reside. The residential confines may be shared by all members included, or they may be separate and independent. This fact, among others, precludes the unqualified applicability to the family structure in Islām of the sociological concept of nuclear family, where unity of residence is one of the basic characteristics.[5]

But it does not necessarily follow that, since the family in Islām is not fully of the nuclear type, it must be "extended" or "polygamous." [6] Neither extendedness nor "polygyny" is a condition to or prerequisite for the foundation of the family in Islām. The Muslim family may be extended, polygynous, both extended and polygynous, or neither. There is no specific provision in Islām that it must be of one type or the other, just as there is none in favor of, or opposition to, the nuclear family type. The organizational form is an open question, unlike the mutual expectations of the membership. Such expectations remain, no matter what form the family may assume. The nature and extent of these will become clear as the discussion proceeds.

C. *The Family Positions*

The social positions[7] which constitute the Muslim family as here defined include, in the first degree, those of the self, the spouse, the immediate ascendants and/or descendants. As far as the mutual expectations of the occupants of these positions are concerned, there is general agreement among the interpreters of Islāmic law. For conceptual convenience, these positions may be designated as "primary," that is, the immediate constituents of the family system. These positions are not necessarily always interdependent or mutually complementary; some of them may exist independently of the others. For example, the self may have a spouse but no ascendants or descendants, and/or may have these but no spouse. However, there may be other positions whose occupants constitute additional categories, such as the agnate, the cognate or enate, and the collateral. But the juristic views on the precise implications of these positions are not unanimous.[8] These positions may be designated as "supplementary." Both primary and supplementary positions make up the *complete* Muslim family system as it is here treated. The basic difference between these primary and supplementary categories is that the mutual expectations of the former are, on the whole, unequivocal, unlike those of the latter where the difference of opinion is sometimes considerable. This distinction, however, does not mean that there are no intercategory implications. Members of both categories share certain mutual expectations. Some of these may not be precisely formulated or universally institutionalized, nevertheless they are prescribed by religion in a general way.

Family rights and obligations are not private family affairs of no concern to the rest of society. It is true that these are assigned to the family members who are enjoined to administer them privately. But, if the situation becomes unmanageable, religion commands society, represented by designated authorities as well as conscientious individuals, to take whatever action is necessary to implement the law, in order to maintain equity and harmony.[9] This is a natural result of the fact that the mutual expectations of the family members are not established only by familial relationship, but also by the membership in a larger social system which derives from a common religious brotherhood. This brotherhood has its own implications. It is so conceived as to reinforce the family ties, complement them, or prevent their abuse.[10]

For example, if a given person's intrafamily position is of a secondary or tertiary degree, there is still a certain measure of mutual responsibility between him and the other members. It is not, of course, the same as the responsibility that obtains between primary relatives. Nevertheless, it is prescribed by religion even though its nature is not formally specified by the provisions of the law. When the family ties are remote or casual, the religious bonds are normatively expected to reinforce the relationship and maintain the responsibility.[11] On the other hand, if the family ties are too strong in certain respects, for instance as between a parent and one particular child, religion prohibits the exploitation of this kind of intimacy in any way that may affect the rights or obligations of other members. Thus, a person may not discriminate among his dependents even if he is emotionally more attached to some than to others. He is not permitted to make a will in favor of any potential successor at the expense of other would-be-heirs or without their approval. Nor is he permitted to let extrafamily attachment and interest or intrafamily estrangement cause him to mistreat his family members. Thus, he may not make any will to nonheirs in excess of a certain portion of his property, i.e., one-third, without the consent of eligible heirs, lest his disposal of the property infringe upon their rights.[12] This problem will be discussed later. What needs emphasis at this point is that familial rights and obligations are not determined by family sentiments alone, nor do they depend solely upon the dispositions and feelings of the parties involved.

The rights and obligations shared by the family members pertain to lineal identity and maintenance, succession and affection, socialization of the young and security for the aged, and maximization of effort to ensure the family continuity and welfare. These aspects of the family structure will be examined in some detail at a later stage in the discussion. But certain points are noteworthy here.

D. The Principle of Identity

To paraphrase a verse from the Qur'ān, every individual whose lineal identity is known must be identified accordingly. He must preserve his rightful identity and no one may deny it to him. Although he has a natural right to lineage and social placement it is also his obligation to identify himself with his true lineage, and it is the responsibility of all those about him to help to that effect. According to the Qur'ān, this is most equitable in the sight of God. If his lineage is unknown, the individual must be identified as the brother and client of his fellow Muslims.[13] That suffices to give him the necessary identity and to assure him of a legitimate place in society.

This point has some interesting implications, particularly with regard to inclusion in, and exclusion from, the family membership. It was not uncommon in pre-Islāmic times for kinship groups to disown original members and admit aliens in their place. It was also common to adopt aliens and confer on them the lineal identity of the adopters, along with what it entailed. But Islām abrogated these practices and insisted on assigning to every individual his rightful identity.[14]

The tribal structure of pre-Islāmic Arabia was so extended that it included, besides the pure-blood tribesmen, a number of what Smith calls "clients." These consisted of three sub-classes: "(a) freedmen, (b) refugees outlawed by their own tribe, [and] (c) groups, like the Jews at Medina, not strong enough to stand by themselves." Freedmen were often adopted by their patrons and, for all practical purposes, were considered members of the patrons' tribe. There was no significant difference between "natural" and adopted sons of the tribe; they shared revenues and liabilities. Likewise, refugees were frequently adopted by the tribe of their protectors. Sworn allies, in al Madīnah at least, had a claim to the inheritance of their protectors and received one-sixth of the estate. On the other hand, the adopting tribe or clan had the right to inherit the property of the adopted members. As a result, persons with means were sometimes invited to establish sworn alliances with other groups even though the recruits were regarded as being of humble status. Occasionally, however, there was unheeded opposition by prospective heirs to such adoptions and alliances.[15]

The implications of these practices must have been far-reaching. It seems that such declarations of adoption and alliance were not, and probably could not be, always mutually binding or equally reassuring. Nor do they appear to have been harmonious with the natural familial ties and expectations which they not merely supplemented but also rivalled and sometimes replaced. Under such circumstances, divided loyalty, role conflict, and "family" disintegration are hardly escapable. A "kinship" unit could disown members without fear of great repercussions as long as "replacements" were easily available through adoption or sworn alliance. Conversely, a person could defy, desert, or renounce his blood kin and join others at will where he might be welcome, especially if he was a brave warrior or a person with means. Any social system operating under these conditions would be precarious and unstable.

With the rise of Islām, a new kind of religious brotherhood was established to override all other ties including even those of blood and marriage should they conflict with it (cf., *Qur'ān* 9:24; 49:10; 64:15). Based on religion, oriented to an eternal supreme being, and centered around the leadership of one man, Muhammad, the new brotherhood had at least the potential of certainty, permanence, and "universality." It did not apparently negate the individual or replace his personality, for within the brotherhood every individual remained responsible for his deeds and through it he was expected to seek self-realization. Individual responsibility and personality were thus complemented rather than threatened or replaced by the new social order because individuality,

according to the Qur'ān, is neither reducible nor transfer-
able (cf., for example, 41:46; 53:38-41). But Islām was
faced with opposition of various kinds. The new brotherhood met with resistance and rivalry, and in its formative years,
apostasy was not unknown. Many, both groups and individuals, renounced their new faith and joined its opponents.
It is not unlikely that the pre-Islāmic practices of adoption
and sworn alliance provided the apostates with some protection or even encouraged defiance.[16] If the pre-Islāmic practice of adoption continued, the attending consequences of
divided loyalty, uncertain identity, kinship estrangement or
severance, and the protection of apostates would probably
have undermined the new social order and the very faith
upon which it was built. To eliminate or minimize the rival
bonds and external threats, and to sustain the new social
order and rest it on permanent solid foundations were the
most likely reasons for Islām's abrogation of the practice
of adoption.

The social factors suggested here would seem to provide
the kind of explanation usually required by, and readily
acceptable to, social science. However, there has been
another "physio-psychological" explanation of the abrogation of adoption in Islām. It is reported in certain biographies
of Muhammad and magnified by certain writers. Briefly
stated, it goes as follows. Before she married him, Muhammad's first wife had a slave, Zayd Ibn Hārithah, whom she set
free and adopted in the traditional way. The freedman became the adopted son of the couple and was widely known as
Zayd Ibn Muhammad. To help him settle down with a
family of his own, Muhammad wanted his cousin, Zaynab
Bint Jahsh, to marry Zayd. She refused and, together with her
brother, protested the request probably because the freedman
did not measure up to her standards and class or because she
had ambitious designs. But then a verse (Qur'ān 33:37) was
revealed which implicitly reproached Zaynab and her brother
and commanded obedience to the decrees of God and His

Messenger. Zaynab married Zayd after all, but their married years were not happy. Whenever Zayd complained of his wife's contempt of him or sought to divorce her, Muḥammad exhorted him to keep her and be mindful of God. One day, however, Muḥammad called upon Zayd, who was not at home and was received by Zaynab. She is said to have appeared so particularly attractive or romantically irresistible that Muḥammad fell in love with her instantly. He had his adopted son Zayd divorce her and when she was divorced he took her to wife. To answer or forestall accusations of incest for marrying the divorced wife of his adopted son, Muḥammad quoted passages from the Qur'ān declaring the abrogation of adoption and allowing marriage to the divorced wives of adopted sons.

This story is exciting, embarrassing, and extremely doubtful if not altogether incredible. It is exciting because it has stirred many critical comments and accusations by Western writers as well as counteraccusations and comments by Muslim writers. It is embarrassing because a great many scholars have labored tirelessly to build a case for or against the person of Muḥammad in order to confound truth with legend, innocently or otherwise, or to disentangle the one from the other. It is even more embarrassing to the social scientist who wants to choose between the sociological and the physio-psychological explanation. Choosing the former is closer to the norms of social science and usually promises a greater explanatory potential. But in this particular case, it may displease the conventional students of Islām who are in the habit of looking at everything related to Islām as divine, super-social, and above criticism, and also those who tend to view the builders of the Islāmic system as socially insensitive distorters and the system itself as lax aberration.

The story itself may be partly apocryphal, since it is not reported in the early sources. The Qur'ān relates only the essential facts. It tells of Zaynab's reluctance to marry Zayd, and of the strained domestic life of the couple. In this version,

Muḥammad exhorts Zayd to keep his wife and to be mindful of Allah—an admonition motivated by Muḥammad's fear of the peoples' expected reaction to the dissolution of a marriage which he had encouraged. Significantly, the Qur'ān criticizes the Prophet's motive and reminds him to fear God's displeasure, rather than that of the people. The Qur'ānic story concludes with Zayd's divorce of Zaynab and her lawful remarriage to Muḥammad. Observers who examine the story in its social context find it incredible and suggest, according to Watt, that it "must be taken with a grain of salt." The story contains too many elements which do not accord with better verified circumstances: Muḥammad's life style, character and career, his community role and age at the time, his continued relations with both Zaynab and Zayd, before as well as after their unsuccessful marriage; Zaynab's advancing age; the long institutionalization of adoption; finally, Muḥammad's sensitivity to his contemporaries' censure—all such considerations cast doubt on the story of a passionate stroke of love. Aside from the credibility or incredibility of the story itself, it is unlikely that an age-old social institution like adoption could be abrogated for such transient personal motives.[17]

The matter of preserving a person's true identity seems somehow epitomized in the position of the married woman in Islām. For while she takes on a new marital identity and may be called wife of so and so, she still retains her old lineal one. There is no diffusion of identity here; the one is not subordinated to or absorbed by, the other. Each entails certain rights and obligations, and both persist independently of each other. This is still the case throughout the Muslim world. Such a duality of identity for the married woman has continued under Islām probably because no other alternatives were practiced, feasible, or desirable. It may also have been adopted to indicate the continuity, at least partially, of the premarital positions, since both husband and wife have certain kinship rights and obligations that are not fundamentally affected by their marriage; marriage does not entirely preclude their responsibility for, and rights over, their blood relatives. And if the married pair and their kins are, in reality as well as religiously, all so bound to one another, it would seem appropriate to symbolize this blood relationship by some external common symbol. A common name derived from a common lineage is probably the readiest symbolic manifestation of this kind of relationship. Furthermore, there is the probability that, unlike absorption of one identity by another, differentiation, even after marriage, is more consistent with, and conducive to, the consolidation of inter-family ties such as ties between the family of orientation, the family of procreation, and the affinal relatives.

Definition of the Muslim family in terms of blood ties and/or marital relationship and on the basis of the attendant mutual expectations excludes certain categories of individuals who had been included in the family and kinship structure of pre-Islāmic times.[18] Under Islām, clients or *mawālī*, slaves, adopted persons, and similar groups were no longer full-fledged members of any family or kinship unit other than their own. This does not deny that they have been "attached" to a particular household or formed "secondary families" within such a household.[19] This may be a further illustration of the principle of identity as envisioned by Islām. It was in such a fashion that Islām abrogated the arbitrary exercise of power by the family heads and tribal councils, who had traditionally been at liberty to admit or expel whom they pleased. On the other hand, the Islāmic principle would tend to minimize the individual's temptation to tamper with his identity or with the implications thereof. It prohibited such fluctuations of identity and affiliation probably because they were at least potentially conducive to serious social and psychological repercussions. Moreover, restricting family positions to the actual blood relatives and/or marital partners may have been conceived as a manifestation of the new order of society, an order which embodied clearly established positions and fixed implications.[20]

There seems to be a relationship between the fact that the Arabs were fanatically proud and boastful of their lineage, genuine or fictitious, and the fact that Islām strongly insisted on restoring to every individual his rightful lineal identity, whether or not this identity was regarded as noble by the current standards. By such insistence, Islām probably meant to temper the pride of the contemporary Arabs with modesty and to impress upon them the Qur'ānic principle that genuine nobility was not a question of lineage, but of piety and good deeds.

Logically, however, the opposite proposition may be advanced. It can be submitted that, by taking this position on lineal identity, Islām actually made concessions to the contemporary Arabs, appealed to their exaggerated sense of pride, reinforced their keen dispositions to claim real or alleged noble lineages, and insured for them the continued legitimacy of such lineages. This logical proposition, moreover, may be supported by the fact that the Arabs used to look with contempt on non-Arabs and also on one another. Even after the introduction of Islām, not all of them were able or prepared to rid themselves completely of their earlier ethnic and tribal prejudices as criteria of stratification and standards of nobility. Nor could they fully internalize or implement the principle of lineal equality. Nevertheless, several basic considerations may make the proposition hardly tenable. For one there is no valid claim that the normative precept of the equality of ancestry in God's sight was completely identical with the ethical outlook of the Arabs, or invariably corresponded with their actual behavior. Secondly, there is no particular reason to suppose that such a precept would be to their liking, or that they would readily abandon their cherished traditions in favor of a norm of equality between the humblest and the most noble stocks. Neither is there clear evidence that established nobility was so conscious of any serious threats from clients and humble allies that it needed the reassurance of Islām to preserve it intact or to set it apart. Nor is it likely that those Arabs of noble ancestry (for whom the new rule could be interpreted as advantageous, as this proposition implies) would be attracted to support a religion which insisted on lineal identity for dignitaries and commoners alike, and which assured the commoners of equal status in the sight of God. Finally, stratifying the early Muslim population on the scale of lineage is hardly compatible with the explicit teachings of the Qur'ān and the established policies of Muḥammad. It was probably no accident, for example, that the first "prayer announcer" (*mu'adhdhin*) was a former black slave (the Abyssinian Bilāl); that the Persian convert Salmān was one of the most distinguished Companions; that the freedman Zayd Ibn Hārithah was joined in brotherhood at al Madīnah with Muḥammad's uncle and was appointed first commander of a major expeditionary force; that the young Usāmah, son of this very Zayd, was designated, first by Muḥammad and later by his immediate successor Abū Bakr, to command an army despite the uneasiness of the more experienced men of older age, nobler stock, and higher status; and that the commander who conquered Andalusia, Tāriq Ibn Ziyād, was a freedman.[21]

To conclude this point, a relevant Qur'ānic passage may be paraphrased thus: Let everyone keep his true identity because by such he is socially placed and differentiated. But let no one be either ashamed or unduly proud of his lineage because this is of no avail in the sight of God, to Whom only pious deeds and spiritual achievements matter.[22]

E. The Traditional Form of the Muslim Family

Although Islām does not prescribe any specific organizational family type, there can be little doubt that traditional Muslim family structure has actually been closer to the extended than to the nuclear type. This is probably the result of continuity, and not the outcome of innovation by the Muslims.

Islām does not prescribe the extended type any more than it forbids it. If it so happened that the family organization in Muslim society assumed, or rather continued, this extended form, there is no provision to give it a universal sanction or disapproval. But whether the extendedness of the Muslim family structure was a function of historical continuity or of other social conditions, Islām apparently accepted this form and took no further stand on it, unlike its position on various other aspects of the family.

This historical development, together with the concomitant religious accommodation, may be highly suggestive. For while Islām was by no means totally indifferent to the social conditions and precedents, it apparently saw no particular need to restrict the family structure to any exclusive form, be it extended, nuclear, or polygynous. This may indicate that such forms in themselves are not crucial to the Islāmic conception of family solidarity and societal cohesion, both of which are of primary concern for Islām, and that emphasis should be placed not on the form but rather on the behavioral components. As a matter of fact, familial rights and obligations in Islām are independent of, and differentiated from, the organizational forms of the family; the former are fixed while the latter are open and malleable.

The position of Islām in this regard was produced by, or is at least in accordance with, a general outlook that seems to presume continuity of precedents so long as they do not violate certain principles or conflict with basic needs. Thus, if we bear in mind that the extended family does not necessarily preclude the nuclear type, at least as a subsystem, Islām seems to have considered the extended form acceptable though not necessary. That form was apparently working and workable. Islām endorsed it, though it did not insist that it must or must not be so always.

The fact that Islām accommodated the extended family type and made no further specifications may suggest that, under certain conditions, such as those surrounding the rise of Islām, the extended family structure would be more conducive to, though not indispensable, whatever functions the family is to serve. Flexibility of the organizational form, on the one hand, and specificity of the mutual, religiously prescribed expectations of the members, on the other, would seem to indicate that the Muslim family structure was or may be conceived as partly divine and fixed, partly human and variable.[23]

F. The Polygynous Form

The family structure in Islām cannot, properly speaking, be characterized as polygynous.[24] The situation here is very much like that of the extended and nuclear family types. The polygynous form is neither absolutely necessary nor unequivocally forbidden; it is permissible. A great deal depends on the individual's discretion and conscience as well as on the social conditions of any given situation. Nothing in Islām indicates that polygyny is or is not a universal rule; or that it must be upheld or abandoned categorically. But once polygyny occurs, certain mutual expectations must be met.[25] This may be another instance of Islām's view of the social forms and its attitude to social change. Islām found polygyny in practice, though there is no conclusive evidence how prevalent the practice was. Among all the logically possible courses of legislation, Islām allowed the practice to continue with certain qualifications. It did not abrogate it, ignore it completely, or prescribe it. This is the bare fact, but the explanation of the fact varies from observer to observer.[26] The question may be put as follows: Did Islām allow this conditional polygyny as an adaptive mechanism? Or was it unable either to uproot it entirely or to liberalize it unconditionally in fear of resistance or protest on the people's part? In other words, had it been necessary or more adaptive to take a polaristic view of the problem by either absolute prohibition or unconditional approval of polygyny, could Islām have done so? A full explanation requires more knowledge than we have about the social structure of pre-Islāmic Arabia. Yet we may propose a provisional explanation.

In view of the changes which Islām brought into the beliefs and social systems of the time, it would seem exceedingly unlikely that Islām allowed conditional polygyny *only* or mainly because it was unable to do otherwise. There are strong indications that, had Islām deemed it necessary or more adaptive to take a different position on the matter, it could, and probably would, have done so. Even if it is hypothetically assumed that polygyny was either practiced or despised—as the conflicting views stand—by a majority of people, who might have objected to Islām's attempt to change the *status quo,* that alone would not have prevented Islām from prescribing whatever course it regarded appropriate. In fact, the basic body of Islām's teachings was met, at least in the early years, by resentment, ridicule, and even defiance. Still, that did not apparently dissuade Islām from pursuing its objectives, however strong the opposition of the people and however firm their unfavorable dispositions.[27] Moreover, when Islām did qualify or abrogate some of its own former provisions, it was not because there had been any mass protest or resentment, but probably because the setting had changed and new situations arisen. In this case the change was, to paraphrase a Qur'ānic verse, for the better or at least for something equally good.[28]

G. Is the Family a Religious Unit?

It is somewhat curious that the family is not necessarily a "religious" unit. While Islām prescribes family rights and obligations, it does not seem to presuppose, at least on the primary level, religious uniformity. Family members are entitled to their rights and are assigned reciprocal obligations which hold whether or not the members subscribe to the same religious beliefs. The principle holds for both primary foundations of the family — ascribed blood ties and the acquired marital relationship.

In the first instance of relationship, for example that of the parent and child, the mutual expectations prescribed by Islām apply whether one or both parties are Muslims. If both parties are non-Muslims, Islām does not interfere in their family affairs unless they seek the help of the Muslim authorities and agree to abide by the provisions of Is- lāmic law.[29] If both parties are Muslims, then the law applies to them, even as it is addressed to both of them. But, if one party believes in Islām while the other does not, Islām ad- dresses its provisions first of all to the Muslim. If the Muslim party is to fulfill his Islāmic obligations to the non-Muslim, he must in turn be empowered to exercise the corres- ponding rights. For example, Islām holds the father re- sponsible, among other things, for the maintenance of the child and the child responsible for the parent's maintenance under certain circumstances. If the father is the Muslim party and is to fulfill his religious duties to the child, even one who is not a Muslim, he must be given the right to reciprocal sup- port by his child, should the need for such support arise. His responsibility for the child must be compensated by the as- surance that the child is also responsible for him. Thus, by the general principle of "reciprocity" [30] the rules of Islām apply to the child if his claims over his father are to be legit- imate and enforceable. It is readily understandable that such judicial technicalities will arise only when there are conflicts that the family members cannot settle privately. Since the family is a primary group *par excellence* and its members are urged to administer their affairs as privately as they can, it may be assumed that such public disputes will be infrequent. They cannot be ruled out, however, and any viable system will have to be prepared to cope with them should they arise.

Difference of religion, even to the extent of polarity, does not, therefore, affect the application of Islāmic law regarding the mutual expectations involved in the parent-child relation- ship. The Muslim parent is enjoined to treat his child in an Islāmic capacity, though the child may not share the parent's beliefs. Similarly, the Muslim child is called upon to treat his non-Muslim parent as if he were a Muslim. Certain mutual expectations and natural affection are inherent in the parent-child relationship. Islām recognizes that they must be maintained irrespective of the religious differences of the parties involved. The sole stipulation is that the relationship must not hinder the Muslim party's fulfillment of other duties, and that the non-Muslim party must not be an avowed, active enemy of Islām.[31]

The same principle is true of acquired, marital relationships, as between a husband and wife, Islām allows "interreligious" marriages. A Muslim man may marry a non-Muslim woman of the People of the Book — a Jewess or Christian.[32] There is a difference of opinion on the details of such interreligious marriages which cannot be discussed at this point, but, so far as the rights and responsibilities of the non-Muslim wife are concerned, the difference of religion is inconsequential as long as their marriage lasts. The position of the non-Muslim wife is the same as that of her Muslim counterpart.[33] However, if the non-Muslim wife happens to survive her Muslim husband, she is not entitled to inherit from him, even as he is not entitled to inherit from her. It would be an overt religious discrimination and infringement upon her rights if the same rule did not apply to her husband and to the same degree. Since the rule applies to both, the question of sex or religious discrimination hardly arises. In fact, a basic rule of "succession" in Islām is that difference of religion precludes eligibility for inheritance. There is no mutual right of inheritance in Islām between any two persons who are not both Muslims. Thus, a Muslim child may not inherit from his non-Muslim parent, nor may a Muslim parent inherit from a non-Muslim child. The principle remains, however, that as long as the marital bonds last, the concomitant mutual expectations hold regardless of the religious differences between the husband and wife.[34]

The whole question of interreligious marriage and succession will be reconsidered in Chapter 7. But what has been said so far may suffice to indicate the point that the family unit in Islām is not necessarily always a religious unit, and that Islām enforces the familial rights and obligations even though the members involved may not share the same religious beliefs.

The fact that Islām has taken this position may lead to some useful insights into the nature of Islām itself as well as the family structure. Why, indeed, did Islām not insist on religious uniformity as a condition for the full implementation of the mutual expectations of the family members? Some tentative explanations may be attempted.

Such a condition may directly or indirectly entail religious compulsion or at least coercive pressure of some kind, and Islām subscribes neither to this nor to anything leading to it. The Qur'ān in a rather confident tone declares that there shall be no compulsion in religion; the true course has become clearly distinguishable from error. Whoever believes in God alone has laid hold of the firmest, most unbreakable support.[35] This declaration of freedom of belief and conscience would make Islām's insistence on religious uniformity of family members an internal inconsistency or obvious contradiction, something that is unthinkable for Muslims. Paradoxically, however, this position may be interpreted as indicative of both weakness and confidence. As a sign of weakness, it may suggest that Islām was unable or unwilling to challenge directly the familial ties by insisting on religious uniformity of kins and spouses, especially if such a uniformity would be involuntary. Any open challenge to these ties might have produced defiance or severance of familial ties, which could ultimately become more disintegrative than integrative. As a sign of confidence, it may suggest that Islām was so certain of its own strength as a viable bond that no kinship ties could challenge it, and that it could benevolently incorporate or accommodate such ties without fear.

Aside from the paradox of weakness and confidence, it is

still probable, however, that religious uniformity was taken for granted and no serious deviation or litigation actually occurred to test the strength of this rule. Should religious differences arise, they would be dealt with. Thus, religion would not appear as incompatible with or threatened by the basic familial loyalties. Rather it might draw support through the fostering of such loyalties so long as they did not create sentiments hostile to religion or hinder the Muslim party's fulfillment of his obligations in other respects.

Moreover, Islām may have taken this position to suggest that, although family solidarity is crucial, it does not, or should not, mean absorption of the individual members by the family collectivity. Personality must be allowed a certain measure of freedom to develop alongside the collectivity, so that individualism may not be forced to submerge or subvert. To avoid apathy, estrangement, and authoritarianism, it would seem necessary to devise some integrative mechanisms whereby the collectivity and personality can coexist and interact to their mutual benefit. One way of ensuring the continuity of this kind of interaction is that the family members, in spite of possible cognitive or religious differences, maintain some mutual expectations of rights and responsibilities. On the other hand, the individual's conscience cannot be totally controlled by the collectivity. To approximate the full development of personality to the level at which the individual can differentiate between intermediate and ultimate ends, some inviolable principles should be emphasized. One such principle, Islām seems to insist, is to hold the individual responsible directly to God, to orient him to something beyond the immediate and the social, to show him how to reconcile his private convictions with social requirements. This is the personality type which would appear closest to the ideal personality of Islām. In many passages the Qur'ān urges the individual to render unto God what is God's and unto man, kin or otherwise, what is man's, to differentiate among the various levels of responsibility and loyalty. It says, in effect, that

man's primary responsibility is to God, and that no man in
the final analysis is accountable for another. Nevertheless
man's direct responsibility to God in no way justifies much
less requires, unkindness to his fellow men or relinquishment
of his responsibility for his non-Muslim kin. On the contrary,
his relationship to God should encourage kindness and affection, in spite of the religious difference.[36]

It is also probable that Islām did not insist on the religious
uniformity of family members because it recognized that such
uniformity is hardly attainable.[37] This means that men must
be socialized to accommodate one another in spite of their
differences and that an effective start toward this end begins
at home.[38] Moreover, Islām may have intended to cultivate,
through the family experience, certain principles of human
relations. For example, natural family ties can be enriched by
religion, by conceiving of God as an integral part of any action
situation. If there is to be any dissent on fundamental questions, let it be the responsible kind that does not affect the
rightful expectations of innocent parties. It is the individual's
responsibility to believe or disbelieve at peril of his future life;
but since the individual is a social being and social life is demanding as well as rewarding, certain mutual expectations
must be maintained irrespective of the individual's belief or
disbelief.[39]

H. The Perpetuation of the Family

Adoption, mutual alliance or clientage, private consent or
access to sexual intercourse, and "common law" or "trial" marriages do not institute a family in Islām, although some of
these relations did so in pre-Islāmic times and some may do
so today in non-Muslim societies. Islām seems to insist that
the foundations of the family should rest on solid grounds
capable of providing assurances of continuity, security and
intimacy, and of being, as much as possible, "natural," mutually binding, and gratifying. Accordingly, Islām recognizes
only blood ties and/or marital bonds as the true foundations

of the family. There is no more natural relationship than that of blood.[40] Similarly, there is no more wholesome pattern of sexual relations than that which joins gratification with conscientiousness.[41] So far human experience has suggested that this can be fully realized only through institutional media, namely, responsible and relatively stable relations. And it is this type of institutional and conscientious sexual relationship which Islām enjoins as a solid foundation of the family structure.

The fact that Islām has established the family on these foundations does not mean that a given concrete family unit is indissoluble. What must continue is the family "institution" itself, not necessarily the concrete structure of any particular family group. Members converge and diverge, change positions or relinquish them altogether; but the family as a normative institution must survive such fluctuations if society is to persist. Islām did not insist on the absolute indissolubility of the family structure. It probably would have been impractical to prescribe such indissolubility; even where it is clearly prescribed, it is not always attainable, perhaps for reasons beyond human rationality. Yet this does not in any way condone unrestrained resort to family dissolution.   (See Chapter 6).

It is true that no system is fully internalized and completely implemented by everyone who subscribes to it. If the system is designed to maximize the welfare of man, as Islām is, [42] it would probably hesitate to alienate men by turning deaf ears to historical experience, to ignore human reality by insisting on the unattainable, or to appease human whims by permitting sanctions. Rather, it would uphold certain principles as inviolable, provide for some measure of readjustment to new situations, facilitate the attainment of the ends desired without necessarily absolutizing the means employed, and stand prepared to cope with emergency or "deviant" cases. In Islām blood ties and marital bonds embody such inviolable principles, but these principles do not require

unconditional perpetuation of any given concrete family
unit. Family expectations are inviolable as long as the family
unit remains intact, but the unit does not persist indefinitely.
Should it break up, there are provisions in Islām to deal with
the situation. If the breaking up is due to death, the rules
of succession apply and the intrafamily positions may have
to be readjusted accordingly. If the reason is divorce, desertion, or incompatibility, certain procedures must be followed to ensure justice and equity. The point to be emphasized is that continuity of the family institution is not identical with, or dependent upon, the perpetuation of any concrete family unit. Members are enjoined to maintain their
family structure intact, but they are not forced to do so
indefinitely.[43]

Bearing upon the perpetuation of the family structure is the
question of *mut'ah,* or "pleasure," temporary marriage, which
was practiced before Islām and continued for a while after the
rise of Islām until it was prohibited along with most other
types of sexual relationship. In an earlier period *mut'ah* was
contracted on a temporary basis and had similarities to, and
differences from, the common contract of marriage. Islām
established the rule that, if a marriage is to be valid, it must
be free from any condition of temporality or restriction in
regard to duration. It must be entered into with the intention
of cherishing its bonds as long as humanly possible.[44] But in
the Islāmic social order, this does not necessarily require the
absolute indissolubility of marriage, because categorical indissolubility may not always be the most wholesome rectifi-
cation of laxity, incompatibility, or stormy unions. And it
does not seem to be the approach of Islām to remedy social
extremities by other extremities. Thus, it did not absolutize
the individual marital bonds, for that may render them meaningless symbols or mere rituals. Nor did it sanction the *mut'ah*
marriage. It must be noted, however, that some branches
of the *Shī'ī* school of thought hold that the *mut'ah* marriage
is permissible in Islām as it had been earlier, though they

consider it neither commendable nor popular. The conflicting arguments and perspectives will be considered in some
detail in a later section.[45]

I. Cohabitation with Captives

Of the numerous pre-Islāmic patterns of sexual behavior,
Islām approves only of contracted normal marriage and
"marriage-like" cohabitation. Any other sexual relation
is absolutely prohibited.[46] The fact that Islām arose in an
environment which had more or less tolerated diverse patterns of sexual behavior, and that it allowed cohabitation
with slaves alongside normal marriage, has been responsible
for some controversial observations. It is sometimes claimed
that, with such a background of sexual variety and laxity,
Islām could not have done more than it did, and what it
did was the best then, according to some apologists, or the
best then and ever, according to others. Other critics claim
that Islām had neither the social interest nor the moral strength
to introduce basic changes in the lax sexual standards of the
time. They usually illustrate the point by alluding to Islām's
approval of cohabitation with slaves and polygyny.[47] We
will reconsider the problem further in Chapter 4. It may be
helpful here to point out some significant facts and suggest
some explanations.

It is a fact that Islām prohibited all patterns of sexual behavior except marriage and marriage-like cohabitation. It is
equally true that both normal marriage and cohabitation with
slaves had been in practice before Islām, and that, as will be
seen, under Islām they took on new features which can hardly
be mistaken for sexual laxity and licentiousness. Probably
nothing could have been easier or more readily popular for
Islām than an unconditional endorsement of the sexual practices of the age. In point of fact, Islām did not adopt this
course. Nor is there evidence that it was inclined to shy away
from sensitive areas such as sex. The Qur'ān, the Traditions
of the Prophet, and the law books have all addressed them-

selves to the problem of sexual behavior so extensively that some observers have thought it out of proportion.[48]

Any serious consideration of sexual mores at the time Islām arose could not have bypassed the problem of concubinage and its far-reaching implications. Islām's approach to the problem was neither outright prohibition nor unqualified approval. This course was probably a reflection of Islām's general conception of piety and human worth as well as of practicality and gradualism. To illustrate the point it is unnecessary to review the entire Islāmic position on the complex details of slavery, of which concubinage is only a variant. But some aspects of the problem are noteworthy.

Before the rise of Islām, there had been many sources of slavery within and without Arabia. Maintaining a continuous and sufficient supply of slaves depended chiefly on warfare. Children born to slave parents constituted the second major source of supply. In addition, individuals were reduced into slavery as a punishment for various crimes or for nonpayment of debt. Gordon points out that in many societies an insolvent debtor became liable to ownership or sale as a slave by the creditor. Many early societies also permitted a free individual to sell himself or others under his jurisdiction into slavery. Under these conditions, and since slavery was conceived as a species of dependent labor, the institution was regarded as essential to the economy of these societies, either to supplement or to replace the existing labor force.[49] It seemed, therefore, perfectly logical to such a philosopher as Aristotle to maintain that "slavery is based on nature, and that certain races are intended to be subject." [50]

In Islām, all sources of slavery except two, were declared unlawful. The two exceptions were birth from slave parents and "war."

Furthermore, other fundamental changes were introduced, of which the most remarkable was probably the rule that slave emancipation became not only a virtuous act, but also a religio-legal obligation to expiate certain offenses, for example, mistaken manslaughter. Therefore, according to the Islāmic regulations, the slave is not to be harrassed, humiliated, or overcharged with labor. He is to be treated in a kind, humane manner to be fed and clothed with the same materials as his master, to be encouraged to seek his freedom, and to be supported by private as well as public funds to enhance its attainment.[51]

It should be noted, nevertheless, that not every war is a legitimate basis of slavery, nor is every prisoner destined to become a slave as has been customary. The war must be justified, defensive, and declared by the caliph or head of state against avowed enemies. Secondly, if the prisoner is found to have embraced Islām before his capture, he is not subject to slavery, but remains free. Third, even if the prisoner has been captured in a legitimate war and has not chosen Islām, Muslims may grant him freedom with or without compensation. Indeed, it is regarded as a highly meritorious act to contribute to the cause of slave emancipation. These rules apply to both female and male slaves. But a woman has another opportunity for freedom by cohabiting with her master.[52] This is the problem which directly bears on the family and on sexual morality and which has led to some conflicting observations.[53]

The details are complex and intriguing, but the general problem may be considered briefly. Although Islām allows cohabitation between masters and slaves, if a master wishes to take his slave to wife, he must first of all set her free and then consummate the marriage. That is also true of a free woman and her male slave. But if the master does not wish to marry her as a freewoman, he may cohabit with her, with significant consequences. Such cohabitation is not considered commendable under normal circumstances. According to Islām, the preferable choice for a Muslim is to marry a free, believing woman. If need be, he may marry up to four. But if he is too poor to marry, or if he is afraid of doing injustice to his free wives, should there be more than one, he may resort to one of three alternatives in the following order of preference: he may exercise willpower and temporarily abstain; he

may marry a slave girl; or he may cohabit with his own slave.
The religio-moral principle behind these rules is expressed in
the Qur'ān:

If you fear that you will not act justly toward the
orphans, marry such women as seem good to you, two,
three, four; but if you fear you will not be equitable,
then only one, *or* what your right hands own; so it is
likelier you will not be partial (4:3 [emphasis added].

Any one of you who has not the affluence to be able
to marry believing freewomen in wedlock, let him take
believing handmaidens that your hands own; Allah
knows very well your faith, the one of you is as of the
other. So marry them with their people's leave, and give
them their dowers honourably as women in wedlock,
not as in license (4:29).

Marry the spouseless among you, and your slaves and
handmaidens that are righteous; if they are poor, Allah
will enrich them of His bounty; Allah is All-Embracing,
All-Knowing.

And let those who find not the means to marry be
abstinent till Allah enriches them of His bounty. Those
your right hands own who seek emancipation, contract
with them accordingly, if you know some good in them;
and give them of the wealth of Allah that He has given
you. And constrain not your slavegirls to prostitution
if they desire to live in chastity that you may seek the
chance goods of the present life. Whosoever constrains
them, surely Allah, after their being constrained, is All-
Forgiving, All-Compassionate (24:32-33) [emphasis
added].[54]

Unlike marriage, there is no legal limit set to the number
of slavegirls with whom a master may cohabit. But like
marriage, he may not cohabit with already married slaves; or
two or more who are sisters or who stand in such relationship
to one another that marriage with them at the time would
be forbidden to him if they were free; or with idolatresses;
nor is he allowed to cohabit with a newly acquired slave

before the passing of a period long enough to determine if she is pregnant. Cohabitation is permissible only with Muslim, Christian or Jewish slaves, just as contractual marriage is. In any case whether a master cohabits with his slaves or not, he may not force them to have relations with other men or hinder their quest for freedom.[55]

In the precepts of Islām cohabitation is not the unqualified prerogative of a master free to exploit his slaves. Rather, it is assumed to be a responsible, conscientious relationship of highly significant and far-reaching consequences. It is not a mere sexual pursuit, nor is sex itself devoid of spiritual implications. As Levy has phrased it, provided it is attained legitimately, "satisfaction of the sexual instinct is encouraged and may be mentioned in prayer or thanksgiving along with other blessings." However, if cohabitation results in the birth of a child, male or female, the master is enjoined to acknowledge it as his legitimate child. Once legitimacy is established, the child is regarded as born free and cannot be subject to slavery. The same rule applies to all the children subsequently born to the couple. One acknowledgment is sufficient to establish the evidence that the master has chosen to cohabit with the child's mother. If this is established, all the children born to them henceforth are born free and occupy the same positions as those of the children of free parents. Further, it is unlawful to sell a pregnant slave or even accept a freedom ransom from her. She may be set free or remain in an intermediate position, between slavery and freedom, till the death of the master, at which time she unconditionally becomes free. Cohabitation in these circumstances could serve as an additional outlet to freedom, a step toward the gradual reduction of the breeding sources of slavery.[56]

With respect to the slave who has given birth through cohabitation, the consequences are important. Reminded of the fact that it is a religious virtue to free a slave, a virtue which is doubly rewarded if the emancipator married his freed slave, and realizing what the birth of a child could symbolize, a master may be motivated to set his slave free before, upon, or after the child's birth. Nevertheless, whether or not he sets her free, she can no longer be legally classified as a slave. She assumes the special rank of a "child's mother" (*'Umm walad*). This means that the master's authority over her is so restricted that he can neither sell her, nor give her away, nor do anything that may hinder her ultimate freedom. If the master dies before he voluntarily liberates her, she becomes, upon his death, unconditionally free and assumes the status of a completely freedwoman.[57]

These are some religio-social and legal implications of cohabitation. The Islāmic rules in this regard are subject to controversial explanations. Jeffery, for example, has noted that, "Several passages in the Qur'ān allow men *sexual freedom* with their slave *concubines.* . . . There is no limit to the number of concubines a man may have. . . . The children born to him by concubines, if he recognizes them, have the same status as those born by his *legal wives.*" [58] Another writer has also noted that a Muslim's female slaves "are allowed to him without restriction. Sûra (Qur'ān) 70,29ff."[59] According to the same writer, this is "one of the earliest compromises by which the Prophet fitted his system to the usages and wants of those around him. This permission naturally furnished a strong inducement to his followers to fight the battles of Islām since the women taken captive in battle would become lawful concubines of their captors." [60]

Such conclusions, however, raise as many questions as they answer: Why did the Arabs have to wait for Islām to allow them the very things which they had been doing all along, but probably in easier, less responsible ways? If Islām was inclined to license this kind of sexual laxity why did it prohibit all sexual relations except in wedlock and marriage-like cohabitation, prescribe punishments for sexual offenses as severe as stoning to death, surround cohabitation with so many regulations, and generally recommend or occasionally demand slave emancipation?

Looking into the problem from another perspective, we should recall that fruitful cohabitation was conceived as an irreversible passage to ultimate freedom for the slavegirl as well as for all her descendents, and that such a course could eventually reduce to a considerable extent one basic source of slavery, birth from slave parents. It has also been suggested that Islām may be said thereby to have redirected man's sexual needs towards moral and humane goals. Capitalizing on the strong sexual drives of men in an area of the world which, in Patai's words, "has always been of high and intense sexuality," Islām encouraged cohabitation with slaves as another avenue to liberation for them and their children. This may be particularly significant if it is realized that the slave's offspring were often the children of wealthy owners who kept slaves for domestic purposes. It is further suggested that, to enhance the cause of liberation, Islām did not limit the number of slaves with whom a master may cohabit because the greater the number, the closer to freedom they become.[61]

At worst, such views can be characterized as latter-day rationalizations or strained apologetics; at best they may be regarded as an idealistic or theoretical projection of the spirit of religion into human history. Whether Muslims in fact observed these rules closely or were at all capable of fully implementing this interpretation of their religion is an empirical question, although it cannot be definitively decided at this point. However, it is untenable to assume that abuses, violations, and exploitations were unknown or rare among Muslims. It is equally untenable to assume categorically that abuse was the rule, that violation of norms was the customary practice or that exploitation went undeterred. Despite the numerous accounts of court corruption, the slaves' role in domestic and public life and the harem world of mystery and intrigue,[62] it requires an overstretch of the imagination to believe that slaves were abundant and easily obtainable (almost like the modern supermarket's commodities) and that virtually every person did or could acquire slaves or maintain a harem of sorts. Demographic, economic, and social factors would render such accounts highly questionable. The military spirit and missionary zeal of the early Muslims, the intellectual in-

terests and scientific pursuits of their successors, the political
conflicts of the various factions and the emergence of regional
nationalism or provincialism, the increasing partisanship and
competitiveness among jurists, bureaucrats, court advisors,
poets and so on[63]—these would make it almost inconceivable
that a society, so ambitious and vigorous in the early decades,
probably affluent but overextended and apparently troubled in
later years, could afford on any large scale the lax, indolent
life to which these accounts refer. An analogy may be suggestive in this respect: The life style touted by *Playboy* and
other sensational media, or the outraged descriptions found in
moralistic-evangelical publications are not authentic accounts
of the mainstream of contemporary American society, but
neither are they absolutely groundless. Rather, they must
be received with a critical and skeptical mind.

At any rate, the Islāmic rules of cohabitation may be interpreted as reflective of Islām's general conception of social
stratification and integration. There are strong indications
that cohabitation contributed manifestly, as well as latently
to social equality and interracial solidarity. By the end of
the ninth century, the pre-Islāmic Arabian ideal of lineage
had almost entirely vanished, and the struggle for a kind of
practical equality had been won. Significant in this context
is the fact that all the caliphs of the 'Abbāsī Dynasty, except
the first three, were the sons of Turkish, Greek, or even Black
slavegirls.[64] But whether Islām gave a new impetus to the institution of slavery as some observers think, or was intended to
gradually exhaust its sources, as others look at it, and whether
Muhammad accepted slavery as an integral part of the social
system or was inclined to eliminate it, the fact remains that
Islām hardly made the elimination of slavery more difficult
than it had been or less attainable than it is now. On the
contrary, it seems to have introduced unprecedented measures,
positive and preventive, direct and indirect, to facilitate the
freeing of slaves. And despite the violations and abuses which
must have occurred, contemporary critics, such as Gordon,
have observed that slavery in Muslim countries:

has always been very different from that which existed in Rome and the Americas. . . . Gang-slavery for work . . . was almost unknown in the Islāmic world. Most of the slaves were employed in wealthy households for domestic service and were well treated in accordance with the prescriptions of the Koran. The one really cruel Muslim institution was that of eunuchs, which involved emasculation. Women slaves in harems became their masters' concubines, or even legitimate wives. Liberated slaves of whatever origin were readily absorbed as equal members of the community and examples of slaves or former slaves reaching the highest positions were numerous.[65]

3   MARRIAGE IN ISLAM

The foundations of the family in Islām are blood ties and marriage arrangements, more or less precisely defined. Behind such conceptions lay the diversity of pre-Islāmic Arabian society, in which almost every imaginable form of marital and sexual relationship had been practiced. The advent of Islām brought, as we have seen, the restriction of permissible sexual relations to marriage and marriage-like cohabitation. The restriction, however, was by no means simply interpreted and implemented; from it emerged complex patterns and rationales, which continue to be subjects of discussion in Islāmic societies.

A. *Control of Sexual Behavior*

Human behavior has always been subject to rules because social life would be inconceivable otherwise. As Hobhouse has put it, "In no part of the world, and at no period of time, do we find the behaviour of men left to unchartered freedom." [1] This is particularly true of sexual behavior, since "sex is capable of impelling individuals, reckless of consequences while under its spell, toward behavior which may imperil or disrupt the cooperative relationships upon which social life depends." [2] It is true that sex is more capable than other drives of being diverted into substitutive forms of expression or sublimation. Nevertheless, modern clinical research and evidence clearly indicate that excessive sexual deprivation produces personality maladjustments that hinder satisfactory relationships and endanger the mental health and efficiency of society. [3]

What the clinical evidence suggests is supported by historical evidence. For example, the unfavorable view of sex among the early Christians was a basic force in the development of a complex system of demonological beliefs about carnal love.

"Innumerable" saints are reported to have been convinced that they were tempted at night by "Voluptuous and lascivious succubi, or female demons, that tormented [them]." Nuns and other Christian women asserted that they were visited at night by the equally seductive and alluring incubus, a fallen angel, who had coitus with them. Pope Innocent VIII, Pope Benedict XIV, St. Augustine and St. Thomas, among other religious leaders, accepted the existence of incubi and succubi as a given. They dealt with the subject both seriously and extensively.[4]

Muslims of early centuries believed that sexual deprivation could lead to mental and physical disturbances bordering on insanity. One observer related that a group of people had decided to abstain for ascetic reasons, but soon they developed physical as well as mental abnormalities, especially depression and fatigue. It was widely believed that sexual deprivation was contrary to the preservation of the human species, harmful to health and destructive of moral integrity. It was, therefore, in the interest of the individual and society that sexual relationships be sanctioned and regulated, not condemned or ignored.[5] This would surely be important if we could accept Patai's characterization of the Middle East as an area of intense sexuality.[6]

Sex, then, is crucial to social survival and personality development. It "is intimately bound up with deep psychological gratifications: the need for security, feelings of personal worth, feelings of power, and the assurance of being loved and lovable."[7] So crucial is sex that no social system can afford to ignore it or be indifferent to its implications. The light in which a religion views sex is probably most indicative of that religion with regard to man, society, and the universe. It seems almost axiomatic that a religious system which devalues sex would be most otherworldly, would initially discourage marriage but defend its insolubility once consummated, would belittle family life and depict women as contemptible sex symbols.[8] By contrast, a system which overestimates sex would be no less injurious to social stability.

B. *Islām's Position on Marriage*

Unlike the doctrine of the Hebrew Essenes and the early Christian ascetics, but in common with the main body of Jewish and other human traditions, Islām recognizes the value of sex and advocates marriage. It strongly discourages celibacy, even for ascetic reasons. The normal, natural course of behavior for a Muslim is to establish a conjugal family of procreation. This is the common practice of ordinary men, spiritual leaders and even prophets. To that effect, there are many passages in the Qur'ān and the Traditions of the Prophet which go as far as to say that when a Muslim marries he thereby perfects half his religion; so let him be God-minded with respect to the other half.[9]

Muslim jurists have interpreted the Qur'ān to mean that marriage is a religious duty and is consequently a moral safeguard as well as a social necessity. As a religious duty, it must be fulfilled; but like all other duties in Islām, it is enjoined only upon those who are capable of meeting the responsibilities involved. The predominant view among the jurists is that, although marriage is a social necessity, it is not *absolutely* necessary for *every* individual. Hence, they have developed a rough typology to classify individuals with regard to their marriageability from the point of view of religion. First, some individuals are apprehensive that abstinence may lead them astray. For these, marriage is a religious duty because they must guard against illegitimate sexuality, and marriage is the natural mechanism of such moral protection. Second, some individuals are capable and desirous of sex but are not so apprehensive of excess; they anticipate no irresistible temptation or lack of self-control. For these, marriage is preferable to abstinence and even to supererogatory devotion, which is voluntarily undertaken to uplift a person's spiritual and moral state. Third, there are individuals who lack potency, for some reason or other. In this case, marriage is still considered preferable to abstinence by some jurists, while others argue that abstinence is preferable because marriage under such conditions will defeat its purpose and deprive the female partners of the moral protection they need and the fulfillment they merit.[10]

Although Islām advocated marriage and took various measures to regulate its functioning, it seems to have realized that marriage is not a light commitment. A person must be fairly certain of his ability to meet the responsibility of marriage before taking a spouse. It is true that in Islām poverty is no barrier to a successful marriage; Allah has, as the Qur'ān puts it, undertaken to provide for every living creature, and He can, and has promised to, enrich the poor mates of His bounty. But, at the same time, Islām recognized that it may not always be possible for everyone to have at his disposal the means to marriage. There can arise obstacles of various kinds and problems of varying magnitude. But Islām's response to these is not in the direction of celibacy, laxity, or aversion to marriage and sex altogether. Rather, it prescribes several specific measures, the last of which is resort to self-discipline and temporary abstinence in the hope that the assured help of Allah will be forthcoming. The Prophet intimated that whoever can marry should do so, but he who cannot, should practice voluntary fasting, which helps him to safeguard his moral integrity and to assume command over his desires. The immediate implication of all this is probably that neither sex nor marriage is dismissed easily or taken lightly.[11]

As might be expected, this doctrine was not always fully internalized or implemented by all segments of Muslim society. There have been some mystic Ṣūfīs who abstained from marriage and regarded family responsibility as incompatible with their personal spiritual aspirations. The rise of such individuals and the circulation of their beliefs may be more indicative of social tension than of personal preference on their part or of actual incompatibility of family life and spiritual ambitions. It seems to have been more in the nature of individual protest and withdrawal than real incompatibility or deficiency of the marriage doctrine proper. Extreme trends advocating abstinence from marriage and withdrawal from

society probably emerged in reaction to the political dissension
and moral laxity that befell Muslim society, affecting particularly its power structure.[12] The general Ṣūfī trend is sometimes believed to have been encouraged by worldly personalities in the power structure.[13] The apparent paradox is
partly explained by the fact that it was in the interest of the
contemporary leadership to divert the attention of the common
people from political interests and mundane concerns in general, so that opposition and rivalry would be reduced to a
minimum. "Asceticism" and its concomitants, were regarded
as a "rational" means to that end. But there is another theory
that political authorities were opposed to extreme Ṣūfīsm even
to the extent of persecuting its advocates because they were
causing public disorder and propagating a worldview which,
if widely embraced, would disrupt social life.[14] Both theories
have elements of validity, but neither seems adequate by itself to account for the facts. It is likely that political authorities on some occasions tolerated or even encouraged, implicitly or explicitly, the Ṣūfī ascetics who might have been
regarded as harmless, otherworldly pacifists. In other circumstances when some of these Ṣūfīs went to the extreme
and made pronouncements that were considered heretical,
the political authorities took action to protect themselves as
well as to maintain order. At any rate, such Ṣūfīs were in the
minority, and not all of them were of the pacifist type, nor
were all influences upon Ṣūfīsm internal to Islām.[15]

C. *The Purposes of Marriage*

The strong emphasis that Islām has put on marriage may be
seen more clearly in the context of the purposes that marriage
is designated to serve. In common with other systems, Islām
favors marriage as a means to emotional and sexual gratification; as a mechanism of tension reduction, legitimate procreation, and social placement; as an approach to interfamily
alliance and group solidarity. But there seems to be a difference
of degree, at least, in that Islām's relatively greater stress on
these ends enhanced to a corresponding degree the value

placed on marriage. The social significance of this difference in emphasis is that marriage was contracted while the prospective mates were still relatively young, and that it was more common among Muslims than among others. Progeny apparently were highly desirable and were received with enthusiasm. It is true that many of these practices go back to pre-Islāmic times, when Arab men preferred to marry young virgins and to seek marriage outside their immediate kinship group, in the belief that it was more conducive to numerous as well as healthy progeny. Such practices continued in Islām and were approved by the Prophet.[16]

What is probably most characteristic of the Islāmic position, is that marriage, apart from these functions and perhaps also because of them, is regarded first and foremost as an act of piety. Sexual control may be a moral triumph, reproduction a social necessity or service, and sound health a gratifying state of mind. Yet these values take on a special meaning and are reinforced if they are intertwined with the idea of Allah, conceived of as religious commitments, and internalized as divine blessings. And this seems to be the focal point of marriage in Islām, even though it does not exclude or underrate the other purposes. To paraphrase some Qur'ānic verses, the call is addressed to mankind to be dutiful to God, who created them from a single soul, and from it, or of it, created its mate, and from the two of them spread abroad many men and women (4:1). It was Allah who created mankind out of one living soul, and created of that soul a spouse so that he might find comfort and rest in her (7:107). And it is a sign of Allah that He has created for men, of themselves, mates to seek in their company peace and tranquility, and has set between them mutual love and mercy. "Surely, in that are signs for those who contemplate" (30:20). Even at the most trying times of married life, and in the midst of legal disputes and litigations, the Qur'ān reminds the mates involved of Allah's injunctions to be kind and charitable to one another and dutiful to Allah.[17]

It is noteworthy that the Islāmic marriage provisions apply

equally to men and women. For example, if celibacy is not recommended for men, the same is true for women; marriage is the normal course for both of them. It may be even more so for women since it assures them of relative economic security, among other things. This added advantage for women does not, however, picture marriage as a purely economic transaction. In fact, the least focal aspect of marriage in the precepts of Islām is the economic factor, no matter how powerful this may have been in other ideologies. The Prophet is reported to have said that a woman is ordinarily sought as a wife for her wealth, for her beauty, for the nobility in her stock, or for her religiosity; but blessed and fortunate is he who chooses his mate on the basis of piety and integrity. The Qur'ān commends marriage to the spouseless and the pious even though they may be poor or slaves (24:32). On the other hand, whatever dowry a man gives his prospective wife belongs to her exclusively and whatever she may have acquired before or after marriage is hers alone. There is no statutory community of property of husbands and wives. Furthermore, it is the husband who is responsible for the support and economic security of the family. He must even provide his wife with the kind of help and service to which she was accustomed before marriage. According to some jurists, the wife is under no *legal* obligation to do the routine housework, although she may do so, and usually does, as the family situation requires.[18]

D. *Marriage: Sacrament or Contract?*

The question of whether marriage is a sacrament or a contract seems hardly applicable in Islām. The traditional conception of sacramental marriage implies, among other things, indissolubility of the marital bond, officiation by a priest, and benediction of the wedding ceremony. The sacramental definition of marriage regards it as "a rite which removes the taboo on sexual intercourse between a man and a woman, while at the same time imposing a lifelong taboo on the intercourse of either of them with a third party." [19]

The idea of sacrament seems to be related to the status of

womanhood and the general attitude to sex. If a given system defines sex as an evil in itself, but unavoidable to prevent greater evils, it is expected that marriage will not be encouraged under normal conditions and will be minimized when there is no other legitimate alternative. In such a system, celibacy will have priority. But when marriage becomes necessary, it is likely to be of the monogamous type and to take on the features of a sacrament, not necessarily because the marital relationship is in itself a sacred bond, but perhaps because sexuality, as a necessary evil, will be restricted to a minimum. That situation will not arise if sex is defined favorably, in which case marriage will be relatively more frequent and the marital bond less difficult to dissolve. The features of sacrament may not come into this picture at all; even if they do, it is unlikely that they will be in the forefront. A favorable view of legitimate sexuality does not seem more conducive to sexual violations than does the counterview. If this is so, the *idea* of sacrament will probably make little difference with regard to the frequency of actual violations of the sexual norms.

On the other hand, the idea of sacrament implies that marital partners are bound together by a sacred bond to which a Supreme Being is also a party. This would appear to suggest that women are equally committed to the bond, that they stand on an equal footing with men, and that they are equally endowed with sacred and moral potentials. A further implication is that the human worth of women is not less than that of men. It is conceivable, however, that in a "guilt-conscious" system, initial disregard for women may eventually lead to the idea of sacrament. It may come about as a result of men's feelings of injustice to women and the desire to remedy it, or as a consequence of women's persistent quest for equality. There is also the theoretical possibility that the idea of sacrament may arise in a system that has a strong ecclesiastical body or regards marriage as an inescapable penalty, a kind of moral sentence that is to be served in full.

The fact that the ancient Mediterranean and Near Eastern

cultures did not define sex as evil and generally held women
in low esteem may explain, at least in part, the absence of the
doctrine of sacrament in their marriage systems.[20] Similarly,
the ancient Hebrews and their descendants considered sex no
evil and, technically if not in fact, generally held women in a
subordinate position.[21] This may explain that, while in Jewish
law marriage was conceived as a divine institution (Genesis
2:24), it was not regarded as a sacrament — "the priestly
benediction is mentioned neither in the Bible nor in the Talmud, and the regular presence of a rabbi at a wedding is not
earlier than the fourteenth century." [22]

The case of Christianity is rather remarkable. Under the
influence of eschatalogical expectations and oppressive social
conditions, some leaders of early Christianity viewed both sex
and marriage quite negatively. To them, celibacy was the
favored status, since it represented the highest virtue on the
Christian value scale. When marriage did take place among
Christians, as it must have in most instances, it was expected
to be of the monogamous, indissoluble type. Also, in common
with, or perhaps in continuation of, the formal doctrinal
Jewish tradition, early Christianity held a relatively low
opinion of the spiritual qualities of women.[23] Jewish influence
and social harassment doubtless made early Christianity's
position equivocal. The elements of monogamy, marriage
indissolubility, preference for celibacy, and preoccupation
with the problem of salvation were highly conducive to the
sacramental idea of marriage. On the other hand, the low
opinion of the spiritual qualities of women, the absence of an
established ecclesiastical body, consideration of marriage as
a private matter, and women's resignation to a traditional
subordinate status seemed incompatible with the sacramental
doctrine of marriage. This early equivocal stance may explain
why the dogma of sacramental marriage was recognized only
in the twelfth century and did not become fully institutionalized until the fourteenth.[24]

It may be interesting to note that this development corresponded with the increasing freedoms granted to women and

with the growing cult of womanhood centered on the Virgin. After the Reformation, however, marriage in the Protestant societies "ceased to be thought of as sacrament, but continued to be regarded as a divine institution." [25]

The case of Islām is still more remarkable. The distinction between sacred and secular was never explicit in Islām. Any action or transaction has religious implications. Legitimate sex is not defined as evil. Women, at least in doctrine, are not held inferior to men on the spiritual level,[26] since they are not thought of as "guilty" of any offenses from which men were, or are, free and immune.[27] Moreover, marriage in Islām was not conditional on officiation by a priest because, strictly speaking, there was no such office. Neither was religious benediction, though highly recommended for the occasion, a necessary requisite for the validity of the marriage. Another factor of importance is that Islām sanctions marriage to non-Muslim women who do not necessarily share the religious persuasion of their husbands, in which case a concept, e.g., sacrament, relevant to one party's persuasion may not apply to that of another. Furthermore, the marital bonds are not indissoluble and conditional polygyny is lawful. These features would seem to preclude the traditional idea of sacrament in so far as marriage in Islām is concerned.

In view of these factors, some observers have been led to stress the contractual nature of marriage in Islām. They maintain that marriage as a contract cannot be concluded without the mutual consent of the parties involved. It is open for additional, but legitimate, conditions and its terms are, within legal bounds, capable of being altered. It is dissoluble if there arise grievances leading to an irreconcilable break in the marital relations.[28] Sometimes, however, the stress on the socio-legal and contractual elements of marriage tends to obscure the religious aspect: "marriage is a contract, but it is also a covenant." [29] It is not quite accurate, therefore, to designate marriage in Islām as either a secular contract or a religious sacrament; it has elements of both. The appropriate designation would seem to be that of a "divine institution."

E. *The Conditions of Marriage*

It is clear, then, that the Qur'ān describes marriage as a solemn covenant between Allah and the human parties as well as between these parties themselves. If it is to be consummated and become valid, certain conditions must be satisfied. Some of these conditions pertain to the contract itself; some to the persons of the contracting parties. The details are intriguing, and the difference of opinion is sometimes considerable. Only the general features can be discussed here.

When a marriage is contracted, there must be a direct, unequivocal proposal followed by a corresponding acceptance thereof. Both proposal and acceptance must be explicit and oral if the contracting parties are present in person. Otherwise, a written form may substitute for the oral. That is not the same as having the contract registered after its conclusion, a procedure which seems to have been introduced in later periods for administrative purposes. The words used in the contract must be directly derived from, or intimately related to, the root word of marriage. Except in certain *Shī'ī* view, the contract must be free from any indication of temporality or limited duration, because this contradicts the very purpose of marriage, which is the intention of making it a lifelong union.[30] There must be at least two competent witnesses so that the progeny's right of legitimacy will be safeguarded. The contract requires the contribution of a "dowry," or marriage gift, by the groom to the bride. If the amount of the dowry is not specified in the contract, the marriage is valid, and the dowry is to be estimated according to the customary standards. In any case, the bride may voluntarily return it in part or *in toto* to the groom.[31]

Related to the condition of witnesses is the question of publicity. Not only is marriage to be intended as a lifelong bond, it must also be publicized widely. An agreement to keep the marriage secret invalidates the contract, in the opinion of some jurists. Other jurists maintain that the contract is valid but that secrecy is nonreligious and thus reprehensible. The idea seems to be that marriage is, in Jeffery's words, "a community matter and Muslim communities in general attach considerable importance to the social ceremonies connected with marriage." Moreover, publicity is the element which distinguishes legitimate unions from illicit ones. This was probably the reason for the Prophet to recommend marriage feasts and sanction folk music and singing at wedding ceremonies.[32]

The contracting woman must be free from all marital bonds. That is, she must not be already married at the time of considering another marriage. If she is widowed or divorced, she must be free from pregnancy; but if she is expectant, she must wait until the infant is born, after which time she may contract a marriage. Neither must she be in a "waiting period," which is the limited span of time that is to elapse before a widow or a divorcée may remarry.[33] Nor must she fall within the forbidden degrees of blood, fosterage, or affinal relationships.[34] She has to be a monotheist and a follower of a divine book.[35] She must be free from adultery and fornication; that is forbidden for the Believers. If she has committed any such offense, it is not lawful for her, in certain cases, to marry her co-offender, in the opinion of some jurists. Nor is it lawful for either to marry anyone within the forbidden degrees of the other party, according to some schools of law. For example, it is forbidden for her to marry the son or father of her co-offender, just as it is for him to marry her daughter or mother. Adultery or fornication is not only a sinful act; it also results in the curtailment of the personal freedom and social privileges of the violators.[36] A free woman of sound mind and full age must give her consent to marriage if the contract is to be valid. In the absence of a legal guardian, *walī*, she must be of sound mind and have reached the age of puberty before she is allowed to marry. In every case the identity of each party must be known to the other.[37]

The contracting man must be a Muslim if the woman whom he wishes to marry is a Muslim herself. If he is already married, his present wife must not be related to the prospective bride in any degree that forbids him from maintaining the two contemporaneously. For example, he may not

marry the sister, niece or aunt of his present wife. Also, if he
happens to have more than one wife, the number must be
within the maximum limit of four. He cannot contract any
new marriage as long as his marital bond to the four is valid
and intact. In the absence of a legal guardian, *walī*, he must
be of sound mind, have reached the age of puberty, and must
give his free consent, if his marriage is to be valid[38]

F. *Dowry, Marriage-endowment, Marriage-gift*
Among the conditions of marriage the question of dowry has
been the subject of consideration from various perspectives.
The conception of dowry is usually associated with a particular type of marriage, namely, marriage by purchase. This type
of marriage "has been widely spread throughout the world and
throughout history . . . [It] has prevailed in all branches of
the Semitic race . . . [But] we should notice that marriage
by purchase did not imply the purchase of a piece of property . . ."[39]
Two basic types of dowry have been practiced. The first
type is that which is paid by the groom or his family to the
bride or her family. It normally consists of money, property,
or movable objects. Sometimes it is made up of gifts which are
offered by the groom's party and which may or may not be
reciprocated by the bride's. It may also consist of service rendered by the groom to the family of the bride. Further, a
wife could have been acquired by means of exchange when a
man agreed to exchange his daughter or ward for another's.
The second basic type of dowry is that which is rendered by
the bride or her family to the groom or his family. This was
common in some ancient societies and is still so in some modern
ones. However, the two basic types of dowry are not mutually
exclusive, nor are their subtypes.[40]
The fact that marriage has been for so long accompanied by
a "bride price" or "groom price" is interesting. The origin of
the bride price, according to a contemporary anthropologist,
"must be sought in a family setup in which a young girl was
an economic asset for her father's family. The departure of the

girl from her own family was an economic loss, and this was compensated by the bride price. From the point of view of the bridegroom's family, the acquisition of a wife meant the addition of a pair of working hands in exchange for the amount paid over to the bride's family." [41] This may explain the origin of the custom, but it can hardly explain its continuation where there are no such extended families, or where the woman herself is the recipient of dowry.

Besides this economic factor, there is also a procreative one, which is not entirely free from economic considerations. The bride price is likely to be stipulated in a patrilineal system where a new union "holds out the promise of increasing the number and strength of the bridegroom's family . . . No comparable advantage occurs . . . to the mother's family . . ." The father not only loses a daughter but also all her future progeny. He should, therefore, receive some material compensation for his losses. Sometimes the payment of a large bride price "may be the expression of the love of the bridegroom for his bride." [42] Yet, here again, this theory may explain only some cases, not the whole pattern of bride price. It is limited by the fact that it applies to a patrilineal system in which the bride's family is the recipient of dowry, or where dowry is regarded as proportionate to the intensity of love. But this does not account for the variants of the general pattern of dowry.

There are situations where the bride's family pays a marriage portion to the groom or his family. This is common in monogamous societies, where the sex ratio is low, where a large number of males never marry, and, finally, where married women lead an indolent life. In such societies, the marriage portion frequently becomes a purchase sum by which a father buys a husband for his daughter.[43] This is true of modern as well as ancient societies. In some cases, however, as in ancient Babylonia, the dowry (marriage portion) brought by the bride remained her property, although the husband had the usufruct of it. In other cases, as in Athens, it was "the wife's contribution toward the expenses of the marriage, and at the same time served as an obstacle to the dissolution of the union for frivolous reasons." The Roman tradition of the *dos* or dower contributed by the bride's father was adopted by the Church to secure for the wife an inviolable provision which would remain hers after the husband's death.[44]

The association of dowry with marriage by purchase has been a source of confusion and inconsistency. For example, one reason for the seriousness of engagement among the Hebrews "was the *mohar,* or dowry, which was given by the groom to the prospective bride's father."[45] Yet, on the other hand, it is believed that the normal marriage in Hebrew society was by purchase where the bride's father provided a dowry which the husband could only manage and which was restored to its source at the dissolution of the marriage.[46] It is not clear, however, whether the *mohar* (marriage price) and the dowry (marriage portion) were contemporaneous and universal. Nor is it certain whether they both went to the wife as personal possessions or were earmarked for future use. The idea of marriage by purchase or marriage price is probably misleading, as is depicting the girl's father as a bargaining beneficiary and recipient of compensation for his economic losses.

With this comparative background, it may be possible to see dowry in Islam in full perspective. Dowry is used here to designate what a Muslim groom gives to his prospective bride. It is her personal property which she is empowered to waive, reduce, return to her husband, or dispense with as she pleases. It is enjoined by the Qur'ān, the Traditions of the Prophet, and the consensus of Muslims. It may consist of money, property, movable objects, or services rendered to the bride herself. There is a Tradition that a Companion of the Prophet wanted to marry a certain woman but had nothing to offer her in dowry. The Prophet asked him to teach her whatever he knew of the Qur'ān, and that sufficed as a dowry. A certain Abū Talḥah proposed to a woman who, in reply to his proposal, said: "A man of your stature is not to be rejected; but you are a non-Believer and I am a Muslim. It is unlawful for me to marry you. If you embrace Islām, that will be my dowry and no more will I ask of you." He then embraced Islām and that was her dowry. Similarly, if a master wishes to marry his slave girl and offers her freedom as a dowry, both the offer and the marriage are valid.[47]

To make dowry the exclusive right of the bride and empower her to dispose of it as she sees fit is sometimes regarded as a radical social change which Islām could not have initiated. Some observers suggest that there must have been a pre-Islāmic custom whereby dowry "was as a rule paid to her and not to her people, so that she cannot often have been left destitute and dependent on her people or clan." [48] This would seem to presuppose that dowries were usually large enough to enable a widow or divorcée to become economically independent of her kinsmen, that she could own and inherit property, and that women were highly stationed in society. But all this is itself problematic and involves obscurity, controversy, or both.[49] Whatever the strength or weakness of this presupposition, it seems important that Islām has made it a divine injunction, not a custom, that the bride alone has the right to dowry and only she may dispose of it as she pleases. Apart from any moral effect that this change may have had on the status of women, the social consequences were equally important. Payment of dowry to the bride herself probably minimized the element of self-interest and power of the guardian in his choice of a husband for the ward. He became mainly concerned with what was best for the woman. This and other changes made by Islām "tended to remove control over their affairs from the women's male relatives and protectors and to vest it in themselves." [50]

The position of Islām on the limits of dowry is also significant. The general principle is that dowry should be estimated according to circumstances with emphasis on moderation. The Prophet is reported to have said that the most blessed marriage is that which is least costly and most easy. Hence, the great majority of jurists set no minimum to dowry. In fact, there were cases in the Prophet's lifetime and thereafter where dowry was as low as two *dirhams,* or less than one dollar. This was acceptable even to leading dignitaries and was regarded as a virtuous act. The two schools of law that set a minimum to dowry, three and ten *dirhams* respectively, made it merely nominal as the amount indicates. On the other hand, all schools of law agreed that there is no maximum limit to dowry. However, moderation is recommended; some jurists preferred it to be within the limit of five hundred *dirhams*, nearly one hundred and fifty dollars, which was the amount sometimes paid by the Prophet himself or received by his daughters.[51]

The fact that there is no fixed minimum of dowry, and that even those who set one made it merely nominal, may suggest several implications. It was probably intended to facilitate marriage since Islām's strong advocacy of marriage is, as already mentioned, unequivocal. It is also likely that it was designed as a measure of narrowing the gaps between the various social strata. The amount of dowry may serve as a status symbol and hence the larger the amount, the higher the status may be supposed to rank. But Islām's interest in discouraging "class" distinctions is believed to be rather emphatic.[52] Other inferences have been made such as likening marriage to sale and the dowry to the price of a commodity, and regarding the absence of a fixed minimum as indicative of a low evaluation of women.[53]

Similarly, the fact that there is no fixed maximum to dowry may indicate that neither sexual gratification as such nor progeny was regarded as the crucial factor in marriage. If they were, a great many people would probably have sought more economical means, such as slave purchase, to achieve these ends instead of having to pay dowries which were often very handsome. In fact, the Qur'ān (4:20) implies that a dowry may be as high as a hundredweight (one *qintār*) of gold or silver. There are some indications that women took advantage of this permissibility to an alarming extent. Just a few years after Muhammad's death, there developed a tendency to demand exorbitant dowries. 'Umar, the Caliph (d.643), was opposed to this tendency and spoke against it in the mosque. He recommended that dowries be reduced to moderate limits. A woman rose from the congregation and said to 'Umar: "Commander of the Believers! Why do you want to deny us a God-given right?" When she recited the relevant keywords of the Qur'ān (4:20), 'Umar admitted that he was mistaken and withdrew his recommendations.[54]

Since Islām has set neither a dowry minimum, according to the majority of jurists, nor a dowry maximum, in the opinion of all jurists, why did it prescribe it in the first place? We have previously noted several theories concerning the institutionalization of dowry.[55] But none of these by itself seems adequate to account for dowry in Islām. The economic explanation which conceives of dowry as a compensation to the father or his substitute for the loss of the girl's economic services is inapplicable to Islām for two basic reasons. First, dowry is the exclusive right and property of the woman in question; she can use it or dispose of it as she pleases.[56] Second, a religio-legal system, such as Islām, that makes dowry as nominal as the offering of an iron ring or the teaching of some Qur'ānic verses seems hardly concerned in this context with economic losses and compensations. Similarly, the procreative explanation, which is also partly economic, has to be ruled out for the same reasons. If progeny was enthusiastically sought by Muslims, as is generally believed, and if dowry was essential to the attainment of this end, as the procreative theory holds, it is very unlikely that Islām would have left the dowry limits so undetermined and its ranges so wide as they are. Furthermore, the fact that passionate love does not necessarily precede marriage but may grow with it or evolve from it, and that dowry can be large or small, would seem to preclude the designation of dowry as an expression of love.

It is sometimes suggested that Islām has enjoined dowry in order to safeguard the economic rights of the wife after marriage and to strengthen her financial position.[57] This view can have great explanatory value only where the dowry is large and when such economic gains are manifest functions of marriage. But this does not appear to represent the majority of cases. Where it is small, as it may be, dowry can only be symbolic. Among the values it symbolizes may be the strengthening and safeguarding of the economic position of the wife. Nevertheless, this seems far from being the exclusive or even the main reason for dowry.

It is also conceivable, as Westermarck and others have suggested, that dowry, especially when paid by the woman's family, "served as an obstacle to the dissolution of the union for frivolous reasons." Another function was that it worked as deterrent to polygyny.[58] But, here again, the assumption seems to be that dowry is large enough to deter the husband, if he is the contributor, from divorcing his wife or taking another one, and that he is relatively poor or highly "rational" and economy-minded. The same is true of the wife if she is the payer of the dowry. Such a number of assumptions would appear, on the one hand, to weaken the power of the theory and, on the other, to leave unexplained the many cases in which dowry is small, where the husband is well-off, or where both husband and wife engage in non-rational behavior, as they may do.

Muslim jurists of later centuries have held the technical view that dowry is enjoined in return for the man's right, at least potentially, to have legitimate access to cohabitation with the woman in question. She is entitled to dowry because she has consented to marriage and made herself accessible. Much discussion among the jurists has centered on this issue.[59] But the exponents of this view appear to assume or to infer that women have no sexual desires and needs of their own, that gratification is not reciprocal, that sex is a cheap commodity in view of the permissibility of nominal dowries, and that marriage is little more than a commercial transaction. The list of assumptions and inferences may be extended. Yet, these seem contrary to the bio-psychological facts and to the very idea of marriage which is depicted in the Qur'ān (e.g., 30:20) as a shelter of peace and comfort, and as a means of mutual love and mercy.

It is interesting to note that the term *mahr* (bride price), which usually connotes commercialization of marriage, is not used in the Qur'ān at all. It occurs very infrequently in the Traditions of the Prophet; when it does, it is usually accompanied by other terms such as *farīḍah* (God-given right), or *ṣadāq* (which is connected with a root word meaning marriage-gift, charity, friendship, fidelity, truth, etc.). The jurists have used these terms interchangeably as denoting the God-given right of dowry. But it is not certain whether in these interchangeable usages the traditional connotations of the term *mahr* were sublimated to the moral and charitable denotations of terms like *ṣadāq, farīḍah,* and so on; or whether these terms themselves took on the traditional connotations of *mahr.* A review of the classical legal texts would seem to indicate that where it occurs, the term *mahr* is used in a sublime moral sense indistinguishable from the meaning of *ṣadāq, farīḍah,* and similar terms. But the law books and usages of subsequent centuries seem to use *mahr* and other alternate terms in a sense very much akin to the traditional meaning of bride-price.[60] This reversal of meaning was apparently correlated with a decline in juristic creativity and the status of women and also with a misconception of the idea of marriage.

So far no explanation has been found adequate to account for the dowry in Islām. The usual explanations addressed to various cultures are inapplicable. Even the idea that dowry is a contribution toward marriage expenses which are normally shared by the bride and the groom or their families is inapplicable. It is true that in contemporary Muslim society the general practice is that the groom contributes a certain portion which sometimes supplements and sometimes is supplemented by what the bride or her family contributes. But that is not the same as the original idea of dowry, though it is not incompatible with it, since dowry is the exclusive right of the bride who may or may not consume it, reduce it, add to it, or dispose of it as she pleases.

In view of these factors, there is still room for further explorations of the idea of dowry in Islām. It seems fairly obvious that dowry is a symbolic, intermediate value. But what

it symbolizes may not be so obvious. Some tentative suggestions may be useful, however. Dowry is probably a symbolic
expression of the groom's cognizance of the economic responsibilities of marriage and of his readiness to discharge all
such responsibilities subsequent to marriage. It may be thought
of as a manifest assurance on his part that the bride's economic
security and rights will be maintained. It is a symbolic acknowledgment that he does or will dissociate the purpose of marriage from the designs of economic exploitations. For "instinctive" or cultural reasons, it is usually the women who need
reassurance of the man's intentions and interest. This reassurance may require more than verbal expressions of love and
seriousness on the man's part, and dowry may be the tangible
symbol of such love and seriousness. To the bride, it is a token
of the groom's desire to enter into a union with her. To her
family, it is a gesture of mutual friendship and solidarity, an
assurance that their daughter will be secure and in good hands.
However, there may be other symbolic meanings of dowry, as
has been mentioned earlier. Nor is it to be overlooked that
what is being suggested here is conceptualized in terms of the
religious and moral ideals which may or may not be in fact
fully implemented. There is no sufficient ground to assume
that the actual has always coincided with the ideal in this case.

G. *Marriage Guardianship*

One of the problems directly connected with the conditions
of marriage is marriage guardianship or *wilāyat al-nikāḥ*.
This is a very complex problem, but it may be worth the attempt to clarify it and see what insights into the social structure it may give. Simply stated, marriage guardianship is the
legal authority invested in a person who is fully qualified and
competent to safeguard the interests and rights of another who
is incapable of doing so independently. It is the authority of a
father or nearest male relative over minors, insane, or inexperienced persons who need protection and guardianship.[61]
There seems to be an overlapping of guardianship in this sense
and other forms of legal representation and delegation. There

is also lack of agreement among the jurists on the guardian's authority and the extent of the ward's rights. To clarify the issue as much as possible, a distinction must be made between the marriage guardian and an ordinary legal representative. The former is normally the nearest male relative in whose absence a community official may assume the responsibility. Whether guardianship is considered as a right conferred on or as a duty assigned to the guardian, the fact remains that it is ascribed by law and neither party can terminate it unilaterally so long as the conditions calling for it exist. Moreover, a guardian is qualified only if he satisfies certain requisites. He must be a free Muslim male, of sound mind, of full age, and of good character.[62] A legal representative, *wakīl,* on the other hand, is a person who has agreed, through private arrangements, to represent another party within the limits of authority delegated to him by the principal party. Such a delegated authority may include arrangements of marriage subject to the approval of the principal party and, in some cases, of the guardian.[63]

As to who must have a guardian in marriage, different positions have been taken by different schools of law. The general view, however, is that minors, insane, and inexperienced irresponsible persons of either sex must have marriage guardians.[64] Yet the lawbooks focus on the woman's need for guardianship and little is said about the need of men for the same. This may be due to the fact that men are generally believed to be relatively more experienced than women and tend to marry their juniors, in which case two basic reasons for guardianship, i.e., minority and inexperience, are eliminated. It is the woman who needs a guardian because she is usually said to lack experience in practical affairs and, hence, may be intrigued into commitments contrary to her interests. Moreover, if she contracts marriage in her own behalf, she may give the impression of being inconsiderate, presumptuous, and inclined to intermingle with men unnecessarily— actions which would customarily stigmatize her character. For such reasons, the jurists argue, a guardian is required to pro-

tect the woman's interest, to safeguard her moral integrity, and
to take all possible precautions to maximize the probability
of a successful marriage. And, because the father's love and
care for his daughter are usually taken for granted, he is the
first man to qualify as her guardian provided, of course, that
he meets the other requisites of guardianship.[65]

Difference of opinion as to what constitutes a woman's lack
of experience and endangers her moral integrity has led to different views on the conditions under which a woman needs a
marriage guardian. These views may be outlined as follows:

1. *Womanhood as such.* Marriage contracts are invalid unless the woman involved has a guardian to represent her.
She cannot give herself or anyone else in marriage, nor
can she appoint a representative other than her lawful
guardian. This applies to every woman irrespective of her
age, physical condition, and marital status, that is, whether
she is a virgin, widow or divorcée. But, as we shall see
later, this does not mean that she can be forced to marry
against her wishes.

2. *Women unauthorized.* If the guardian so authorizes, a
woman may give herself and others in marriage, and may
also appoint any representative she wishes. This assumes
that the guardian trusts her judgment and is reasonably
confident that her interests will be protected. In the absence of such authorizations, a marriage guardian is necessary to the validity of the contract.

3a. *Immaturity and minority.* A woman, maiden or otherwise, who is mentally sound and has reached the age of puberty may independently negotiate marriage contracts and
give herself or others in marriage. If her chosen match
turns out to be unsuitable, or if she accepts a dowry less
than that of her equals, the guardian may object to her
choice and request annulment of the contract. Any un-
justified objection on his part can be overruled by the
legal authorities upon the woman's request. But if he
raises no objection, her choice and marriage are valid.

3b. A woman who is in the approved state of mind and

physical growth is free to negotiate contracts and give
herself in marriage. No guardian has any right to object
to her choice, whatever the choice may be.

4. *Virginity (Maidenness).* If a woman is "virgin" she cannot marry without a guardian. But if she is a widow or
divorcée, she may marry independently and make her
own arrangements.

5. *Nobility and Wealth.* A former slavegirl or a poor woman
of low rank may be wise to appoint an agent to represent
her in marriage; that is seemly and advisable. But if she
acts in her own behalf, her marriage is valid. On the other
hand, a "noble" woman of wealth and high status must be
represented in marriage by a guardian or a community
official.[66] This view is probably taken because such a
woman has much to lose if she is not well-advised.

Obviously all shades of opinion on this question are represented. It is important to note that each side tries to
support its position by reference to the Qur'ān and other principles of law. It is also important to notice that the main concern of all parties is claimed to be the protection of the moral
integrity as well as the material interest of the woman involved.
In the opinion of some jurists, it is in her best interest to have
a marriage guardian. Other jurists prefer that she should act
independently but with the careful guidance of a guardian. Still
others consider it best to let her act freely without supervi-
sion.[67] The substantive arguments will not be examined here.
It seems that these different opinions have arisen not
from a disagreement on the underlying principles of law but,
rather, on the interpretation of certain texts and the application of certain principles. The Qur'ān and the other sources
of law which are invoked in support of the various arguments
are held by all parties as binding. But the interpretation of the
texts or the application of the principles is another matter
which is largely determined by the jurist's personal discretion.

It is possible to identify certain positions with certain Muslim regions, but it is unlikely that the customs of any particular
locality were the sole determinants of the position identifiable

with that locality. Neither the law schools nor the individual jurists were strictly regionalized. Muslim society of those early centuries had no regional boundaries. It is known that many leading jurists traveled to the centers of learning throughout the vast Muslim territories and often changed their minds upon gaining new experience or finding new evidence. Pilgrimage, in particular, was a significant factor in physical mobility and social experience. Even jurists who grew up in the same environment and generally adhered to the same school of law took different positions on marriage guardianship.[68] Nevertheless, the influence of the prevailing social conditions in coloring these shades of opinion cannot be ruled out entirely. In addition to varying social conditions and the personal discretion of the jurists, another factor seems to have been operative, namely, the nature of the language in which the Qur'ānic precepts and the Prophet's instructions are stated. These are expressed in terms so general and probable or equivocal that they can be interpreted in more than one way; they are not mathematical equations. Whether this inconclusiveness is an advantage or otherwise, and whether it is inherent in the language or so intended to allow for fresh adaptations, is another question and, to be sure, a controversial one.

The role of the marriage guardian may be defined as a right conferred on him by law, empowering him to act on his ward's behalf with or without regard for her wishes. It may also be considered as a duty assigned to him by law and by virtue of his responsibility for the ward's welfare. If guardianship is defined as a right of the guardian, as some writers seem inclined to do, and if rights can be conceived without corresponding duties, the guardian is depicted as a person endowed with coercive rather than advisory powers. He is primarily interested in preventing any match that may bring dishonor to the family or tribe.[69] But, in view of the particular relationship between a kinsman guardian — who is often a father — and his ward, and keeping in mind Islām's opposition to the tribal conception of honor and its own advocacy of brotherhood and equality, it seems very unlikely that guardianship was endorsed for reasons other than the welfare of the ward. It is, of course, conceivable, perhaps even imperative, that the guardian should consider the ward's interests as his own. Thus, when he acts on the matter, he may appear as if he were defending his interests while, in fact, he is defending those of his ward.

Definition of guardianship as a mechanism devised principally to protect the honor or pride of the ward's family seems to have led to conflicting comments. For example, a contemporary writer has noted that, "It is, firstly, the kindred and, secondly, the woman herself, who must be protected from a *mésalliance;* but in no case may the guardian derive any material advantage from arranging a match or consider anything but the best interest of his ward. If he does so . . . his action, according to all schools, will be *ḥaram* [forbidden and irreligious] . . . ." Authorities of all schools of law are, according to the same writer, unanimous in characterizing marriage guardianship as ". . . 'the right to assist a woman at her marriage.' Guardians are expected to act in the ward's interest and, generally speaking, in conformity with her wishes."[70] This observation appears to confound the Islāmic conception of guardianship with the pre-Islāmic idea of tribal honor and pride, and to define guardianship as a right *over* the ward rather than a right *of* hers or a duty *to* her. It is probably this misconception which is responsible for the inconsistency of the respective parts of this statement.

Muslim jurists who insist on marriage guardianship seem to consider it a duty rather than a right of the guardian, or at least a synthesis of both. While the guardian has the right to negotiate and conclude a marriage on his ward's behalf and to give his consent or object to her "unwise" choice, it is his duty to exercise this right in her best interest. He is enjoined to take her wishes into consideration. To fulfill this duty, he must have the right to participate in the decision-making process and avail of his experience in helping her. But, to have this right, his ability to exercise it in the best interest of the ward must be demonstrated. As a precautionary measure, he must

meet certain moral and personal requisites. These are stipulated to insure that in all probability he will neither neglect his
duty nor abuse his right.[71]

However, in spite of these precautions, negligence and abuse
do occur and guardians do make unwise decisions. But there
are provisions to cope with such situations. Deliberate negligence or abuse is forbidden. Should a guardian's religious conscience fail him, or should he act against the interests or the
wishes of the ward, she, if a major, has a religio-legal right to
override his decisions. She may request the legal authorities to
annul any contract concluded against her will or which falls
short of her expectations. There were such cases in the time
of the Prophet who revoked the marriage contracts upon the
request of the women concerned.[72]

H. Marriage of Minors

The foregoing discussion raises two interrelated questions:
(1) the marriage of minors and (2) compulsion in marriage.
Marriage in minority would seem to imply a betrothal or
some formal agreement, deferring final consummation to a
later date.[73] This type of child "marriage" is probably best explained by the desire to draw families together and to facilitate
social integration.[74]

Given the low sex ratio and racial plurality of Muslim
society, the need for social integration and the high
value of sexual purity and virginity, it may become understandable why Islām set no age limits on marriage. Preliminary
arrangements may have been made at an early age, but consummation usually took place when the parties were fit for
marital congress, which depended, among other things, on
their physical conditions.[75] However, the lawfulness of such
marriages does not necessarily mean that they were predominant. Nor were they peculiar to any society, region, or generation. For example, in Abyssinia in the sixth century a law was
issued prescribing forcible intermarriage between Christians
and baptized Jews. Accordingly, no boy or girl over thirteen
was to remain unmarried, because such early marriages "would

lead to speedy amalgamation of the communities." [76] At various times, very youthful marriages prevailed among the Jews, and in the second half of the seventeenth century, "the bridegroom was frequently not more than ten years old and the bride was younger still." [77] The Roman law stipulated that a man may marry at the age of fourteen and a woman at the age of twelve. This law was adopted by the Church and is still preserved in various countries, including some regions of the United States of America. In England, marriages at these respective ages "were valid without the consent of parents until the year 1753. . . " [78]

Such a general and somewhat persistent phenomenon is not fully explicable in terms of any one culture or age. Some common reasons must account for marriages of this type. Whatever these common reasons, Islām seems to prescribe that, no matter at what age betrothal may take place, final consummation must be delayed until the parties are ready for marital relations, a condition usually determined by puberty.[79] In any case, the law prescribes that all marriage arrangements must be made in the best interest of the minors involved. It is unlawful to do anything disadvantageous to them. To guard against possible misjudgment, Islām has made certain specific requirements. First, marriage in minority is invalid without the consent and participation of the guardian. In this respect, Islām agrees with other religious and legal systems of ancient and modern times. Second, Islām does not entrust this responsibility to any parent or guardian *per se,* but to those who, in addition to parenthood, must have certain qualifications sufficient under normal circumstances to ensure a good sense of judgment and conscientiousness. Third, Islām has, according to many jurists, given to minors the so-called "option of majority." A minor who has reached the age of puberty is free either to uphold or annul a marriage contract that was concluded on his or her behalf while in minority. Taken together, these measures seem to suggest that, in the final analysis, the minor's interest and welfare are the focal point of the law.[80] Even the jurists who do not recognize the minor's "option of majority" insist that no one other than a qualified *father* or *grandfather* is authorized to conclude a valid marriage on the minor's behalf. This is based on the assumption that a father, who is also qualified as a guardian, would normally do what is best for his ward. Thus, it is probably not so much an affirmation of the father's authority over the ward as a protection of the latter's interest, even if that overrides the "option of majority." [81]

I. *Compulsion versus Freedom in Marriage*

As regards compulsion in marriage, several preliminary points must be noted. First, in no society is there unchartered freedom of marital choice. The social structure defines and limits the so-called "field of eligibles," if only because of rules governing incest and ethnocentric preference. Second, the more functional and interdependent the family, the higher the probability that marriages will be "arranged" and the marital freedom of the principals curtailed. Third, arranged marriages do not necessarily ignore the wishes and consent of the principal parties, nor does the freedom of choice of the principals preclude the influence, wishes or consent of the parents. In practice, "The actual influence of the woman's wishes is, of course, often a question of fact rather than of right." [82] Fourth, in almost every known society, the parents are believed to have exercised authority, great or small, in the marriages of their children. This authority may be based on custom, law, veneration for parents, the power to disown the children, or the mere recognition of the children's helplessness and dependence on the parents. [83]

With these facts in mind, it may become clear why there are seemingly conflicting views on the question of the children's consent and the nature of parental authority. The underlying reason is probably that some observers tend to simplify or polarize the problem of consent which, as Hobhouse has put it, "is no simple one." [84] The literature of pre-Islāmic Arabia is almost exclusively devoted to the consent of women. According to some accounts, women were not free in contracting marriage. It was the right of the father or some other male guardian to give a woman in marriage regardless of her age and marital status.[85] On the other hand, there are reports that she was free in the choice of her mate, and no one could force her to marry against her wishes or without her consent. Sometimes she herself took the initiative and concluded the marriage in her own behalf. The girl's mother was usually consulted and her counsel heeded.[86]

It seems clear that both positions are exaggerated and resemble ideal types. Social reality is probably never so simple or dichotomous as these conflicting reports indicate. It is very unlikely that they are generalizing about the same situation or describing the same society. If these reports have any factual basis, the only possible explanation would probably lie in the diversity of the pre-Islāmic mode of life. What happened in Makkah or al Madīnah was not, and apparently could not have been, a replica of what took place in the interior Bedouin environment. Nor was the mode of marriage of the wealthy, noble, or endogamous tribes the same as that of the wanderers, freed slaves, humble, or exogamous tribes. The partial evidence available suggests that below a certain middle point the lower the social standing of the parties, the greater the woman's freedom of marital choice and expression of her wishes. This is because nothing much is at stake here. On the other hand, the closer the parties to the summit of social standing from a certain middle point, the greater was the consideration given by parents to the woman's wishes. Few parents or guardians probably could ignore these wishes or leave the matter entirely in the hands of the woman concerned. There are indications that when the prospective suitors were of alien tribes, the girl's consent was sought. Parents hesitated to marry their daughters off to strangers without sounding out their wishes. But where endogamy or matrilocality was the norm, there was no need for consent since the girl was apparently well taken care of. On the other hand, in settled communities, such as that of al Madīnah, it is reported that parents often used to marry their daughters off without asking for their consent,[87] though not necessarily against their wishes or inclinations.

From an Islāmic standpoint, compulsion in marriage is probably more imaginary than real, notwithstanding the jurisprudential niceties. The question is wrapped up in many hypothetical folds that seem to have little to do with reality. Taken as presented in the law books, the problem may be outlined in the following way.

1. All schools of law agree that if it is feared that a woman will engage in sexual misbehavior, the guardian or even the sovereign may force her to marry to protect her and other people from her misbehavior.[88] Public morality and the individual's own integrity take priority over personal freedom when they come into conflict.

2. There is also agreement that a father may give his daughter in marriage, with or without seeking her consent, provided she is (a) under age (nine years old or younger), (b) virgin, and (c) is given in marriage to a suitable, socially equal husband.[89] Whether a father, who is legally and religiously qualified to be a guardian, would actually force his daughter to marry under these circumstances, and whether any reasonable suitor would be keen on such a marriage is, of course, an empirically interesting question. In any case, this position derives from a Qur'ānic verse (65:4), which indirectly implies that it is lawful for a girl who has not yet experienced menstruation to marry. Some minor girls were married in the time of the Prophet and thereafter, although consummation did not follow immediately. The argument runs as follows: Since the marriage of minors is lawful, and since they are not legally or religiously responsible, they have no independent legal personality and no valid consent to give or withhold. The father then is not really ignoring his minor daughter's consent because, as the argument would put it, there is no such consent in the first place in any strict legal sense. Rather, he may be taking it upon himself to do what he believes to be in the interest of his ward and in fulfillment of his religious responsibility.[90]

3. If a woman is "virgin," of sound mind, and adult, i.e., has reached the age of puberty, it is lawful, according to some jurists, for the father to give her in marriage with or without her consent, provided the prospective husband is suitable and of equal status. The explanation offered is that such a woman who has had no marital experience is in no position to know where her real interest lies. She is as inexperienced as the girl who is underage. These jurists do not deny the Traditions of the Prophet where he is reported to have said that the consent of a virgin is to be sought and her silence is evidence of her approval. But they interpret these Traditions as meaning that it is only "commendable," not necessary, to seek the girl's consent.

On the other hand, in the light of these Traditions and according to the majority of the Companions of the Prophet, other jurists deny such authority to the father and hold the girl's consent a necessary condition for the validity of her marriage. This is the position which, according to some leading jurists, is in conformity with the teachings of the Prophet, the spirit of Islāmic law, and the common interest.[91]

4. If a woman is "virgin," whether adult or underage, and her father gave her in marriage, without her consent, to a husband who is not her equal, the general view is that such a marriage is invalid. The reason is that the father has done something contrary to her interest and in violation of his trust. As a legal guardian, he is authorized only to do what is beneficial to his ward. Marrying her to an unequal suitor is neither in her interest nor to her benefit.

However, there are other opinions held by a minority of jurists. These are: (a) the marriage is valid because equality in marriage is not a necessary condition, and the "defect" of inequality does not invalidate the contract, (b) the marriage is invalid only if the father was aware, before the contract, of the husband's unequal status, and (c) the marriage is invalid if the girl is underage; otherwise, the contract is formally legal, but she may revoke it by other means if she so desires.[92]

5. A woman who is of age and is a widow or divorcée is free

to make her own choice. The father may not force her to marry against her wishes. This is supported by the Traditions of the Prophet and by common practice, because such a woman is experienced and would normally understand the implications of marriage. She is unlikely to be easily misguided. Contrary to this "consensus," a particular Sūfī-jurist, al Hasan al Baṣrī (d. 728), said that the father has the right to marry her off even if she objects. Another early jurist said that this father's right holds only if she is a dependent of his and a member of his household. Both these opinions are said to be very unpopular among the jurists. However, the opinion of the predominant majority is divided on whether it is the age or previous marital experience which is the significant element in the situation. According to some jurists, if the woman has had a former marriage, she is free to make her own choice even if she is underage. With her experience, she can well protect herself. Other jurists maintain that if she is underage, whether or not she has been previously married, the father may marry her off with or without her consent. It is argued that her previous marriage does not change the fact of her being underage.[93]

6. All jurists agree that it is at least commendable, though some hold it necessary, for the father to seek the consent of his maiden daughter before he gives her in marriage. This is what the Prophet said and did with his own daughters. It was his practice to tell the girl in question from behind a curtain that so and so had proposed. If the girl kept silent, that was indicative of her approval of the marriage. But if she shook the curtain, it meant objection on her part, and the Prophet would disregard the proposal. The reason usually given for asking the girl's consent is that it would please her and cultivate congeniality between the parties. It is also commendable, according to a Tradition, that the girl's mother be consulted because, apart from personal gratification, she, like the father, has compassion for the girl and is equally interested in her welfare.[94]

7. The legal right of compulsion, where it applies, may be

exercised only by a father who is also qualified to be a guardian on the assumption that his care and compassion for his daughter are ordinarily a matter of course. Some jurists confer this same right on the grandfather in the absence of the father in the belief that the former is equally compassionate and experienced. Some other jurists authorize any guardian to exercise this right but recognize the minor's "option of majority," whereby the marriage contract may be revoked by the minor upon reaching the age of majority. This applies to male and female minors alike.[95]

In summary, the juristic views on compulsion in marriage are varied. Some permit certain guardians to impose the status of marriage on their wards. The basis of the guardian's authority in this respect is his assumed concern for the welfare of the ward. There are wide differences of opinion concerning the factors which justify compulsion. These include virginity, minority, womanhood, as such, and dependence on the guardian.

Textual and historical evidence seems to suggest that these juristic views are little more than academic or mental exercises. Nowhere does the Qur'ān or the Prophet speak with approval of such coercive authority. There are authentic reports that some fathers gave their daughters in marriage without their consent, but probably not without good intentions. Yet such marriages were revoked when the women concerned objected to them. There are no cases, as far as the available reports indicate, where imposed marriages were allowed to continue. It is reported that some families, particularly in al Madīnah—just as in some contemporary Muslim societies—used to marry their daughters off without asking for their explicit consent. But whether this necessarily means coercion on the parent's part or resentment on the daughter's side is a matter of interpretation. It probably meant that tradition-bound parents used to arrange the marriages of their children and to take the latter's approval for granted. To assume that arranged marriages automatically preclude consent or even romantic love seems unwarranted.

A father who has, besides his assumed love and care for his children, the qualifications of a legal guardian, would be expected in tradition-bound societies to know better the "field of eligibles" and to have at least a general idea of his ward's inclinations and expectations. Moreover, given the fact that a ward's modesty (*hayā'*) and respect for parents are among the highest Islāmic virtues, and that marriage is a union of more than two individuals, it is unlikely that there could be any patterned grand-scale coercion. The children's approval of what the parents do on their behalf is probably expected or taken for granted. They may not say anything either to approve or disapprove a father's selection. But silence is taken by Muslim jurists as an indication of approval, not of coercion or resentment. In reality, however, there must have been abuses, although a ward who disagrees with a guardian's arrangements has various mechanisms to make his or her desires known and to revoke such arrangements. In law, there are various grounds to annul any marriage contract that is disadvantageous or disagreeable to either principal. Since in Islām, every act is also a religious act, it is thus expected to be conceived and executed with the best intention and to the satisfaction of God. If it results in harm or inequity, Islām demands that this must be remedied. If coercion in religion itself is forbidden by the Qur'ān, how much more so with respect to marriage! Some jurists have theorized that in certain cases fathers or guardians may impose the status of marriage on their wards. It will be revealing to investigate whether they will actually do it, or have, in fact, done it. And if they have, was the compulsion allowed to pass as valid and irrevocable? The evidence, however inconclusive, seems to indicate the contrary.[96]

J. *Mate Selection: Equality (Kafā'ah) in Marriage*

The question of "social equality in marriage"[97] is but one dimension of the general problem of mate selection. The idea that love is blind and is the decisive factor in mate selection is not the universal norm of any society, notwithstanding some popular misconceptions. The belief that "love and marriage go together like a horse and carriage" has been drummed into the heads of western young people so insistently that they consider it entirely natural, indeed, necessary. The idea is quite without historical support. Love and marriage are two modes of experience that are by no means identified with each other or with normality. Mate selection has been governed by rules and considerations that may or may not include the priority of love.[98]

Mate selection, therefore, is neither random nor strictly personal; rather, it is patterned and hence largely predictable. In this connection, two major theories have been advanced. According to the theory of homogamy, "people tend to marry people who are in various social ways like themselves . . ." But, on the other hand, marital choice "is not altogether a matter of similarities; rather, it seems to some extent to be a matter of *social* similarities and *psychological* differences." [99] This is the theory of heterogamy or complementary needs, according to which "every individual seeks within his or her field of eligibles for that person who gives the greatest promise of providing him or her with maximum need gratification." [100]

Although the two theories have a particular reference to the white middle class of American society, they seem to suggest some generalizations. Mate selection is not a random choice. In every society there is a field of eligibles for every marriageable person. The field of eligibles may be narrow or wide, depending on the stratification system and cultural values of the society. Where the field of eligibles is strictly defined, people would be more inclined to choose mates like themselves and, hence, largely homogamous. Where it is wide, consideration of complementary needs will have a relatively greater prominence and some social similarities will be more tolerably interchangeable with need gratification. However, the two theories are not mutually exclusive, if only because both use the common concept of the "field of eligibles." In view of the seemingly conflicting evidence, attempts have been made to reconcile them in a useful way: homogamy operates at the level of "social" characteristics, while heterogamy or the complementary needs theory applies at the level of psychological traits or personality needs. This reconciliation is reached mainly by the so-called "developmental approach," according to which courtship is viewed as not being mechanically predetermined by either social or personality variables, but as the end product of a long series of variegated interactions.[101]

Every society envisions an ideal mate who may or may not actually fall within a given person's field of eligibles. To the pre-Islāmic Arabs, the ideal wife was one who had honor and noble ancestry (not necessarily identified with wealth), virtue and good manners, youth and virginity, fecundity and moderate beauty, modesty and chastity, intelligence and affection, integrity and eloquence, energy and productivity, grace and cheerfulness. A woman who approximated these standards was considered by men of the highest social standing a most desirable mate.[102] On the other hand, the ideal husband had to be young and of Arab descent. It was disgraceful for Arabs to marry their women to non-Arabs. The literary evidence suggests that young women preferred young mates, however poor and destitute, to old suitors of wealth and fame. Moreover, the ideal husband had to be affectionate and honest, companionable and cheerful, generous and brave, noble and faithful. He had to be the social equal of his mate in lineage, honor and fame. The tribe of Quraysh, in particular, adopted the additional practice that their daughters could be married only to suitors who followed the same tribal religion.[103]

The pre-Islāmic society of Arabia may not have been highly differentiated, but there can be little doubt that it was stratified and had some criteria of social equality. When Islām was established as the community religion, the ideological situation changed and a new criterion was adopted. Accordingly, every individual was to be ranked first on the basis of his religious virtues which may or may not agree with certain traditional values. All Muslims were regarded as equals in the sight of God and brothers of one another; the only recognizable criterion of ultimate distinction was that of piety or God-mindedness (*taqwā*). There are authentic Traditions that the Prophet ranked the religious virtues of a prospective mate above everything else. He himself encouraged the marriage of some former slaves to women of the Quraysh tribe, whose members enjoyed the highest social standing and to whom such marriages would probably have been inconceivable, were it not for the "egalitarian spirit" of Islām. "Social equality" was thus replaced by the new concept of "religious equality." [104]

What made the new principle of religious equality acceptable to the Arabs was most probably a combination of several factors. With the rise of Islām, there emerged a new community whose members were drawn. together by a religious identity superseding the old forms of solidarity. In this community, practically every member was an "achieving" person and, in some capacity or other, rendered valuable services to the community. Theirs was a pioneering spirit of endurance, self-denial, and profound communality. The Prophet's leadership and his full sharing with them the ups and downs of life must have been effective in levelling the traditional social barriers of lineage, wealth and race. [105]

Moreover, while the community was in the making, there was ample opportunity for aspirants to demonstrate their virtues. Islām affirmed the new principle of religious equality and recognized piety as the ultimate valid criterion of distinction. But, on the other hand, it did not altogether reject the traditional values of the Arabs; rather, it rechanneled them and placed them in a religious context. For example, generosity was no longer a mere personal or tribal virtue, but also, and above all, a religious merit. Modesty, affection, faithfulness and other traditional prerequisites of an ideal mate now became tributaries to the new ideal personality, namely, the pious, God-minded Muslim. Piety under Islām embodies most of the traditional values of the Arabs, but it excluded their traditional conceptions of honor and lineage which were no longer compatible with the emerging dynamic community.

This community had the task of propagating a new faith and
was subject to threats of extinction. It had to consolidate its
ranks and respond to the challenges of a hostile environment.
Under such circumstances, social barriers were probably forsaken and levelled. This would surely happen in the context of
a religious *weltanschauung* affirming human equality, social
solidarity, and brotherhood, as was the case with Islām and its
emerging community. This religious philosophy of life, the dynamic leadership of the Prophet, the re-channelling of the Arabian values, the rise of new opportunities for achieved distinctions, the internalization of a religious calling—such factors,
combined and tied to a new sense of community, seem to have
made possible the transition from the pre-Islāmic standards of
marriage to the Islāmic principles.

In the new order, it became lawful in theory and accepted
in practice for any free Muslim man to marry any Muslim
woman so long as his religious integrity remained intact. What
was required in marriage was the "religious" not the traditional
"social," equality. Thus, a non-Muslim man is forbidden to
marry a Muslim woman because he is not her equal in religion.
Nor is it lawful for a debaucher to marry a continent, decent
woman for the same reason. If religious compatibility obtains,
any other consideration is of secondary importance. This is the
logic of the Qur'ān and the Sunnah of the Prophet particularly as interpreted by jurist critics.[106]

In view of these unequivocal precepts and in light of the
social conditions of the early Muslim community, the pioneering jurists disregarded the traditional requirements of social
equality in favor of the religious integrity of the suitor. That
position seems to have been more than a religious fad. It was
apparently internalized and fully implemented during the first
and part of the second century of Islām. Yet, that was not the
end; individual jurists, in opposition to their respective schools
of law, and a major branch of the Shī'īs have always upheld the
doctrine of religious equality, beyond which nothing was crucial. They support their position by textual evidence as well
as authentic precedents. Even the leading jurist and Tradition-

ist, Ibn Hanbal, the father of one of the major schools of law, seems to have been reluctant to stipulate social equality as a prerequisite of marriage.[107]

The case of the Shīʿīs is interesting. This is the only group that has disregarded the traditional conditions of social equality and continued to affirm the doctrine of religious equality whereby any free Muslim of religious integrity is eligible to marry any woman of the highest social standing. It is unlikely that the difference between them and other schools in this respect arose from dispute over the textual or historical evidence; such evidence is accepted by all, at least in principle. But some jurists go beyond the evidence for reasons which will be discussed later. Nor is it likely that the Shīʿīs adopted this egalitarian attitude only because many of them were of non-Arab descent who lived in regions where obstinate social barriers had been a matter of course and where they had greater opportunities to demonstrate the Islāmic principles of human equality and brotherhood. Many leading jurists, some of whom, as Abū Hanīfah, were also of non-Arab descent, lived in these very regions under the same circumstances. Yet, they strongly endorsed certain conditions of social equality.[108]

The explanation of the Shīʿīs' position may be sought in the context of their social structure and political orientation. They were a minority, sometimes persecuted, sometimes suspect. In a sense, they resembled the early Muslim community and probably adopted its position for similar reasons. Their political doctrine has taken the form of extreme hereditary elitism in the sense that, to them, only particular descendants of the house of ʿAlī, the Prophet's cousin and son-in-law, are eligible to be the rightful Caliphs. They probably have been more endogamous than other Muslim groups and generally led a rather exclusive life.[109] It is not unlikely, therefore, that their being a minority in these circumstances reinforced their belief in egalitarianism, which is best reflected in the doctrine of religious equality, either as a mechanism of internal solidarity or as a protest against the society around them, a society whose very constitutional foundations they rejected. Nor is it altogether improbable that extremism of one type breeds and attracts other extremisms. When a group adopts an extreme position on a vital issue, such as the constitutional foundations of the state, it is more likely that the group's views on other matters of importance will take on extreme features as an offshoot of the original position or as a tempering counterbalance. The Shī'īs were extreme political elitists. But, probably conscious of the early egalitarian social character of Islām and, perhaps, of their political elitism, they advocated the doctrine of religious equality more strongly than other Muslim groups. By so doing, they may have meant to dispel the suspicion of outright elitism or to soften their political elitism by stressing egalitarianism on the nonpolitical levels. In any case, what their political doctrine and marital egalitarianism have in common would seem to be extremism.[110]

Apart from this particular Shī'ī group and some individual jurists who have continued to stress religious equality, the majority of the law schools have adopted the doctrine of social equality as a prerequisite of marriage. The points of the scale vary in articulation and number from school to school; but they all set some criteria (e.g., lineage, honor, profession, piety, etc.) whereby a given suitor can be said to "measure up" socially to a prospective bride.[111] The tendency among some observers is to attribute the rise of this doctrine to the deep-seated pride of Arabian society and its inability to act in full accordance with "the equalizing character and democratic spirit of Islam" and to implement "the Koranic dictum that *all Muslims are brothers.*" [112] But this does not seem to account for the facts bearing on the issue. If the doctrine were a revival of some pre-Islamic dispositions, it would probably have had a greater appeal to the jurists of the Arabian environment and less acceptance among those of other regions. What actually happened was the contrary. The explicit doctrine of social equality was not even mentioned by Mālik, who flourished in al Madīnah in the second century of Islām and was the master of one of the major schools of law. It is curious, however, that his followers in North Africa and elsewhere adopted some criteria of social equality; probably in response to some societal needs or through interaction with other schools. Besides, it was the schools of Iraq, Syria, Egypt, and beyond that stipulated certain criteria of social equality as a prerequisite of marriage, and elaborated the doctrine in a way that seems remote from what was practiced in pre-Islāmic Arabia. Furthermore, if the doctrine were a revival of a pre-Islamic practice, it would be difficult to understand why a leading and influential jurist like Abū Hanīfah of Iraq was among its staunch advocates, while he himself was of non-Arab descent and his loyalty to the reigning Arab dynasty was suspect.[113] It is unlikely, therefore, that the doctrine of social equality was merely a revival of a pre-Islāmic practice. The explanation may be found in the social setting contemporaneous with the rise of the doctrine itself.

The introduction of Islām into Egypt, Iraq, Syria, and beyond brought the Arab Muslims into direct contact with the natives on a large scale hitherto unexperienced. This expansion, the rise of political rivalry among various dynasties, and the removal of the capital city from al Madīnah to Damascus and later to Baghdād, must have created problems for and changes in the attitudes of those Muslims. There was no longer the same cohesive, homogeneous and fully-integrated community of earlier decades. Their number increased, their geographical boundaries expanded, their ambitions variegated and often conflicted, their enemies ceased to be a serious threat to them, their leadership became provincial and lacked the inspirational drives and the support of fresh revelations. On the other hand, the societies which were incorporated into the Muslim Empire had been under Roman and Persian rule for generations, and possessed long traditions of social stratification, urbanization, racial and cultural admixture.[114]

This new social setting must have appeared to the Arab Muslims exceptionally complex. If they had succeeded in levelling the social barriers in the early, compact Muslim community, the new setting with its heterogeneous elements must have stood as an obstinate reminder of social distinctions. This would be particularly the case because, as Gibb has noted, the Muslims, at least in the beginning, did not interfere with the life styles and social institutions of the conquered peoples.[115] On the other hand, the native converts had not themselves directly experienced the sense of religious cohesiveness and social levelling of the early Muslim community. Whether they voluntarily regarded the incoming Arab Muslims as a high social stratum, because they were the ruling class, or were forced to regard them as such, it seems that the new environment was impregnated with social barriers and even perhaps conducive to more. Such a situation naturally presented fresh conflicts between the ideal and the actual, between the desirable and the attainable. Two types of reaction can be derived from the juristic views on the general situation. Some jurists maintained that the principle of religious equality should prevail and the new social order must adapt thereto. Other jurists, who later became the majority, accepted the principle but seem to have felt a need for its re-interpretation in the light of the emergent social reality. It was probably their conviction that the new societies could not be transformed completely to adapt to the principle of religious equality any more than this principle could be superimposed upon them. Instead of taking a polaristic position, these jurists, unable to deny religious equality altogether or to disregard the prevailing social reality, adopted a compromising position. They recognized social equality as a factor to be counted in marital arrangements.

One point of compromise seems to be that a great majority of these jurists did not view social equality as an absolute prerequisite of the validity of marriage. It is a right which can be easily waived by the parties concerned. Another point seems to be that some of the criteria of social equality are interchangeable. For example, according to some jurists, a poor but learned man of humble origin is socially equal to the daughter of a notable or rich, but unlearned, father. A third point is that a man is regarded equal to a woman in wealth so far as he can provide for her, even though he may not have as much money or property. Moreover, all these jurists agree that a man may disregard the considerations of social equality and marry below his social class.[116]

It was in this setting that the doctrine of social equality emerged. The jurists who subscribed to it tried to support their view by reference to a Tradition in which the Prophet is said to have stratified the members of Quraysh as equal to one another but superior to the members of other tribes, and these tribes as equals among themselves but superior to the non-Arabs, who themselves are equal to one another. He is also reported to have enjoined, among other things, that women should be married only to their equals (akfā'). They argue, further, that the Arabs deserve this high position because the Prophet was one of them. Also, it is natural that people boast and look down on the lowly. Furthermore, marriage is contracted as a lifelong union and serves noble purposes such as companionship, congeniality and interfamily affinity, conditions which obtain only among compatible equals. It is especially humiliating to the woman to marry down and cohabit with a man below her social status. Unequal matching, therefore, hurts the socially privileged party, particularly the woman.[117]

The opponents argue, in turn, that the alleged Tradition on social stratification is inconsistent with the authentic pronouncements and precedents of the Prophet, contrary to the letter as well as the spirit of the Qur'ān. It is unlikely, therefore, indeed one might say inconceivable, that the Prophet would have endorsed such a scale of stratification. Besides, the counterargument continues, the authenticity of this Tradition is highly dubious on technical grounds. In the second Tradition, the keyword is "equals," a general, equivocal term, whose Arabic denotations include capable, efficient, suitable, etc. To translate this term into fixed scales of social equality is probably too arbitrary. Moreover, this alleged "Tradition" is sometimes attributed to 'Umar I, not to the Prophet. The notion that people are boastful, that hypogamy is humiliating to the woman, and that the Arabs deserve a specially high rank-

ing because of the Prophet seems to violate the very principles
for which he and Islām stand.[118]

This sketchy review of the conflicting arguments clearly indicates that the doctrine of social equality in marriage has no
conclusive religious support, notwithstanding the claims and
rationalizations of its advocates. The basis of the doctrine was
most likely social. The social conditions of the time can help
to explain the doctrine which is inexplicable in terms of the
strict religious precepts of Islām. It seems that the jurists were
faced with the dilemma of how to apply the principle of religious equality to the newly conquered, highly stratified, and
traditionally heterogeneous societies without creating new
problems. The majority chose to interpret the principle in such
a way as to accommodate the new situation without losing
sight of the principle altogether. In this process they seem to
have been more preoccupied with social reality and family
stability than revolutionizing the family or preaching a principle which, to them, was laudable but, under the circumstances, impractical. However, it is clear from the nature of the rules that the doctrine of social equality on the
whole "is not so much a legal prohibition," as it is "a rule of
worldly wisdom . . . The true nature of the rule is that it is not
an absolute prohibition to marry [outside one's social class],
but it allows the . . . [judge] to rescind the marriage . . . in certain cases of *mésalliance* . . ." [119]

The practical result of the difference of opinion is this: If a
woman marries down (hypogamy), the guardian may seek
annulment of the marriage according to the advocates of social
equality. Likewise, if the guardian marries her off to a man
below her social standing, she may seek revocation of the
marriage. If both she and the guardian agree to the marriage, it is valid except in the opinion of the few who regard
social equality a necessary condition. To the advocates of religious equality, hypogamy is valid and class differentials are
inconsequential as far as the marriage validity is concerned.[120]

This was a case where social reality or necessity came into
conflict with an established religious principle which did not

recognize social barriers among Muslims. The majority of jurists adopted a compromising position because they were probably more concerned with the welfare of the family than contesting a certain principle. To them in their milieu the welfare of the family seems to have required some measures of social equality to maximize the probability of marital success. It is curious that they sought to support their position by adducing religious evidence, however questionable. They could have presented their view as a response to the necessities of the new situation and that would have been sufficient, since it is a supplementary principle of law that in case of necessity the unlawful may be regarded as lawful. But, instead, they produced religious evidence however doubtful their adversaries may regard it. The probable reason is that they wanted to give their view a manifest religious color so that it would gain a wider acceptance. Or they may have wanted to show that no gaps existed between the new social order and that of the Muslim community of earlier decades. It seems that they regarded it more integrative to stress the idea of accommodation than to stand inflexible on a principle according to which the new society could be characterized as deranged or deviant.

There appears to be a general agreement among the advocates of social equality that when the two parties are not socially equal, it is the man who must "measure up" to the woman. A woman may marry above but not below her social level, whereas a man may marry below but not above his. Although these stipulations are not absolute, since they can be easily waived by mutual agreement of the parties concerned, and have a questionable affinity to the authentic precepts of Islām, the reasons behind them are both interesting and indicative. It is argued that if a man marries below his social level, it would neither hurt his own status nor lower that of his dependents. The children identify with the father and rise or decline in status as he does. The wife's status is determined by the husband's, whose own position is established and who will not be vulnerable to disgrace or blame if he marries down. A man who marries down may not improve his status; neither

will it decline. The woman who marries up assumes her
husband's status. But if she marries down, she loses her premarital status and assumes a new one which is not as high.
That may be a source of disgrace to her and her family, and
thus create marital instability. To spare the woman this disgrace and the disadvantageous shift of status, she or her family has the right to insist that the suitor be, at least, her social
equal.[121]

This reasoning seems to stress that the Muslim family is
patrilineal as well as patriarchal in certain respects. The status
of the conjugal unit is determined by that of its male head;
members identify with him. Structurally, this means that he
holds the balance of power and is the decision maker. Leadership, especially of the "instrumental" type, is his, as he is the
provider for the family and the bearer of its social status. If
this leadership is to be real, he must be certain of his status.
This is most likely to obtain when he marries his equal or
down. But if he marries up, his position may be subject to uncertainty: personalities may conflict; roles may become diffused and blurred and family stability may be endangered. To
minimize this risk, it is deemed advisable for a man to marry
his equal. If class exogamy is desirable or necessary, he had
better marry down.

The case of women is not the same. When a woman marries,
she assumes the status of her husband. If she marries her equal
or up, she has lost no prestige that a status may carry. But if
she marries down, she may, sooner or later, feel that she has
lost her premarital prestige and whatever compensation or
reciprocity she hoped for may not materialize. This situation
can create emotional problems and social conflicts and it is
quite probable that such a marriage will fail unless the woman
is exceptionally devoted and wise, or the man is willing to exchange roles with the woman. Yet, even if there is a role exchange, it cannot be certain that this will keep the family unit
intact. It may, therefore, be considered in the interest of the
family as a unit and of its members as individuals that the
woman marries her equal or up, not down.

The question, however, does not seem to be that only the husband can raise his wife's status because, being a man, he is the superordinate party, while the wife cannot because, being a woman, she is the subordinate one. Even if this superordinate-subordinate typology is to be accepted, it does not appear to have been the reason for differentiating between men and women with respect to class exogamy. There are indications that a wife could raise the low status of her husband. It is reported that a young woman complained to the Prophet that her father had married her off to a cousin of hers, without her consent, in order to improve his ignoble condition, that she did not consider him to have the same social standing as herself. Muḥammed allowed her to revoke the marriage if she wished. But she then replied that she had no objection to the marriage; rather, "she wished women to understand that their fathers had no authority over their daughters' affairs." This clearly indicates that the woman could raise the lowly status of her husband. But it is uncertain that this action could be socially acceptable and psychologically assuring in a stratified society, or whether it could be implemented as a commendable pattern. The advocates of social equality in marriage seem to think it highly improbable. And here apparently lies the reason for their view on the advisability of male hypogamy and female hypergamy.

4 MARRIAGE (CONTINUED)

A. *Plurality in Marriage*

Although pre-Islāmic Arabia was characterized by various forms of marriage and cohabitation, as we have shown, the Arabian family was of the extended type and, with a few exceptions, as in Makkah of later years, kinship considerations were the foundation of social life. When the immediate family is controlled by the extended family "the society is," as David has put it, "familistic." In such a society, "plural mating [in the form of either polygyny or concubinage] is very likely to occur, because in a kinship dominated society any means of enlarging the family contributes to one's power and prestige." [1]

There can be little doubt that plural mating occurred in pre-Islāmic Arabia if only because there was no institutionalized taboo against it. It was practiced among the various branches of the Semites, including even those who embraced Christianity.[2] But it is not certain how common plural mating was. Some scholars tend to exaggerate its incidence among the pre-Islāmic Arabs; others seem to infer the opposite.[3] From a broad historical and comparative perspective, it seems that the custom was permitted and occasionally practiced. Under normal circumstances its "disadvantages" may well outweigh its "advantages," and it would be unlikely, therefore, to find it as a universal norm in any society. Moreover, in pre-Islāmic Arabia, as in other societies, the wife and/or her kin resented plural mating. Cases are reported where it was stipulated or pledged that the prospective husband would take no partner other than his only wife.[4] In fact, there are indications that this attitude continued in Islām and was endorsed by some of the major schools of law. If a husband takes a second wife, the first may justifiably refuse to be a co-wife and request a divorce.[5] We may infer, then, that under normal conditions plural mating occurred, but was uncommon, resented, and protestable.

B. *Polyandry*

The question of polyandry is also a controversial issue. Some writers claim that this form of marriage was common in pre-Islāmic Arabia at a particular *stage* and certain vestiges thereof were found at the rise of Islām. This notion is usually connected with a theory of matrilineality leading, eventually, to patrilineality. An examination of the evidence adduced to support this theory and of the findings of other investigators would seem to lead to the conclusion that this form of marriage was neither universal in any society nor representative of any historical stage. Polyandry is likely to prevail under such conditions as these: a very high sex ratio, lack of sexual jealousy, severe poverty, internalization of the conceptions of common property, benevolence with regard to sex, and insignificance of the economic output of women. It is very unlikely that these conditions will obtain, in combination, long enough in a society to give rise to perpetual, institutionalized polyandry. Even if some of these conditions, such as poverty, prevail other conditions, e.g., sexual jealousy or acquisitiveness will most probably check the tendency toward total societal polyandry. However, various kinds of laxity, sexual hospitality, and sex communism have existed in some societies for various reasons. But these are exceptions and do not take the form of institutionalized marriages and reciprocal commitments.[6]

The extent of polyandry in pre-Islāmic Arabia is therefore uncertain. Matrilineality had existed but it had no conclusively causal relation with polyandry. Female infanticide, poverty, and sexual laxity were known, but not to any degree demonstratively conducive to polyandry as an institutionalized form of marriage. Conceptions of honor, pride, and shame, which are believed to have been responsible, at least partly, for female infanticide, would not ordinarily favor patterned polyandry.[7] Yet this does not preclude occasional recourse thereto. There are accounts that it was practiced. In certain cases a woman would cohabit with a group of men whose number was under ten. When she gave birth she summoned all of them (no one could refuse to respond to her call) and told them the

news. Then she herself would decide who the father of her
child would be.[8] This implies that the woman must have
been powerful enough to express her choice and have men
abide by her decision. If so, it is likely that not many
women could have been in this favorable position. Further,
the reports on these cases give the impression that it was not
any man, but some particular men, who could have had this
kind of intimacy with one woman, and that the reason for
this kind of relationship was, perhaps, the quest for good
breeding.[9]

In another variant of polyandry also known in pre-Islāmic
Arabia, the number of men involved was greater than
that of the first variant and the relationship was characterized
as prostitution. When the woman in question gave birth physiognomists were called to determine the child's lineage and
the man named as father had to accept their decision. Women
who were involved in this kind of relationship, we are told,
lived in isolation and disrespect. They were in the main slaves
of non-Arab stock; it is contended that seldom would Arab
women put themselves in this position. There are indications
that slave owners used to force their slavegirls to enter the
practice and turn over their earnings to the masters. At any
rate, while this may have been a form of sexual behavior, it
can hardly be designated as a pattern of marriage.[10]

C. *Other Forms of Marriage in pre-Islāmic Arabia*

In addition to these, pre-Islāmic Arabia had at one time or
another experienced the following forms of marriage and
cohabitation.

1. *Marriage by contract.* In this type of marriage men proposed to women through their fathers or guardians. When the
proposal was accepted a dowry was set and the marriage consummated. It was a full-fledged marriage with all the contractual responsibilities and normal marital consequences.

2. *Istibḍāʿ cohabitation (wifelending").* Husbands sometimes permitted their wives to cohabit with men of distinction in
quest for select offspring. The offspring would be identified not

with the natural, but with the social father, the husband, who abstained while his wife cohabited with the other man, the natural father.

3. *Mut'ah marriage.* This type was contracted for a limited period of time and in return for a price payable by the man to the woman. Apparently, it was practiced by strangers and travellers.

4. *Lovers' secret cohabitaticn (akhdān).* It was acceptable for men and women to cohabit in secret without any contract as long as they wished. But once the relationship was disclosed, it was regarded as disgraceful and then terminated.

5. *Marriage by exchange.* A man could exchange his wife or daughter for another man's wife or daughter. No further reciprocity or dowry was required.

6. *Marriage by purchase.* It was customary to acquire a wife for a price (*mahr*) payable to her father or guardian. This practice had some exogamous effects. The Arabs often hesitated to marry their daughters out of their own tribes, and nothing could induce them to overlook that feeling except a high price (*mahr*) offered by the suitor. They were also sensitive to their daughters' future and would usually prefer to marry them off to men who could afford a high price, perhaps under the assumption that the women would be more secure and cherished by their husbands.

7. *Marriage by capture.* This form is believed by some scholars, e.g., Smith, to have preceded marriage by purchase and is one of the heatedly debated points in the history of marriage.

8. *Marriage by inheritance.* Widows were inherited like property by the heirs of their deceased husbands. If an heir wished to marry the widow, he could do so for the very same dowry paid by the deceased husband. He could also contract her marriage to another man and receive the dowry himself. He was also empowered to debar her from remarriage altogether and force her to remain in the state of permanent widowhood.

9. *Maqt marriage.* It was acceptable for a man to marry his father's widow or divorcée.

10. *Service marriage.* Some tribes adopted the practice that when a man was unable to pay a bride price he agreed to serve the girl's father or kin for a period of time sufficient to earn the bride price.

11. *Errébu marriage.*[11] The basic feature of this type was that when a Semite father had no sons of his own he would adopt a young man, treat him as his natural son and marry him to one of his daughters on the basis that the groom would bear the lineal identity of the adopting father and continue to preserve the family name.

12. *Experimental (sifāḥ) cohabitation.* Some tribes used to allow men to cohabit with young women before marriage. If the partners liked one another during this premarital experiment, they would conclude a marriage contract; otherwise, there was no commitment on either side.

13. *Concubinage.* A man could have as many concubines as he was able to afford. Concubinage co-existed with polygyny among the Semites, especially the Hebrews, for two basic reasons. Childless wives preferred their husbands' cohabitation with slavegirls to becoming co-wives. They were confident that the slaves, unlike free women, would not, and could not, compete with them for the husband's love and favors. When a slave gave birth, the child was not identified with the natural mother, the slave concubine, but with the wife of her master; the wife assumed the role of the social as well as the natural mother of the child. Besides this social reason, there was an economic one. Polygyny was costly; only the rich could afford it. It was much more economical to keep concubines and at the same time reap the fruits of their services.[12]

D. *Islām's Position*

In this diversified environment, Islām rose, and to the people who had experienced or witnessed those various forms of sexual behavior it addressed its precepts. Whether all these forms were actually practiced at the rise of Islām or some of them had long died out, Islām approved only of marriage by contract, marriage-like cohabitation with slaves, and, according to the Imāmī S̲h̲ī'īs, the *mut'ah* temporary marriage. Any other form or means of sexual behavior was unequivocally forbidden. Marriage by contract and cohabitation with slaves have been briefly discussed in the last two chapters. The question of the *mut'ah* was also raised but not adequately explored.[13]

E. *The Mut'ah Union*

There is agreement that the *mut'ah* temporary marriage was practiced before Islām and for some time after the rise of Islām. It was a personal contract between a man and a woman to cohabit for a limited period of time in return for a certain remuneration payable by the man. It required no witnesses and did not entail the mutual right of inheritance. That much seems fairly certain. Beyond this, ambiguity and conjecture come into the picture. Some scholars, notably Smith, maintain that it was a kind of marriage which no one need know anything about. Since there was no contract with the woman's kin and the kin might know nothing about the arrangement, it must be concluded, according to Smith, that "the woman did not leave her home, her people gave up no rights which they had over her, and the children of the marriage did not belong to the husband. . . . [This] is simply the last remains of . . . mother kinship . . ."[14]

Aside from the validity or invalidity of this conclusion, the old Arabian custom was apparently regarded as expedient in times of war and on travels. It was not among the first forms of marriage or cohabitation which Islām prohibited. In fact, a major branch of the S̲h̲ī'ī school, as already shown, contend that it was never prohibited by the Qur'ān or the Prophet. They argue that in principle, everything is lawful unless it is specifically and authoritatively classified as forbidden. Since everyone agrees that the *mut'ah* marriage was originally lawful, any claim to its subsequent prohibition must be supported by sufficient evidence. But since there is no such evidence, the *mut'ah* remains lawful on the precedential basis. To reinforce their argument, they invoke the consensus of the "upright"

group, that is, their own group leaders, and interpret certain
verses of the Qur'ān (4:3, 23) in a way that would seem to
permit the *mut'ah* marriage. They also claim that it was not the
Prophet, but 'Umar, the second Caliph after Muḥammad,
who prohibited it, and that all reports tracing this prohibition
to the Prophet are of questionable authenticity.[15]

All Muslims other than this Shī'ī group consider the *mut'ah*
marriage unequivocally forbidden. They support this view by
the Qur'ānic verses which explicitly prohibit any form of sexual relationship except through marriage or marriage-like cohabitation with one's slavegirl (e.g., 23:5-6; 70:29-31). They
cite Traditions from the Prophet and affirmations thereof by
his Companions and their successors to the effect that the
mut'ah union is "the sister of harlotry." They report that even
some of the early Shī'ī Imāms, such as 'Alī himself (d. 40
A.H.), al-Bāqir (d. 114), Ja'far (d. 148) were of the same
opinion as the rest of the Muslims. In fact, they consider it
inconceivable to view the *mut'ah* as having any claim to validity and insist that marriage, according to the Qur'an, is as
strong a social bond as blood relationship. To serve its purposes, they argue, marriage is valid only if it is contracted on
a permanent basis with the earnest desire of both parties to
lead, together, a normal, permanent life. Since illicit sexuality
is forbidden in Islām, and since the *mut'ah* is a disguised form
of fornication, Islām cannot condone it. If it did, the argument
continues, it would be self-inconsistent and would defeat the
purpose of marriage.[16]

It is agreed, howover, that it was during the Caliphate of
'Umar (13-23 A.H.) that the *Mut'ah* practice was ruthlessly
condemned and absolutely forbidden. What preceded that
period is rather obscure. Some scholars claim that the practice
persisted during the Caliphate of Abū Bakr (11-13 A.H.).
The Shī'īs seem to interpret this as lending further support to
their doctrine that the Prophet did not prohibit the *mut'ah*
and it must, therefore, have been accepted as lawful.[17] Some
contemporary writers are inclined to attribute the persistence
of the practice, however illicit, till 'Umar's Caliphate to the

fact that it was fairly common in Arabia before Islām, was overlooked for some time after the rise of Islām, and was justified as being useful in times of war and on travels.[18] There is another theory that the practice was forbidden by the Prophet himself, but certain jurist Companions did not take the prohibition in the absolute sense. Rather, they likened it to the prohibition of the flesh of dead animals which may be lawful in case of necessity or compelling needs. Thus they ruled that it was permissible to practice the *mut‘ah* in similar circumstances of necessity. When they found that this concession was being abused and people were becoming increasingly undiscriminating in taking advantage of it, they revoked the ruling and suspended the concession. This took place in the Caliphate of ‘Umar. Henceforth, the opinion of non-Shī‘ī Muslims became unanimous that the *mut‘ah* was absolutely forbidden.[19]

Examination of the conflicting arguments and of the rather apologetic attitude of some contemporary Shī‘īs seems to indicate that the religious, textual basis of the doctrine of the Shī‘ī *mut‘ah* marriage is equivocal. It is difficult for a non-partisan student of Islāmic law to find clear religious or jurisprudential evidence in support of that doctrine. Even if one is to be extremely skeptical, the most that can be said is that the conflicting arguments at best stand on a par as far as the jurisprudential evidence goes. It is not helpful, therefore, to seek an explanation of the Shī‘ī doctrine in terms of the religious or jurisprudential evidence exclusively; such evidence is highly debatable and can by itself hardly explain the Shī‘ī position. Nor was it entirely a question of political partisanship. It is sometimes suggested that they did not agree with the majority of Muslims because they believed that it was ‘Umar, not the Prophet, who prohibited the *mut‘ah* marriage and voiced the strongest condemnation of its practice. Since they were opposed to ‘Umar's assumption of the Caliphate, they rejected his ruling on the matter.[20] But it seems doubtful that their political attitude to ‘Umar had any funda-

mental effect in this regard. If it had, they would most
probably have been equally opposed to the changes, rulings,
and innovations that were introduced by 'Umar or by other
non-Shī'ī Caliphs and jurists. But they did not adopt such an
attitude of outright opposition.[21]

A satisfactory explanation of the Shī'ī position would seem
to make it necessary to go beyond the jurisprudential evidence
and the political attitude toward a certain Caliph. Such an
attitude and evidence can at best give only a partial, inadequate explanation. These Shī'īs were from the start, a minority
group, whose political opponents prevailed over them and
from time to time subjected them to persecution, imprisonment, exile, or forced separation from their families. They
lived in a state of revolt against the religio-political authorities.
One of their cardinal doctrines was the belief in the Hidden
Imām, the counterpart of the Messiah, who absented himself
in a cave and whose time of return is known only to God. This
belief apparently became firmly entrenched after they had
given up hopes of political victory through open revolt. They
began as a protest group, who soon internalized the idea of
revolt and later adopted a policy of resignation, awaiting the
return of their Hidden Imām.[22] A group in these circumstances
of revolt and suspense, unable apparently to disregard sexual
needs altogether or practice methodical celibacy, and probably, at the same time, apprehensive of family responsibilities
or attachments in fear of becoming subject to exile, imprisonment, or separation from their families, would very likely seek
for some supplementary means of gratification involving minimal risks. Since normal, permanent marriages and marriage-
like cohabitation with slaves were neither always available to
every man nor particularly encouraging under those circumstances, and since all other forms of sexual relationship were
unequivocally forbidden, the *mut'ah* must have appealed to
them as the most natural solution to the problem. It entailed
a minimal responsibility and risk. To them, it could be de-
fended on some jurisprudential grounds, however shaky these

might appear to the adversaries. Had the Shī'īs adopted a different political platform and their original attitude been less "revolting," had their social position been less precarious and their opponents more tolerant, and had the Qur'ān been more specific in its usages of the derivatives of the word *mut'ah*, they would probably have seen the *mut'ah* marriage in a different light, as the rest of the Muslims have.

The Shī'ī position is a sectarian one which was adopted by a minority sect in diametrical opposition to the vast majority of Muslims. Once endorsed by the religious leaders of the classical formative period, it became easily accepted by the succeeding generations and was apparently transmitted without questioning as an integral part of the authoritative traditions. A change in the circumstances under which a given doctrine, such as the *mut'ah*, was originally adopted does not necessarily always lead to a corresponding change in the doctrine itself; the latter may continue to exist as a "survival," which can hardly be explained in terms of the new contemporary conditions. And if a satisfactory explanation of the Shī'ī doctrine of *mut'ah* is to be sought, it is most likely to be found in the earlier historical context. The explanation submitted here appears preferable, notwithstanding the fact that the Shī'ī life became in time routinized and settled, that they ceased to be the persecuted "rebels" or the scattered resigned fatalists, or that they now have their own viable political and religious institutions. Neither can the *mut'ah* doctrine be easily explained in terms of Islāmic precepts or by the principle of the presumed continuity of the pre-Islāmic custom, for not only is this debatable, as we have seen, but also because the same precepts and principles, are shared by other Muslims who, nonetheless, prohibited the *mut'ah*. Nor can the doctrine be readily explained in terms of universal drives, intense regional sexuality, or pre-existing local customs. These, too, were common to the Shī'īs and their adversaries, to Muslims and non-Muslims alike. These factors seem to narrow down the range of explanation to a considerable extent, almost to a predetermined course. Since the doctrine is sectarian and upheld by a minority group, a most probable explanation appears to lie in the very circumstances surrounding the rise as well as the early developments of that sect. This is the kind of explanation we have submitted in the present context.

Although the Shī'īs endorsed the *mut'ah* marriage, they differentiated their conception of it from that of pre-Islamic times. They endeavored to make it appear as close to permanent marriage as possible. It is designated as a "disjoint" or temporary union; but it is like permanent unions in that it requires a valid agreement based on an earnest desire to enter into a marital, though temporary, relationship. It is concluded through the usual procedures of proposal and acceptance. The woman involved may act in her own behalf or choose a third party to represent her. She must be marriageable at the time, that is, she must not be in a "waiting period" that follows a divorce or widowhood. Similarly, she must be free from the usual impediments to a normal permanent marriage whether they be due to blood, affinal, or foster relationships or to religious differences. The *mut'ah* contract is valid only if the proposal is expressed in one of three specific verbal forms. The remuneration payable to the woman must be specified in the contract and the period for which the union is to last must be defined. If the parties failed to specify the period, the contract takes the form of a permanent union. Likewise, if they agree to change the character of the contract into a permanent marriage, so it becomes. When the term of the contract expires and no children are involved, the parties become free from any commitment to one another, and the woman enters a "waiting period" which is usually half the waiting period of a divorcée. If the man dies before the end of the term, the woman's waiting period is the same as that of any widow. Should the woman conceive or give birth during the *mut'ah* union, the child belongs to the natural father and all the usual father-child mutual rights and obligations apply, just as in normal permanent unions. But unlike the latter, there is no limit to the

number of women with whom one man may conclude *mut'ah*
contracts. In such contracts, no witnesses are required, and
none of the principal rights and duties of provision, inheritance, etc. (which are entailed in permanent marriages) apply
unless the *mut'ah* contract so stipulates. Furthermore, the contract may be terminated prematurely either unilaterally or by
mutual agreement.[23]

Compared with the pre-Islāmic practice, the *mut'ah*
seems to have undergone some considerable modification at
the hands of the Shī'īs. They introduced to it several features of
the normal permanent marriage. They assured the children
involved of a legitimate social placement, narrowed the "field
of eligibles" for the *mut'ah* union, and facilitated its transformation into a permanent marriage. These features may clearly
imply that they took the problem much more seriously than the
pre-Islamic Arabs had. In certain fundamental respects the
mut'ah contract became indistinguishable from permanent
marriage; in others it remained "the sister of harlotry."

F. *Polygyny*

We have noted that the Muslim family system could not be
characterized as polygynous in the technical sense of the term,
even though Islām permitted conditional polygyny without
either an outright prohibition or an unqualified sanction, that
the position of Islām was in all probability due neither to
inability to do otherwise nor to laxity or appeasement.[24] Some
further exploration of the far-reaching implications of the
problem may be helpful at this point.

Modern research has shown the true complexity and multi-
dimensionality of polygyny. Some conclusions seem to indicate
that polygyny is not necessarily "irrational" or even non-
rational; not always a privilege of the man and a curse for
the woman. Nor is it altogether "antisocial" and invariably
sensual, contrary to certain evaluations in which some moral-
ists easily engage and on which social scientific research has
shed new light. Polygyny has been attributed to a variety of

reasons: personal, social, physical, economic, and so on. However, on a societal level these reasons interact with one another and, at the same time, with other social forces such as traditions, public morality, custom, and law. This inter-action may result in the reinforcement and public recognition of these reasons, in which case polygyny is likely to become more or less acceptable. But it is not improbable that it may result in the opposite, in which case polygyny is likely to be outlawed and unrecognizable by the public. Yet, to sanction a practice does not necessarily mean that it will prevail; and to outlaw it is no assurance that it will cease to exist in all forms.

It has been suggested that low sex ratio is conducive to and correlated with polygyny. But this is only one of several fac-tors and perhaps the most superficial of all. There is no nec-essary connection between polygyny and low sex ratio as such. It is conceivable, if not indeed observable, that the one can obtain independently of the other. Low sex ratio does not nec-essarily lead to polygyny except, perhaps, when the former has long interacted with a host of other variables. It is generally held that men's sexual needs are greater and more demanding than women's. Analogy with subhuman primates, as Linton has noted, suggests that men may have natural predispositions toward polygyny, based on their higher capacity for physical dominance and aggressive sexual arousal. This capacity, if it does exist, is *reinforced* by the presence of more marriageable females than males in most societies. In view of this biological and demographic reality, a society may, to paraphrase Linton, consider it desirable to give these surplus females an oppor-tunity to breed, thus maintaining the manpower of the group. Moreover, the society may consider it equally desirable that the offspring of these surplus females should be reared under normal familial conditions. The presence in any society of many unmated adults, particularly females, and of children lacking proper family care may prove to be a disturbing threat to public morality and also to the stability of marital relationships. This is the more so in societies where marriage is the natural respected career for women.[25]

Other reasons for polygyny have been suggested. On the individual level, a man may be attracted to more than one woman and seriously wish to marry them. Such attractions may be the result of a desire on his part for sexual variety, offspring, wealth, or authority. In some cases, polygyny may serve as a status symbol not only for the man, but also for the woman. To him, it is a mark of prestige and wealth. As for her, it is a matter of distinction to be married to such a man, not to mention the fact that with two or more women the household burden becomes lighter for each one of them. This is true at least in traditional societies. On the group level, polygyny may serve as a pact of interfamily alliance or, as in ancient times, intertribe and interstate friendship.[26] That such reasons seem to be *post factum* interpretations does not negate their predictive and explanatory power. They can still help to explain why polygyny occurs as it does or why it is likely to occur as it may. In the light of these reasons, it becomes understandable why polygyny is likely to exist or be advocated in societies where adoption, for example, is not legalized and the desire for children can be satisfied only through legitimate procreation; where sexual continence is highly evaluated and sexual expression is tightly restricted to wedlock; or where status indices are limited and/or fixed.

As a complex phenomenon, polygyny may help to solve some personal or social problems. Yet, it may as well generate new ones within and/or without the household. Obvious instances are jealousy among the co-wives, competition for husband's favors, and maneuvering among the sons for advantages. A subtle effect of this is that polygynous families tend to stress *formal* organization and hence lose much of the spontaneous intimacy and congeniality associated with the family. Societies which approve of plural marriage, as Linton has put it, "go to great lengths to define the . . . marital rights and duties . . . [P]olygynous patterns require an elaboration of formal organization which exceeds that needed even for ex-

tended consanguine groups . . ." On the other hand, a polygynous husband is, to paraphrase the same writer, inevitably
caught in a dilemma. If his wives cannot agree, he is subjected to increasing conflicting pressures which leave him
little peace. If they agree, they do too well, in which case they
and their respective children tend to become a closed circle
from which he is largely excluded.[27]

Such problems do impose practical restrictions on polygyny.
Other limitations stem from economic, demographic, and social factors. Polygyny is very unlikely to prevail where marriage and maintenance are costly; where the sex ratio is nearly
equal; or where women enjoy an independent high social position.[28] The list can be extended and more limitations can be
cited. One may, therefore, conclude with Westermarck that all
the evidence from the ancient world "would seem to indicate
that polygyny was an exception . . . [A] multitude of wives is
the luxury of a few despotic rulers or very wealthy men." [29]
Put in stronger and more general terms, Levy has recently
suggested that, "Reference to polygyny is *never* more than
reference to an *ideal* structure for any society. Only a [small]
minority of males ever achieve it, and they almost certainly
constitute an elite by that fact alone in such social contexts." [30]

However limited or costly, polygyny has been permitted by
religions with which Islām has close affinities, and has occurred in many societies with which Muslims have interacted.
It was permitted and practiced in ancient Egypt, Persia, among
the Slavs, the Indo-European peoples, and the pre-Islamic
Arabs. Where monogamy was the law, as in the Code of Hammurabi, exceptions were made to allow a man to take a second
wife or a concubinage was acceptable and practiced, though
the concubines had no rights and the children were bastards.
Similarly, Greco-Roman marriage was strictly monogamous,
but liaisons between married men and mistresses were not
uncommon.[31]

The case of the Hebrews and their successors is highly
indicative of the complexity of polygyny. According to
some accounts, the Hebrew family, along with the whole fam-

ily system of the Middle East of historical times, has been characterized as polygynous. The Bible set no limit to the number of wives and/or concubines a man might take. All the Judges must have had several wives each (Judg. 8:30; 10:45; 12:14). King Solomon is said to have had seven hundred wives, princesses, and three hundred concubines (1. Ki. 9:16; 11:3 cf., S. of Sol. 6:8). His son had eighteen wives and sixty concubines (2 Chron. 11:21). Each of Rehoboam's twenty-eight sons had many wives (2. Chron. 11:23). Even the wise men of the Talmud have given good advice that no man should marry more than four wives, the number Jacob had. Monogamy may have been regarded as the "ideal" form, but polygyny and concubinage were not unknown. On the other hand, some scholars tend to argue that, although polygyny had been the rule among the Hebrews as nomads and was common in the times of the Monarchs and Judges, in process of time monogamy came into favor. Some rabbis prohibited plural marriage, others allowed it only in the case of a childless wife. Various social circumstances, along with the rabbinical institution of marriage control and settlement, operated as a check upon plural marriage.[32]

A tendency toward exaggeration seems to be at work in this area. Some writers are inclined to take the lawfulness of polygyny and its frequent occurrence among the Hebrew nomads, the Monarchs, and Judges as indicative of a "universal" practice. But such inferences can hardly be established. There is no necessary connection between the lawfulness of a given practice and the common occurrence thereof; that is, if an act is lawful or tolerable it is not necessary that the act will be done, and even when it is done it does not follow that it will be undertaken frequently or by a large number of people. Nor is it likely that the commoners would, or ordinarily could, follow the example of the Monarchs or the Judges.

Conversely, some observers tend to translate the involuntary social and economic limitations upon plural marriage into moral virtues and to view such external restrictions as internal moral traits. This may obscure some important aspects of the problem and shift the focus from *explanation* to *evaluation,* an error which is not uncommon especially among those who study systems or generations other than their own. As Day has noted, in the Judges' time plural marriages "were undoubtedly common, but they probably seldom led to such unpleasantness as would seem to be indicated by the stories of domestic infelicity found in Genesis, which were coloured to suit the monogamous ideas of a later day." [33] However, there can be little doubt that the Jews have throughout the ages more or less practiced polygyny, that the polygynous among them have been on the whole no more and no less in number than the polygynous members of other societies in comparable situations, and that they have no exceptional predispositions in favor of either polygyny or monogamy. This may be illustrated by the fact that European Jews of the Middle Ages were still practicing polygyny, and the practice can still be found among those living in certain Muslim countries.[34]

The development of the Christian position on polygyny is also interestingly relevant. The New Testament, according to some scholars, assumes monogamy as the normal form of marriage, but it does not expressly prohibit polygyny except in the case of bishops and deacons. Some of the Fathers accused the Jewish rabbis of sensuality, yet no church council in the earliest centuries opposed polygyny. Nor was any obstacle placed in the way of its practice. St. Augustine clearly declared that he did not condemn it. Occasionally Luther spoke of it with considerable toleration and approved the bigamous status of Philip of Hesse. There was a time, in 1650, when some Christian leaders resolved that every man should be allowed to marry two women. It is reported that the German reformers, even so late as the sixteenth century, admitted the validity of a second and a third marriage contemporaneously with the first, in default of issue and other similar causes. In 1531 the Anabaptists openly preached that a true Christian must have several wives. The doctrine of the Mormons is well known. Even today, some African bishops support polygyny on moral grounds and in preference to other alternatives. Excessive casualties of men in war have, from time to time, led groups and individuals to advocate legalized polygyny. Some Western intellectuals have speculated that the West's adoption of polygyny is probable or even necessary. Apart from these doctrinal arguments, there have been many cases of polygyny, explicit and disguised. Several kings are believed to have taken more than one wife each and to have kept concubines. In certain ages it was the established privilege of royalty to keep mistresses, a variant of polygyny. There are indications that polygyny was not unknown during the reign of Charlemagne even among priests.[35]

Christians are, nevertheless, believed to have been on the whole far less polygynous than either Jews or Muslims. Several interpretations of this have been offered. It has been suggested that the first Christian teachers had no reason to condemn polygyny since monogamy was already the universal rule among the peoples to whom Christianity was addressed. But, as Westermarck has pointed out, "this is certainly not true of the Jews, who still permitted and practiced polygyny at the beginning of the Christian era."[36] Nor can it be said that Christianity introduced monogamy to the Western world, or reinforced it out of "respect" for women or for social reform. The monogamous orientation of Christianity was probably the product of a religious philosophy "which regarded every gratification of the sexual impulse with suspicion and incontinence as the gravest sin. In its early days the Church showed little respect for women, but its horror of sensuality was immense."[37] And because the chief concern of the Church was to save souls by preventing the deadly sin of fornication, the form of marriage was reduced to the simplest possible terms. On the other hand, monogamy was the only legitimate form of marriage in the Western societies to which Christianity was first introduced. It was not a preconceived social philosophy, but most probably a combination of aversion to sex, suspicion of women, and preoccupation with soul saving that gave Christianity its doctrinal monogamous character. This combination was further reinforced by the strong tradition of formal monogamy in Greece and Rome and also by the fact that Christianity took root first in the lowest brackets of free classes, who probably could not afford polygyny anyway.[38]

This sketchy review of polygyny in the broad religious and historical context has been intended to serve not merely as an introductory background, but also, and more importantly, as a general interpretation of the position of Islām. The religion of Islām belongs to the monotheistic family of religions which developed in the same cultural area of the Near East. Given the fact that similar conditions generally invoke similar reactions, it may be concluded that most of the points which have been discussed so far apply to Islām. For example, the reasons for, and the limitations upon, polygyny among non-Muslims more or less apply to Muslims. It is not necessary at this point to examine the sweeping claims that Islām raised the status of women almost to a rank of deification any more than it is necessary to examine the equally sweeping claims that Islām introduced or reinforced polygyny, and that the practice has been confined to Muslims almost exclusively. However, it appears reasonably clear that had Islām been averse to sex, like doctrinal Christianity, or had its initial contacts with Europe followed the same path as Judaism and Christianity, the situation would probably have been different. That is, if Islām were suspicious of women or averse to sex, and if it had come to a Europe of formally monogamous traditions to be the religion of the vast majority, Islām would probably have adopted a more strict type of monogamy or Europeans would have been more openly and frequently polygynous. Similarly, had Muslims, like the Jews and Christians, come to Europe as minorities of refugees or proselytizers, they would very likely have adopted a different attitude to polygyny. Nevertheless, this does not mean that the Muslim family system is simply a replica of or is identical with any other system. The rules of polygyny in Islām are said to have been established in response to certain pressing situations and also, but perhaps more significantly, to regulate future behavior in a way that could provide for legitimate alternatives. This may become clear from the discussion to follow.

Islām permits polygyny. This is a voluntary behavioral measure which the individual may or may not apply depending on certain factors. It is neither an offense, nor an injunction, nor an article of faith. Contrary to some modern interpretations, and in spite of the fact that the Qur'ān implies that the family of Adam and Eve, together with other "prominent" families, had been monogamous, Islām appears to assume neither monogamy nor polygyny as the normal form of marriage.[39] What it seems to assume is that marriage is a universal phenomenon which may conceivably take various forms, that man is endowed with a conscience which he can and is expected to heed, that in every action situation a sense of God-mindedness and transcendental responsibility must be brought to bear upon the web of social relations, that similar situations may create reaction differentials in different individuals. The capacity to cope with and adapt to a "crisis" situation varies from person to person and is, in any case, finite. God expects of man only what is possible and holds him responsible for what is humanly attainable. God's relationship to man is a relationship of mercy and equity. On this basis the relationship between man and man should be built.[40]

The key passage in the Qur'ān (4:3) where polygyny is designated as permissible may be rendered as follows:

> And if you fear that you will not act justly towards the orphans, marry such women as seem good to you, two, three, four; but if you fear that you will not be equitable, then only one, or what your right hands own; so it is likelier that you will not be partial (or become destitute).[41]

This is usually interpreted in conjunction with another passage (4:129) where the Qur'ān says:

> You will not be able to be equitable between your wives, even so you be eager. Yet, do not be altogether partial so that you leave her (i.e., the wife discriminated against) as it were suspended. If you set things right, and are God-minded (or godfearing), God is All-forgiving, All-compassionate.[42]

Some contemporary scholars interpret the first passage

(4:3) to mean that polygyny is lawful *only* if there is fear of injustice to the orphan wards, and it is *forbidden* if the husband is not sure of treating his co-wives equitably. Since equity is prerequisite to polygyny, and since the second passage (4:129) states that men will not be able to achieve equity, then polygyny, in the final analysis, is actually unlawful. This interpretation seems to have been associated with two major factors. Internally, polygyny has been both abused and displaced as can be readily seen. Externally, more and more Muslims are becoming increasingly sensitive to some Western criticism of polygyny. However, the classical position is still predominant among the contemporary religio-legal authorities. With the early interpreters of the law, they maintain that:
1. The permissibility of polygyny is established by the Qur'ān (4:3), by the precedents or Sunnah of the Prophet, and by the consensus of Muslim jurists throughout the ages.
2. Polygyny was initially permitted to prevent injustice to women, particularly female orphans, and to promote continence.
3. It is lawful to those who have reasons for it, who can treat their wives equitably and provide for them sufficiently.
4. The unattainable justice to which the Qur'ān makes reference (4:129) is the absolute equity, which demands the husband to have the same undiscriminating feelings towards his co-wives and to control fully his emotional inclinations so that his sentimental sympathy will not be greater for one wife than for another. It is this kind of *absolute* equity which is impossible to achieve. Yet this does not condone discrimination. What the Qur'ān requires is what is humanly attainable, that is, justice to wives in terms of companionship, provisions, considerateness, and such controllable aspects of the family life. Feelings and emotions may sometimes defy control, and it may be in vain to decree that an individual develop or maintain the same intensity or extensity of feelings for a number of persons, even if they be his children, wives, or close friends. It might be added, parenthetically, that no party, even in a monogamous

diad, can be said to have the same invariable feelings for the other party.[43]

The status of polygyny in Islām is no more and no less than that of a permissible act. And, like any other act lawful in principle, it becomes forbidden if it involves unlawful things or leads to unlawful consequences such as injustice.[44] The Qur'ān (4:3) is unequivocal in stating that if there is fear of injustice a man may marry only one wife or what captives his right hands own. This constitutes one of the religio-moral limitations which Islām has placed on polygyny. The problem, is how to determine injustice and cope with it in this situation. Islām seems to take the position that the individual can best judge his own inclinations or dispositions and, with the proper kind of divine guidance, cope with the situation, either to prevent injustice or to remedy it should it occur. As long as injustice remains in the conceptual or emotional stage, formal law can do little about it; and it is here that Islam would seem to entrust a great deal of the "corrective" action to the individual, who is assumed to be responsible and God-minded. Also, it is here that the belief in a Final Judgment may have some impact. But if injustice takes the form of concrete, detectable behavior, then the law-enforcement authorities are enjoined to take action to ensure justice and equity.

Besides this and the other common limitations upon polygyny, Islām has added the following stipulations. First, it is forbidden for a man to take more than one wife if he cannot provide for them adequately and treat them equitably; and under no circumstances may he exceed the limit of four wives. Secondly, all schools of law, except the Shī'īs, have endorsed the doctrine of "suspended repudiation," according to which a wife may stipulate in the marriage contract that divorce would become effective should the husband do certain things unfavorable to her, like taking a second wife. They have also endorsed the principle of "delegated repudiation," in which case the right to divorce is vested in the wife who may exercise it should there arise circumstances disadvantageous to her, e.g., becoming a co-wife. Thirdly, no one may impose the status of polygyny upon a woman or a man. If harm or injustice is done to the woman, she may refer to the judicial authorities for protection and/or divorce. The Ḥanbalī school of law regards stipulations against a second marriage binding on the husband (4:41) and enforceable, while the Mālikī school takes the concept of "prejudice" (ḍarar or harm) in a broad enough sense to allow a wronged wife a judicial divorce.[45]

In addition, certain moral exhortations and legal rulings are interpreted as checks against the abuse of polygyny. For example, Muḥammad is reported to have proclaimed God's condemnation of the "sensual" men and women. When asked whom he meant, he replied: they are those who marry frequently in pursuit of carnal pleasures.[46] It may also be pointed out that a considerable portion of the marriage endowment (dowry)—usually between one and two thirds—is ordinarily deferred, to be claimed by the wife in the case of divorce and/or widowhood. This can, and it often does, serve as an indirect limitation upon polygyny. At any rate, the severest restriction is probably the fact that a second or third or even fourth marriage is a full-fledged contract that entails the same rights and obligations as the first one. A marriage may be second or third in the temporal sequence, but not in the religious, moral, or legal ranking.

The question may be raised: Why did Islām take this particular position? What were the conditions leading to this stand? In answer to the question several factors may be suggested as potential, common reasons or as actual, specific circumstances behind the Islāmic orientation. Among the usual potential reasons are cited the default of issue, chronic illness of the wife, the relatively tempered and moderate sexual needs of the woman, which may not match the compelling drives of the man. This does not exhaust the potential reasons for which a man may desire a second wife. The list is clearly partial as it stresses only the most serious and common reasons. With regard to the actual, specific circumstances of Islām, scholars of various persuasions have observed the following:

1) The Muslims had a great need for progeny to build up and reinforce the nascent community.

2) There was an increasing number of helpless widows and orphans who had lost their supporters for one reason or another and who urgently needed providers, fosters, and guardians to take proper care of their moral and material welfare.

3) The lack of public funds or "state budgets" to meet the urgent needs of such helpless dependents was obvious.

4) The marriage bonds were generally lax at the time and in need of reform. Polygyny was a measure of regularization and stability.[47]

Commenting on these reasons, Stern has suggested that "Muhammad by his sanction of polygyny was introducing a regularized type of polygamous marriage to meet the emergency of the situation . . ." The idea was to replace the ill-defined marriage practices, which provided no protection for the women, by a well-defined institution and to incorporate the superfluous women into the community, instead of allowing them to act as a disintegrative factor.[48] It may be submitted that, left short of complete incorporation into the normal community life, such superfluous women could become the target of exploitation by irresponsible, uncommitted men; or, in pursuit of their own need gratification, they may be driven to violate the social norms and thus undermine the moral fabric of society.

Although the immediate demographic needs and economic factors may have been influential in the sanction of polygyny, the most fundamental single reason was probably the moral consideration. The demographic and economic factors can at best explain the initial sanction to meet an emergency situation. But the sanction was more than a temporary legislation. On the other hand, the economic and demographic situation seems to have approximated a state of stabilization toward the end of Muḥammad's life. Nearly all Arabia joined the band of Islām, and the rules of collective economic security were fully enacted by the way of compulsory poor-due (*Zakāh*) and relatively sufficient administration, as well as distribution of public revenues.[49] What appears most revealing, therefore, is not the demographic and economic factors, however enlightening these may be. Rather, it is the moral factor that seems to gen-

erate a greater explanatory power. The insight into this situation lies in Islām's strong condemnation of fornication and
adultery, its recognition of certain human drives as meriting
satisfaction or sublimation in a wholesome fashion, and its
intent to dissociate the intimate relationships from exploitation and abuse. To this effect, Islām prescribed various measures to prevent illicit relationships and to distinguish proper
from exploitative or delinquent sexual behavior, so that the
risk of deviance in the disapproved direction could be restricted to an absolute minimum. Indicative of this approach
are the following points.

1) Muḥammad strongly stressed the role of "guardians" in order to
avoid the possibility or resemblance of fornication; a villain may easily
intrigue an unguarded woman into a dubious marriage without any
serious intention on his part to keep the marital bonds.

2) Islām prohibited the *taḥlīl* (a form of marriage in which a man
marries a thrice-divorced woman solely to make her once again lawful
to her former husband). When a man divorces his wife irrevocably, he
cannot remarry her unless she has been voluntarily married to another
man. If the second marriage happens to end in a voluntary divorce, then
she may remarry her first husband, provided thy feel that they can keep
the limits of God. This condition is most probably meant by the Qur'ān
as a reproachful deterrent to arbitrary, hasty divorces. But when a man
marries such a thrice-divorced woman only to legalize her eventual reunion with her former mate, the act is nothing but a variant of adultery
and is therefore forbidden.

3) Islām also prohibited the *mut'ah,* temporary marriage and accepted only the contracts in which the parties intend to consort with one
another permanently and which are consummated with the approval of
guardians in the presence of qualified witnesses.

4) To avoid any uncertainty and remove even the doubt of resemblance of illicitness, Islām required the publicity of marriage, recommended marriage festivities, and insisted on the elimination of all
impediments to a full-fledged, perpetual, and wholesome marriage.

5) The penalty of fornication and adultery can be as severe as capital
punishment by stoning the guilty till they exhale their very last breath.[50]

It is this moral consideration which seems to provide the
best explanation of the sanction of regulated polygyny in
Islām. Marriage in principle is highly regarded by the religion.
Sex as such is not condemned and sexual needs are fully recog-

nized. Pre-Islāmic Arabia had known and practiced polygyny, along with various forms of loose sexuality. The early years of Islām left a number of helpless widows and orphans to whom the rest of the community must have felt some moral obligations and whose complete incorporation into the social fabric of society must have called for more than economic welfare or half-hearted patronage. Men and women, when denied the satisfaction of natural needs, or forced to enter into and keep monogamous unions, may be driven to engage in illicit relationships and thus become forces of social disintegration. It was most probably in response to or recognition of these basic human needs that Islām allowed the continuity of polygyny, the likely alternative to which would be, in some cases at least, fornication, adultery, or promiscuity.

The question seems to impose itself: why did Islām not resort, instead, to other mechanisms such as self-restraint, sublimation, discipline, and the like? The fact is that Islām did resort to these mechanisms; but they may not be always adequate in every situation. Polygyny does not necessarily exclude their presence or applicability; rather, it may complement them by filling any gaps that may result from human failures. Perhaps even polygyny itself can be regarded as one of these very mechanisms in view of the moral burdens it involves. In this sense, polygyny and these other mechanisms are not mutually exclusive; they may be actually complementary.

Polygyny in Islām is a subject to which every observer seems to project his own particular mind and age. The same idea evokes different opinions from scholars differentially situated in the social and intellectual world. This is probably clearly manifested in the comments of some contemporary Western writers. For example, Stern has noted that the introduction of the Islāmic type of polygyny "apparently did not meet with the approval of the Anṣār [the Muslim natives of al Madīnah], and there was possibly a certain amount of dissatisfaction even amongst the Muhājirīn [Makki immigrant] women." [51] Simi-

larly, Roberts doubts if Muḥammad recognized the "evils of
polygamy" and seriously questions "whether the prophet could
have abolished polygamy entirely had he wished to do so." [52]

Such remarks can only obscure more than reveal. Stern's
remark may be interpreted in several ways with varying implications. But whatever the implications, the remark seems
misleading and incomplete—if there were Muslims dis-
satisfied with polygyny, there must have been others who
were also displeased with any limitation or regularization
of it. This, too, should be pointed out, at least as a logical
supplement of the caution to see the problem in full perspective and avoid the possible misunderstanding of how the
law was made or received. One undoubted fact is that the ruling on polygyny was not addressed to any special sector of the
population or made in response to the demands of any "pressure group." This becomes readily apparent from a careful
examination of the relevant passages of the Qur'ān (e.g., 4:
1-3).

Roberts' remark may be also misleading. It probably reflects a mind preoccupied with the "evils" or negative effects
of polygyny to the complete exclusion of any possibility of
"positive functions" of the institution. It attributes to Islām
and Muḥammad ideas which seem inconsistent with the letter
as well as the spirit of the Qur'ān. For instance, how could
Muḥammad fail to recognize the evils of polygyny when the
Qur'ānic sanction is couched in a context of trembling fear
and warning, and is voiced in the keys of justice and equity?
It might be true that there were Muslims who regarded the
ruling too "liberal" or too "conservative" and thus resented it.
The Qur'ān makes no secret of such possible resentments or
half-hearted acceptance of some of its rules. It does not assume
an angelic any more than it does a satanic nature of the human
being. Nor does it rule out or ignore the occurrence of evil
deeds and abuses. Its approach seems to emphasize the principle that it is in man's power, with the help of God, to learn to
adapt; that behavior can be learned, unlearned, and relearned;
that the degree of man's control over and knowledge of his en-

vironment is limited; and that, when in doubt, man should rely on God and always adapt himself to God's guidance. Two examples may illustrate the point. The Qur'ān says:

> Prescribed for you is fighting, though it may be *hateful* to you. It may happen that you will *hate* a thing which is *better* for you; and it may happen that you will *love* a thing which is worse for you; God knows, and you know not. (2:216; emphasis added.)
>
> O believers, it is not lawful for you to inherit women against their will; neither debar them, that you may go off with part of what you have given them, except when they commit a flagrant indecency.
>
> Consort with them honorably; if you are *averse* to them, it is possible you may be *averse* to a thing, and God set in it *much good*. (4:19; emphasis added.)

It can be readily seen that this is not the approach of a legislator who looks upon man as either infallible or hopeless, or who assesses the human situation in absolute, dichotomous terms. It is necessary therefore to view remarks like those of Stern and Roberts as reflections of certain styles of thought and modes of existence. This is important to keep in mind when considering whether polygyny is a male privilege or a female blessing. Jeffery, a contemporary scholar, has no doubt that it "is solely a male privilege in Islām, however, for no woman may be married to more than one man at a time." [53] But Ibn Qayyim, a medieval Muslim scholar, made some sociologically interesting observations. He suggested that if polyandry were institutionalized along with or instead of polygyny, society would disintegrate, legitimacy and lineage would be lost, male spouses would try to eliminate one another, disturbance and disputes would abound. Polygyny, not polyandry, was permitted, he claimed, for the following reasons:

> 1) Because of role differentiation and habitual seclusion, natural confinement and disposition to the household activities, women are less sexually animated than men; their sexual needs are relatively moderate.
>
> 2) Contrary to the common misconception, women are not more sexually inclined than men. The leisurely carefree life women usually lead may appear to support this misconception. But the fact of the matter is that it is not so; a man may be capable or even desirous of having more than one intercourse at a time. The woman's post-intercourse reaction is different; her passionate sensations submerge as she lends her-

self easily to meek feelings and temporary depression, which leave her no desire for more at the time.

3) Men labor, sweat, and run great risks to provide for women. God, the appreciative and just, allowed polygyny in compensation for these extraordinary efforts and responsibilities. (Parenthetically, if this statement is taken out of context, it would seem to support Jeffery's observation.)

4) What men undergo in making a living for their women is more burdensome than the amount of discomfort which women may suffer because of jealousy. The male's duty in this regard outweighs his option of polygyny, and the female's discomfort is overcompensated by the care and protection due to her in marriage.[54]

What is implied in these observations is that polygyny is not entirely a blessing for one sex and a curse for the other. Nor may it be viewed in this light. It is more enlightening to approach the subject analytically as a corollary of the principle of equity in Islām and as a legitimate alternative applicable to some difficult, "crisis" situations. Such an approach is more likely to give the student a broader perspective of role differentiation as well as the structural and moral foundations of Muslim society.

To this point the discussion has dealt briefly with the complex phenomenon of polygyny from a historical crosscultural perspective. This practice is not entirely peculiar to any age or system. The differences in this regard may be more of degree and formality than of kind and principle. In the religious context of Islām, polygyny is a voluntary course which was legalized under certain conditions and which, in the social context of Muslim society, might have been or actually was abused. Like any complex social action, polygyny entails normative ideal elements as well as behavioral externalities which may or may not completely correspond to one another. Some writers, mainly Muslims, have been almost invariably preoccupied with the normative ideal aspects, taking little or no interest in the actual realities of Muslim life. Others, mainly Westerners, have been preoccupied almost exclusively with the external, perhaps sensational, abuses of the practice, weighing them against some abstract idealized standards which probably never existed anywhere at any time. The result is that both groups of writers seem to talk past one another leaving the problem more obscured than explained. However, polygyny cannot be entirely divorced from its actual behavioral context; otherwise, it will remain a pure formal conception without any meaningful relevance to reality. Nor can it be totally divorced from its normative ideal context; any social action divested of normative regulations is little more than aberration.

Aside from these preoccupations, the discussion has addressed itself primarily to the general nature of polygyny, its *raison d'ètre*, the actual as well as the potential factors which a legislator may take into account in the legalization or prohibition of the practice, and of which "practitioners" are or should be made aware. We have not discussed to what extent and with what effects the practice has been used or abused, how frequently the norms have been violated or fully enacted, or what the relevant variables are in any given case. Nor have we compared and contrasted polygyny with monogamy in the context of absolute or universal morality. Neither have we answered any specific questions so much as we have raised some researchable ones and brought to focus the ambiguities, complexities, and commonly persistent misconceptions of the problem.

G. *Eligibility for Marriage: Endogamy, Exogamy, and Incest Boundaries*

Marital union, being a special variant of the general category of social interaction, is subject to extraordinary control mechanisms. In no society is a person completely free to marry whom he wishes; the choice is necessarily limited by a number of factors. One of such limitations is the law of endogamy and exogamy. As Merton has put it, "all marriages are intermarriages in the sense that the contractants derive from different social groups of one sort or another. This follows immediately from the universal incest taboo, which forbids marriage at least between members of the same elementary family unit and derivatively restricts marriage to members of different family groups." [55]

While all marriages are in this sense intermarriages or exogamous, the extent of exogamy, and derivatively of endogamy varies from group to group and from time to time. The barriers setting limits to exogamy include religion, race, lineage, and social status. The strongest of these, however, seems to be religion. But this in turn fluctuates with group solidarity and self-sufficiency. If a group is internally cohesive and faces no external threat or has no designs for expansion, it will most likely take a strong stand against exogamy. Such a stand may take the form of religious proscriptions as can be seen from the historical experience of the Jews, the Romans, the Christians, and so on. On the other hand, there are factors that narrow the field of endogamy and thus necessitate a certain degree of exogamy. Included in these are the incest taboos, affinal bonds, and lactation or "milk" fosterage.[56]

Little is definitely known about the incest relationship in pre-Islāmic Arabia. Inconsistent conclusions have been reached by various scholars and even by the same scholar in different contexts.[57] Much of the confusion in this regard probably stems from a controversial clause in the verse (4:23), in which the basic forbidden degrees are clearly enumerated. The verse may be rendered as follows:

> Forbidden to you are your mothers and daughters, your sisters, your aunts paternal and maternal, your brother's daughters, your sister's daughters, your mothers who have given suck to you, your suckling sisters, your wives' mothers, your stepdaughters, who are in your care, being born of your wives you have been in to—but if you have not been in to them it is no fault in you—and the spouses of your sons who are of your loins, and that you should take to you two sisters together, *except what had taken place (or unless it be a thing of the past),* God is most assuredly ever All-forgiving, All-compassionate . . .

The italicized clause can be interpreted to mean that (1) All or most of the forbidden degrees mentioned in the verse were actually permitted and/or practiced before Islam, and (2) the prohibition stipulated in the verse was not retroactive. For example, the Qur'ān now made it unlawful for a man to marry the widow or divorced wife of his father, but if such a marriage had already taken place before the rule was made, the marriage remained valid; the new law did not affect it because the prohibition was not retroactive. The same is true of a man who was married to two sisters together; such marriages, already in existence, were not affected by the new law of prohibition. This is how the clause has been interpreted by some scholars.[58] But this interpretation seems to read into the clause much more than it can bear and to take it out of context. When taken as it stands in the passage and read independently of the historical legal process, the clause may support this interpretation. Yet, in view of the ambiguous evidence concerning the forbidden degrees before Islām, the controversial nature of the whole issue, the alleged laxity of marital bonds among the pre-Islāmic Arabs, and the instruction by Muḥammad to the polygynous new Muslims to release any wives in excess of the legal limit, it is exceedingly unlikely that Islām would honor the incestuous marriages that were already contracted or in existence when the law of prohibition was introduced. Moreover, the Qur'ān may sometimes prescribe a certain course of action and add that God forgives what is past (e.g., 5:98). This is because what is done cannot always be undone and it would be inequitable to hold any person responsible for what he cannot undo. Furthermore, what was there in the situation to prevent the dissolution of the incestuous unions, if any existed at the time, after the Qur'ān declared them forbidden? To assume that the exceptive clause meant the validation of the existing incestuous marriages and only the prohibition of initiating fresh ones is rather untenable, unless the marital ties of the time were sacramental or indissoluble. What the clause seems to mean is this: These degrees are forbidden to you except what *had* taken place, i.e., that which cannot be undone. Also the exception usually refers to the nearest noun in the passage, i.e., the taking in marriage of two sisters together, which might have been practiced before the law was made. But that does not mean the continued validity of unions of this type that were previously contracted.

However, there are literary indications that the majority of pre-Islāmic Arabs detested the idea of marriages between close relatives even though there was no legal bar against it. They believed that such marriages were detrimental in that they produced weak or defective progeny—a notion similar to the modern genetic explanation of incest taboo in terms of the alleged harms of inbreeding. Some Arabs even prided themselves on their exogamous unions. Further, a statement is attributed to the Prophet and is said to have been confirmed by 'Umar I which strongly recommended exogamy to prevent population "shrinking." [59] What is interesting here is not so much whether the biological theory is helpful or whether the Arabs actually knew the genetic implications of inbreeding, for all this is still highly problematic. Rather, the curious thing is that the Arabs seem to have interpreted certain statements in such a way as to fit their own preconceived ideas. The proud utterances of some exogamous Arabs would appear more meaningful and better explicable if placed in the sociological, not the biological, perspective. Exogamy may very well symbolize high status, security, self-confidence, and freedom from inhibitions or any fear that made cousin marriages preferable in the first place. Similarly, the statement attributed to the Prophet does not necessarily mean a warning against any alleged biological defects of close endogamy. It lends itself more easily to the sociological interpretation because exogamy could facilitate the propagation of Islām, a primary concern of the Prophet and his followers, and also reinforce the religious ties by the newly acquired interfamily bonds.

There are also some other minor arguments in favor of exogamy among the pre-Islāmic Arabs. According to Smith, marriages with war captives were of constant occurrence. Besides, a man in quest for friendship might find a wife by agreement in a friendly tribe or he might shun marriages within his own tribe to avoid the ugly family quarrels. These factors, together with the practice of female infanticide, "would render a law of endogamy almost impossible when every tribe was anxious to have many sons to rear up as warriors." [60]

It cannot be inferred, however, that the pre-Islāmic Arabs were undiscriminatingly exogamous. Rather, they were selective and in certain respects inflexible. The Arab tribes, however lowly, were strongly opposed to giving their daughters in marriage to non-Arabs, however noble in their own right. Some tribes subjectively stratified their status higher than that of others and would not allow their daughters to marry below their "class." [61] Apparently there was no objection to female hypergamy as there was to hypogamy; females could marry above their social rank but not below. In addition, intermarriages between the tribes of Makkah and al Madīnah were relatively rare. The two towns were inhabited by traditionally hostile groups of different origins. Their modes of life were also different. The Makkīs lived in an open, trade-centered society and were thus relatively more disposed to exogamy than the Madīnīs. However, their exogamy was limited; it seldom transcended the confines of subtribal clans or allied tribes The society of al Madīnah was more of the closed agricultural type. The Madīnis would intermarry with allied clans, neighboring tribes, local Jews; but hardly with the Makkīs.[62]

With the coming of Islām, the situation changed. The basic forbidden degrees became unequivocal and most of the traditional barriers to intermarriages were removed or readjusted. The forbidden degrees in Islām constitute three broad categories: (1) consanguineal (blood relatives), (2) affinal ("in-laws"), (3) lactational (relatives in milk fosterage and through wet nursing). The details of these aspects can be readily found in any standard source of Islāmic Law. However, the third category and its implications are sociologically interesting and deserve some detailed discussion.[63]

All Law schools accept the authenticity of the Tradition which stipulates that the forbidden degrees due to lactation fosterage are the same as those due to consanguineal relationships. For example, a man's foster sister is as unlawful for him as his own natural sister. The details of how much milk is

suckled, at what age it is received, *how* it is given, and so on
are the subject of wide disputes among the jurists and do not
concern us here.[64]

To explain the incest taboo several theories have been suggested, but none is considered adequate by itself. It is generally held that an acceptable theory must be consistent with the known facts and provide a satisfactory explanation for all or most of them. Because of their failure to satisfy
these conditions, the following theories are rejected: (1) the
theory of alleged, harmful biological effects of inbreeding,
(2) the theory of alleged instinct against inbreeding, (3) the
theory that familiarity breeds sexual indifference, and (4) the
psychoanalytic theory of Oedipal involvement. Instead, an eclectic theory has been suggested and seems widely accepted. It
synthesizes principles of sociological theory, behavioral psychology, cultural anthropology, and psychoanalysis.[65] Of
significant relevance to our discussion is the principle
of "stimulus generalization" from behavioral psychology. "According to this principle, any habitual response, learned in
connection with one stimulus or situational configuration, will
tend to be evoked by other stimuli in proportion to their sim-
ilarity to the former. To the extent, therefore, that any secondary or remoter relative resembles a sexually tabooed member
of the nuclear family, the avoidance behavior will tend to be
extended to him." [66]

This principle may help to explain several of the forbidden
degrees in Islām, particularly those having to do with lactation
or fosterage. The Qur'ān (4:23) states very briefly that unlawful for men are their milk mothers and sisters. But the
prohibition is extended, as we have noted to other milk
relatives. This extension derives from the Traditions of the
Prophet. The principle of "stimulus generalization" does seem
to render these Traditions much better understandable sociologically. Some Islāmicists incline to explain things in terms of
what appears to be little more than arbitrary, personal dispositions of Muḥammad. For example, Stern has concluded
that "Muḥammad's attempt to introduce the idea of a wide

foster-relationship (with a similarly wide circle of prohibition) was [probably] made with the view to replacing, to a certain extent, the practice of relationship by adoption which *he* had repudiated . . ." [67]

The custom of wet nursing (*radā'* or *irdā'*) might have been ancient, but wet nurses "were used in Biblical times only in exceptional cases. . ." [68] In Makkah, however, it was the custom of many families to send their infants away with foster parents to be looked after by wet nurses from Bedouin tribes. The practice apparently was not followed in al Madīnah. In Makkah, there probably was, according to Stern, a close association between this practice and the "strong objection" of the Makkīs to intercourse with a nursing mother, which was believed to have ill effects on the child's health. The Madīnīs did not subscribe to the same belief, which may account for the fact that they did not customarily send their children away to foster parents. [69] But this explanation does not seem in full accord with the facts. Whether or not the Makkīs actually had any objection to intercourse with nursing mothers, the custom of seeking wet nurses for infants was most likely due to some other consideration.

Makkah was a trading center with a mixed, somewhat heterogeneous population. Life in this commercial influx was not much conducive to the internalization of the traditional values that were believed to be best cultivable in the rugged but healthy desert life. This "urban" environment was even believed to corrupt the pure Arabic dialect, a corruption which was regarded as an intolerable stigma. Under these circumstances, prominent families—the custom was by no means universal—deemed it necessary to send their infants away to foster parents in the desert for some years, so that they would grow up healthy and acquire manliness, bravery, generosity, eloquence, etc. Moreover, the practice was followed even when there was no prospect or fear of intercourse with the nursing mother. For example, Muḥammad's father died before the conceived infant was born, yet his mother sent him away with a wet nurse, although the widow did not marry nor was she then contemplating a new marital career. Also, if the natural parents were motivated by the fear of ill effects of intercourse upon the child's health, what could assure them that the wet nurse would also abstain from intercourse while she was nursing, a period of two or more years? It would seem more likely, therefore, that the custom of placing infants temporarily with foster parents or wet nurses had its deeper origins in the social environment rather than in the mist of superstition, and that the extension of the sphere of the forbidden foster relatives was due more to the principle of "stimulus generalization" than to Muhammad's attempt to replace adoption, which he had repudiated, with fosterage.[70]

The forbidden degrees or incest confines in Islām may be viewed as narrow or wide, depending on the scale used. They are wider than the confines of many ancients, including the Athenians, Spartans, and pre-Islāmic Arabians, among whom marriages between siblings and/or half siblings were legally permitted and actually practiced. Also, while the Islāmic prohibitions generally agree with those set down in the Old Testament, the former are wider than the latter in that marriages with nieces and nephews are allowed in the Old Testament but forbidden in Islām. Moreover, in Islām there is no law corresponding to the Biblical levirate which requires a man to marry the childless widow of his brother.[71] Islāmic law neither enjoins nor forbids the levirate. However, when compared with modern Western standards, divested of their Biblical affinities, the forbidden degrees in Islām would appear rather narrow. The example that is usually brought up in this regard is preferential marriage with the father's brother's daughter (patrilineal cousin marriages). According to R. Levy, "Islam has perpetuated the practice, which has thus acquired the force of law." [72] But there seems to be a series of misconceptions calling for clarifications.

First, Islām neither proscribed nor prescribed cousin marriages. In fact, if the Tradition attributed to Muhammad and confirmed by 'Umar I is authentic, Islām would seem to command kin exogamy.[73] Secondly, there is no evidence that the preIslāmic Arabs, especially those of al Madīnah, were entirely averse to cousin marriages and only began to show preference for this type after Islām. On the contrary, Levy has observed that in pre-Islāmic times the marriage of cousins "prevailed amongst a majority of the Arabian tribes." [74] Yet, thirdly, some observers, as Stern, suggest that prior to Islām the practice was by no means an established custom; its subsequent prevalence at al Madīnah "was probably due to a great extent to Muḥammad's reform of the law of inheritance which allowed the woman her share. If she married her paternal cousin, this share was not lost to the clan." [75] Here again, this explanation appears to assume that the Madīnīs, and other Muslims after them, tilled the land jointly, understood the economic advantages of collective land ownership, and detained the shares of married women. These assumptions lack the support of evidence. However, even if the Muslims adopted preferential cousin marriage, it was not because Islam "required" it or perpetuated its appeal, but probably because it was placed in the category of the "permissibles." Moreover, the term paternal "cousin" (bint 'amm or ibn 'amn) is equivocal. It may denote the first, second, third or even a remoter cousin. In contemporary Arabic, the word uncle ('amm) is sometimes used freely as a term of respect for persons whose age is about that of one's father. Incidentally, it is also customary among many Arabs, Muslim and Christian, immigrants in North America to refer to one's spouse as his or her paternal cousin even though they may not be consanguineally related. Where cousin marriages occur, they do so whether or not there is any property involved and irrespective of the residential location of the couple concerned. There is no established pattern in favor of either paternal, maternal, or cross-cousin marriages. The instances with which the present writer is familiar seem to cluster equally along the three legal lines. It may be interesting to note that the Qur'ān (33:50) includes the daughters of both paternal uncles and aunts as well as the daughters of maternal uncles and aunts among the women whom the Prophet, and derivatively other Muslims, may wed. However, it is possible that some individuals are motivated by socio-economic factors to marry their cousins or the surviving widows and widowers of their siblings. But this is strictly volitional; Islām does not prohibit it any more than it prescribes it. To say that Islām *prefers* paternal cousin marriages is incompatible with the outward, international outlook of the religion and the behavioral precedents of its followers who moved into new territories and intermarried with the natives of various regions.

The fact that the forbidden degrees in Islām are not too narrow, like those of ancient societies, or too wide, like those of modern times, may be interestingly suggestive. While Islām sought to preserve and reinforce the traditional family unit, it also probably aimed at the same time to create links between this unit and other similar units to mould the whole into an open, interconnected and interdependent society. But if every family, clan or tribe is endogamous and closed into itself, there will be no society beyond the kinship border lines. When the forbidden degrees are too narrow, e.g., restricted only to the elementary members of the nuclear family, kinsmen may develop internal role conflict and confusion, or the kinship unit may become self-contained and find itself gradually cut off from other units which will themselves be in the same predicament. On the other hand, if the forbidden degrees are too wide and inclusive of cousin marriages or successive sororate, the restrictions may, in some cases at least, be more dysfunctional than otherwise. Proscription of cousin marriages and successive levirate or sororate does not necessarily appear more "functional" than prescription of the same. It is not inconceivable, for example, that a widow or widower with children and/or property may find it more convenient socially, economically, and morally to marry the former spouse's sister or brother. Nor is it entirely improbable that some marriageable persons will be better off if married to their cousins. While Islām does not enjoin such marriages, it does not prohibit them either; it places them in the category of the permissible, so that if the individual, for any legitimate reason, needs to resort to them he will be free to do so. On the other hand, if it be in his interest to marry exogamously, he will not find himself hindered by endogamous rules.

H. *Religion and Exogamy*

One of the most persistent impediments to exogamy is religion. This is true of Islām as it is of other religions, notwithstanding some significant differences. For example, according to Talmudic law and the Rabbinical code intermarriage with all gentiles, including Christians, was forbidden for the Jews. It was only in 1807 that the great Jewish Synod, convened by Napoleon, declared marriages between Israelites and Christians valid if contracted in accordance with the Civil Code. Yet "such marriages cannot be invested with the religious forms," that is they cannot be solemnized by the religious rites of Judaism. The Rabbinical Conference held at Brunswick, Germany, in 1844 resolved that the intermarriage of Jews and Christians or other monotheists is not forbidden, provided the parents are permitted by the state to bring up their children in the Jewish faith. But this resolution "has been strongly criticized even by some of the most pronounced advocates of reformed Judaism. No section of Jewish opinion favors marriage between parties who are not of the same religion." The Christians - - Constantine, later emperors, and various councils - - also prohibited intermarriages with the Jews. During the Middle Ages such marriages were universally avoided. While St. Paul indicated that a Christian must not marry a heathen, and Tertullian called such an alliance fornication, "the Church, in early times, often even encouraged marriages of this sort as a means of propagating Christianity; and it was only when its success was beyond doubt that it actually prohibited them." [76]

The case of Islām is different in some fundamental respects. The general rule is that religious homogamy takes preference as the first choice. When both parties adhere to Islām, the probability of mutual harmony is highly assuring. But it is

not an absolute condition that mates be of the same religion.
Muslims may intermarry with non-Muslims. Such intermarriages are as valid and binding as "intramarriages" are. However the permission is not unqualified. No Muslim, male or
female, is permitted to marry anyone who has no divine book
or God-sent Prophet to follow. The Qur'ān (2:221 cf., 60-10)
stresses the point thus:

> Do not marry idolatresses, until they believe [in God]; a believing
> slavegirl is surely better than an idolatress, though you may admire
> her. And do not marry idolaters, until they believe; verily a believing
> slave is better than an idolater, though you may admire him.

This injunction limits the field of non-Muslim eligibles to
those who believe in God and have a divine scripture. Another
limitation is that no Muslim woman is permitted to marry a
non-Muslim man. This is the unanimous resolution of Muslims
from the days of the Prophet till the present time. That leaves
only the possibility of religious intermarriages between Muslim men and non-Muslim women who believe in God, follow
a prophet, and have a divine scripture. These are notably
Jewish and Christian women. Muslims almost unanimously
allow such intermarriages. In one of the few chapters revealed toward the very end of Muḥammad's life, the Qur'ān
(5:5-6) says:

> Today the good things are permitted to you, and the food of those
> who were given the Book (i.e., the Jews and the Christians) is per-
> mitted to you; and permitted to them is your food. Likewise (law-
> ful to you are) believing chaste women in wedlock, and in wedlock
> chaste women of them who were given the Book before you if you
> give them their due dowers and desire chastity, in wedlock and not
> in license or as taking secret lovers.

Based on this statement, the opinion of the overwhelming
majority of Muslims is that intermarriages are permitted between Muslim men and non-Muslim women if the latter believe
in God and recognize the Book that was given to them before
Islām. But some "individual" jurists and also some Shī'īs disagree wholly or in part with the majority's interpretation of the
statement. Mālik, the father of the Mālikī law school, held
that such intermarriages are lawful only if they involve free

women, not slave girls, because the passage of the Qur'ān speaks of chaste women of the Book and freedom from slavery is a constituent of chastity; a woman who is not free is not chaste, and if she is not chaste and not a Muslim, she is not lawful to the Muslim. A small minority of early jurists rejected the idea of intermarriages completely on the basis of their interpretation of certain statements where the Qur'ān (3:118, 5:51; 12:106; 60:1) warns against the intrigues, impure beliefs, and ill feelings of the people of the Book as well as the polytheists. The Shī'ī Imāmīs also disagree among themselves and with the rest of Muslims. Some of them view religious intermarriages as forbidden altogether. They argue that disbelief in Islām is the equivalent of idolatry. Since idolatry is an absolute impediment to marriage in Islām (Q.2: 221; 60:10), it is unlawful for a Muslim to marry any one who is not like himself. Others, however, agree with the majority of Muslims on the permissibility of such intermarriages. Still, other members of this Shī'ī branch adopt an intermediate position to reconcile the conflicting interpretations. They allow intermarriages if they are contracted on a temporary, *mut'ah,* basis and forbid them as permanent, continued bonds. The reconciliation of these passages and opinions is a highly technical, controversial issue which will not be discussed at this point.[77]

The foregoing discussion raises certain questions that need to be considered briefly. First, a distinction must be maintained between the permissibility and the advisability of intermarriages with women of the Book. For, according to the majority of Muslims, while these intermarriages are lawful in principle they may not be always advisable for practical reasons. The distinction is important to keep in mind because speaking against the advisability of the action may be misconstrued as a stand against the permissibility of that action, which of course is not necessarily the case.

Secondly, this lawfulness is established with the understanding that the man involved assumes the "instrumental leadership" in the family of procreation, where he is the protector, the head of the household, the status bearer, and the party responsible for the upbringing of the offspring in his own religious faith. This is derived from the Qur'ānic verse (4:34) in which men are described as the *Qawwāmūn*, i.e., the protectors and maintainers of women and the managers of their affairs. However, in his role as the instrumental leader, the man has no jurisdiction over the religious beliefs of his non-Muslim wife. Nor may he interfere with her freedom of worship and conscience. Islām, in Roberts' words, "'does not demand that these . . . women, whom a Muslim takes in marriage, should adopt [his] religion . . . , but allows them to retain their own . . .'" [78]

Thirdly, the Muslim male is permitted to intermarry with a non-Muslim female because it may serve as a gesture of good will toward non-Muslims, or as a practical implementation of the principles of Islām in concrete, though apparently "adverse," situations of interaction.[79] This probably reflects the Muslims' hope that, once exposed to the true principles of Islām in a favorable encounter, a person is very likely to become appreciative of these principles and to rectify any former misconceptions. When a non-Muslim woman marries a Muslim, who is enjoined to honor and cherish her, respect her rights and whole-heartedly acknowledge her religious freedom as well as her Scriptures and prophets, it may be expected that she will somehow reciprocate. By her increasing knowledge of Islām and experience of daily living with such a Muslim partner, she may adopt his faith or discover that it is not, in fact, a renunciation but rather an enrichment of her own. Whether or not she does so, she is legally well protected against coercion or pressure of any kind and loses none of the rights due to her in a marriage to one of her coreligionists.[80]

It is conceivable, however, that other explanations could be entertained, at least theoretically. One might say that this permission was actually designed as an indirect form of pressure to enlarge the following of Islām. A non-Muslim wife may find herself isolated or helpless in a household headed by a Muslim and thus feel pressured to give up her faith for his. Or, it can be said that such a law was a shrewd foresight on Islām's part, introduced in anticipation of pluralistic future societies, or in preparation for any possible demographic imbalance. Other notions may be entertained, such as sexual exploitation, male superordination, humiliation of the non-Muslims, etc. But all such suggestions hardly seem to echo even the lowest tone, or fit in the context, of the Qur'ānic passage (5:5-6) where the provision is stated. Besides, this type of intermarriage is voluntary for both parties, and the non-Muslim females are portrayed in the same light as their Muslim counterparts, with equal emphasis on chastity, eligibility for and receipt of dowers, the sanctity of wedlock, and the condemnation of license.

Finally, the prohibition of intermarriage between a Muslim woman and a non-Muslim man has always been maintained by the religio-legal authorities. An explanation of this position may be attempted in the following way. It seems that such intermarriages, if permitted, would be considered by Muslims impractical and disadvantageous to the women involved as well as to their coreligionists. A Muslim wife of a hypothetical non-Muslim husband is not believed to have the same assurances of religious freedom and personal rights as does her counterpart with a Muslim spouse. The principle of "reciprocity" is not fully implemented; while the Muslim woman does acknowledge and honor the religion of her hypothetical husband as an integral part of her own faith, he does not reciprocate. She accepts Moses, Jesus, and all the authentic messengers of God, even as she accepts Muḥammad. She makes no discrimination between them, nor is she prejudiced against any of them. When she hears the name of Moses or Jesus, or when reference is made to their Scriptures, she may only respond with reverence and homage; that is an essential aspect of her being a Muslim. To accept Islām means a committed affirmation of the previous divine messages and an unreserved honoring of all the messengers of God. This is something she must do and delights in doing as a Muslim. But is there any reciprocity on her mate's part? Does he accept

and honor her religion as she does his? If he does so, then he—
for most practical purposes—may be regarded as a Muslim.
In this case, their intermarriage may have some ground for
legality. But if he does not do so, at least four logical alternatives present themselves: (1) the Muslim woman may lose
her "most valuable" asset, i.e., faith, and renegade; (2) she
may experience unnecessary tensions and mental conflicts from
which the non-Muslim man is not totally immune; (3) the
marriage may break up; (4) both partners may gradually grow
skeptical, or simply become "liberal" and indifferent to religion
altogether. Whether any of these alternatives is acceptable or
advisable from a religious and societal point of view is an open
question. Of course, love may be invoked at this junction as
omnipotent, capable of solving all problems, emotional, ideological, or social. But love is perhaps one of the most abused
words; and if it were so omnipotent as is sometimes claimed,
social interaction would be much simpler and human life
much less problematic.

Besides the relative lack of security and freedom for the
Muslim woman and also the lack of reciprocity on the part of
her hypothetical non-Muslim mate, there may be other reasons
for the prohibition of this type of intermarriage. It seems
that since Muslim authorities believe Islām to be the highest,
most complete form of religion, it is forbidden for the Muslim
to subject his conscience to non-Muslims and entrust them
with the management of his intimate affairs. Because the male
partner is the status bearer in the family and the instrumental
leader of the household, he must be a Muslim if the wife is so;
she may not be led to subordinate her spiritual status. If he is
a Muslim, the question of subordination does not usually arise, because this is a case of expected harmony and convergence of beliefs, attitudes, and practice. It would be degrading for her to intermarry with a man who does not reciprocate religiously and who, according to her belief system, is
spiritually inferior. It is true that Islām acknowledges and in-
corporates the essence of all the former revelations; but Muslims believe that it has also added perfection and coverage

unattained by its predecessors. It would appear exceedingly difficult, therefore, to place the Muslim woman in a position where she believes herself to be spiritually or religiously superior but must accept a partner who, in his capacity as the family head, has the authority to confer on her his own social and probably also religious status.

This is similar in a way to the cultural, not necessarily the statistical, norm of almost all known societies where it is generally accepted and expected from the female to marry above or at least on her social class level, but not below. In an open class system, a male may descend in marriage without risking much loss of status. The case of the woman is different; even if she can "bargain" and exchange her high social status for some desirable qualities of her mate of a lower social status, faith is no object of bargaining, not according to Islām at any rate. Muslims take their faith to be the zenith of spiritual and moral achievements; there is no higher level to long for or aspire to. Nor may a Muslim allow himself to retrogress. When a Muslim man intermarries with a non-Muslim woman, he is not descending religiously; he may even "help" his mate to "ascend" to his own religious status if he is conscientious enough and if she so desires. However, neither he nor she will lose what they may cherish most, i.e., their private beliefs. On the other hand, if a Muslim woman intermarries with a non-Muslim man who does not wish to adopt her faith or reciprocate, she will probably have to "descend" to his level and thus lose her most valuable private asset. In an intermarriage situation, the Muslim woman will be the loser if there is no religious reciprocity, convergence, or consensus. Her very faith may be at stake, her serenity threatened, and her marriage precarious. For these explicit and/or implicit reasons, this type of intermarriage is forbidden. This is not apparently the simple question, why can the Muslim woman not raise the religious status of her mate? Religion is the most private relationship between man and God; it cannot be imposed or conferred. Nor is it the question of discrimination between men and women in Islām.

The rights and obligations of both men and women are equal, though not necessarily identical in details.[81]

This explanation derives from ideological, psychological, and sociological factors. Yet it is, to a certain extent, inferential and even perhaps *post factum*. It infers from the general attitude of Islām toward other religions and of Muslims toward non-Muslims, from the intrafamily and sex differential roles, from the principles of reciprocity and cooperation in marriage, and from the historically established practice of female hypergamy. It is one of the provisions which have been upheld with a rare unanimity. That in itself may be suggestive. The question does not seem to be that of a categorical prohibition of interreligious marriages as such; we have seen that *some* Muslims, specifically men, may intermarry with *some* non-Muslim women, though with certain reservations on the advisability thereof. Nor is it apparently a matter of an absolute prohibition of female hypagamy; we have also seen that, according to some jurists, such is unconditionally legal and, according to others, it is valid with the approval of guardians. The "double standard" notion may conceivably enter into the situation. But this would be likely only if Muslim men's interreligious marriages were unconditionally permissible and ad-visable, or if they were demonstratively more advantageous to them and less morally binding than unions with their coreligionists, or if male hypagamy was defined as a privilege and female hypagamy as a disadvantage. Since this is not the case, the "double standard" notion is not very helpful.

However, looking into the general historical realities of Muslim society, which were not always in complete conformity with the teachings of the religion, we may find some further insights. Almost invariably, Muslim women led a secluded life behind the confines of their households. A man's honor was measured primarily by the extent of protection, shelter, and continence he could secure for his womenfolk, especially on the consanguineal side. In fact, the word *harem* or *harīm* and its derivatives denote, among other things, holiness, sacredness, man's inviolable honor, etc. As a result, women were generally believed to be fragile and inexperienced in the sphere of practical affairs. Their "instrumental roles" were almost always subordinate, at least technically. Men provided for them, bore full responsibility for their protection, and legislated or interpreted the existing legislations for them. Men's concern for their honor and protection apparently extended beyond the maiden years as it came to bear upon mate selection. A marital union between an inexperienced, fragile or naive Muslim woman and an unreciprocating, inflexible non-Muslim man must have been conceived by the law interpreters as "dangerous." As a rule, Muslim men would not or believed that they should not expose their womenfolk to such a risky relationship. They would be apprehensive of the responsibility, humiliation, shame, and disgrace that are bound to result in case of conversion on the women's part. This apprehension may in part be the product of a lack of confidence in the strength of the Muslim women's convictions, or the non-Muslim men's characters, or both. To protect their women from exposure to uncertainty, to avoid the risk of degradation or disgrace, to honor their religion by placing it outside the category of the "exchangeables" in mate selection, and to save their "honor" from being at the mercy of those who are not "trustworthy,"—these were probably the major reasons for the prohibition of intermarriage between Muslim women and non-Muslim men.

Beyond the forbidden degrees of consanguinity, affinity, milk fosterage, and religion, and so long as the prospective mates satisfy the usual conditions of marriage,[82] a family unit can be established. Social class, race, birth or color are not serious impediments to a full-fledged, permanent union. Jurists who uphold the doctrine of "social equality" of partners as a consideration for marriage, view it only as a precaution that can be dispensed with under appropriate conditions of security, a right that may easily be waived by the woman or her marriage guardian. It is not an absolute condition. Rather, they say, a stipulation of assurance to maximize the probability of a stable, successful union that would contribute to the uninterrupted

So far, the discussion has been concerned in the main with the formation of the family. This chapter will focus on the web of domestic family relations, on those social and legal effects of a marriage contract that has been properly concluded and fully enacted. Such effects may be outlined in the following fashion.

1) The wife becomes entitled to maintenance and to her "prompt" portion of the dower.

2) Sexual intercourse becomes lawful and the children born of the union are legitimate.

3) The husband is entitled to exercise the marital authority associated with his role as husband.

4) Where there is an agreement between the parties, entered into at the time of the marriage or subsequently, its stipulations will be enforced, insofar as they are consistent with the provisions of the law.

5) A wife does not change her basic identity: She retains her maiden name, her religion, or school of thought if she so desires, and her legal personality. Neither the husband nor the wife acquires any "right" in the other's property by reason of marriage, according to the almost unanimous opinion of the jurists.

6) Mutual rights of inheritance are established if both parties adhere to the same religion.

7) The rules of incest due to affinity become effective.

8) After the death of the husband or the dissolution of the marriage, the wife becomes entitled to the "deferred" portion, if any, of the dower; but she may not remarry before observing the legal "waiting period" (*'iddah*).[1]

Analysis and elaboration of this outline constitute the subject of the present chapter. To begin with, the relationship between husbands and wives is too intimate and varied to lend itself easily and entirely to the formal regulations of legal systems, however comprehensive. It probably defies the most subtle formalities of the codes of law since it operates on levels that are not always accessible to legal detection. Yet the family is too crucial a social network to be entrusted entirely to the individual's conscience or left to his capricious whims. Certain major aspects of the family life are therefore subject to specific legal rules; others derive from and rest upon general religio-moral (henceforth to be called ethical) principles. Islām seems to have realized this fact and perhaps even focalized it. The Qur'ān and the Sunnah neither lost sight of the ethical principles of the family operation nor ceased to present God as an integral element of any action situation. So much was this the case that jurists apparently took it for granted and felt no further need for added emphasis. This may explain, on the one hand, why the Qur'ān and the Sunnah contain relatively minimal details regarding the legal specifics of family life and why, on the other hand, many jurists focused their attention on the intricate, formal elaboration of these minimal details, almost to the exclusion of their ethical foundations.[2]

A. *The Moral Foundations of Marital Roles*[3]

The ethical principles of the husband-wife relationship are believed to derive from a conscientious commitment by both sides to the divine designation of marital union as an abode of peace and serenity, a link of mutual love and compassion— all being God's sign for those who reflect (Q. 30:21, cf. 2:184).

The role of the husband normatively evolves around the principle that it is his solemn duty to God to treat his wife with kindness, honor, and patience; to keep her honorably or free her from the marital bond honorably; and to cause her no harm or grief (Q. 2:229-232; 4:19). The role of the wife is summarized in the Qur'ānic statement that women have rights even as they have duties, according to what is equitable; but men have a degree over them; God is All-mighty, All-wise (2:228). This degree is usually interpreted by Muslims in conjunction with another passage which states, among other things, that men are protectors of women and managers of

their affairs because God has made some excel others and
because men expend of their means. The righteous women
are therefore devoutly obedient and conscientiously guard
what God would have them guard (4:34).[4] This degree may
be likened to what sociological parlance calls "instrumental
leadership" or authority in the household due to role differentiation on the basis of sex. However, there will be further consideration of the point later in this chapter.

MARITAL ROLES

A. *The Wife's Rights; the Husband's Obligations*

Translated into behavioral norms, these ethical principles
behind the marital roles allocate to the wife certain rights,
which are the husband's duties, and corresponding obligations,
which are his rights. Because the Qur'ān and the Sunnah of
the Prophet have commanded kindness to women it is the
husband's duty to consort with his wife in an equitable and
kind manner. A specific consequence of this divine command
is that the husband is responsible for the maintenance of the
wife, a duty which he is enjoined to discharge cheerfully
without "reproach" or "injury."[5] The wife's right to maintenance is established by authority of the Qur'ān, the Sunnah,
the unanimous agreement of jurists, and reason or common
sense. It is inconsequential whether the wife is a Muslim or
non-Muslim, rich or poor, and, according to many authorities,
minor or adult, healthy or sick. She is entitled to this right
by virtue of the fact that she is devoted to the husband's companionship and is confined to his household, or by the very
reason of marriage, i.e., being his wife and "trust."[6] Maintenance, however, is not a pure mathematical equation or a
calculated business transaction, in which she provides comfort, affection and compassion in return for maintenance. The
essence of marriage is compassion, of which she is entitled
to receive at least as much as she gives. The husband, too, is
instructed to be a source of compassion and security for his
mate, to initiate and reciprocate in kind, not only to receive.

A component of his general role is to bear the family financial responsibility in a generous, charitable way, so that his mate may be assured of security and hence perform her "expressive" role devotedly.

1. Maintenance and Its Components
a. Residence
The wife's maintenance entails her incontestable right to lodging, clothing, food, and general care. The rules and patterns of marital residence have stimulated interesting research with significant bearings on lineality, authority, the family type, the size of the dower, and so on. In Islam, however, there seem to be no prescribed patterns of residence. The elementary family unit may be neolocal, bilocal, patrilocal, or matrilocal. What is prescribed is the husband's responsibility for the wife's shelter. He must lodge her where he himself resides, according to his means, without causing her to suffer. The specific location of residence may be chosen bilaterally or by the husband alone. It may also be determined by circumstances, e.g., the husband's vocation, the housing conditions, etc. Should there be an irreconcilable conflict between his and her choice, his decision will be implemented, so long as it is not contrary to her welfare, since his is the ultimate responsibility. Because of the flexibility of residence rules, it was probably easy to follow the custom according to which the married couple usually lived with the bridegroom's family and were considered members of it.[7] The continuity of this custom did not seem to be in conflict with the law, nor would its discontinuity. This may be significant in that it can allow married couples to feel free legally, as well as morally, to lead their own lives as they see fit or as circumstances demand. For example, if life conditions call for geographical mobility, they can adapt to the situation without fear of violating the law or breaking away from any sacred traditions and customs.

The wife's lodge must be adequate so as to ensure her privacy, comfort, and independence. This is interpreted by three major schools of law to mean that the lodging quarter must befit the means and life style of both mates. However, it is the wife's home in her capacity as wife; she has the exclusive right to it. None of the husband's relatives, dependents, or any other person may live with her in the same lodge unless she voluntarily agrees to it. Yet, in the opinion of another school of law, a commoner wife of low rank has no right to refuse living with the husband's relatives in the same quarter. But if she is of high ranking, she may exercise this right unless the marriage contract stipulates otherwise. Should she agree in the marriage contract to share the lodging with his relatives, she must honor the agreement, but she must be provided with at least one private room for her own use and must not be subject to any harm by sharing the premises with her in-laws. The main concern here seems to be the welfare of the wife and the stability of the marriage. The husband's responsibility for the wife's shelter does not entitle him to impose upon her any disagreeable arrangement of residence. The whole matter rests upon the Qur'ānic passage (65:5-6)[8]:

> Lodge them where you are lodging, according to your means, and do not press them, so as to straiten their circumstances . . .

> Let the man of plenty expend out of his plenty. As for him whose provision is stinted for him, let him expend of what God has given him. God charges no one beyond his means. After difficulty, God will soon grant relief.

b. *Other Components of Maintenance*

What is true of lodging is also true of clothing, food, and general care. The wife has the right to be clothed, fed, and cared for by the husband, in accordance with his means and her style of life. This right is to be exercised without extravagance or miserliness. For instance, if the wife has been used to having a maid or if she is unable to attend to her domestic affairs, it is the husband's duty to provide her with at least one maid if he can afford it. This is derived from the statements of the Qur'ān and the Sunnah. Some of these statements are specific and direct: some are not clearly so. In one passage, the

Qur'ān states that it is for the husband-father to provide for the
wife-mother and to clothe her equitably; no self is charged
beyond its capacity (2:233). The Muslim is instructed to be
neither miserly nor extravagant lest he become blameworthy
or denuded (17:29). Men are taught to maintain their adorn-
ment at every place of worship, and to eat and drink without
being prodigal, for God loves not the prodigal (7:31). Moreover, the Prophet is reported to have declared that the best
Muslim is one who is the best husband. On various occasions
he called upon his followers to take good care of, and show
kindness toward, their wives. He warned that the man who
remains in the state of anger with his wife is a man whose
prayers will not be answered and whose good works will not
be accepted.[9]

c. Maintenance in Sickness

The Qur'ān and the Sunnah have enjoined care for and
kindness to the wife. Yet the application of this general principle to the case of a sick wife has stimulated curious arguments, differences of opinion, and legal niceties. According
to some jurists, a sick wife who, on account of her failing
health, is unable to discharge her marital duties has no legal
right to maintenance by the husband. They argue that the
right to maintenance is a function of a full-fledged marriage in
which the wife fulfills all her commitments. If sickness hinders
her performance seriously, then the husband is not legally
responsible for her maintenance until she recovers and re-
assumes her duty. It cannot be objected, according to this
argument, that because she is his wife, lives in his household,
and gives him companionship, he must provide for her even
though she may be sick and incapable of playing her full role.
If he is to be responsible for her maintenance because of the
marriage—a contract for which she has already received her
marriage gift (*mahr* or dower)—then she would be acquiring
two rights (the dower and the maintenance) for one and the
same reason, i.e., being a wife, or she would be receiving "two

compensations for one and the same loss." This is, according to the argument, unlawful and unjust.[10]

Another group of jurists argue that formally, or analogously, a husband is not responsible for the maintenance of a sick wife because she is actually unable to meet her marital responsibilities. But they realize that, in accordance with the principles of istiḥsān (a moral and practical consideration that overrules the formalities of law),[11] it is his obligation to provide for her because she is still his mate, whose companionship he enjoys even though illness may impede her performance in certain respects, e.g., the sexual fulfillment. A variant of this doctrine maintains that the raison d'être of the wife's right to maintenance is marriage as such or the husband's trusteeship (qawwāmīyah) over the wife. This right remains inalienable so long as she is his wife and he is the trustee. Her physical condition is inconsequential in this regard; it neither lightens his obligation nor negates her right.[12]

The problem of maintenance of a sick wife is provocative, although it seems more apparent than real, that is, more of an academic exercise than a practical issue. It probably indicates that the later in time, the farther some jurists drifted away from the spirit of the law and its ethical foundations. It is curious that neither the Qur'ān nor the Sunnah raised the problem in any way that can be likened to the approach of those jurists. Moreover, none of the disputants produces any authoritative evidence in support of his argument against the adversaries. Not even would these juristic doctrines seem to be addressed to responsible conscientious litigants; such litigants would probably refrain from harming one another and yield to the dictates of their religious consciences, in which case it would be unnecessary for them to engage in these legalistic casuistries. It is not unlikely therefore that this was mostly an "intellectualistic" problem or, if it was a real one, the formal doctrines of the jurists were concerned with cunning litigants, whose religious consciences were inactive. That the issue seems to have been more conceptual than real or was raised in later generations may be inferred from an observation by the medieval scholar Ibn Taymīah (d. 728/1328). He pointed out that a sick wife is unquestionably entitled to full maintenance by the husband in the opinion of the four founders of the major schools of law.[13]

Related to the problem of a sick wife's maintenance is the cost of her medical care. The formal consensus, not the unanimous opinion, of the majority of jurists is that the husband is not legally responsible for the cost of medicine, the physician's fee, etc. Some jurists, however, maintain that if the husband is financially comfortable and the cost of medical care is modest, he is responsible for it. Others argue that even if he is not *legally* responsible for the cost, it is still his *religious* duty to bear the responsibility out of compassion, courtesy, or in conformity with the social norms. Those who exempt the husband from the responsibility do not consider the cost of medical care to be part of the obligatory maintenance. They draw an analogy between wifedom and leased property; tenants are not responsible for the repairs and improvement of the premises. Their obligation is to pay only the rent; the rest is the owner's charge. Like a tenant, a husband is not responsible for the cost of any treatment his wife may undergo to restore or improve her health. But a minority among the Shī'ī jurists consider medical care a means to save life and preserve health. Hence it is as essential as food, shelter, and clothing are and is therefore part of the husband's responsibility. It is interesting to note that this position has been adopted by the courts of Syria and North Africa because it was considered closer to the spirit of the law even though it emanated from a partisan and traditionally adversary group. It is also interesting that contemporary Muslim scholars are impatient with these formalistic interpretations of the law which, on the one hand, enjoin the husband to furnish his wife with maids—an obvious luxury— but, on the other, exempt him from the responsibility for her medical care. To these scholars, this is plain mockery, casuistry, and abuse of the purposes of the law.[14]

Moreover, such formal interpretations contain no authoritative evidence. Nor do they seem compatible with the ordinances of the Qur'ān and the Sunnah, which unequivocally call for kindness, compassion, and consideration. Here again, the question arises: were these jurists fighting windmills or tackling a real problem? How could they overlook the strong directives of the Qur'ān and the Sunnah, and focus, instead on such a formalistic approach?

The view that a husband may be exempted from the obligation of maintenance and payment for an indisposed wife's medical care cannot be explained in terms of any authoritative text from the Qur'ān or the Traditions. Not only is there no such possible explanation, but also the very view is perhaps one of the clearest instances of "deviation" from the orientation of the basic sources of Islamic law. Nevertheless, its rise among certain juristic circles is interesting. Some explanation in nontextual terms may be proposed for consideration.

Aside from the possibility of intellectualistic riddles or formal casuistries, this view, together with the accompanying analogy between wifedom and "leased property," was probably a reflection of certain social and intellectual trends. Among these, the following would seem relevant. The demographic composition of the Muslim population was growing diverse as well as complex. An urban life style on a new large scale, with the concomitant relative anonymity and individuality, was increasingly in vogue. Under such circumstances, marital bonds would be regarded not so much as alliances of families, clans, or tribes or as "companionship" ties as individual "contracts" largely oriented to specific formal exchanges of service. Women, as a rule, became increasingly secluded in the background and excluded from the world of men. With the keeping of standing armies and the transformation of political conflicts from the old tribal or local level to that of grand ruling dynasties and regional nationalities, the traditional value of sons as tribal warriors or defenders of tribal honor declined. And with this decline, the social value of women as mothers or procreators of such sons must have also declined. In addition, the "companion role" of women seems to have been seriously challenged by other rivals, old and new. For example, singing girls, slaves, and commoners appear to have been more experienced and thus more desirable as companions than ordinary housewives were, a phenomenon which is not unknown in human society. In fact, if some of the popular accounts of Muslim life of the eighth century onwards are to be trusted, the vivid picture of Muslim society would display a rakish, world of too many loose companions and common performers, a world of song and wine, of misplaced romance and infidelity. Ordinary women appear to have been little more than helpless dependents and liabilities. Those of power and status are portrayed as having invested their energies for the most part in plots and intrigues, often against rivals of their own kind. With the traditional mother role so depreciated, and with the companion role so contested by other rivals, probably little was left for the normal housewife other than being an object of sexuality. Even that role was not confined to her exclusively.[15]

From the intellectual viewpoint, the period of legal creativity or originality was almost over. Jurists were either barred from, incapable of, or unwilling to join in tackling the basic issues of politics and society. Instead, they redirected their intellectual energies to formal questions, that is, to minute technical arguments in which they probably found some fulfillment and satisfaction. This also is not an entirely unusual phenomenon; there are parallels to it in intellectual history, particularly in periods following great upheavals or breakthroughs. The development of sociology itself may stand as evidence of this. The sociological debates of the thirties in the United States, the statistical disputes over Weber's formulations, Durkheim's theorizing and Marx's prophecies, are clear manifestations of the same phenomenon. As a contemporary sociologist has recently suggested, "the history of ideas reflects a slow but steady exhaustion of the intellectual attitude; the process is reminiscent of the loss of energy asserted by the Second Law of Thermodynamics and may be defined as *mental entropy.*" [16]

It was most likely under these sociocultural conditions that the "exemption" view gained popularity among some jurists. However, there may have been other logical possibilities, of which two are particularly noteworthy. First, this particular orientation was probably a consequence of the universal gap between the "ideal" and the "actual," the "normative" and the "normal," or between what is required and what is performed. There is no reason to suppose that the Muslims were significantly different in this regard from any other group. These formal interpretations of the law were perhaps entertained to deal with men and women who might tend to exploit one another, those in whose actual conduct deviance from the ideal was beyond the limits of tolerance.

Second, the issue was probably raised at first as a curious hypothetical problem; but toward the later part of the second century of Islām and beyond, it was reformulated in more specific but still formal terms. There is perhaps indirect evidence of this in the suggestive remark of Ibn al Qayyim. He noted that the pioneering interpreters of the law felt no necessity to formalize family regulations. Early Muslims were, according to him, conscientious enough to implement the moral teachings of their religion without the need to be reminded that such was a *legal* duty. Religious motivation was sufficient to insure mutual kindness and compassion. In later centuries, people and conditions so changed that it became necessary to supplement the moral principles with specific legal formulations.[17] This may suggest that such a change, coupled with increasing complexity and diversity of Muslim society, made many jurists reluctant to probe into and judge the motives of litigants. In default of active religious conscience and in the face of an open family conflict over the cost of medical care and maintenance of a sick wife, a conflict unlikely to arise in a stable family unit, some jurists seem to have responded to this "abnormal" situation in an evasive and perhaps equally "abnormal" way. They probably felt that if the conflict develops so as to reach a court of law, if litigation replaces consideration and the parties involved would rather abide by the court ruling than respond to the dictates of conscience, the safe course would be the formal one. Professional medical care does not seem to have been a fashionable pattern of the family life in those days. And while it is conceivable that a husband might refuse to bear the cost of this "unusual" item of service, it is also conceivable that a wife might exploit the situation. Now if a conflict over this matter reaches the court, it seems clear that there is a moral failure on one or both sides. The medical profession, if there was one, and the administrative machinery of the time were not so efficient as to determine soon enough whether a given treatment was really needed or a certain fee was justified. Instead of passing a categorical judgment on the motives of litigants, some jurists apparently evaded the moral issue and adhered to the formalities of the law, leaving the rest up to the individual conscience. The same jurists could conceivably have held the husband responsible for the cost of the wife's medical care and would still remain evasive or morally uncommitted. But this was not to be; the reason is perhaps the fact that there is no community of property between husbands and wives. The wife's assets are her own. She may use them as she sees fit and she can meet her own medical expenses out of such assets. She is not entirely dependent on the husband nor is she denied the right to possessions and property. At any rate, the whole issue seems as hypothetical as the arguments about it seem "formal" and conceptual. In the course of research for this work, the present writer has not found any cases of reported conflict between husbands and wives over who was to be responsible for a sick wife's maintenance and care. This may not deny the rise of domestic disputes over such matters. But whether they were settled privately or otherwise, the fact remains that jurists seem to have been fighting windmills, not tackling real issues, and found intellectual gains in pursuing the unusual.

d. *Maintenance in Recalcitrance (Nushūz)*
There is one case where all jurists agree that a wife loses her right to maintenance. This is the case of recalcitrance or

nushūz, which is manifested by the wife's aversion to her husband, hatred toward him, disinterest in his companionship, or attraction to another person. Such a defiant, refractory wife is not entitled to maintenance by her husband. But jurists differ on the details of what exactly constitutes recalcitrance. For example, some hold that a fit healthy wife who denies her bed to her husband is refractory and thus loses her right to maintenance. Others are of the opinion that maintenance is not a function of sexual accessibility, but is the result of a marriage contract that confines her to the husband's home. And as long as she so confines herself and does not leave the home without his consent, she is obedient and her right to maintenance stands valid. It is religiously forbidden for her to deny him her bed, but that does not affect her legal right to maintenance.[18]

Recalcitrance may be overt or covert. Jurists seem to be concerned with the overt type that has become a legal case calling for a court decision. The covert type is dealt with in the Qur'ān in a way aimed at solving the family problem as privately and peacefully as possible, without allowing the issue to become a public record. The Qur'ān states that if a husband is fearful of his wife's recalcitrance, he may follow a three-step redemptive course. First, he must exhort her with sound advice and guidance. If that does not solve the problem, he must take the second step by "abandoning" her bed. And if that does not remedy the situation, then the third and last step is to apply physical disciplining, e.g., slapping or hitting in a symbolic way that is not humiliating, injurous, or deformative. If he abuses this disciplining authority in any way, such as using the second or third step where the first suffices, his own action is forbidden and legally punishable. It is understood from the grammatical structure of the Qur'ānic statement that the fearful husband should hasten to *exhort* the would-be refractory wife and then allow sufficient time before he resorts to the second or the third measure. It is also understood that such disciplining is justifiable with moderation only in the case of a wife who is not wronged, who heeds no advice, whose obstinate attitude is not changed by temporary separation in bed, and whose husband is not at fault.[19]

It is noteworthy that the Qur'ān allows for the possibility of the husband's covert recalcitrance. In this case, the wife is instructed to initiate the peace-making process, and the husband is enjoined to reciprocate, so that the two may settle the problem between themselves quietly. But should that course fail, two arbitrators representing both sides are chosen to make peace. It is interesting to note that a certain law school empowers the legal authorities to discipline a refractory husband in the same way he would discipline his refractory wife. The court executes this right on the wife's behalf. It would first exhort him; if this proved ineffective, it would then allow the wife to deny him her bed without losing any of her marital rights. If that too fails, the court shall apply physical disciplining.[20]

However, the husband's recalcitrance may become overt, as when he refuses to provide for his wife. If he persists in this attitude, the Hanafī school authorizes the law enforcement agencies to imprison him until he renounces his position and discharges his responsibility. But the consensus of the rest of the jurists is that the wife has the right to seek a divorce from him. If she so wishes, the court must comply with her request and grant her the divorce.[21]

e. Maintenance on Poverty

Failure to provide for the wife may sometimes be involuntary. If the husband's financial situation does not allow him to discharge his obligations to her, it is the opinion of the Hanafī school that his obligations remain, and the wife shall be supported by her relative who would be responsible for her if she were not married. Also, she may be informed that she has the option of borrowing on his behalf in proportion to her needs. In either case, whatever she spends becomes a claim or debt against her husband, which he is to pay when his financial situation improves. According to this school, the husband's

financial inability to maintain his wife is no ground for divorce.
Nor shall he be completely free from the obligation. An extreme variant of this position is adopted by the Zāhirī (Literalist fundamentalist) school. It maintains that marriage must be
preserved irrespective of the husband's financial condition. If
she has the means, the wife must support herself and also her
poor husband, who is not responsible for repaying anything of what she has expended. But the great majority among
the Muslim jurists grant the wife a right of choice. She may
bear with him and keep the marital bonds, if she so desires.
Otherwise, she may seek separation from him, and the court
shall agree with her request. This kind of separation is a revocable divorce (ṭalāq), according to some jurists, or an
annulment (faskh) or merely a separation, according to others,
because the husband does not in fact make any divorce pronouncements or authorize any one else to do so in his behalf.[22]

Every school attempts to support its position on the issue by
citing the Qur'ān, the Sunnah, common sense, and moral arguments. Those who favor the wife's right to choose between
separation/divorce and endurance argue that it is disadvantageous and harmful to the wife to preserve a marriage that
does not give her the needed security. Rather than *forcing* her
to suffer from poverty, she should be allowed to decide for
herself either to bear with her destitute husband or seek separation by a court ruling. Those who favor the preservation of
the marriage, regardless of the husband's financial situation,
argue that separation/divorce is *more* harmful than a temporary endurance in which the wife is directed to claim the support of her relatives or to borrow on the husband's behalf. It
is a general rule that whenever there are two differentially
harmful courses, the less harmful of the two must be chosen.
Financial hardships are harmful, but more harmful is divorce
or separation. It is better, therefore, for both parties to endure
together and await relief. Financial problems are involuntary,
but not insurmountable. It is quite possible, indeed promised,
that relief follows difficulties. The husband should be given a
chance to solve his problems instead of a court confrontation

ending in divorce or separation. The very authentic sources which hold the husband responsible for his wife's maintenance also stipulate unequivocally that God does not charge a self beyond its capacity. They, moreover, urge creditors to be patient and kind so as to await the relief of the debtor's straitened circumstances. How much more would this apply to a wife-husband situation! At any rate, in his concluding summary of the discussion of the conflicting arguments, Ibn al Qayyim points out that the spirit of Islāmic law demands the following: if the man deceives his wife by misrepresenting his financial status or deliberately refuses to support her, leaving her helpless, then she has the right to seek separation from him. But if she marries him without any prior knowledge of his financial problems, or if his position hardens after ease, then she has no right to seek separation on account of his poverty.[23]

To review these opposed positions from a sociological standpoint, it may be helpful to note that the schools whose members insist upon retaining the marital bond, irrespective of the financial strains, were prominent in Iraq and, to a lesser extent, Muslim Spain. These were the two seats of power: the 'Abbasī Eastern Dynasty of Baghdad and the Umawī Western Dynasty of Spain. On the other hand, the schools whose members empower the wife to choose between separation/divorce and endurance with a destitute mate developed and flourished mainly in the other regions of the Muslim Empire. Unlike Spain and Baghdad, these were relatively remote from the great centers of political gravity and power struggle. It is true that scholars of various regions exchanged views with one another and were familiar with the different positions on the significant issues. It is also true that no region was exclusively monopolized by any given school. Moreover, every major school developed into several branches each of which adapted itself to the local conditions.[24] Nevertheless, it may be suggestive that Iraq and Spain were the cultural centers of the doctrine of marriage preservation, while scholars of the other regions adopted the doctrine of "option." The difference between the two doctrines is difficult to explain in terms of the authentic sources of law or

the extent of adherence by the respective schools to the spirit of
the religion. This renders a provisional sociological explanation
the more worthy of pursuit.

With the shifting of political power to Iraq and Spain, social
diversity probably exceeded every hitherto known precedent.
New ethnic and cultural elements of Persian, Turkish, Frank-
ish, and other origins came on the scene, not only as subordinate assimilations, but also as influential forces. The administrative system became increasingly complex, and many of the
practices of the former Persian and European empires influenced the new Muslim rulers. Mobility, social as well as
geographical, frequent change of fortunes, some kind of urbanization, along with an increasing social and spatial distance
between the early simple Arabian environment and the new
majestic seats of power and adventure—all became recognizable features of the Muslim Empire both in the "East" and in
the "West." Coupled with this is the fact that the traditional
tribal ties of the early Arabs loosened and the native kinship
systems apparently produced no viable substitutes. Also, it
was a man's world for most practical purposes, however influential behind the scene some women may have been. Laxity
and luxury became widespread. Confidence in the governing
authorities apparently left much to be desired in that political
turmoil of revolts, "nationalistic" fragmentations, plots and
counterplots.[25]

Under such circumstances of unstable cosmopolitanism, it
is, perhaps, not unusual to detect a sense of resignation even
among the intellectuals and the interpreters of law. The
situation being what it was, it was probably regarded as
humiliating, aggravating, or disgraceful for a man to be forced
to separate from his wife on account of poverty. On the other
hand, it would be considered unseemly or risky for the wife
to leave him destitute or seek another spouse, even if one could
be found soon enough. The law interpreters who had first-
hand experience of these conditions did not react to the situation as detached lawyers, but rather, it seems, as religious reformers. They wanted the law to serve its moral purposes, at

least on the family level. To them, this was achievable by ruling in favor of preserving the marital bond, irrespective of the husband's poverty. It was thought preferable and manly for both parties to endure temporarily, awaiting God's promised relief. This position may conceivably be understood as intending to serve the following purposes: (1) the preservation of the elementary family unit, to minimize the risk of spouselessness which could become another serious threat to public morality as well as the future of the offspring, if any; (2) the restoration of kinship ties and community solidarity without breaking up the marital ones. The wife is entitled (a) to claim the obligatory support of her kinsmen, or (b) to borrow for her needs on her husband's behalf. Thus the kin would be able or even forced to affirm their cohesion and sense of responsibility; the people with means, the creditors, would show their responsiveness to human needs and social solidarity; the husband would be allowed time to solve his problems and pay his debts; and, above all, the marriage would be saved.

However, it is not entirely improbable that the juristic ruling on the wife's endurance with a destitute husband was related to some other variables. Under the sociocultural trends alluded to earlier, women were *de facto* denied much of their law-given freedom in marital affairs. They were probably regarded as incapable of or ineligible for either the initiation or the termination of marital contracts independently of some male agents or representatives. Dissolution of the marital bond, in particular, seems to have been considered a man's right, however strongly exhorted or emphatically enjoined he may be to exercise it judiciously. And as long as a man wanted to keep his wife, he should, according to this view, be empowered to do so, in spite of his involuntary poverty and her ensuing deprivation.

Turning to the other regions of the Muslim Empire, it can be reasonably said that their share of diversity, cosmopolitanism, and laxity was considerably less than that of the central seats of power. The traditional kin ties were still more or less strong. There was close affinity in space and outlook with the

early Muslim Community. Moreover, dissolutions of marriage
and remarriages, at least when justified, were not apparently
thought of as moral stigmas or earthshaking vices. Spouselessness was not likely to become the inevitable lot of normally
desirable women, especially those whose kin took a protective
interest in their welfare. A wife's deprivation was probably
more injurious to her kin's pride than to herself. Economic
fluctuations and social change were apparently much slower
and less likely than they were in the centers of power struggle.
In these circumstances the law interpreters seem to have
deemed it religiously valid and humanly equitable to give the
wife of a destitute husband a choice. She may retain the marital
bond and endure by her own volition, or she may seek dissolution of the marriage to become free from her marital commitments. Religion demands maintenance and security for the
wife; but this is difficult to achieve if the husband is destitute.
It would be non-religious and unequitable to force her to settle
for less than a free choice. On the other hand, religion calls for
compassion and cooperation between marital partners. Assuming that each party would show the decency and manliness
expected of a conscientious Muslim, it could be anticipated
that the husband would do his utmost to minimize his wife's
deprivation and she would do hers to stand by him, sharing his
ups and downs. But expectations are not always fully met; and
if the wife has no choice except to endure, she may become
more of a liability than an asset, in which case deprivation may
increase rather than decrease. One solution to the problem is
to allow the more dependent party, the wife, the alternative
choice of separation/divorce. The fact that jurists presented
this solution as an alternative, and not as the only course of
action, probably implies considerable confidence in the integrity of some women and an awareness of the fragility of the
character of others. Some wives may prefer to endure with
their mates; these should be allowed and even encouraged to
do so. Others may not be so able or willing; these should not
be coerced, nor should their quest for freedom be hindered
unnecessarily. The wife's right to choose between the two al-

ternatives may have significant, though indirect, bearings. It may motivate the husband to intensify his drive to improve his lot, so as to keep his family and pride. It may also encourage him to show the best in his character, to acquire personal qualities that can be a source of consolation for a wife who has proven her integrity and understanding under adverse conditions. Here, too, the intent of moral reform and allowance for variations in the human response seem to underlie a legal doctrine dealing with interpersonal relationship, the simplest form of social interaction.[26]

2. *Dower and Other Economic Rights*

The wife's right to maintenance is only one aspect of her marital role. There are several other aspects to be considered. She is entitled to a marriage gift, or dower (*mahr*) that is her own. This may be prompt, deferred, or divided, depending on the agreement of the parties involved. The prompt portion is payable before or upon consummation of the marriage. The deferred portion becomes due in case of divorce or widowhood. The wife, however, may remit the dower wholly or partly if she so desires.[27] She is entitled to the dower as a wife, i.e., by virtue of marriage. But this seems to be an extension of her rights as a person with full personal rights. Her new marital rights as a wife do not override or absorb her former rights as a person. Nor do her marital obligations negate her independent personality insofar as private possessions and acquisitions are concerned. According to Islāmic law, women, married or otherwise, are allowed to hold property in their own names or to dispose of it independently as they wish, to retain their separate estates, to remain mistresses of their doweries and of any goods they may acquire by inheritance, by gift, or by the fruits of their own labor and investment. The fact that Islām took this position almost fourteen centuries ago is sometimes viewed as astonishing and remarkable. Demombynes notes in this connection that Qur'ānic Law has given the wife "a status which is, in many respects, more advantageous than that bestowed by modern European law." [28] Similarly, Lichten-

stadt has observed that the Qur'ānic attitude "is astonishingly
ahead of its own time and environment." And by ruling in
favor of the woman's right to personal property, "the Prophet
anticipated Western legislation by many centuries." [29]

This doctrine of economic independence was probably too
far in advance of its own time and environment to be implemented easily even though it may have been accepted as
a part of the religious teachings. Western writers, who view
the doctrine with an almost enthusiastic astonishment or admiration, hasten to cast doubt on its practicability in everyday
life. They claim that it is difficult in practice for a woman to
exercise these economic rights, although she is certain of
maintenance and service according to her rank. This difficulty,
it is suggested, seems to arise from the fact that law books and
custom, according to Demombynes, "give the husband absolute authority over his wife and children"; and other than these
economic rights, "the theoretical subjection of the wife to her
husband is," says Jeffery, "almost complete . . . [which] seems
to be a survival from pre-Islamic custom . . ." [30]

On the other hand, some Muslim jurists probably regarded
the doctrine of the wife's economic rights as too far-reaching
and tried to set certain limits to it. Thus in the Mālikī school
of law, but in no other, the husband acquires some "rights"
over the wife's property. First, he has the right to *live* in his
wife's house. This is not a right to ownership or possession, but
to the use of the premises for residence. There seems to be an
assumption that if she owns a house and he neither owns nor
can provide her with one, then he may reside in hers. Such an
assumption is necessary; otherwise the ruling would be contrary to the unequivocal ordinance of the Qur'ān regarding the
husband's responsibility for the wife's lodging, a contrariety
which Muslim jurists would not ordinarily condone. Second,
alienation of any portion exceeding one-third of the wife's
property is invalid without the husband's consent. Here again,
it is not a question of sharing with her the ownership or possession of the estate, but of limiting her freedom to dispose of

her own property, which will, in any case, remain her own as long as she lives.[31]

The fact that his consent is required only after the one-third limit is highly suggestive. The husband is, at least potentially, an heir of the wife. Like any other heir, he has potential interests in and rights to the property of the would-be bequeather. To preserve the legitimate, though potential, rights of the heirs and prevent possible abuse of property, the bequeather's freedom to dispose of or alienate the property must be guarded. For, if a bequeather were to become needy, it is his potential heirs who would be responsible for his welfare. Not only is his property a potential asset to the heirs, but he himself is also a potential liability. To render obligations and rights mutually complementary, the bequeather is neither denied his freedom completely nor allowed to exercise it without limits. To draw a border line of balance, the law, based on the Sunnah, sets as a limit one-third of the property, more than which a bequeather may not give by will or by gift without the consent of his potential heirs. As long as he acts within the one-third limit, he is free to dispose of his porperty as he wishes; if he exceeds that limit, the potential heirs' consent is required, and they may or may not go along with his desires. It is not, therefore, a *special* right of the husband to the wife's property; it is a *general* right of every potential heir to the property of every potential bequeather.[32]

It is rather difficult to determine the social or cultural basis of this Mālikī position, however little it actually differs from that of other schools. The difficulty arises from two sources. First, it is not clear exactly when, where, or by whom the doctrine was first formulated. Secondly, the Mālikī school was not confined to any specific locality; it has exponents in almost every region from Spain to Madīnah. However, since this doctrine appears to have been voiced by late writers, and since it ultimately amounts to giving the husband a right to use his wife's house in case of need for a lodge,[33] it may be suggested that the point seems a little more than a formal restatement of a general moral precept. Such a precept derives mainly from the religious exhortations and prescriptions regarding compassion, kindness, brotherly feelings, and solidarity, not only among marital partners, but also among all Muslims.[34]

3. Nonmaterial Rights

The wife's material rights, however extensive or limited, are not her only assurances and securities. She has other rights that are more of a moral than a legal nature; and they are equally binding and specific. A husband is commanded by the law of God to treat his wife with equity, to respect her feelings, and to show her kindness and consideration, especially if he has any other wife. While the Qur'ān realizes the impossibility of absolute equity between co-wives, it does not accept this human impossibility as a justification for any mistreatment. A co-wife has the right to be treated impartially with due consideration for her feelings and security. She is not to be shown any aversion by the husband or subjected to suspense and uncertainty. A corollary of this rule is that no man is allowed to keep his wife with the intention of inflicting harm on her or hindering her freedom. If he has no love or sympathy for her, she has the right to be freed from the marital bond; it is his duty to grant her that freedom and not to stand in her way to a new life.[35]

Since roles are complementary, the wife's rights may be taken as the husband's obligations, and *vice versa*. What has been discussed so far as the wife's rights can therefore serve as an outline of the husband's duties. When turning to the other components of the wife's marital role, i.e., her obligations, we shall be examining, at the same time, the rights of the husband, whose obligations have been considered implicitly or explicitly in the discussion. To minimize redundancy and maintain a theme of continuity, we shall then concentrate on the obligations, as we have done on the rights, of the wife.

B. The Wife's Obligations; the Husband's Rights

The main obligation of the wife as a partner in a marital relationship is to contribute to the success and blissfulness of the marriage as much as possible. She must be attentive to the comfort and well-being of her mate. She may neither offend him nor hurt his feelings. Perhaps nothing can illustrate the point better than the Qur'ānic statement which describes the righteous people as those who pray:

> Our Lord! Grant unto us wives and offspring who will be the apples of our eyes, and guide us to be models for the righteous.[36]

This is the basis on which all the wife's obligations rest and from which they flow. To fulfill this basic obligation, the wife must be faithful, trustworthy, and honest. More specifically, she must not deceive her mate by deliberately avoiding conception, lest it deprive him of legitimate progeny. Nor must she allow any other person to have access to that which is exclusively the husband's right, i.e., sexual intimacy. A corollary of this is that she must not receive or entertain strange males in her home without his knowledge and consent. Neither may she accept their gifts without his approval. This is probably meant to avoid jealousy, suspicion, and gossiping, and also to maintain the integrity of all parties concerned. The husband's possessions are her trust. If she has access to any portion thereof or if she is entrusted with any fund, she must discharge her duty wisely and thriftily. She may not lend or dispose of any of his belongings without his permission.[37]

One of the essential criteria of determining the wife's obligations is "the purpose of marriage." Whatever serves that purpose or follows from it falls within the range of her duties. Otherwise, she is under no legal obligation. Jurists hold the purpose of marriage to entail enjoyment, companionship, and gratification. From this, they conclude that the husband has no right to force the wife to attend to him or to manage the household. She is under no legal obligation to do any of the housework, because such work is not required by the marital contract nor is it one of its purposes. However, it is recommended that she do the usual routine work; this is not only normal, but also more conducive to the perpetuation of companionship.[38]

Muslim jurists as well as social scientists recognize legitimate sexual access to be one of the essential aims of marriage

and a universal function of the family. It is the wife's obligation
therefore to be sexually responsive and to make herself attractive, available, and cooperative. The husband's right to sexual
access is inalienable. A wife may not deny herself to her husband, for the Qur'ān speaks of them as a comfort to each
other. Due consideration is, of course, given to health and
decency. Moreover, the wife is not permitted to do anything
that may render her companionship less desirable or less gratifying. If she does any such thing or neglects herself, the husband has the right to interfere with her freedom to rectify the
situation. To insure maximum self-fulfilment for both partners,
he is not permitted to do anything on his part that may impede
her gratification. He must not interfere with the natural course
of the sexual act. For example, he may not apply any contraception technique such as *coitus interruptus* or external "superficial" ejaculation (*'azl*) without her consent, because it denies
her due gratification and decreases the offspring unnecessarily.
Neither should he seek intercourse without some foreplay or
preliminary love play, nor allow himself to experience orgasm
before her; this leads her easily to frustration. Ibn 'Abbas (d.
68/687-8), a pioneering authority, sums up the point as
follows:

> Most certainly, I like to make myself handsome for and attrac-
> tive to my wife, just as I like her to beautify herself for me. God says
> that women have rights even as they have obligations in an equitable
> manner.[39]

1. Obedience

The wife's obligations are many and varied. But the question of her obedience to the husband has probably stimulated
more comments than any other single problem. There is, on
the one hand, what may be called the classical Muslim approach; and there is, on the other hand, the modern Western
approach. The former seems less emphatic and less sweeping.
For example, al Jaṣṣāṣ (d. 370/980) adds to the wife's obligations that she must obey her husband and refrain from dissent,
because the Qur'ān (4:34) states that men are guardians and

protectors of women—God has made some of them excel others—and because men expend their means (to maintain and protect their womenfolk). He goes on to say that it is understood, of course, that such obedience is not absolute or unqualified; it applies to matters that fall within the sphere of the permissible categories of action, lie within the range of the husband's rights, and do not violate the rights of God. For instance, she may not enter into a voluntary fast without his permission, because her observance may interfere with her marital performance and thus infringe upon his rights. But when it comes to the obligatory fasting of the month of Ramadān (in which every adult able Muslim must fast from dawn to sunset), she does not need his permission because this is her obligation to God and, in a sense, to herself.[40] There are, moreover, several passages in the Qur'ān and some Traditions to the effect that it is forbidden to obey any person in what is wrong or sinful. A child may not obey his parents if they ask him to do the wrong or believe the untrue. The Qur'ān praises the wife who refused to share her husband's false beliefs or condone his wrong doings. It also acclaims the attitude of the son who did likewise with his parents.[41] Dissent may therefore be even necessary at certain times. Every individual Muslim has a multitude of obligations to God, to himself, and to those on whom he depends or with whom he associates. The obedience of an adult person is not, and may not be, the exclusive right of another person, parent or partner.

Similarly, Ibn Qudāmah cites the complementary marital roles and adds that the husband's rights, however, are greater than the wife's. This is because God says that men have a degree above women (Q-2:228), and the Prophet declared that, if a human being were to prostrate before another, he would have ordered wives to prostrate before husbands for the God-given rights of the latter over the former.[42] Ibn Qudāmah's statement does not refer to obedience, partial or complete; but it does focalize the husband's qualitative rights over the wife. Such focalization is difficult to explain in terms of the Qur'ān or the Sunnah, because these authentic sources demand equity.

The "degree" of men above women is qualified by certain stipulations which would, in the final analysis, leave no room for
the categorical inferiority of one sex to the other and which,
when fully observed, would be conducive to harmony and
equity.[43] This focalization seems rather to be a subjective
disposition on the author's part or the reflection of some popular attitudes toward the social ranking of men and women.
If this was the case, it was then an obvious deviance from the
religious norms and also from the legal principle of the equitable proportionality of rights and obligations. At any rate,
even this position is expressed in a relatively vague but mild
tone.

In contrast, some Western writers have taken a more as-
sertive position. For example, Jeffery has categorically stated
that, "Wives must always be submissive and modest (IV, 38
[more accurately, Q. 4:34])" and, aside from certain economic rights, "the theoretical subjection of the wife to her
husband is almost complete." [44]

Demombynes has, likewise, stated that "law and customs
give the husband absolute authority over his wife and children.
. . . The husband is superior to his wife: 'men having a degree
above them,' says the Qur'ān (2:228)." [45] The problem seems
to rest ultimately on the "degree" of men above women and on
the "guardianship" (qawwāmīyah) of the former over the
latter, as stated in the Qur'ān (4:34). These two bases will be
examined later.

a. Manifestations of Obedience

The wife's obedience to the husband is qualified, as already
indicated, by at least two conditions: (1) it is required only if
what is asked of or expected from the wife is within the permissible categories of action, and (2) it must be maintained
only with regard to matters that fall under the husband's rights.
This is the general frame. Translated into specific manifestations, obedience comprises the following:

1) She must not receive male strangers or accept gifts from them without his permission. Nor must she lend or dispose of any of his possessions
without his approval.

2) The husband has the legal right to restrict her freedom of movement and prevent her from leaving her home without his permission. She must comply with this right unless there is a necessity or legitimate advantage for her to do otherwise. However, it is his religious obligation to be compassionate so as to relax his right to restrict her freedom of movement. If there arises a conflict between this right of his and the wife's parents' right to visit and be visited by their daughter, his right prevails. Yet it is religiously recommended that he be considerate enough to waive his right and avoid estrangement within his conjugal family or between any member of this family and close relatives, e.g., the wife's parents.

3) A refractory wife has no legal right to object to the husband's exercise of his disciplining authority. Islāmic Law, in common with most other systems of law, recognizes the husband's right to discipline his wife for disobedience.

4) The wife may not legally object to the husband's right to take another wife or to exercise his right of divorce. The marital contract establishes her implicit consent to these rights. However, if she wishes to restrict his freedom in this regard or to have similar rights, she is legally allowed to do so. She may stipulate in the marital agreement that she, too, will have the right of divorce, or that she will keep the marriage bond only so long as she remains the only wife; should he take a second wife, the first will have the right to seek a divorce in accordance with the marriage agreement.

5) Finally, if the husband insists on patrilocality or neolocality, the wife must comply.[46]

b. The Basis of Obedience

The question of the Muslim wife's obedience and the husband's authority has been viewed from what seems to be a limited perspective. It is taken by most writers to be based almost entirely on two statements in the Qur'ān and some supplementary Traditions of the Prophet. The Qur'ān (2:228) states that women have rights even as they have duties in an equitable manner, but men have a degree above women. Again, it states (4:34) that men are the guardians, protectors, or custodians of women because God has made some of them excel others and because men expend of their means to maintain women. This is the range within which the problem has been discussed by those who are interested mainly in admiration or condemnation of Islāmic law. Students of the Muslim family have made little use of the sociological insights into role

differentiation, power structure, and division of labor wthin
the family. Since our objective is neither admiration nor condemnation, certain observations may be highly suggestive
and therefore noteworthy in this connection.

First, as Gordon Allport has pointed out, the problems suggested by the concepts of status, power, authority, etc. "run
through all human and animal relationships. . . . Sociologists
find superordination and subordination in all the groups they
study. The social psychologist sees ascendance-submission or
dominance-compliance wherever two persons are in contact
with each other." [47]

Secondly, Bernard and others have observed that "practically universally the status of wives as measured by rights and
privileges is, according to the institutional pattern, inferior to
that of husbands." This is true even of the so-called equalitarian family system of the United States and is traceable to
the instructions of Paul, who "commanded wives to submit to
their husbands . . ." [48] Such observations seem to lend support
to the contemporary view that, "In virtually all societies, children and women are subject to the authority of the man who
lives with them . . ." [49]

Thirdly, it has been argued by Parsons and others that in the
family there are actually multiple power structures independent of each other. While the husband might be more influential
in some decisions, the wife would be in others. One of the
structural requirements which the family has to meet is that of
leadership; and like any enduring group, the family has to differentiate roles on the power axis. This leadership is of two
types, normally not combined in the same person. They are:
instrumental leadership, which deals with the "external system," and *expressive leadership,* which deals with the "internal
system." As Zelditch has shown, "in all but a very few
societies, instrumental roles, which include political and economic leadership, are played by the husband-father, while expressive roles are played by the wife-mother." [50]

These observations seem to suggest that authority is a necessary element of any group structure. It is not "generalized"

or anonymous; rather, it is allocated to specific positions in the structure and is delegated to the occupants of these positions. Moreover, authority is not of one type or one dimension, since it can be instrumental or expressive, overt or covert, a privilege or a duty. Parenthetically, while authority is a requisite of any viable social system, it does not necessarily follow that it will be absolute, unchecked, inexchangeable, or unshared. It is possible, perhaps probable, that uncritical observers may be led to amplify overt, instrumental authority to the disregard of the equally operative but perhaps less conspicuous covert, expressive authority. Conclusions reached by such observers are hardly acceptable at their face value; they should be subjected to careful scrutiny and structural analysis. Generalizations have been made about the inferiority and subordination of women throughout history. Yet the new sociological insights into the nature of the power structures within the family may cast some serious doubts on the unqualified validity of such generalizations. Men may have "believed" themselves superordinate or superior and acted according to their own "definition of the situation." Women also may have behaved at least externally, as though they were submissive and subordinate. But whether they were actually so in all respects and always is an open question. This may have some interesting implications for the Muslim wife's obedience to her husband and the perspective from which the problem has been viewed.

The authentic, textual basis of obedience in Islām is, as already indicated, the two statements of the Qur'ān (2:228 and 4:34). The first of these declares that women have rights even as they have obligations in accordance with equity; but men have a *degree* above them. This degree is, some writers believe, evidenced in the fact that a woman is worth half a man in certain cases of inheritance and in the bearing of witness to some legal transactions.[51] But this alleged evidence does not seem to explain the degree because the evidence itself needs an explanation. Both the degree and the evidence may better be explained by some other variables, such as role differentiation or role allocation.

The question of inheritance may exhibit some "arithmetic inequality" or lack of role identicalness; but it does not necessarily mean inequity, much less a categorical ranking of women as being half men in worth.[52] Similarly, the question of the bearing of witness is raised in the Qur'ān in a suggestive context. The Qur'ān (2:282) stipulates that when a loan is contracted it should be written down and witnessed by two men. But if the two be not men, then one man and two women should be called in to witness, for if one woman forgets the other woman will remind her. The interesting fact here is that the passage speaks of the bearing of witness to such a transaction as a religio-moral obligation which must be discharged in the interest of justice and for God's sake. Witnesses are strongly warned not to conceal the testimony lest their hearts become sinful, for God has knowledge of everything. If the Qur'ān views the bearing of witness in this dutiful manner, a more reasonable conclusion would probably be the following: considering the testimony of two women equal to that of one man is a concession in the woman's favor, aimed at lightening her moral burden and relieving her conscience, rather than a curtailment of her equal rights. Moreover this Qur'ānic stipulation was probably made in recognition of the social fact that at the conclusion of such contracts women were not usually present; and if they were, they might not be interested enough or closely attentive to the degree that would warrant their responsibility for giving the necessary testimony. Thus, instead of disregarding the validity of the women's testimony altogether or holding them as equally responsible and equally experienced in financial matters as men, the Qur'ān took what Muslims may call a cautious position: it prescribed the witness of two trustworthy men or one man and two equally trustworthy women.

This explanation seems more consistent with the position of Islām on the general status of women. In various spiritual and mundane respects women alone are granted certain concessions and exemptions. For example, a woman is exempted from observing the obligatory prayers during menstruation and after child delivery through the early stage of nursing, a period which may extend from three to fifteen and forty days respectively. She is also enjoined not to observe the obligatory fast of the Ramadān month during such times. Instead, she must postpone the fast until she is physically fit. Moreover, she is not financially responsible for any person, not even for herself even though she may have possessions and capital. Whether she be a wife, mother, daughter or sister, she is assured of adequate maintenance by the respective male whom the law designates as the provider.[53] Beyond that, the fact that the Qur'ān regards the testimony of two women equal to that of one man in certain contractual cases does not necessarily mean inherent mental deficiency or inferiority of women.

The Qur'ānic passage clearly states that, in principle, women are capable of discharging the duty of giving testimony. Islāmic law recognizes their right and capacity to do business independently. But not every woman is capable of discharging this duty or exercising that right. Nor is every man, for that matter. To qualify as a witness, one must have a certain degree of practical experience sufficient to constitute reliability and insure justice. Lack of sufficient experience in some aspects of life is not a necessary indication of mental or human inferiority. Every person is lacking in one way or another. Women ordinarily lack sufficient experience in mundane affairs, but it does not necessarily follow that such lack is inherent, complete, or generalizable. In fact, women are the sole experts on certain feminine matters which may involve legal decisions, and their testimony in this regard is both conclusive and exclusive. In addition, there are situations in which the woman's testimony may have a legal value equal to that of a man's or even where her testimony may nullify his. For example, the Qur'ān (24:6-9) states that if a man accuses his wife of infidelity but has no witnesses other than himself, he must testify by God four times that he is of the truthful and, a fifth time, that the curse of God shall be upon him if he should be of the liars. To establish her innocence and exoneration, the wife must testify by God four times that he is of the liars and, a fifth time, that the wrath of God shall be upon her if she should be of the untruthful.[54]

The explanation of the degree of men above women still remains to be sought. Neither the giving of testimony nor the differentiated distribution of inheritance seems to be a satisfactory explanation. The Qur'ān is, Muslims believe, self-explanatory in many respects. Some of its passages explain and are explained by others. A case in point is the question of the degree (Q. 2:228). There is a suggestive insight into the nature of that degree in the passage (4:34), the second of the two statements providing the textual basis of obedience.[55] Here, the Qur'ān states that men are *qawwāmūna 'alā al-nisā'*, which in all probability means that men are guardians over, protectors and maintainers of, or responsible for women. The degree of men above women is the former's guardianship over and responsibility for the latter because, as the passage has put it, God has made *some of them* excel *others* and also because men expend their means. The degree is "operationalized" as the man's role of guardianship, a role which is based on the differential capacities of men and women. It is this role differentiation, together with differential capacities, that may provide a satisfactory explanation of the degree.

It is probably interesting to note that the Qur'ān does not state it categorically that men are superior to women or that God has made men excel women. The passage (4:34) is unequivocal in specifying the financial role of men as a factor in their designation as guardians of women. But when the verse speaks of excellence, it does not allocate it to any particular sex. Much less does it associate excellence with men exclusively. The interesting fact is, however, that almost all writers, Oriental and Occidental, classical and modern, have, with varying degrees of emphasis, interpreted the verse in question to mean the superiority of men to women.[56] This interpretation is probably better understood as a reflection of certain psychological dispositions or of the *actual* status of women, which has been low on the whole, at least on the surface. The assertion, by some observers, of the categorical superiority or excellence of men is difficult to explain in terms of the spirit or even the letter of the verse.

The verse declares that men are guardians, etc. of women. Guardianship entails authority of the guardian over the person(s) guarded. But authority is not the equivalent of power, much less of absolute power. Nor does it necessarily mean a dichotomous, absolute ascendance-submission relationship. The verse does not mention authority in any direct sense; at most, this can only be inferred as a function or consequence of guardianship. But authority is not the only function, because guardianship also entails responsibility. The distribution of both authority and responsibility is a dimension of the division of labor; it is not an affirmation of "instinctive" or absolute or mutually exclusive characteristics of the sexes.

Moreover, there is a grammatical point that may be suggestive. The verse states that men are guardians, etc. of women *because God has made some of them excel others.* The Arabic original of the italicized objective pronoun (them) is the plural masculine. If taken literally, it would mean that God has made some men excel others. But if it is interpreted in conjunction with the first part of the verse, where men and women are mentioned, the pronoun *them,* though strictly masculine, can be taken so as to refer to both men and women. In this case, excellence is attributed to some generalized men and women. This would be based on the grammatical rule of *taghlīb,* according to which a plural consisting of singulars differentiated on some levels may be identified by one of its components and still include the rest. For example, the sun and the moon may form a plural which can be called the "two moons." It would seem that the referents of the objective pronoun *them,* of whom some excel, include members of both sexes for at least two reasons. First, if excellence is conferred by God on some men to the exclusion of other men and also of *all* women (a necessary conclusion of taking the original pronoun literally as a plural masculine), it would be difficult to explain why the Qur'ān clearly designates men in general as guardians of women, or why it allocates rights and duties to the male sex on the merit of only *some* members thereof. Secondly, the object of the verb "excel" is defined neither by the masculine nor by the feminine pronoun, nor is the content of excellence specified in the verse. There is no direct indication of *who* is excelled or in *what* excellence is. Furthermore, it is a grammatical rule that the pronoun refers to the nearest preceding noun unless otherwise indicated. The nearest referent of the pronoun *them* in the verse is actually women, not men. If the interpreters of the Qur'ān adhered to this rule of Arabic grammar, they would have concluded that God has made some of *them,* i.e., women, excel. But they, instead took the verse to mean that God has made some men excel. They went further to specify or define those who are excelled as women, and further still to conclude that men as such, not only some of them, excel and hence are superior to women as such, not only some of them. Such an interpretation and conclusion seem to draw no substantiation from the verse. They must have been reflections of the prevailing social conditions and mental dispositions. Not originating in any textual authentic declarations, they must have been adopted by men who actually believed themselves superior to women, in an age when external appearances probably lent support to such a belief, and in places where instrumental authority overcast expressive authority. The verse, which is somewhat equivocal, was adduced perhaps to rationalize those contemporary conditions and to give those men at least the appearance of evidence in support of their views, so that they would not be taken as contrary to the principles of religion.

In view of this analysis, a reinterpretation of the verse may be worth attempting. Men are guardians, etc. of women because men and women are not completely alike; they are differentiated and differentiable in various respects. Some of them, men and women, are endowed with what others, men and women, lack. In matters of guardianship and exercise of authority, men are generally more qualified than women and can better deal with the external problems of the family social system. Hence they are entrusted with the *instrumental* authority of the household. But this does not exhaust the quality of excellence, nor does it exclude the capacity or eligibility of women to excel in some other areas, e.g., *expressive* authority. If the two types of authority are "differentiated" but held to be equally essential to the family operation, then the question of the superiority of one sex to the other is actually irrelevant and hardly arises. But if they are "stratified" to present one type of authority as superordinate and another as subordinate, then whoever exercises the former type will be "superior" to the one who does the latter. However, it is doubtful whether students of the family would regard such a stratification useful or tenable.

At any rate, the idea that men are superior to women and have power over them without reciprocity or qualifications stemmed from sources apparently alien to the spirit as well as the letter of the passage under consideration. A contemporary Muslim sociologist has noted that the husband is entrusted with the instrumental authority for two basic reasons. First, since he is the party responsible for the general, and particularly the economic, welfare of the family, it would be unequitable and perhaps risky to allocate this authority to any other person. Secondly, this type of authority requires more rationality than emotionality. Because of their practical, acquired experience and external involvement, men are generally more capable of meeting that requirement. This is not to say that rationality and emotionality are mutually exclusive; they are complementary and indispensable to the family as a viable operative social unit. The investment of instrumental authority in the husband does not mean that he excels or is superior in every way. Men excel in certain respects and so do women. The husband's authority is not the absolute or despotic type. It is restrained by the ethical principles of the Qur'ān and in no way allows him to ignore his wife's potential contribution to the decision-making process. It is a type of authority which, according to the same observer, is based on equity, guarded by compassion, and guided by conscientiousness, principles which underlie the husband-wife relationship in the Islāmic scheme of society.[57]

A contemporary Muslim theologian has drawn attention to an interesting fact. Islām requires leadership in every group activity, be it permanent or temporary. For example, whenever two or more persons congregate for worship, they must choose one of them who is best qualified to lead the congregation in prayers. Likewise, when they travel together, they must appoint one of them to assume leadership of the group. Leadership is, therefore, a requisite of any group activity and is to be invested in a person who is best qualified for it.[58] What this seems to suggest is that the family leadership is not created for the husband; the "office" is not founded for the man. Rather, it is allocated to him and he is appointed to it because he is better qualified for the placement. This means that in his assumption of the family leadership the husband is bound by the rules of the office. If he violates the rules or abuses the office he ceases to qualify for it. His authority is not categorical, nor is his leadership unquestionable. They are neither imposed nor claimed, but allocated and subject to checks.

INTERGENERATIONAL ROLES

A. *The Child's Rights, The Parents' Obligations*
1. *General Guidelines*
    Islām's general approach to children may be summarized in a few principles. First, it is a divine injunction that the child is not to be the cause of harm to its parents (Qur'ān 2:233). Secondly, by *implication* the parents should reciprocate and cause the child no harm. The Qur'ān contains relatively fewer specific references to the parents' duties to their children. The reason is probably that normal parents would usually need little admonition to attend to their offspring; such care is expected as a natural drive, a social obligation, or an affective response.[59] Nevertheless, the Qur'ān recognized that parents

are not always immune from negligence or overprotectiveness. On the basis of this recognition, it proceeded to establish general principles and point out certain facts with regard to children. Thus, it prohibited infanticide and warned against the continuance of that pre-Islāmic custom.[60]

In addition, the Qur'ān also recognized rather clearly that children are joys of life as well as sources of pride and strength, seeds of vanity and false security, fountains of distress and temptation.[61] So it hastened to point out the greater joys of the spirit and to warn parents not to be deceived by the multiplicity of their children or to go astray on their account.[62] Furthermore, the religio-moral basis of this position is that every individual, parent or child, relates to God as a person and is independently responsible for his own deeds. No child can absolve the parent from his responsibility before God, nor can the parent intercede on his child's behalf. Each has a direct, personal relationship to God and is commanded to give first priority to the rights of God. These rights are *inclusive;* under normal circumstances they harmoniously incorporate as well as reinforce the intergenerational rights. But if there arises a crisis, such as some unavoidable conflict over the choice of religion or practice of faith, then every individual must do what is conducive to his spiritual welfare, i.e., choose the side of God. Yet this does not invalidate the principles of intergenerational concern, kindness, and mutual obligations, especially in matters of subsistence and general care.[63]

Finally, Islām seems sensitive to and conscious of the child's crucial dependence on the parents. Their role in forming its personality and the far-reaching effects of socialization are clearly recognized by the Prophet. In one of his unequivocal and perhaps most suggestive statements he declared that "every child is born into the true religion [i.e., into a pure natural state of "Islām"], its parents later on making it into a Jew or Christian or pagan." [64] It is with this understanding and in the light of these principles that the intergenerational roles will be discussed in this chapter.

2. The Right to Life and Equal Life Chances

One of the most inalienable rights of the Muslim child is the right to life. Parents are unequivocally commanded by God not to take their children's lives. Preservation of the child's life comes, in some passages, third in the hierarchy of Muslim commandments. The Qur'ān (Q. 6:151; cf., 17:23ff.) declares: (1) that it is forbidden to associate with God any object of worship; (2) that the Muslim must be good to his parents and (3) that it is forbidden to kill one's children because of poverty; "We will provide for you and for them."

This injunction may sound meaningless when severed from its historical setting. But it will become significant when viewed from a sociological perspective. Infanticide, exposure, and the sale of children to slavery or concubinage were frequent practices of ancient societies of the Near East, as well as in Europe and elsewhere. According to several Biblical accounts the father's power over the life and the death of his children was taken completely for granted. As Patai has put it, ". . . the patriarch's absolute power over his family included the right to decide at the time a child was born to him whether to let it live or condemn it to die." [65] Yet in spite of his "absolute" power, "the Hebrew father," according to Bardis, "enjoyed less influence than his Roman counterpart . . . [and] he does not seem to have abused his authority." [66]

The position of Christianity was rather paradoxical. "As in the case of women, Christianity was inconsistent regarding children." The Church disapproved of infanticide partly because no infant was to die unbaptized. Selling children into slavery "was regarded a serious sin. Constantine the Great permitted child sale only when the parents were unable to support their offspring. . . . Still, throughout Western Europe, both infanticide and the sale of children were rather common until about A.D. 1000, particularly whenever war and famine were raging." [67]

There can be little doubt that pre-Islāmic Arabia practiced infanticide. What is not clear is how extensive it was, which of the two sexes was more affected by it, and what reasons led to

it. Classical Muslim writers seem to exaggerate the spread of
the practice, partly because the Qur'ān condemns it very
strongly and classifies it as a grave offense, and partly because
they viewed Islām as a *total* social revolution.[68] On the other
hand, modern writers show a tendency to minimize the intensity of the practice. Contemporary Arab scholars appear reluctant to accept the uncritical generalization that pre-Islāmic
Arabian life was savage or barbaric in every respect. Such
scholars probably do not wish to underestimate the "remedial"
influence of Islām on Arabian life, yet they hesitate to dis-
credit their ancestors completely.[69] This position may be best
understood in terms of the rise of Arab nationalism and the
general tendency to cherish Arab history, both Islāmic and
pre-Islāmic.

That infanticide in pre-Islāmic Arabia was not common is
also the view of Western writers, but apparently for different reasons. It is generally believed that the incidence of
female infanticide was more frequent than that of the male,
and while it "was a very general custom among the ancients,"
Roberts maintains that it "prevailed among only a few of the
Arabic tribes . . .*Subsequently we have here something against
which the prophet could speak out boldly, without fear of
much opposition.*" [70] A relatively socioeconomic explanation
is suggested by Bell's view that female infanticide could not
have been extensive for, in a sense, "daughters were valuable
property." [71]

The fact that it is generally held that more female than male
infants were put to death by parents may clarify the reasons
for infanticide. When a tribe resorted to infanticide without any
sexual discrimination, the reasons were apparently of an economic nature; poverty and the barrenness of the vast desert
made it difficult to maintain children. The Qur'ān alludes to
this practice, warning parents against it but assuring them of
God's help (Q. 6:151; 17:31). In these passages the Qur'ān
uses the word *children* without specifying the child's sex. From
this usage it has been inferred that whenever poverty was the
reason the infant's sex was immaterial. In other words,

wherever infanticide was sexually indiscriminate, it most probably was due to poverty.[72]

However, there were situations that involved only male infants and others that concerned females exclusively. It was customary in some tribes that a father would vow to the gods to sacrifice one of his sons if he was to be blessed with ten of them.[73] When the practice involved female infants only, the usual reasons are believed to have been (1) the fear of poverty that would result from providing for such unproductive children, and (2) pride or avoidance of the disgrace that would follow if the tribe's women were captured by the enemy or became scandalous through loose behavior.[74] A less common explanation of female infanticide is that it was due to the girl's physical retardation or deformity.[75]

Perhaps the least traditionally common explanation of female infanticide is the religious one, which seems to enjoy increasing credibility. Smith, Bell, and others made brief references to this religious factor.[76] But it was Wāfī, a contemporary Muslim sociologist, who formulated the religious theory in sociological terms. Briefly, it states that pre-Islāmic Arabs believed girls to be profane creatures of Satan or some god other than their native gods, and such creatures were to be eliminated. The cultural basis of this belief was another belief according to which all land and animal products were dichotomized. Some products were considered to have been made by the native Arabian gods, to belong to them, to have totemic symbolism, and to be pure. Other products were believed to be the creation of Allah or the God in whom the tribes did not believe. Such were regarded impure products which should be eliminated or offered in sacrifice to the tribal gods. This dichotomization was extended to the human offspring. All born infants were thus classified into (1) the pure sex or the male species, the creation of the good tribal gods, and (2) the impure profane sex or the female species, the creation of Allah or the discredited god. The Arabs felt that it was their religious obligation to exterminate such profane creatures, whose blood was impure and polluted. For this reason, they buried these female creatures alive to avoid any contact with their defiled blood if other methods of death had been used. Those Arabs extended their beliefs even to the heavenly planets. They attributed to Allah, the discredited god, all the female creatures in those heavenly spheres. For example, they classified the angels as members of the female sex and derisively called them the daughters of Allah (Q. 16:56-62; 43:15-19; 53:21-28). It is true that the two statements of the Qur'ān (6:151 and 17:31) refer to poverty as the reason for infanticide. But this is infanticide in general, without any sexual differentiation because the Qur'ān in this context uses the word "children" or offspring, not daughters, girls, females, or women.[77]

This theory seems to have more explanatory power than any alternative explanation, although it is far from conclusive. If there was such a widespread religious belief among the Arabs about the sacred-profane (male-female) dichotomy, the practice of female infanticide would have been much more common than the evidence indicates. This may be the strongest criticism of the theory. But perhaps only a few tribes fully subscribed to this belief or took it seriously. However, the religious explanation seems more tenable than the "poverty" and/or the "pride" theories. Smith, like other scholars, has suggested poverty and pride or fear of disgrace as the basic reasons for female infanticide. But to reconcile these two apparently incompatible reasons, he imputed the pride motive to the noble chieftains and the poverty variable to the commoners.[78] Yet, to accept the economic explanation it must be assumed that daughters were economically less useful and more burdensome than sons. Such an assumption may be difficult to hold in view of the general belief (1) that daughters brought their fathers handsome bride-prices, (2) that they participated in wars and raids, and (3) that they shared in the chores of their parents.[79]

Moreover, the manner in which the female infant was put to death appears to weaken the economic hypothesis. Girls were sometimes spared till the age of six, at which time they were adorned and then cast by their fathers into a pit in the wilderness without any blood being shed or touched. This is altogether different from the customary infanticide and seems to have no economic basis. In fact, Smith himself points out that this was rather a kind of human sacrifice "such as we know the Arabs to have practised." [80] Furthermore, the pride explanation is highly problematic. It would appear to presuppose a number of things which may be difficult to uphold, as the relatively high standards of sexual morality, discrimination by the captors between the captured males and females, disposition of the Arabs to avoidance rather than confrontation, and so on. All this would seem to leave the religious explanation of female infanticide as the most likely one.

At any rate, whatever the reasons for and the frequency of infanticide, Islām categorically condemned the practice and reaffirmed the infant's right to life and equal life chances. Parents and others used to discriminate between male and female children, with their favors showered on the former. The Qur'ān disapproved of this discrimination and admonished parents to receive their infants, male or female, joyfully as the gift of God. It reproached those who were disposed to gaiety upon the birth of a baby boy but prone to depression, anxiety or shame if the infant was a baby girl. The Prophet showed in words as well as in deeds that the birth of a child should be a festive occasion marked with joy, charity, and thankfulness.[81]

3. The Right to Legitimacy

Like the inalienable right to life and equal life chances, the child in Islām has the equally inalienable right to legitimacy. Of all the logical possibilities of placement and of the pre-Islāmic patterns of descent acquisition, Islām chose what may be termed the "principle of legitimacy," which, in the summary words of Rose Coser, "holds that every child shall have a father, and one father only." [82] By so doing, Islām probably meant to put an end to the Arabian practices that left the individual sometimes without any secure identity.

In pre-Islāmic Arabia and among the Semites in general,

matrilineality was more or less observed either exclusively or together with patrilineality. This practice even continued into Islām in some instances. For example, al Hasan ibn 'Ali (d. A.H.61/680) was often called the Prophet's daughter's son, a title of honor in this case. As a historical fact, then, matrilineality seems indisputable, but the explanations of the fact are highly problematic and variegated. They include such evolutionistic hypotheses as promiscuity, matrilocality, and ignorance of the biological implications of paternity.[83]

However, a closer examination of Arabic literature, especially pre-Islāmic poetry, suggests to some scholars that when a pre-Islāmic Arabian was named after his mother or called the son of the mother of so and so—e.g., *ibn* Hind or *ibn umm* Zayd, i.e., the son of his mother Hind or the son of Zayd's mother respectively, it was due to one or more of the following reasons:

1) It was an expression of honor for and appreciation of the mother.

2) It was a status symbol for some Arabs to take pride in the true or alleged noble stock of their mothers.

3) Sometimes the mother was more renowned than the father, and the children were thus believed ennobled by affixing their mothers' names to their own.

4) Sometimes, also, the mother resided with her own family of orientation after divorce or desertion by the children's father, in which case they were identified for all practical purposes by the mother's name.

5) Occasionally, a person would be called the son of so-and-so, i.e., his mother, simply in contempt.

6) In some cases the father was survived by his own mother or mother-in-law, who then undertook the upbringing of her grandchildren, and they were identified by her name in addition to their own given names.

7) It was not unknown that a child was named the son of so-and-so who was its wet-nurse or governess even though she was neither the natural mother nor the grandmother.[84]

The "normal" mechanism to establish legitimacy, immediate-

ly before Islām at any rate, was either acknowledgment and/or
adoption by the real or the would-be father, or by his tribe.
The child could not assume its father's status without his approval. But the father's approval was not always binding; he
could at any time revoke his recognition and completely disown the child, particularly if the child had committed any act
disagreeable to the father or his tribe.[85] This situation must
have generated confusion and status anxiety in the minds
of some individuals.

With Islām came a different system that was apparently
designed to reduce to a minimum the possibility of status anxiety and also the stigma of illegitimacy. Under this new system, the "principle of legitimacy" was restored and reinforced;
every child was to have a father and it was to be the one real
father, whose fatherhood, once established, would be irrevocable. Accordingly, every child may be reasonably assured of
placement. Much of this security rests upon the individual's
conscience and his religious sensitivity. However, these moral
instructions may be designed to supplement the specific legal
procedures and to generate an active sense of moral responsibility. In one of his strong declarations, the Prophet said that
a woman who misplaces a child's legitimacy by relating its
descent to someone who is not responsible for its conception
has committed a grave offense, alienated herself from God, and
will be denied the bliss of eternity. Likewise, a father who ob-
scures his child's legitimacy by denying his responsibility for
its conception has offended God and inflicted upon himself
universal disgrace. This seems so institutionalized in Islam
that, in the words of Jeffery, "the stigma of illegitimacy seldom
clings to a child in the Islāmic family; even the children of
slave concubines are legitimate members of the family with
family rights." [86]

It was probably to ensure the child's right of legitimacy that
Islām adopted what may sound highly unusual or extreme
measures. For example, the conception-birth span is set by
various schools of law at a minimum of six lunar months and a
maximum of four years. Thus, if a husband and wife cohabit

and she gives birth six months thereafter, the infant will be regarded a legitimate child of its parents. Similarly, if she gives birth within four years after widowhood, divorce or separation and before remarriage, the infant shall be legitimate. However, a child born before six months from the beginning of legal cohabitation, or after four years since the cessation of legal cohabitation, will be legitimate if the husband recognizes it and if there is any evidence or likelihood that it is his, not the procreation of any other identifiable parent. Should there be more than one claimant of the child, as was customary before Islām, and there is no conclusive evidence in favor of any particular party, the matter may be settled by consulting some experts, i.e., physiognomists in the pre-Islāmic fashion, or by lot. But if it is established that the child was conceived out of wedlock, then the child's descent will derive from the mother only, while the adulterer, the father, will be denied paternity as a punitive measure for his misconduct. The social meanings and implications of this punishment will become clear as the discussion proceeds. Moreover, it is forbidden to marry a pregnant woman or cohabit with a newly acquired slave until the expectant gives birth and the slave is proven to be free from pregnancy. This is to avoid any confusion of descent and misplacement of legitimacy. Furthermore, if the husband questions the legitimacy of his wife's child which is born while she is his legal spouse, he is advised of the serious consequences of making any hasty expression of his misgivings. But should he accuse his wife of infidelity and deny her child's relationship to him, this will lead to a course of mutual "imprecation," to end with the special type of irrevocable divorce known as *li'ān*, after which he may never remarry her or have any claim on her. This is a warning that legitimacy is not to be taken lightly or denied at will. However, if there is absolutely no possibility of relating the child to its real or very likely father, which would seem rare under such extended time provisions, the child will be related to and identified by the mother's name. "Adoption" is not legal at all, even if the child's real parents are unknown, in which case the person involved shall be called the brother in faith and client of his fellow Muslims.[87]

When paternity is denied to the adulterous father and the child is related to the mother only, this is considered penalizing the father for his misbehavior as the Prophet's statement indicates.[88] It may also be a punishment to the mother for her sharing of that misbehavior. Yet she is given the apparently incontestable right of maternity and, in spite of her misconduct, her relationship to the child is neither severed nor questioned. Perhaps this is in recognition of what Queen has called the universal phenomenon of mother-child attachment, at least in the early years.[89] Or it may be in response to the child's various needs which normally a mother only could satisfy adequately, especially perhaps a mother who may wish to compensate the child for her negligence. Moreover, it may be in recognition of the unique relationship of the mother to the child, a relationship which the Qur'ān characterizes thus:

> We have enjoined on man to be kind to his parents: in travail upon travail did his mother bear him, and in years twain was his weaning (31:14). . . . In pain did his mother carry him, and in pain did she give him birth (46:15).

Nevertheless, the question may arise: why should the child be deprived of a legal father or denied a father's name? The child has committed no offence, and it is unjust to "penalize" an innocent party. Adoption may remove the stigma of illegitimacy and assure the child of a normal happy childhood. So might the question and its corollaries go. But the basic question and its concomitants would seem hardly relevant to the Islāmic environment or appealing to the Muslim mind. Muslims maintain that illicit relationships constitute a grave offence against God as well as against society. Part of the penalty for this offence is to deny to the guilty the fruits of their liaison. Following this logic, parenthood should be denied to both the man and the woman, who are equally responsible for the conception of the child. But the Prophet's statement stipulates that the child relates to the mother and the father gains nothing.[90] This differentiation in recognizing the mother as the legitimate parent of the child may be based on the fact that while paternity can be subject to doubt, maternity is usually unmistakable. Added to this factor are the possibilities already suggested.[91]

As for the child, it may be in its interest to deny it to a father of such questionable integrity and character. This denial, however, does not affect the child's basic rights to security and full community membership. In fact, such a position may be a testimony to the child's own credit, to the society's openness, to the social response of the community, and to the degree of social integration.[92] It would seem to reaffirm the basic principle that every Muslim individual has equal access to whatever is of value for Muslim society, hindered neither by a family name nor by the lack thereof. The chief criterion of excellence in the value system of Islām is personal piety and religio-moral achievement. No one may claim the credit of another, nor is any one responsible for or penalized by the actions of anyone else.[93] Whenever an offence is committed against God, e.g., adultery or fornication, it is only God Who exempts or forgives the offender. Thus, if there is any stigma of illegitimacy, it would cling not so much to the innocent child as to the guilty parents, and its effects shall not be allowed to hurt the innocent. If the stigma is to be removed, it is not by placing the child for adoption and "covering up" for the offence of the parents; such may actually brand the child and confirm that inevitably it is somehow penalized by or held responsible for the actions of others. The stigma need not arise in the first place for an innocent party; but if it does, reparations obtain by way of giving the child complete access to equal life chances and the right to grow up free from prejudice or stigmas of any kind.

Prohibition of adoption does not negate the "generalized" responsibility of society to the child. Nor does it lessen the binding effects of the stronger bond of brotherhood in faith.[94] Actually, Muslims might contend that if adoption were permitted it could give the impression that illicit liaisons are tolerable and gratifying; that an individual, (the adopter,) is capable of atoning for the offence of another, (the adulterer), even if the offence is clearly against God; that the individual is free to relinquish his commitment at will or claim what is not his at will; that substitutes may replace the originals permanently. But none of these implications fits the Islāmic scheme of society, a scheme which stresses the unity and "organic solidarity" of the Muslim community without obscuring or fusing the individual units.[95]

Even beyond the realm of possible implications, one consequence of adoption is almost certain. When an alien child is fully adopted by new parents, it will probably upset the role structure of kinship as regards inheritance, provisions, solidarity, and perhaps marital chances. It may bar natural relatives from their God-given rights or exempt them from their God-ordained duties, and thus tamper with the order of society. Tampering with the natural priorities of the kinship system may generate at least covert hostility and/or estrangement among the kin. This is clearly contrary to the teachings of the Qur'ān.[96] The coming of an adopted child to an adopting family may even create uncertainty in the minds of some potential heirs, rightful claimants, or prospective mates. It is also possible that the adopted child may, unknowingly, enter into incestuous relationships by marrying close relatives of the natural parents or otherwise become subject to confusion. Adoption under these circumstances may place an individual child and provide it with adequate substitutes for its natural parents. But it may well "displace" other relatives and hurt their legitimate interests or affect the kin's mutual obligations. To help one adopted individual by alienating other individuals or causing estrangement among the kin is probably not the lesser evil. Nor would it seem conducive to family solidarity, which is usually necessary for social stability. Generalized social obligations to the needy or fatherless and the honoring of kinship commitments are not mutually exclusive in Islām. But if adoption were permitted to accommodate the fatherless at the expense of the adopter's kin, it may render social responsiveness and kinship solidarity incompatible, or at least relegate the true kinship to a secondary position. Islām relegates kinship only when it seriously interferes with one's personal relationship to God or hinders the realization of one's spiritual potential, part of which is, however, kindness to the kin.[97]

The fact that Islām prohibited adoption and preferred legitimacy, even through the mother only, to paternity by an adulterous father or adopter may be sociologically significant. It seems to suggest that paternity is neither a favor bestowed by a person upon another nor a negotiable concession. Rather, paternity is both the father's obligation to and right upon the child. It is the basis on which various legitimate claims may be made by either party. This is probably a partial explanation of the ruling that an adulterer is punished, among other things, by rejecting his claims to paternity and depriving him of the paternity rights.[98]

Another suggestion may be that children were highly valued and eagerly sought after. To minimize disputes and confusion in this regard, Islām ruled that they were to be conceived in wedlock, placed with, and entrusted to, devoted parents of unsuspected characters. Under these conditions adulterers could hardly qualify. Adopters might if the matter did not implicate other relatives or engulf other considerations. Paternity and descent are highly consequential relationships with far-reaching implications. Such crucial relationships cannot rest entirely on individual whims if they are to be effective. Paternity, to be wholesome, must, among other things, be placed firmly where it actually and rightfully originates.

Adopting a child of known parents may, and often does, entail serious consequences of emotional, material, and social nature. It may upset the life style or responsibility aptitude of the procreators, the adopters, the adopted children, and possibly other relatives as well. If the natural procreators are, for any reason, incapable of raising a child, Islām's injunction is not to re-place the child even if they, under distress or tension, so desire. The answer to the problem is not to cut the child's roots of natural descent altogether by placing it with eager, possibly overprotective, "parents"-to-be. This may encourage

some individuals to relax their sense of moral responsibility.
Islām's answer would rather seem to call upon the brotherhood
of faith to help needy parents to raise their children in as
natural an environment as possible. When the welfare of the
child requires its placement with another family, this shall be
done in the interest of the child, in the name of Muslim society as a whole, for the sake of God, and without changing
the child's lineal identity or denying parenthood to the natural
parents. The new family, whose members must be lineally
as akin to the natural family as possible, takes care of the child,
not to acquire a status of parenthood or displace the procreators but to fulfill the common obligations of kinship, to reaffirm the principle of solidarity and social responsiveness, and
to show compassion toward the needy. Whatever the new family invests in raising the child will be either a deed of private
charity or subject to material compensation, depending on
the situation. But in no way does it affect the child's personal
or lineal identity.[99]

When the child's parents are unknown, no other parent(s)
may claim parenthood of the child by way of direct or indirect
adoption. The Qur'ān states that adopted children are not the
real offspring of the adopters; they must be related to their true
procreators when known or knowable. Otherwise, they are the
brethren in faith and clients of their fellow Muslims (Q. 33:
4-5). The specific background of this Qur'ānic ruling has been
a battleground of polemics and counterpolemics.[100] What interests us here, however, is the sociological meaning of the
ruling. It would appear that under the Islāmic system, motivation for adoption stagnated or even ceased. With the new
regulations of polygyny and divorce, the replacement of tribalism with the brotherhood of faith, the guarantee for every
individual in the Muslim community of certain fundamental
rights, and the supremacy of personal merits over mere kinship affiliations, the traditional desire for adoption ceased to
be so burning as before. Moreover, Islām most emphatically
insists that every child must be related to and identified by its
legitimate descent, if it at all can be established, and would

accept any possible evidence in support of complete legitimacy. But it would not permit adoption for the purpose of forging legitimacy. Adoption for this purpose may devalue legitimacy itself and turn the whole question into a mockery.

This discussion has significant bearings upon a special class of parentless children, foundlings. It is the consensus of jurists that whoever finds an abandoned child must attend to it immediately because, as the Qur'ān has put it, saving one life is like saving the lives of all mankind, and also because this foundling may prove to be a societal asset. It is a duty, as well as a charitable deed to rescue the foundling; failing to do so in the best possible way is a heinous sin.[101]

It is also the agreement of jurists that if a Muslim claims the foundling to be his child, actually convinced that it is not the procreation of another man, the claim shall be accepted and will suffice to establish the child's legitimacy and all the concomitant mutual rights. But if no man claims the child, it remains the trust of the finder, who will be responsible for its upbringing and socialization. The Public Treasury shall supply the funds necessary to raise the child unless the trustee volunteers to undertake it at his expense and privately. However, if the trustee is found lacking or incapable of discharging his duties responsibly, his trusteeship over the child shall be terminated and put under the direct jurisdiction of the chief public official of the region. In case the Treasury can provide no adequate funds, it becomes the generalized duty of the Muslim community to raise the money required to meet the foundling's needs. In this way the vital needs of the child will be met adequately, and its upbringing shouldered by Muslims jointly.[102]

As far as the child's vital needs and fundamental rights are concerned, including complete security and unhindered community membership, it is inconsequential whether legitimacy is unestablished, unclaimed, or unassigned. Nothing in this regard can absolve the Muslim community from its social responsibility to the child. Nor can such considerations of legitimacy impede the satisfaction of the child's vital needs and the full enjoyment of its rights. It would appear then that paternity as such is not an end unto itself. Rather, it is a means to other ends, i.e., specific allocations of specific duties and rights to facilitate social interaction and moral reciprocity. Loss of original paternity or obscurity of legitimacy neither entitles nor compels another specific party to assume independently the roles involved in parenthood. If legitimacy is unknown and unknowable, attempts to forge it may lead to confusion of descents, prohibition of the lawful, or permission of the forbidden, especially in matters of incest and succession. Paternity and legitimacy are highly consequential, very personal, specific, and indispensable when they can be established with any degree of certainty. But when they are unknown, it is unjust in the view of Islām to replace the diffused or unknown with specific substitutes. The closest measure to equity in this respect, it would seem, is to adopt equally diffused substitutes that are specific enough to guarantee the individual's basic rights and common enough to insure social responsiveness and solidarity. Outright adoption of the foundling is as forbidden as it is for any other child and for the same reasons. But every individual Muslim is called upon to show parental compassion to and take brotherly interest in the foundling, just as if he were its real parent or sibling.

4. *The Child's Right to Socialization and General Care*

To take good care of and show compassion toward children is one of the most commendable deeds in Islām. The Prophet, in Jeffery's words, "was fond of children and he expressed his conviction that his Muslim community would be noted among other communities for its kindness to children . . ." It is a charity of a higher order to attend to their educational needs and teach them proper manners. Interest in and responsibility for the child's welfare are questions of first priority. According to the Prophet's instructions, by the seventh day the child should be given a good, pleasant name and its head should be shaved, along with all the other hygienic measures required for healthy growing. This should be made a festive occasion marked with joy and charity. At least a ram or an ewe should be sacrificed and distributed among the poor. Also the weight of the child's hair in silver or gold should be given away in charity and thankfulness.[103]

Apart from these festivities and so long as the marital bond obtains, the parents are jointly responsible for the upbringing of the child. During its early years, the father shall provide the material necessities and the mother care for the bodily welfare. Jurists argue as to whether, when, where, and how the mother should nurse the child, in return for material compensations or as a duty. But they agree that the child must be provided with adequate care and if it needs a hired nurse or hired services, the father shall be responsible for that. The two parents together shall attend to the mental and spiritual socialization. For example, the Prophet urged parents to demand that their children begin practicing the regular daily prayers by the age of seven. If the children do not start the practice by the age of ten, they should be disciplined by physical means—without causing them harm or injury, of course—only to show disapproval of their behavior.[104]

The parents' responsibility for the child's welfare remains binding as long as the child is a minor or incapable of taking care of itself. When both parents are Muslims and fulfil their parental obligations adequately, the child's socialization to the Islāmic environment will in all probability be successful. Every child is, as the Prophet implied, born into the true religion, the natural state of Islām. It is the parents who reinforce this propensity or change it. Part of their religious responsibility is to try to raise the child as a Muslim and in the best possible Islāmic way. However, they may not, even if they could, impose their religion on the child, which becomes accountable upon reaching the age of majority, usually marked by puberty. By this time the child is presumed to be capable of making responsible decisions. What parents are enjoined to do then is to show the child in words as well as in deeds the Islāmic way of life, hoping that this early socialization will be effective in later years. Actually, there is some indication that the parents' righteousness benefits the minor child and their misconduct contaminates it. But as children come of age, they stand on their own feet; it is neither the duty nor the right of the parents to tamper with their religious choice by any means other than peaceful, sincere advice, something that the Muslim owes in any case.[105]

There are certain obligations which the parents must fulfil irrespective of the child's religious identity. They are responsible for the welfare of their minor poor children, whether or not these adhere to the same religion as their parents. As long as the child is poor and a minor, it is the father's duty to support it. This right of support and maintenance overrides the father's desire to have the child adopt the same religion as his own and does not depend on the child's particular religious inclinations. But if the child happens to have means, conceivably through gifts, bequests, endowments, etc., then the child's expenses should be drawn from its own resources so long as these are adequate for its material needs. However, the child's age is not the crucial criterion of maintenance allocation. The father is responsible for the support of his poor needy children even after their coming of age. For example, an adult son who is incapable of self-support will be entitled to maintenance by the father. The daughter is entitled to the same right until she actually marries. This right holds even if she is capable of earning a living, because it is not usually expected of the girl to work for a living. But if she does or has independent resources, she must support herself so long as she can; otherwise, the father shall supplement her funds to make sure that she is well provided for.[106]

When both parents are Muslims and their marriage is intact, there is a high probability that the child's socialization will be smooth and free from any major crisis over the question of religious choice. But if the parents do not follow the same religion, the minor child will follow the parent with the *better religion*. This is tantamount to saying that the child shall follow the father and shall be considered for all practical purposes a Muslim. Since it is forbidden for the Muslim woman to marry a non-Muslim man, not *vice versa,* a valid intermarriage involving a Muslim party can only obtain between a Muslim man and a non-Muslim woman. And since Muslims believe their religion to be the "best religious choice," it is evident therefore that the minor child shall follow the "better" religion and the "better" parent, i.e., Islam and the father respectively.[107] This injunction holds because the child is a minor and incapable of accountability. The rationale is that inter-religious marriage is permissible in Islām with the understanding that it does not cause the Muslim partner to relegate his commitment, part of which is to assume responsibility for the household and impart to his children the best in his value system, including his religious preferences.

It may be interesting to note that the social basis of this injunction was a case which involved a husband who embraced Islām and a wife who did not. Their marital bond dissolved, but each claimed the right to take custody of their minor daughter. When the case was brought before the Prophet for a decision he told the father to stay on one side and the mother to stay on another. Then he asked them both to call the girl. At first, the girl went to her mother's side. But the Prophet, says the report, prayed that she might make the wise choice and then asked the parents to call her once again. When they did, she went to the father's side. Accordingly her guardianship was given to him because, presumably, she would be much better off under the direct care of her Muslim father. From that time on the rule has been upheld that the child must follow the religiously better parent, the Muslim father.[108]

This narrative, assuming its authenticity, is nevertheless rather puzzling. Was the Prophet determined to give the father the guardianship of the girl in any case? But if so, why did he wait for the girl's second response? Muslims cannot conceive that the procedure was casuistic or game playing. It is also very unlikely that the Prophet delayed his decision because he was unwilling in principle to grant the mother's request or worried about her personal displeasure. What seems to have been the probable reason is that he wanted to clearly sound out or retest the girl's true inclinations. He could have had no doubt that she would be better off with her Muslim father; but he probably wanted to make certain that her inclinations coincided with his judgment. It is a legitimate question to ask: what would the ruling have been, if the girl had chosen her mother for the second or nth time? To this hypothetical question the answer of the great majority of jurists would probably be this: the girl's guardianship would have been assigned to the father in any case, because she would be best entrusted to the Muslim parent, and her choice would be disregarded on account of her lack of experience. Yet there may be some indication that in all likelihood the girl's guardianship would have been assigned to the mother in accordance with her wish. This is reflected in the legal position of the Hanafī school of law[109] which maintains that the mother, Muslim or otherwise, is more deserving and thus should be given custody of her child. The duration of custody depends, among other things, on the child's sex and particular needs.

This minority position is probably reinforced by the ruling that when divorce or widowhood is involved the children's custody shall be determined solely in terms of their own welfare. The cardinal concern here is to safeguard their interest and promote their well-being. This is the principle upon which all jurists agree. It is on the interpretation of what maximizes the minor's well-being that they disagree. For example, the minor will be placed under the care of its fit mother up to a certain age—seven, puberty, marriage. However, if the mother remarries sooner, some jurists maintain that she is still entitled to the youngster's custody; others assign the child's guardianship to the father; still others would replace it with a fit female relative, e.g., maternal grandmother. These differences of opinion are sometimes minute and hair-splitting, but they all seem to focus on one goal: the safeguarding of the child's well-being.[110] That its well-being is conceived in such different ways could be the reflection of the differences in time, space, and local standards. At any rate, the child's right to care is so inalienable that not even a mother, the closest person to the child, can tamper with it, as the following point indicates. Some jurists argue that, since the mother is the first adult entitled to take charge of the child's nursing and general care, it is *her personal obligation* to discharge this duty, which she cannot relinquish so long as she is fit. Other jurists contend that it is the mother's *right* to take care of the child; if she surrenders this right, the child shall be placed where its own rights are best safeguarded.[111]

Responsibility for and compassion toward the child is a matter of religious importance as well as social concern. Whether the parents are alive or deceased, present or absent, known or unknown, the child is to be provided with optimum care. Whenever there are executors or relatives close enough to be held responsible for the child's welfare, they shall be directed to discharge this duty. But if there is no next of kin, care for the child becomes a joint responsibility of the Muslim community, designated officials and commoners alike.[112]

B. The Child's Duties; the Parents' Rights

1. General Guidelines

The parent-child relationship is structurally complementary. Parent and child in Islām are bound together by mutual obligations and reciprocal arrangements. But the age differential is sometimes so wide that parents have grown physically weak and mentally feeble. This condition is often characterized by impatience, degeneration of energy, heightened sensitivity, and perhaps misjudgment. It may also result in abuses of parental authority or intergenerational estrangement and uneasiness. It was probably with a view to these considerations that Islām has taken cognizance of certain facts and made basic provisions to govern the individual's relationship to his parents.[113]

The fact that parents are advanced in age and are generally believed to be more experienced does not by itself validate their views or certify their standards. Similarly, youth *per se* is not the sole fountain of energy, idealism, or wisdom any more than it is antithetical to these very characteristics. In various contexts the Qur'ān cites instances where the parents were proven wrong in their encounter with their children and also where the children misjudged the positions of their parents.[114]

More significant, perhaps, is the fact that customs, folkways, traditions, or the parents' value systems and standards do not in themselves constitute what is morally good, cognitively true, and aesthetically beautiful. In several statements the Qur'ān strongly reproaches those who stray away from the truth just because it is new, contrary to the familiar, or incompatible with the parents' values.[115] Furthermore, it focalizes the fact that since the individual is directly responsible to God, he must make his religious choice independently of all others including even his parents. His values and responsibilities are his own concern. Whenever "loyalty" or obedience to his parents is likely to alienate him from God, he must side, as it were, with God. For example, if the parents endanger his spiritual welfare or invite him to do wrong things, he is under no obligation to obey them. They are empowered, it is true, to exercise certain rights and they merit compassion, consideration, and mercy. But if they step out of their proper sphere of rights to intrude upon his own or upon those of God, a demarcation line is drawn and must be diligently guarded.[116]

Just as the parents have no right to impose their religious convictions upon their children, these are similarly restrained. Neither are they necessarily obligated to follow the footsteps of the parents unless, of course, they see spiritual gains in doing so. The demarcation line between the rights of God and those of the parents must be guardedly maintained. Basically, however, these two sets of rights are mutually complementary and reinforce one another. They seem to be designed in such a way as to reduce to a minimum the possibility of conflict. This is probably best indicated by the fact that the parental rights come second only to the highest value in Islām, namely faith in God and exclusive worship of Him. The same idea is reiterated in the Prophet's statement that what pleases one's parents is also pleasing to God, and what annoys them likewise annoys Him.[117] Nevertheless conflict does arise, and accommodation may be difficult to obtain. In such situations, the rights of God must be rendered supreme.

2. Iḥsān

One of these rights is to provide the parents with certain basic securities, irrespective even of their religious preferences. Parents may disagree with or differ from their children with respect to religious values and moral standards. But this does not affect the parents' basic rights upon their children, so long as the former do not engage in or contemplate active conflict with the latter. The Qur'ān sums up the whole matter in a master concept called *iḥsān*, which denotes what is right, good, and beautiful. It means in the Islāmic context, among other things, kindness, compassion, charity, reverence, conscientiousness, and sound performance. It is the Muslim's religious duty as well as virtue to show *iḥsān* to his parents, be they Muslims like himself or otherwise. Concrete behavioral manifestations of this Divine Ordinance of *iḥsān* to the parents include active empathy or "role taking," compassionate gratitude, patience, prayer for them even after their demise, honoring their commitments on their behalf when they can no longer do so, sincere counsel, and veneration.[118]

3. Deference

It is also implied in the concept of *iḥsān* that the parents have the right to expect obedience or deference from their children, if only in partial return for their investments and authority. But parents, like any other persons, may not expect such obedience if they demand the wrong or ask for the improper; if they do, disobedience becomes not only justifiable but imperative. Obey or disobey, the children's attitude may not be allowed to become one of indiscriminate submissiveness or irresponsible defiance.[119]

4. Support and Maintenance

An integral part of the children's absolute religious duty is to provide for their parents in case of need and help them to be as comfortable as possible. Jurists disagree on some details and, as usual, their differences at times appear highly complex.[120] However, they agree on several general principles. First, every individual is responsible for his own maintenance and should try to be self-supporting, especially as far as subsistence is concerned. To this rule there is one exception, namely the wife, whose maintenance is the husband's responsibility whether she is poor or wealthy. Secondly, no individual in particular is held responsible for the maintenance of any other individual of a different religion. To this rule also there are some exceptions, namely one's wife, immediate parents, and children. These categories are entitled to maintenance irrespective of their private beliefs. Thirdly, parents are entitled to maintenance by their children when the former are in need and the latter capable of supporting them. Fourthly, a poor man is not responsible for anyone else's support except his wife, parent, and child. In this case, whatever is spent on their maintenance by other relatives or by the Muslim community will be considered a free community service, according to one school of law, or a debt to be paid when possible, according to another. Fifthly, maintenance includes adequate provisions for food, lodging, clothing, and general comfort for the parents and their dependents, even though these may not be directly related to the providing children, who are required, for example, to provide for the father's wife and maid, and to help him to remarry if this is needed for his comfort. The parents' need-level, the children's capacity for support, the constituents of comfort, and other variables shall be determined in accordance with the standards of the time, but with a view to equity, kindness, and moderation—*iḥsān*. Finally, support for poor parents shall be shared by their children equally without regard to the children's sex, according to one interpretation, or in proportion to their shares of inheritance, according to another.[121]

Support for parents was apparently so taken for granted that a certain pioneering savant, al Shaʿbī (d. ca. 105/723), thought it improper to speak of it in terms of legal rulings. It

was built into the religio-moral system of Islām to be kind to
and thoughtful of parents. So much was this natural and internalized that it needed neither coding nor any specific emphasis. But this position was abandoned by the succeeding
jurists who elaborated the intergenerational duties of mutual
support and care. These jurists did not subscribe to al Sha'bī's
interpretation of the child-parent relationship for some interesting sociological reasons. Ibn al Qayyim insightfully observed that al Sha'bī's doctrine was conceived at and practicable
or appropriate for a time when Muslims were highly conscientious, leading a simple life, and freshly infused with religious
enthusiasm. As those conditions changed, there arose a need
to formulate in specific legal terms the duties of children to
parents, as well as other mutual obligations of siblings and
collaterals.[122]

INTRAGENERATIONAL AND MISCELLANEOUS KINSHIP ROLES

A. *Brother-Sister Relationships*

A general review of the relationship between brothers and
sisters in the heart of the Muslim world of both ancient and
modern times reveals some interesting patterns and contrasts.
From the very early days of life in that part of the world, that
relationship was sometimes marked with rivalry, jealousy, and
hostility. Sibling rivalry often involved the parents as favoring
one child, almost invariably the youngest, to other children.
This was further aggravated by the practice of polygyny as well
as other social considerations. For example, there are indications that even among contemporary Middle Easterners sibling rivalry is conscious, deliberate, and contemplated by some
families so that the child may, in Patai's words, "stand up to
its rivals upon becoming an adult." It is also probable that
these families' early ancestors might have felt that "exposure
to competitive stress within the family was the best way
for preparing the sons for life . . . where . . . might meant
right . . ."[123]

However, the sibling relationship, especially between brothers and sisters, was more often than not profoundly
amicable. There are indications that brothers were allies, help-
mates, and reliable supporters of one another. So commonly,
it seems, was this the case that their solidarity, compassion, and
natural fealty became proverbial or set apart as lofty ideals,
whose implementation is both desired and desirable. The
Qur'ān, for example, speaks of the Believers as constituting
one brotherhood and refers to the Muslim individual as the
brother of every other Muslim. This appears to suggest that
brotherhood must have meant a strong bond, an appealing
sentiment, a familiar rallying cry, and above all a special relationship. The Qur'ān was calling upon these people to interact with one another as brothers. Unless brotherhood had actually meant something particular to these people and their
ancestors, the Qur'ān's call would have fallen upon deaf ears.[124]
Moreover, there is literary evidence that in pre-Islāmic times,
brothers (a) loved their sisters and their sisters' children,
(b) shared their wealth with their sisters, (c) married experienced, older widows and divorced women in preference
to young maidens because the former could take better care
of their husbands' sisters, (d) heeded the sisters' counsel and
sometimes implemented it, and (e) protected their sisters and
respected their wishes. On their part, sisters reciprocated and
often favored their brothers over their own husbands; blood
bonds were deemed stronger than marital obligations.[125]
    In the Islāmic context, however, brothers' relationships were
reorganized either to take new dimensions or to discontinue
old ones. The very concept of brotherhood was broadened to
include the entire body of the Believers. Brotherhood in faith
transcended brotherhood in blood, although it did not necessarily replace it completely. The principle of ihsān, with all its
denotations, was to be implemented in and applied to the
brothers' relationships. But in spite of the enjoined compassion
and mutual support, every individual brother or sister is still
held independently responsible for his or her deeds and directly
accountable to God. Whenever there is an irreconcilable con-

flict between one's relationship to God and the demands of consanguineal brotherhood, one's spiritual welfare comes first in priority.[126]

Blood brothers and sisters share their "gains" and "losses" collectively. When they inherit from a deceased relative, e.g., a parent, they share the assets together. Likewise, when they are enjoined to support a needy deserving relative, the responsibility is shouldered by them together. The distribution of such gains and responsibilities is agreed upon by jurists in principle, although some differentiate between the sexes, doubling the male's share of both gains and liabilities.[127]

With reference to the mutual obligations of brothers and sisters, there is a general agreement that this intra-generational relationship must be governed by kindness, love, equity, and all that is denoted in the concept of *iḥsān*. This is what the statements of the Qur'ān and the sayings of the Prophet command. But jurists disagree as to the specific application of *iḥsān* in this connection. Some schools take it to mean primarily specific, fixed responsibilities for brothers and sisters as far as their maintenance needs are concerned. It is the re- ligio-moral duty of the Muslim to support his needy brother or sister adequately. Failure to discharge this kinship duty is not only indicative of ingratitude and disrespect for blood ties, but also punishable here and now as well as on the Day of Judgment. Other schools interpret *iḥsān* among brothers and sisters to mean a general sentiment of compassion and consideration that does not necessarily amount to any specific compulsory pattern of aid and, above all, does not involve recourse to liti- gation. Needy individuals accordingly, are the collective re- sponsibility of the whole community, not only of their blood brothers and sisters.[128]

B. *Miscellaneous Kinship Roles*

Here we must briefly consider the general relationships of relatives other than the individual's parents, children, brothers, and sisters. These relatives include intra- as well as inter-generational agnates, cognates, and collaterals. In these

miscellaneous categories certain basic principles apply, just
as they do in the case of intergenerational structures. The
Muslim is commanded to be kind to his relatives of whatever degree. They are bound together by kinship bonds since
they are supporters and heirs of one another. Their relationships should be guided by the same general principle of *ihsān*.
But affinity or kinship considerations may not be allowed to
become so excessive as to cause injustice or deviation from
the "path of God." [129]

On these guidelines jurists agree. But it is a different matter
when they consider their application through fixed patterns of
aid, i.e., maintenance in case of need. Some jurists hold that
relatives in these categories are not, strictly speaking, responsible for one another's maintenance; what is obligatory is only
some kind of general concern for each other's welfare. The rest
is the collective responsibility of the Muslim community as a
whole. Other jurists interpret the statements of the Qur'ān and
the Traditions in this regard as clearly meaning the mutual
obligations of fixed maintenance. But the criterion of enforc-
ing this specific rule varies. According to the Hanbalī school of
law, it is the right of mutual inheritance which determines who,
among relatives, is responsible for whose maintenance in case
of need. Relatives who are potential heirs of one another, e.g.,
cousins, are legally responsible for one another's maintenance.
If A is in need and A's cousin B is the closest relative with adequate means, then B must support A because B would be the
natural heir if A were to leave any property, and also because
A would have to do the same for B if the situation were re-
versed. This is in conformity with the rule: gains compensate
for losses and are proportionate thereto. The Hanafī school of
law, on the other hand, maintains that the criterion, in addition
to or even in lieu of inheritance, is the *mahramiyyah* relationship i.e., the special kind of relationship that includes relatives
to any of whom one's marriage is unlawful or incestuous. For
example, it is forbidden to marry one's paternal or maternal
aunts and nieces. An affinity that is so close is strong enough to

be a basis for the mutual obligation of maintenance whether or not there is any potential right of inheritance.[130]

C. *Family Planning; Birth Control*

Before this discussion is brought to an end, some further important aspects of the family life are noteworthy. These relate to abortion and the use of contraceptives, both of which may be grouped under the concept of family planning or birth control. The problem has aroused very keen interest among the contemporary students of the family as well as "social engineers" who are concerned about the "population explosion." This is a relatively modern phenomenon which has arisen as a result of several interrelated factors. However, classical Muslim scholars addressed themselves to the problem of abortion and contraception for what appears to have been personal, private, or academic reasons rather than demographic or population crises. Their primary concern was with the lawfulness or unlawfulness of these practices.

In response to certain pressing questions by some concerned Muslims, a prominent contemporary authority has summarized the classical religious doctrine in the following way. First, it is unanimously agreed that abortion after the "quickening of the embryo" is religiously forbidden and legally punishable; if the fetus emerges alive, the offender shall pay a full bloodwit; otherwise, a lesser fine is imposed. In either case, the act is displeasing to God, and the offender will be subject to punishment in the future life. The quickening of the embryo is definitely established by the end of the fourth month after conception. Secondly, if it becomes certain that abortion is the only way to save the life of an endangered mother, then abortion is lawful, according to the general rule of recourse to the "lesser evil." But, thirdly, jurists disagree with respect to abortion during the first four months of conception. Some hold it lawful on the ground that it entails no destruction of any real human life, since quickening of the embryo is ascertained only after four months. Others forbid it because it is still a destruction of life in some form, a killing of what is a potential self.[131]

With respect to family planning, the statement continues, a distinction must be made between the policy of *limiting* reproduction and the policy of *planning* it, that is, between societal compulsory laws and individual voluntary measures. Limiting reproduction by way of making compulsory indiscriminate legislations to limit procreation to an absolute minimum or maximum is contrary to the law of God, nature, and human reason. But family planning by way of voluntary, individual measures to space or regulate the family size for economic or health reasons is lawful. It is contrary neither to the law of God nor to nature. In fact, Islāmic law seems to urge this kind of family planning. First, the Qur'ān extends the lactation-nursing period up to two full years. But the Prophet warned against suckling the child by its pregnant mother. The two facts together appear to call for some checks on unregulated conception and indirectly require the use of some measures of contraception. Secondly, jurists agree that it is lawful for married people to prevent conception, by mutual consent, temporarily or permanently, if the prospective children are likely to be disposed to any hereditary disease of any parent.[132]

It may be interesting to note that this position is not unanimously adopted by contemporary Muslim scholars. Nor is the use of contraceptives a general practice. However, there seems to be a slow but growing acceptance of both the doctrine and the modern practice among Muslims of all walks of life. The reasons for this change are many and varied. The religious doctrine itself is being reinterpreted by some and revived by others. In recent decades, certain religious authorities hesitated to recommend family planning as a general public policy, even though they themselves made use of it privately. What was quietly practiced is now advocated publicly on a large scale. Economic and political pressures are increasingly felt. The international concern over the population explosion is brought closer to the attention of many Muslim leaders and commoners alike. Central political directives and governmental regulations are reaching the masses in a relatively more systematic and persistent way. The declining occurrence of epidemic diseases seems to have introduced new elements into population growth. Some of the traditional pro-natality factors are becoming less focal in Muslim life.

However, it seems somewhat paradoxical that Muslims, whose religion is not opposed in principle to family planning— as we have seen—are among the peoples with the highest birth rates. Kirk has recently observed that among contemporary Muslims "natality (1) is almost universally high, (2) shows no evidence of important trends over time, and (3) is generally higher than that of neighboring peoples of other major religions." [133] Islām's ideologically neutral or even somewhat favorable attitude to family planning seems to have been overweighed by what Kirk calls "general factors" and "special Muslim features" favoring high birth rates. The basic general factors are the following: (a) Sons are valued for many purposes; (b) Islām shares with other religions the injunction to marry and multiply, (c) Islām has a strong tradition of military conquest and cultural domination; (d) Islām has a history of conflict with and resistance to the West, with which Muslims identify the techniques and philosophy of birth control and family planning; (e) Muslims share with other religions some important fatalistic themes, e.g., God's care, provision, natural birth, etc. Under the special features he includes the following: (a) marriage institutions with polygyny, easy divorce, and early marriages, (b) emphasis on sexuality and opposition to celibacy, and (c) women's inferior position, in which they marry young, are illiterate, and have no voice in family affairs. These three factors affect natality through the proportion of the reproductive life spent in marital unions, and within such unions the practices determining exposure to pregnancy.[134]

While these observations may be generally accurate and valid, they seem to draw from the historical traditional patterns rather than from the contemporary scene. It may be true that many Muslims still live in the past and cling to such traditional patterns. It may also be true that some of them suspect the modern techniques of contraception as products of the "infidel pagan West." But the greatest difficulty of Muslims in this regard seems to be ignorance or unawareness. There are many who are not conscious of any national or international population problems, or who are unaware of any modern techniques of contraception, or who do not know how to obtain them, much less to apply them effectively. Likewise, there are those who do not know where religion stands on the matter. In fact, all this may be inferred from Kirk's presentation of the religious doctrine approving birth control and from his concluding summary that "the traditional Islāmic way of life is culturally favorable to high natality in the absence of voluntary restriction of births within marriage." [135]

D. *Recapitulation*

To conclude this discussion, some recapitulatory remarks may be helpful. First, all schools of law agree (a) that kindness (*iḥsān*) to kindred of whatever degree of relatedness is imperative, (b) that kinship considerations should not be allowed to curb the individual's spiritual maturation or delay his moral growth, and (c) that every individual is directly responsible to God and personally accountable for his own deeds. Secondly it is the incontestable duty of the Muslim to provide adequately for his wife, rich or poor, and for his needy parents as well as children regardless of their particular religious views. Thirdly, with the exception of the Mālikī school, jurists agree that (a) grandparents, great grandparents, and so forth up are entitled to the same rights and charged with the same duties as the immediate parents, and (b) grandchildren, great grandchildren, and so forth down have the same rights and duties as immediate children. Fourthly, both the Hanafī and Hanbalī schools, though using different criteria, extend the sphere of fixed mutual obligations, e.g., maintenance, beyond the limits of vertical descent. That is, they hold the individual responsible for the support of certain relatives even though they may not be his parents, grandparents, etc., or his children, grandchildren, etc. Finally, all schools derive their doctrines from the same basic source of law; but the Hanafī and Hanbalī schools are regarded more kinship orientated than the Shāfi'ī which, in turn, is more so than the Mālikī school.

It may be interesting to attempt a sociological explanation of these various interpretations of the law with regard to the set limits of kindred obligations. The positions of the Shāfi'ī and Mālikī schools are very similiar, almost identical. Mālik flourished in al Madīnah, and his thought was very much influenced by local conditions. al Shāfi'ī also was influenced by Mālik and shared with him a certain "Arabian" outlook. It may be convenient therefore to designate their view as the *central* position of al Madīnah-Makkah region. On the other hand, the Hanafī and Hanbali doctrines are also quite close. They developed and flourished in what is now the Syrio-Iraqi region, and hence may be designated as the *northern* position. These designations, however, do not coincide with the familiar characterizations of these schools as traditionalist, rationalist, or literalist.[136]

In contrast to their counterparts in the north, the Muslim communities of central Arabia at Makkah and al Madīnah were relatively simpler in social organization, more homogeneous in population, closer in time and space to tribalism, and farther from the seats of political conflict. Moreover, in these communities Islām "replaced" a social system based primarily on tribal solidarity and established its own bonds of religious brotherhood. Before Islām, interdependence of the immediate family members of central Arabia was probably minimal, since there was always the clan or tribe to act on behalf of its members to meet their needs or allocate their responsibilities. With the advent of Islām, these people were already familiar with collective, communal, or tribal solidarity and interdependence. When Islām called for a total community involvement or reciprocity among the Believers, the idea itself was not probably so new to them is was its *raison d'être*, which in this case was religion and not kinship. Thus the external manifestations of the kinship structure were very likely the same as before Islām;

only their philosophy, their foundation, took on the new Islāmic coloring. Jurists living under these conditions would be probably inclined to keep to a minimum the interdependence of the immediate family members, to maximize or reinforce the collective communal solidarity. This is what Mālik and al S̲h̲afi‘ī apparently did. Unlike their colleagues in the north, they placed much of the kinship responsibility on the community as a whole and limited the individual's set obligations to the most immediate nuclear family members. Any other obligation will be met by him as a member of the community and not of a particular family or kinship unit. This is also true of the Sh̲ī‘īs who compel no one in particular to provide for relatives outside the nuclear family, but consider provisions for such relatives a community duty. Their sense of community solidarity and closeness, like that of the Mālikīs and S̲h̲afi‘īs, made them involve the community as a whole in the vital concerns of the family. This central position therefore took the whole community as a social unit, whereas the social unit for the northern position was the family in its extended form.[137]

A. *An Overview*

As a human historical phenomenon family dissolution or marriage termination is, like marriage contraction, pervasive, persistent, and variegated. In Pitt's words, "every society has structural means for ending a marriage which cannot fulfill its function . . ." [1] Yet as some other contemporaries have summarily put it, "in virtually every society divorce is subject to some social disapproval." [2] These observations apply to human society in general, irrespective of time, place, or level of civilization. There are probably as many reasons for marriage dissolution as there are for marriage contraction. These reasons spread over a very wide range, stretching from the unavoidable death of a spouse or involuntary barrenness to the trivial cooking mistake of burning the husband's food or putting too much salt in it, not to mention the man's arbitrary dislike of his spouse or capricious preference for another woman who seems more pleasing to him.[3]

Voluntary dissolution of the family through divorce or similar procedures appears so "natural" or inevitable that almost every normative system, past or present, has made some specific provisions for it. A system that is not adequately responsive in this regard will not prevent the dissolution of the family. Rather, it most likely will be either ignored, abused, modified, or defied. When there is a lack of correspondence between the normative law of the books and the law in action, people engulfed in family crises may be compelled to bypass the written law or commit perjury and enter into collusion in order to obtain a release. Frequently, "spouses seek a divorce because they find it very difficult to continue living with each other, and not, or not primarily, because of any gross wrong-doing on the part of either spouse." [4] Perjury and collusion may become implicitly recognized and even socially sanctioned as devices for terminating a marriage at least *de facto* if not *de jure*. When a code of norms prohibits or severely restricts (a) the absolute divorce, the parties involved can, and they do, resort to (b) the limited divorce, which accords legal recognition to the separate households, but denies the principals the opportunity for legal remarriage, or to (c) the annulment which asserts that, owing to some condition existing at the time of contraction, no valid marriage could have been concluded and therefore the parties are free to marry.[5] The method of annulment has been widely used, especially by Christians of former centuries. Except for a few, the early Church Fathers condemned absolute divorce. But, as Bardis put it, "despite the Church's opposition, a special form of divorce became quite common during the Middle Ages. This was the dissolution of marriage by asserting that a previous clandestine union had been contracted."[6] The rules covering that special form of divorce were, in Lord Bryce's words, "so numerous and so intricate that it was easy, given a sufficient motive, whether political or pecuniary, to discover some ground for declaring almost any marriage invalid."[7]

B. *Islām and Marriage Dissolution; Divorce*

Although marriage dissolution through divorce is universal and hence inevitable in principle, the frequency of its occurrence, the reasons for it, and the reactions thereto vary in time and space. In the region where Islām was first preached, marriage dissolution was practiced by the people among whom early Muslims grew up and with whom they made external contacts. Jews, Christians, Arab pagans, and Persian Zoroastrians more or less resorted to the practice, with either the explicit, the implicit, or the mutilated sanction of their respective system.[8] With regard to Hebrew law, in particular, a remark has been made which applies in a general way to the case of Islām. According to Driver, "Hebrew law . . . does not institute divorce, but tolerates it, in view of the imperfections of human nature (. . . Mt. 19:8), and lays down regulations tending to limit it and preclude its abuse."[9]

The phenomenon of marriage dissolution had existed before Islām and has persisted ever since. Indeed, if the contemporary world situation is indicative of any trend, it appears to foretell a continuing increase in divorce rates; the gradual decline in some societies is offset by the continuing rise in others.[10] However, Islām has taken a position between categorical proscription and unqualified liberalization of divorce. It neither instituted the practice nor ignored its reality and occurrence. An outright prohibition would probably remain an "ideal" or merely a state of mind, but hardly a pattern of actual behavior, because absolute self-control is not always attainable. Such a prohibition, then, would seem incompatible with Islāmic ideology which, as a matter of principle, prescribes only what is humanly attainable.[11] On the other hand, any unregulated liberalization of divorce is socially inconceivable and would almost certainly result in chaos, peril, and such traits that are destructive as well as intolerable. Instead of demanding the impossible or catering to the intolerable, Islām adopted a position which has been variously characterized as "lax" and loose by some observers, "rigid" and inflexible, or moderate and perfect by others.

Such characterizations, however, seem to be oversimplifications. Divorce or repudiation in Islām is distributed along a continuum encompassing all the religio-legal categories from the one extreme of prescription through the other of proscription. It is obligatory, e.g., where there is no conceivable way of reconciliation or hope for peace between the parties. It is highly recommended or nearly obligatory if the wife is unfaithful or defiantly inattentive to her religious duties. It is forbidden legally and/or religiously during the wife's monthly course and also during the interim in which an intercourse has taken place. It is strongly undesirable or nearly forbidden where there is no good reason for it, because it would be harmful and Muslims are forbidden by their religion to initiate harm or inflict injury upon one another. Finally, it is lawful when there is a valid ground for it, like recurrent inconsiderateness or failure to realize the objectives of marriage. Even then, it is designated by the Prophet as the most repugnant, in the sight of God, of all lawful things; it is an act which shakes the throne of God as it were.[12]

The permissibility of divorce in Islām is thus only one of several religio-legal categories and represents an alternative course of action, which is admissible in response to certain basic human needs. But beyond this general response, there are some peculiar factors bearing on the position of Islām. One of these is that, in Islām, things as such *are* lawful in principle. They *become* forbidden or undesirable, obligatory or commendable according to other elements of the situation. Another factor is that the marriage contract in Islām is neither a civil act nor a sacramental vow, but a synthesis of both. Its dissolution therefore is admissible; it is not unrestricted like some civil liberties, and it is not indissoluble like some sacramental vows. Finally, Islām has been characterized as the religion of the middle but straight and well-balanced course.[13]

Marriage dissolution through divorce or repudiation is recognized as both real and lawful in principle, however undesirable or repugnant. This recognition has elicited different reactions from different scholars. For some, divorce in Islām is a mechanism of discipline and compassion, a necessary and sensible corollary of the freedom given to men and women to choose their marital partners.[14] For others, Islām's position has been an object of strong and varied criticisms. In Jeffery's representative words, "The lightness with which the marriage tie was regarded in early Arabia has carried over into Islām, as evidenced by the facility with which a man may divorce his *wives* and by the high frequency of divorce which has *always* characterized Muslim society. The Qur'ān grants man *complete liberty* of divorce and demands of him *no justification* for divorcing his wife. Thus he can divorce her at his own caprice, but no such facility exists for her." [15]

Criticisms have also been voiced with concern by some Muslims, who unlike their Western colleagues, usually hasten to point out the perfection of the revealed law and attribute any abuse thereof to the individual's negligence or lack of integrity. As far back as the second decade of Islām, the first half of the seventh century C.E., some people began to misuse their right of divorce. Until then, it had been accepted that if a man told his wife that she was "divorced thrice" the word thrice counted only as one revocable divorce. When some people used this thrice formula carelessly, 'Umar, the Second Caliph, reacted with indignation. He consulted with his companions and it was decided to consider such a formula as a triple irrevocable divorce. The interesting fact here is that this new provision was conceived as a punitive measure to discipline the divorcing men and protect the divorced women.[16] A few centuries later, Ibn Taymiyyah observed that many people were using divorce formulas like ordinary casual forms of oath. But he realized that the breaking of an oath was easily expiable by feeding or clothing ten poor people or by freeing a slave, whereas the breaking of a "divorce oath" meant the breaking of a marriage and a home. So he ruled that such divorce oaths were void and inconsequential as far as the marriage bond was concerned. He also opposed the earlier decision of 'Umar and other leading schools of law with respect to the "thrice formula," counting it as one revocable divorce, not three. What 'Umar had considered disciplinary measures against irresponsible men turned out, with the change of time and conditions, to be harmful to innocent women. Ibn Taymiyyah sought, by his rulings, to redress this situation.[17]

Taken as a sociological index, such considerations seem to indicate (1) that Islāmic law regards both marriage and divorce as highly sensitive and consequential matters; (2) that people's reactions do not always correspond with the intent or spirit of the law; (3) that, in the early centuries of Islāmic history, the simplicity of divorce was thought of as more harmful to men than women; but (4) that recent centuries have witnessed a general reversal of the effects of divorce.

As many Muslims fail in their behavior to meet the moral expectations of their religion, so do some critics appear to fall short of a full appreciation of the logic of social legislation in Islām. It may be difficult for Muslim scholars to comprehend the scientific basis of such assertions as those made by Jeffery, Levy, or Roberts about what they have called the incredible simplicity or unjustifiable facility of divorce in Islām. It seems simplistic to attribute to Muslims, as Roberts does,[18] a greater need for, and a higher frequency of, divorce because of the separation of the sexes and the women's wearing of the veil. The mixing of the sexes, even in modern enlightened times, and the discontinuity of the veil have neither prevented nor curtailed the frequency of divorce. If anything, they seem to have increased its frequency. On the other hand, the wearing of the veil over the face has little or nothing to do with Islām.[19] Besides, it is strongly recommended by the Prophet that prospective marital partners should be enabled to know each other well enough to build their future relations on love and compassion but, of course, without undue familiarity, indulgence, exploitation, or illicit experimentation.[20] Moreover, the fact that women have had less freedom to divorce their husbands does not necessarily mean that it has led to an increase in divorce rates. Rather, it may be one of the effective restrictions on divorce, for it has been observed that, at least in Western societies, the long-run trend in divorce rates is upward and, partly, the increase "is tied to the *emancipation* and the *equalitarian* status of women . . ." [21]

C. *Dimensions of Divorce in Islām*

To understand divorce in Islām as most Muslims do or believe it should be understood, it is necessary to go beyond the face value of such simplistic misconceptions whether they originate with certain disoriented Muslims or mistaken outsiders. The problem must be examined in the full context of the family structure, the religious precepts, the human situation, and the historical circumstances. This will be our point of departure in the analysis of the various aspects of the problem.

1. *A Misleading Analogy*

Divorce, the universally unavoidable phenomenon, which has been called by the Prophet of Islām the most repugnant of all things lawful and the act for which God's throne shakes, as it were, will not ordinarily be taken lightly. Only those who are contented with superficial forms or simplistic analogies will probably so take it. Divorce in Islām may appear unbelievably easy to one who compares the early simple forms of contraction in Islām with the modern complex bureaucratic procedures, or who mistakes the ideal for the actual, or who makes a "cross cultural" analogy but between the *professed moral values of one system* and the *behavioral practices of another*. At any rate, divorce may have been relatively easy and simple, but so was marriage as well as revocation of divorce itself. Within a certain time limit, i.e., "a waiting period," a divorce could be revoked by saying or doing, initiating or reciprocating, anything indicative of a desire for reconciliation such as a gesture of love, a look of compassion, an expression of regret, or a direct revocation.[22]

2. *Divorce as a Moral Act*

Divorce, like marriage, is more than a simple legal bill. It is couched in a context of moral and human principles of a high order. Islām commands marital partners to consort with each other in kindness or to part with kindness. It calls upon them to do everything within their power to maximize the probability of marital success and to minimize the inconveniences of marriage dissolution. Outsiders are forbidden to do anything that may reduce this probability or harden reconciliation and sympathy. It warns against any hasty judgment, enjoins kindness and understanding, and reminds one of how it is possible to dislike something in which God may have placed much good. It assures the parties that if they mean well God will help them to achieve accord; but if they must part, and they separate in good faith without intent of injury or harm, God will enrich them out of His all-reaching bounty. Finally, it portrays the action situation as a stage closely watched by and expectedly oriented to God, whose omnipresence is an essential element of the situation. The actors are assumed to be conscientious and rational. The Qur'ānic statements dealing with divorce begin and conclude with strong moral exhortations. The whole question of divorce is enveloped in emphatic moral teachings and thus seems to be regarded primarily as a moral act.[23]

3. *The Grounds of Divorce*

The fact that Islām requires no publicity of the grounds of divorce does not necessarily mean that it views divorce lightly. Such grounds are probably entrusted to the individual's conscience; publicity thereof may not be of any great positive consequence. They can be unspoken, unpronounced, but genuine; they can be pronounced and accepted, but actually false. Perjury and collusion cannot be ruled out completely. In Islām, however, with God being a necessary element in the definition of the action situation, the Qur'ān seems to assume that the normal Muslim, man or woman, in most cases and most of the time will act responsibly, conscientiously, and God-mindedly. It assumes, further, that with dutiful authorities, sensitive publics, and sound characters divorce will be used as the very last resort. It is highly unlikely that rational, conscientious individuals will lightly take the separation from their loved or loveable ones, the breaking of their homes, and the inconveniences of divorce (which will be discussed later in this chapter). Man, whose behavior is taken by social science to be oriented to need gratification, will not ordinarily resort to this difficult course of action without some serious reasons. Moreover, as some contemporary Muslim scholars have remarked, disclosing the specific grounds of divorce is no more incumbent upon the wife than the husband where she is the party to seek a divorce.[24] Furthermore, if disputants were required by law to disclose their specific reasons for divorce, they might sometimes feel compelled to commit perjury, enter into collusion, engage in recrimination, reveal embarrassing or harmful facts, and possibly endanger the family institution. Insistence on disclosing the grounds of divorce is unlikely by itself to prevent the irreconcilable, determined parties from somehow terminating their marriages. Also it may well hinder their subsequent rehabilitation and lessen their chances of remarriage. It is probably because of these reasons, and not for the lack of grounds of or insensitivity to divorce, that Islām did not make crucial the publicity of the divorce grounds. As a contemporary scholar has noted, in marriage and divorce motives may be very personal or psychological and therefore difficult to evaluate. If there is evidence of abuse in this respect, the proper authorities must annul the action and redress any attendant harm.[25]

While Islām takes for granted the continuity and permanence of marriage,[26] it does not entirely exclude the other possibility. People's hearts and minds change in different ways for different reasons. The change may be so unavoidable and profound as to lead to estrangement or alienation among the parties involved and thus defeat the purpose of marriage or cause anxiety. It is here in this context that the Qur'ān alludes to the general grounds of divorce. It declares that if the parties fear that they will not be able to observe God's limits or implement His law of marriage, then a divorce may be negotiated.[27] When they must part for good reasons, not only will they be free from guilt, in the sight of God, but also they will be enriched out of the encompassing bounty of God.[28] The general ground of divorce in the Qur'ān is therefore the hopeless failure of one or both parties to discharge their marital duties and to consort with each other in kindness, peace, and compassion. Although this is a question which rests ultimately within the individual's sense of morality and relationship to God, jurists have developed indices of that failure and specified the major situations which may be accepted in litigation as grounds for a divorce or annulment. Some of these relate to the husband alone; some to either party or to both.

Apart from the differences concerning the detailed technicalities, jurists agree in principle that certain situations peculiar to the husband's position justify the wife's request for a divorce and the implementation of that request. Long absence without knowing the whereabouts of the husband, long imprisonment, capture by war enemies, refusal to provide for the wife, severe poverty, and impotence are the major circumstances under any of which a wife may, if she so desires, seek a legal release from her marriage bond by way of divorce or annulment, depending on the particular situation. There is another set of circumstances which may involve either party. These are: desertion, serious chronical diseases, insanity, deceptive misrepresentation at the conclusion of the marriage contract, incongruity, mistreatment, and debauchery or moral laxity. If one party is involved in any of these situations, the other may justifiably seek a divorce or annulment. There are also circumstances which necessitate the dissolution of marriage. Some of these are (a) the wife's acceptance of Islām when her husband remains a non-Muslim, (b) apostasy of a Muslim party, particularly the husband, and (c) established invalidity of the initial marriage contract.[29]

It is interesting to note, first, that the wife has more grounds for seeking a divorce and is accorded a greater justification than the husband. Perhaps this is a reflection of the religious dictum that women are entrusted by God to men and therefore should be treated with kindness. Also it may be due to the fact that a man with unfulfilled needs may resort to the alternative of polygyny, if he must, but she cannot do the same. He could maintain a "defective," indisposed or impotent wife without running great moral or financial risks. In fact, attending to such a wife is a charitable virtuous deed. Secondly, when one or both parties are entitled to take the course of divorce, it does not necessarily mean that they must or will definitely use it. Divorce is the very last resort, and if it must take place, the parties are enjoined to be charitable and kind to each other as if the marriage bond were still intact.[30]

4. The Timing of Divorce and the Preceding Steps

The timing, the preceding steps, and the consequences of divorce, as well as other related factors, already or to be considered, all seem to represent checking points and impose certain limitations on divorce. To begin with, before a divorce takes place as a final legal action, several conditions must obtain.

a. The husband who wishes to initiate a divorce must be of age and capable of "discrimination," a state usually measured by reaching the age of puberty.

b. He must be sane, conscious, alert, and free from excessive anger. If he acts while under the influence of intoxication, his divorce pronouncement is void, according to some jurists; valid according to others, provided the intoxicant is of the prohibited kinds and is used voluntarily. Parenthetically, validation of a divorce pronouncement by an intoxicated, jesting, or thoughtless man is probably intended to discipline the man and awaken him to the seriousness of his action, something perhaps similar to what 'Umar did with people who took the divorce formula lightly.

c. He must be free from external pressure. If he is forced to divorce his wife against his will and he, under pressure, so pronounces her, the pronouncement is void, according to all schools of law except the Hanafī, whose position in this respect is regarded by other jurists to be clearly incompatible with the statements of the Prophet.

d. There must be a clear intention on his part to terminate the marriage. Some schools, however, accept as valid the divorce pronouncements of a jesting and thoughtless or forgetful husband.

e. Finally, if a divorce is to take place according to the Prophet's Sunnah, i.e., instructions, the wife must be of age and in a state of "fresh purity." That is, she must be fully recovered from the menses of the regular menstruation and the usual postnatal fluxes, whose maximum time spans are about ten and forty days respectively. In addition, she must not have had an intercourse at any time during this period of fresh purity, which covers the whole interim between the monthly courses. If she is experiencing her period or the postnatal flux, or if there has been an intercourse after recovery and purity therefrom, the wife's state is considered impure and there can be no Sunnah divorce. Under these circumstances, a divorce pronouncement is both religiously forbidden and legally void according to the Shī'ī and Zāhirī schools of law. Other jurists regard it religiously forbidden but legally valid. This difference of opinion is merely formal, for all jurists insist that the man should repeal his pronouncement and keep his wife until she has had a monthly period. After that, she enters a state of fresh purity, completes it without any intercourse and goes through a second monthly period to a second state of purity. At this stage, if no change of heart or mind has taken place, a divorce may be pronounced.[31]

This so-called Sunnah divorce requires the wife to be in a state of fresh purity for the following reasons. First, menstruation is called by the Qur'ān "hurt"; its term is a difficult time of fatigue, depression, irritability, tension, etc. Much of this is due to the wife's physical condition, which makes her sexually both undesirous and undesirable, and also to the husband's unfulfilled needs. Intercourse is forbidden during all such times of impurity. All these factors may lead some parties to act hastily or misjudge each other. It is required therefore that they wait for these periodical difficulties to pass and then act, if they must, under normal conditions. Secondly, when the wife enters her period of purity, she is usually fresh and pleasantly companionable, both desirous and desirable, more considerate and responsive. She has not only the capacity, but also the opportunity to strengthen the marriage tie and command the husband's love, compassion, and devotion. If, in spite of this, there is a desire to dissolve the marriage it will be, presumably, for some serious reasons other than a passing fatigue, momentary depression, or casual unfulfillment. A divorce contemplated under these congenial circumstances is unlikely to be rash, thoughtless, or irresponsible.[32]

Among the factors bearing significantly upon divorce is the light in which Islām views the contraction and dissolution of marriage. Although, as previously shown, marriage is neither a civil act nor a sacramental vow, the Qur'ān defines it as a solemn covenant, a God-given blessing, and a means of love and compassion. To maximize the probability of continued marital happiness, without unnecessarily hardening the lot of the marriageables, Islām gave unequivocal preference to piety and integrity as the most commendable criteria of mate selection. It also made the binding ordinance of kindness and compassion the supreme moral principle of marital relations. But since man falls short of complete control over the self and the environment, failures occur and shortcomings upset the marital unison, if only as exceptions to the rules. In response to such circumstances, Islām allows the grieved parties to seek a release from their unfulfilled and perhaps unfulfillable covenant of marriage. Under normal conditions, in a properly concluded and properly maintained marriage, estrangement is unlikely. But if it develops, as it sometimes does, it will be probably only symptomatic of far more serious failures which should be recognized and redressed. Divorce, however repugnant and loathsome in the sight of God, is one prescription which may be administered as the very last resort. It appears, therefore, that the Islāmic definition of marriage and divorce was probably conceived as a moral check on the dissolution of marriage.[33]

Divorce in Islām is designated as the very last and the most detestable recourse. Before the breaking-point is reached, certain phases in the marital cycle must pass. First, as soon as the marriage is concluded, the partners are enjoined to do their utmost to implement the teachings of Islām, so as to render their married life an abode of bliss and compassion. If this level of harmony is not attained because of some conflict, attention should be paid to the source of conflict. Secondly, should conflict, overt or covert, originate with the wife, the husband is directed to consider the whole situation carefully, to search his own soul, to judge his wife as a *total* person, to act patiently, responsibly, and charitably. Thirdly, if the conflict becomes chronical and the husband fears the wife's defiant recalcitrance, he is instructed to follow a phased disciplinary course of three steps. He should allow sufficient time intervals and move from one step to the next only after having tried in earnest the previous one and found it of no avail. This disciplinary course has three phases: (i) kind exhortation, (ii) temporary abandonment in bed or deliberate abstinence from the usual sexual intimacy, and (iii) symbolic beating without inflicting any physical harm or injury.

Fourthly, in case recalcitrance and conflict persist, the husband may yet consider a severer course of abstention more indicative of his displeasure. This is the course of 'īlā' (vow of continence), which means that he may take an oath by God to abstain completely from intercourse with his wife. This was a pre-Islāmic practice of indefinite suspense, and it may be likened to the contemporary form of "legal suspensive separation." In Islām, however, after taking the oath of 'īlā', the husband is allowed a maximum period of four months to reconsider the situation and make up his mind. If there has been an improvement sufficient to encourage him to resume his full marital status, a reunion is highly commendable, and the parties are God-forgiven. Otherwise, if the period expires without any significant change, a divorce will be acceptable to God.

Fifthly, if the conflict originates with the husband and the wife fears his cruelty, desertion, or aversion, it is their joint obligation to settle their differences together for, as the relevant Qur'ānic statement has put it, "peace is best." She may try in her own way to make peace, and he should respond to her initiative. The two together must cooperate to solve their internal problems between themselves.

Sixthly, should these private measures, alternatives, and remedies fail to bring about a viable harmony, one final detour must be taken before the breaking-point of divorce. A family council of two arbitrators representing both sides shall be selected to look into the situation with a view to settling the dispute. If they see any possibility of reconciliation and so recommend, it should be attempted. But if they recommend a divorce as the only solution after the failure of arbitration, then a divorce may be entered into, unless the principals choose otherwise.

Finally, if a divorce is to be pronounced in accordance with the Sunnah, all the other necessary conditions enumerated at the opening of this section must be fulfilled.[34]

D. The "How" and the Types of Divorce

1. The Sunnah Divorce and Its Variants

Divorce can be classified in various ways along several dimensions. One of these classifications is the Sunnah and the contra-Sunnah divorce. The former has three basic variants.

a. The Simple Revocable Divorce

When it becomes clearly evident, after the exhaustion of all the other peaceful means of reconciliation, that divorce is the only recourse left, this should be concluded according to the Sunnah. That is, if eligible, the man will pronounce his freshly pure wife divorced, using specific terms, before two qualified witnesses, and in a *simple revocable divorce*. What follows this kind of divorce is as significant as the preceding and concomitant conditions. This form of divorce does not terminate the marriage completely, much less does it necessarily entail any resentment or unkindness. The man is unequivocally obliged, among other things, to keep the woman in the same home or at least furnish her with a comfortable residence, which will be easily accessible to him. She may not be evicted from her home nor should she leave it, unless she has committed a manifest offense of indecency. Moreover, he must provide for her adequately as if no divorce had taken place. These particular obligations continue through the probationary "waiting period," which usually lasts for about three months, except if the wife is pregnant. In this case, the waiting period expires with the termination of the pregnancy. If pregnant, the woman is forbidden to conceal her condition, because pregnancy may be a good omen for both of them. "Keeping" the woman in this way, under the man's eye and conveniently accessible to him, or discovering her pregnancy may change the situation favorably because, to paraphrase the relevant Qur'ānic passage (65:1), who knows? Perhaps God will bring about thereafter some new congenial situations. If during the probationary period there develops a desire for reconciliation, which is probable in the light of these conditions, it should be fostered. The man may resume his full marital status by simply revoking his previous pronouncement in words or in deeds, e.g., by paying the woman a suggestive compliment, kissing her, etc. To facilitate the reunion, nothing else is required other than this initial revocation. If the probationary period expires without revocation, the divorce becomes ultimate in the sense that she becomes free either to marry anew or reunite with her former husband. But this reunion requires a new marriage contract with all the standard requisites, a stipulation which may deter some rash actions.[35]

b. The Double Revocable Sunnah Divorce

Having made the first pronouncement of divorce, the man may wait for the woman to recover from her very next monthly course and enter into a new state of fresh purity. Then there will be three lawful alternatives, the first two of which have already been mentioned in connection with the simple revocable Sunnah divorce. The three alternatives are (a) revocation, (b) waiting for the probationary period to expire, at which time the divorce becomes ultimately final, and (c) making another pronouncement in the same way as the first and with the same implications of residence, provision, revocability, etc. Should the third alternative of making another pronouncement be chosen this will be the *second revocable Sunnah divorce.*

c. The Triple Irrevocable Sunnah Divorce

Here again, after the second revocable divorce, the same three alternatives with the same implications obtain. If the third alternative be chosen once more, it will be the *triple irrevocable divorce.* At this point, it becomes clear that reconciliation is extremely remote, if not impossible. The thrice-divorced woman, whose final waiting period has expired, is free to marry whomever she wishes. But she is absolutely forbidden to her first husband unless she has remarried in a normally consummated union and, for some valid reasons, become divorced or widowed. Only then may she be lawful again to her first husband through a new full-fledged marriage contract. This is the form of *taḥlīl* or "re-marriage legalization." [36]

The *taḥlīl* form has provoked much condemnation, criticism, and ridicule. Muslim scholars, however, maintain that it gives a warning signal to the parties concerned. The same view is incorporated into Levy's remark that, "The law was probably enacted in the first place as a check upon easy divorce, but (in actual conduct) it runs counter to the general ideas of sexual purity held in Islam." If properly heeded, *taḥlīl* alerts the parties to the fact that, after a third pronouncement of divorce, revocation is impossible, and even a new marriage contract is also forbidden without *taḥlīl*. When a thrice-divorced woman is free to remarry and is seeking peace in earnest, she may find a suitable second mate and settle down for good. There is no ground for holding her responsible for something of which she may be innocent. Nor is there any particular reason to assume that she will remain unmarried. If, however, after its consummation the second marriage stumbles at any time and is broken beyond hope of reconciliation, or if she is widowed, the woman may wish to return to her first spouse. This is permissible provided (a) that the second marriage was not intended only for the purpose of *taḥlīl,* (b) that the second marriage has been dissolved by way of a valid divorce/or widowhood, (c) that the probationary waiting period has expired, and the woman is completely free from hinderances, (d) that the first spouse is still eligible, and (e) that both parties believe that they will observe more closely the bounds of God after their reunion. Whether any person, man or woman, would find these conditions acceptable is, of course, another question. These procedures are clear limitations on the use of divorce and may stand as repulsive prospects. This seems

the case even with the generous assumptions, (a) that a
thrice-divorced woman will easily find a suitable second mate,
who intends to maintain her permanently, but whose marriage somehow stumbles, and (b) that she thereafter will
freely want a reunion with her first spouse, who in turn is
willing to try once more and expects to be successful. It presents a very rare combination of some very unusual circumstances. The situation appears even more restrictive if the
thrice-divorced woman has no great prospects of remarriage
and the man knows that any reunion between the two of
them is forbidden without such a remarriage. This is the
idea of tahlīl as conceived by Islām and as interpreted by
Muslim scholars. Admittedly some parties have abused this
form extensively. What was meant to be a disciplinary check
against the thoughtless rash and a release for the helpless
innocent has become the subject of condemnation, abuse,
and disgust. Sometimes thrice-divorced women are humili-
atingly married off casuistically to invalid or minor persons,
who are forced or bribed to divorce them immediately so that
they will become, by the end of the waiting periods, lawful
once again to their first mates. This is absolutely contrary
to the teachings of Islām and is unanimously condemned. A
marriage which is contracted with the explicit or implicit
stipulation of tahlīl is both religiously forbidden and legally
void, according to the majority of jurists. Other jurists consider the stipulation of tahlīl forbidden and void, but the
marriage itself is valid, and no party may be forced to dissolve it against his or her wish. In other words, it is a perfectly valid and viable marriage, with the normal probability
of continuity like any other marriage contract. Moreover, the
Prophet is reported to have said, "marry and do not divorce,
because divorce shakes God's throne, as it were, . . . and
because God does not like men and women who relish variety
in sexual experience." Again, he declared that, "condemned
by God are the second as well as the first husband." This
condemnation is inflicted both upon the man who marries
a thrice-divorced woman intending only to divorce her in

order to legalize her reunion with her first husband, and upon the man for whom the legalization is intended.[37]

A husband is allowed two revocable divorce pronouncements. The third, if used, will be absolutely irrevocable, unless there has been an *unintended taḥlīl*. However, if the man revokes the first divorce during the waiting period or thereafter through a new contract, the revocation or the new contract makes the parties lawful for each other; but it does not discount the revoked pronouncements. This means that, once made, a pronouncement counts, whether or not it is directly revoked within the waiting period, or followed by a new contracted reunion thereafter. Also, the range of revocability covers only two pronouncements, whether they are made in closely consecutive terms, within the span of the waiting period, or after long marital intervals.

The Sunnah divorce, with its regulations, variants, and maximum limit of three pronouncements, was clearly introduced to eliminate pre-Islāmic abuses of marital relations. Previously, the wife's physical or emotional condition was immaterial to the man who wanted to divorce her. Moreover, divorced women were often hindered from reunion with their desirous former mates by some interested third party. Another practice, which seems to have continued into the early years of Islām, was that men used to keep their spouses in a vicious circle of indefinite suspense; they were neither fully married nor free to remarry. The circle runs thus: divorce pronouncement, an almost completed waiting period, then another divorce pronouncement, followed by another almost completed waiting period, followed by another pronouncement, etc. Such practices were forbidden by Islām. Some relevant statements may be rendered as follows:

> And their husbands have the better right to take them back in that period (of probationary waiting), if they wish for peace and reconciliation . . .
>
> Divorce is only permissible twice: after that, the parties should either hold together in fairness and on equitable terms or separate with kindness . . .

If he divorces her finally, she shall not be lawful to him after that, until she marries another husband. If he divorces her, then it is no fault in them to return to each other, if they suppose that they will maintain God's bounds. Those are God's bounds; He makes them clear to a people that have knowledge.

When you divorce women, and they have reached their term, then retain them honorably or set them free honorably; do not retain them by force, to transgress; whoever does that has wronged himself. Take not God's signs in mockery, and remember God's blessings upon you, and the Book and the Wisdom He has sent down on you, to admonish you . . .

When you divorce women, and they have reached their term, do not debar them from marrying their husbands, when they have agreed together honorably. That is an admonition for whoso of you believes in God and the Last Day; that is cleaner and purer for you; God knows and you know not.

(Qur'ān 2:228-32).[38]

2. The Contra-Sunnah Deviant Divorce

Any divorce pronouncement which is not made in accordance with the Sunnah procedures, as outlined here, is considered contra-Sunnah, unprecedented, or *bid'ī,* that is, an act of deviation in the disapproved direction. Such a pronouncement is both religiously forbidden and legally void, according to some schools of law. The majority of jurists hold it as religiously forbidden, but formally valid. Some of these maintain, however, that, while it is formally valid, the man must rescind it even by a court order. Others among these hold that it is highly commendable, but not necessary, for the man to rescind his contra-Sunnah pronouncements. Those jurists who viewed as legally valid such unprecedented pronouncements followed 'Umar's discretion. When people were abusing divorce, he, in consultation with other leading Companions, decided to punish the thoughtless by holding them accountable for their careless pronouncements. This check, it is believed, was effective at the time because marriage then was a costly undertaking, a situation which no longer obtains. For this reason, some contemporary Muslims question the relevance of 'Umar's decision to the modern scene.[39]

3. Irrevocable Divorce

a. Levels of Irrevocability

The unprecedented contra-Sunnah "divorce" is, in certain instances, merely nominal; it entails no actual divorce formula, yet in most cases it dissolves the marriage bond irrevocably. However, irrevocability is not peculiar to this type. It may result also from some forms of the Sunnah divorce. Thus there are the four logical possibilities: (a) revocable Sunnah divorce, (b) revocable contra-Sunnah divorce, (c) irrevocable Sunnah divorce, and (d) irrevocable contra-Sunnah divorce. The discussion here is concerned with the last two irrevocable types, apart from the Sunnah-contra-Sunnah typology.

Irrevocability itself is of two levels: intermediate and ultimate. The intermediate means, among other things, that resumption of the broken marital relationship is forbidden without a new marriage contract. This arises, for example, in the case of 'īlā' (the vow of continence) or khul' (divestiture).[40] The ultimate irrevocability means that resumption of the broken marital relationship is absolutely forbidden, as in the case of a triple divorce, unless there has been a taḥlīl (a normal marriage to a second man followed by a valid dissolution through divorce or death).[41]

b. The Basic Variants of Irrevocable Divorce/Dissolution

Irrevocable dissolution of marriage may take one of several forms with different consequences.

1. 'Ilā (Vow of Continence). It was customary before Islām that some men took vows of continence for various reasons and abstained from intercourse with their wives for unspecified periods of time. As a measure of discipline and also as an indirect deterrent to divorce,

Islām retained the practice in a significantly modified way. The maximum term of the vow is set at four months. If reconciliation is reached within this period, the vow is nullified, and the parties are God-forgiven. But if the term expires before reconciliation, the marriage becomes irrevocably dissolved with or without a confirmatory pronouncement of divorce, according to different schools of law. The term *'īlā'* was so defined because it was believed that a wife could tolerate her husband's abstention up to four months without abnormal reactions. And for this reason, 'Umar decided not to separate the fighting soldiers from their wives more than four months.[42]

2. *Zihār (Injurious Dissimulation).* This also was a pre-Islāmic form of divorce, in which a man said to his wife, "Be thou to me as the back of my mother." Some Muslims are reported to have done it. The Qur'ān refers to an encounter between a woman who was affected by this form of divorce and the Prophet, whose instructions were sought by the woman. The exchange is thus reported:

> God has heard the words of her that disputes with thee concerning her husband, and makes complaint unto God. God hears the two of you conversing together; surely God is All-hearing, All-seeing.
> Those of you who say, regarding their wives, 'Be as my mother's back,' ... they are surely saying a forbidden (dishonorable) saying and a falsehood ...
> *(Qur'ān 58:1-2).*

Islām condemned the practice. But if a man makes this pronouncement, his wife becomes forbidden to him until he atones for his wrong deed. He must (1) free a slave, if he has the means; or (2) observe day-time fasting for two consecutive months before touching his wife; (3) if unable to fast, feed sixty needy persons.

If he does not make the atonement voluntarily, he must be forced by some proper authority to comply before he is permitted to resume his full marital status. Some schools, however, give him a period of four months, as in the case of 'īlā'. If no atonement takes place within this period, the ẓihār pronouncement amounts to an irrevocable divorce.[43]

3. *Li'ān (Double Testimony/Recrimination)*. This form of mutual imprecation was apparently a familiar practice in the ancient Near East. The Code of Hammurabi, the Old Testament, and the Qur'ān all make reference to the practice. However, Islām's approach to the problem is somewhat different. When a man accuses his wife of adultery, but has no witnesses other than himself, he must testify by God four times that he is of the truthful, and a fifth time that the curse of God shall be upon him, if he should be of the liars. To avert chastisement, she shall testify by God four times that he is of the liars, and a fifth time that the wrath of God shall be upon her, if he should be of the truthful. At this point, the marriage becomes dissolved and absolutely irrevocable; they could not be expected to live peaceably together after having reached such extremities.[44]

4. *Khul' (Divestiture/Self-Redemption)*. This is another irrevocable form of divorce, which is initiated by the wife rather than the husband. If she is unhappy in her marriage for her own reasons, and he has no overt fault or guilt, she may seek a divorce from him. She shall return to him the dowry and other marriage gifts, to compensate for his material and/or moral losses. He may, however, waive his right of compensation and simply agree to divorce her in compliance with her request. In fact, there are instances in which women sought the divorce, and their requests were granted by

their mates without asking for or getting anything in
return. The Qur'ān (2:229) refers to *khul'* thus:

> It is not lawful for you (men) to take of what you have
> given them (women) unless the couple fear they may not
> maintain God's bounds; if you fear they may not maintain
> God's bounds, it is no fault in them for her to redeem
> herself. Those are God's bounds; do not transgress them.
> Whosoever trancgresses the bounds of God — those are
> the evildoers.

Whenever the husband is clearly at fault, he must
be directed to discharge his full duty to his wife. But
should a man mistreat his innocent mate or pressure
her to seek self-redemption — and she so desires —
the marriage will be dissolved, and she will not return
anything to him of what he has given her. Nor will he
be permitted to take anything from her. Conversely,
she is forbidden to request a divorce from her innocent
husband unless she has some valid, even though personal,
justifications, because, as the Prophet has put it, for
any wife who so acts the smell of Paradise will be
forbidden.[45]

5. *Divorce Before Marriage Consummation.* A man may
choose to divorce a woman after the conclusion of the
contract but before the final consummation of the marriage. This divorce will be irrevocable and no waiting
period is required. According to the Qur'ān (2:236-7)[46]

> There is no fault in you, if you divorce women while as yet
> you have not touched them nor appointed any marriage-
> portion for them; yet make provision for them, the affluent
> man according to his means, and according to his means
> the needy man, honorably — an obligation on the good-doers.
> And if you divorce them before you have touched them, and
> you have already appointed for them a marriage-portion,
> then one-half of what you have appointed, unless it be they
> make remission, or he makes remission in whose hand is
> the knot of marriage; yet that you should remit is closer

to piety. Forget not to be bountiful and generous one towards another. Surely God sees the things you do.

6. *From Revocable to Irrevocable Divorce.* If a revocable divorce, simple or double, was pronounced, and the waiting period expired before revocation, the divorce becomes irrevocable.[47]

7. *The Triple Divorce.* This is the ultimately irrevocable divorce. Any resumption of the broken marital relationship is absolutely forbidden without *tahlil.*[48]

8. *Figurative Pronouncements.* Many jurists insist that the divorce pronouncements should be made in clear, direct, and unequivocal terms. Other jurists maintain that if the terms are figurative, i.e., indirect or equivocal, and the man actually means to divorce his wife, the divorce becomes valid and irrevocable.[49]

9. *Miscellanea.* Although most of these divorce forms are considered contra-Sunnah and unprecedented, there are a few miscellaneous formulas which have been excessively abused and strongly condemned. Such formulas have one characteristic in common; they are conspicuous deviations from the expected behavior patterns of conscientious, responsible men. On this account they have been the subject of condemnation by Muslim scholars and criticism by others. It is relatively easy for Muslim zealots to condemn (1) the lightness with which some Muslims take the whole question of divorce, (2) the substitution of a divorce formula for an ordinary oath in the market place or during a casual conversation, (3) the use of a triple divorce formula in the same sitting or in the same breath, (4) the acceptance by some late jurists of divorce pronouncements made under the influence of intoxication, pressure or in jest, and (5) the casuistic recourse to the *tahlil.* Such practices

are easy targets because they contradict the spirit of Islāmic law and defeat the purpose of divorce in Islām. They are indicative of serious lacks of conscientiousness and moral integrity. These sensational practices have occupied many jurists for several centuries and have crowded the files of litigation before the courts of law. And it is these very deviations which seem to have drawn disproportionate attention from non-Muslim critics. They take these practices or "malpractices" as though they were typical of Muslim society and essential to the family system of Islām.[50]

E. The Agents of Divorce

It is probably a serious misconception to say, as some Westerners and especially Muslim feminists seem to imply, that the exercise of divorce is the exclusive right of men. It is also a misconception to hold, as some Muslim scholars may be tempted to do, that both men and women have "equal" rights of divorce in every respect.[51] What appears equally bestowed upon them is the right to seek and obtain the dissolution of an unsuccessful marriage. To be sure, the mechanisms or channels vary in kind and accessibility from case to case. Some channels are open to the man only; some to the woman only, with or without judicial intervention; and some to both, directly or through judicial process, with or without the partners' consent.[52]

1. The Man's Right to Divorce

Rightly or wrongly, it is the assumed general nature of the male to court the female. In terms of human relations, man usually initiates the marriage by proposing to the woman. In Islām, he further settles a dower on her, maintains her, and assumes guardianship over the household. In recognition of these factors, he is allowed in certain cases to initiate and pronounce the dissolution of the marriage tie. But he is enjoined to do so with discretion, kindness, and equity.[53] Considering (1) the general detestability of divorce in Islām, (2) the Prophet's description of a good spouse as the greatest joy of life, (3) the man's investment in marriage, and (4) the increase of divorce rates as a partial result of the woman's right of divorce in modern times, it is unlikely that a husband would ordinarily want to part with his spouse for trivial reasons. At any rate, the Muslim man's right in this respect is not absolute, nor may he abuse it.[54] Only in certain limited cases may he independently dissolve the marriage tie without the consent of the wife or the permission of a court of law. These cases are: (1) divorce proper or repudiation in accordance with the Sunnah procedures and with the conditions, stipulations, and implications outlined above; (2) 'īlā', or vow of continence, which is not repealed before the expiration of the probationary period of four months; and (3) ẓihār, or injurious dissimulation.[55]

2. The Woman's Right to Divorce and Marriage Dissolution

Since marriage is described by the Qur'ān as a partnership of peace and compassion, and since every right corresponds with an obligation, the wife is entitled, like the husband, to initiate and actually dissolve the marriage tie independently. In certain cases she may do so without the permission of any court of law or the husband's consent. These cases are: (1) what is commonly called "delegated divorce," in which the man agrees in the marriage contract to transfer, irrevocably, his right of divorce to the woman, so as to empower her to free herself from the marriage bond if and when she so desires; and (2) what is also commonly called "suspended" or "conditional" divorce, in which a man stipulates at the time of marriage that if he does a certain thing(s) contrary to his wife's wish, she will be free to divorce herself from him. It should be pointed out that some of these forms of divorce are unacceptable to certain jurists who, nevertheless, accord the woman in principle the right to seek her freedom through alternative channels. Moreover, if the wife is aggrieved or betrayed, she may initiate and

actually obtain a divorce through the proper judicial proces-
ses. The husband's consent to her request is immaterial if
she has valid reasons for divorce. It becomes the duty of the
proper authorities to enable her to gain her freedom from
the marital bond. Grounds for such action include: (a) the
so-called "option of puberty," in which the wife is entitled
at puberty to either retain or dissolve a marriage that was
previously contracted on her behalf by a fully qualified
guardian, (b) long absence of or desertion by the husband,
(c) mistreatment, (d) impotence, and (e) physical or financial inability.[56]

3. Divorce cr Marriage Dissolution by Mutual Consent

Here both the husband and wife agree privately to dissolve the marriage tie peacefully. This may take one of two
legitimate forms: (a) khul' (self-redemption or divestiture),
which is initiated by the woman but eventually consented
to by the man, and (b) mubāra'ah, a mutual bilateral agreement to terminate the marriage and free each other from
the marital bond. The court of law will enforce their terms
and intervene only if unlawful stipulations are involved.[57]

4. Divorce or Marriage Dissolution by Judicial Process

In this category, the dissolution of marriage takes place
by the ruling of some judicial agency, with or without the
parties' consent. In this case, termination of the marital relationship is not the private concern of the principals; rather
it implicates the judicial as well as the executive authorities. This situation obtains mainly in the case of (a) li'ān,
double testimony or mutual imprecation, and (b) annulment,
in which a marriage contract is found void or incomplete
and must be annuled.[58]

F. The Consequences of Divorce

Different types of divorce and marriage dissolution produce
different consequences. Some of these have been already
indicated in connection with certain specific types of

divorce that have been considered so far. What remains in this section, however, is to outline the general consequences of divorce, apart from the specific forms this may take.

1. Remorse-Elation

The parties' first reaction to divorce is either a sense of remorse or elation, or probably a combination of both. If it is remorse, the parties are encouraged and given the opportunity to rectify their mistakes, atone for their guilt, and repeal their action. If it is elation, it is tempered with pending obligations and concern for the future readjustment. Whatever the feeling of the parties may be, a divorce pronouncement does not necessarily mean an immediate dissolution of the marriage tie. Much less does it imply the parties' unkindness, resentment, or bitterness toward each other. There are certain mechanisms to revoke the pronouncement and ways to resume the marital relationship even after an irrevocable divorce. In fact, Muslim jurists unanimously have agreed that in certain types of divorce the surviving party of either sex inherits from the deceased one as if there were no divorce. Reconciliation is highly commendable wherever here is hope of harmony; and equity with kindness is mandatory at all times, within as well as without wedlock.[59]

2. 'Iddah or Waiting Period

An immediate consequence of divorce or dissolution of marriage is the commencement of a waiting period or probationary term. This usually lasts about three months, to allow for three monthly courses or the equivalent thereof. If there is a pregnancy, the period lasts as long as the pregnancy does. The typical explanation of this rule is that it is required to establish whether or not the woman has conceived. If there is no conception, she becomes eligible for remarriage at the end of the period. But if there is a conception, she must wait until the childbirth, so that the child's legitimacy and identity will be secured.

While this explanation may be "manifest function" of the

waiting period, there is another which seems equally significant, even if less manifest. The waiting period is a term of probation, reconsideration, and transition. Perhaps a longer period will be torturous and a shorter one too tempting. In any case, it allows one a gradual release from the marital bond and a relatively smooth transition from one status to another new one without much abruption. It may thus be considered an added precautionary measure and the last checkpoint.[60]

3. Maintenance in the Waiting Period

The fact that the waiting period is at least a partial extension of the marital link is probably indicated by the rules of maintenance during that period. The woman whose divorce has been initiated and pronounced by the husband is fully entitled to complete maintenance as long as she is still in the waiting period. She has the right to continue her occupation of the same home as before the divorce, or to be furnished with relatively comfortable lodging facilities. She may not be expelled from her home, nor should she move therefrom, unless she has committed an evident offense of indecency. Along with this right, the man, the repudiator, is fully responsible for her food, clothing, and, if necessary, service, just as if the marriage were still completely intact, by which time she will probably have adjusted to the new changes in her life.[61]

4. Custody of the Children

Young children remain in the custody of their divorced mother, unless she is otherwise unfit. Divorce as such does not disqualify her or affect her right to custody. While she nurses the young children and cares for the rest, it is the father's responsibility to bear the full cost of this care and equitably compensate the mother therefor. In addition, he alone is responsible for their housing, clothing, and food, even though they are in the mother's custody or home. While this may be a potential source of tension and litigation, it may also be an effective channel of reconciliation and harmony.[62]

5. Dowry Settlement

If divorce does take place after the consummation of marriage, the divorced woman must receive her complete dowry or any deferred portion thereof. Besides this inalienable right of the woman, it is highly commendable that she be treated by the repudiator as generously and kindly as possible. The same principle of generous treatment applies also to the woman who is divorced before the consummation of marriage, in which case she is entitled to at least one-half of the dowry, although she is exempted from the observance of a waiting period. However, these specific terms are probably only the irreducible minimal obligations. The whole question of post-divorce settlement is described in terms of generosity, piety, kindness, compassion, and good will. Such principles, when implemented, clearly transcend the legalistic formalities and give divorce a moral coloring. Perhaps nothing can illustrate this better than the Qur'ān (2:236-7, 241-2) [63]

> . . . make provision for them [divorced women], the affluent man according to his means, and according to his means the needy man, honorably, an obligation on the righteous.
> . . . Forget not to be bountiful and generous one towards another. Surely God sees the things you do . . .
> There shall be for divorced women provision honorable—an obligation on the righteous, pious. So God makes clear His signs for you; haply you will understand.

6. Remarriage

One of the major consequences of divorce is the freedom to remarry. Being divorced does not necessarily stigmatize the parties involved, nor must they spend the rest of their lives in loneliness or laxity. One "mistake" does not incapacitate the mistaken party forever; one misjudgment is no reason for continued discomfort. Sins are forgivable by God, and so must they be by man. There is always a second chance to approach God and atone for one's wrong-doings. Perhaps this is the logic of the permissibility of remarriage. The divorced parties are offered every possible opportunity to remarry one another if they intend peace and desire harmony. As we have seen, there are ways to revoke certain divorce pronouncements and to conclude new marriage contracts in certain irrevocable cases. Even if there is no reunion between the divorced parties, they become free at the end of the waiting period to marry whomever they wish.[64]

Concluding Remarks

To conclude this chapter, some essential aspects of the problem should be kept in mind. First, divorce in Islām is relatively easy and formally simple, and so is its revocability. But whether this formal simplicity is also morally simple, and whether it is a "virtue" or vice, is a different question. Secondly, there are various mechanisms and grounds to dissolve a marriage, but there are also various alternatives to redeem it, even after dissolution. Probably this was a result of the gradual transition from a diversified pre-Islāmic Arabian society to a new expansive Muslim society and heterogenous population and folkways. Or, it may have been the consequence of a tacit recognition of the changeability of the human mind and, particularly, the so-called intemperate Arabian character. Thirdly, it is noteworthy that Muslim scholars, especially in modern times, concentrate on the Sunnah divorce as the ideal moral solution and condemn the contra-Sunnah types to the extent of almost completely denying their connection with Islām and disowning those Muslims who resort to such types. On the other hand, non-Muslim scholars take particular interest in the latter types of divorce, to the extent of almost completely denying the existence of the Sunnah types. The result of these partisan-like, polemical views is confusion for the student and obscurity of the problem. In our own presentation, we have tried to examine the problem from a different perspective. We have discussed the various dimensions of divorce, both the Sunnah and the contra-Sunnah types, the ideal "norms" as well as the behavioral deviations. Fourthly, the Qur'ān and the Prophet's statements present the problem of divorce in a highly moral context. The legal formalities are buried, as it were, in a rich soil of exhortations, to manliness and piety, rememberance of God and kindness. Any attempt to analyze divorce in Islām out of this context, or to separate the legalities from their moral grounds, will be quite inadequate. Finally, a view of divorce as a whole, and particularly a consideration of the "why," the "when," the "how," the "who," and the "what," will probably show how divorce may be conceived as a moral, self-restricting, and self correcting act. Perhaps this explains the Prophet's statement about divorce being the most repugnant of all things lawful.

A. Social Implications of Inheritance

Inheritance laws are believed to be closely allied to and strongly indicative of the society's normative system, social structure, and principles of family organization. A particularly consequential affinity existed in ancient times between the family worship and the family property. It was, as De Coulanges pointed out, "a rule without exception, in both Greek and Roman law, that a property could not be acquired without the worship, or the worship without the property." This was the principle from which all the rules of succession among the ancients were derived. The first such rule was that the domestic religion being . . . hereditary from male to male, property is the same. As the son is the natural continuator of the religion, he also inherits the estate."[1]

Similar affinities existed in other societies between the law of inheritance and various aspects of the social structure. For example, inheritance among the Hebrews "largely follows lines of descent within the family. From this rule it follows that males are preferred to females as heirs, since the line of descent is patrilineal."[2] In pre-Islāmic Arabia, on the other hand, inheritance was based on the principle of "comradeship in arms." The chief criterion of eligibility was the ability to contribute to the strength of the individual tribe through effective participation in the popular sport of tribal warfares. This resulted, among other things, in the exclusion from inheritance of women, minors of both sexes, and invalids, as well as in the preference of the paternal to the maternal lines.[3]

Inheritance laws may also index the intrafamily relations and the direction of social change. Where the daughter was considered incapable of participating in or continuing the domestic religion, she was deprived of inheritance, as was the case in ancient Greek law, according to which she did not inherit at all, neither before nor after marriage. But where marriage meant, as in Roman law, adoption of the husband's religion and renunciation of the father's, the married daughter did not inherit from the father.[4] The role of the oldest son and the influence of the levirate are seen in various regulations of inheritance among the Hebrews. In the beginning the oldest son inherited almost the entire estate. At a later stage, he was given only a double share. Sons living within the father's household were allowed to inherit from him, whereas those who had moved out did not inherit. While husbands inherited from their wives, there is no mention whether the latter inherited from the former. It seems probable that wives did not inherit because it was unnecessary; they were cared for by their children or through the levirate rules. Moreover, it was in the changing times of Moses that daughters were permitted, with certain conditions, to inherit in default of sons and in preference to the agnates. While the rules of inheritance in pre-Islāmic Arabia are said to have been basically determined by the war-like mode of life, the Hebrew Jewish laws are believed to have been patterned to suit an agricultural sedentary society. More significant, perhaps, is the notion of the relationship between the doctrine of God's Chosen People and the succession rights. It is suggested that this doctrine gave the Jews a special sense of cohesiveness and solidarity. This sentiment was mirrored in the inheritance law, which aimed at keeping the estate intact as long as was possible, instead of breaking it down into small shares or lots.[5]

Some scholars subscribe to the idea that inheritance laws register new trends of "human evolution" and industrial development. The struggle between individualism and collectivism, between the individual's yearnings and the social tendencies of humanity, is revealed in the law of inheritance. While individualism demands equality among all recipients or eligibles, the social mission of the family often demands a deviation from this equality principle, and forces one or more individuals into the background.The individual's right is thus forsaken for the group's sake. Because the group's interest is assumed to be best served by keeping the property intact, the female is sometimes less favored than the male sex, and even the members of the same sex are treated differently to minimize the division of the property.[6] Moreover, it is the conclusion of some observers that, in the nineteenth century, primogeniture fostered the development of industry in urban centers, whereas division of the property among the sons favored the development of local industries in homes or small workshops.[7]

B. The General Characteristics of Inheritance in Islām

Comparatively speaking, and in the light of the preceding overview, it would be difficult to identify the Islāmic law of inheritance as either collective or individualistic, traditional or modern. It would seem inaccurate to describe it as designed for an agricultural society or for commercial communities, adapted to the military mode of life or to the missionary vocation. Appealing as they may be or have been, these labels do not adequately demonstrate the meaning of succession in Islām. To be sure, illustrations can be found in support of individualism or modernism just as easily as they can be rallied to support collectivism or traditionalism. In fact, some contemporary Muslim scholars have pointed out, perhaps with a sentiment of implicit pride, that the Islāmic law of inheritance fosters the collective social spirit, because it favors the distribution of property among many heirs and thus holds in check the concentration of wealth. While this orientation may have some ground in certain Qur'ānic statements,[8] it is probably also prompted by the international impact of modern socialist thought. Yet a counter argument can be made in favor of individualism, since every heir within certain grades inherits, and since all parents, sons, daughters, spouses, brothers, and sisters are treated equally and/or equitably, as will be seen later in the chapter. However, such illustrations seem out of context and may be more misleading than helpful and representative.

What this suggests for our discussion is that the characteristics of the Islāmic law of inheritance must be sought from a different standpoint. In fact, the very term *different* would seem to characterize this Islāmic law more accurately than anything else suggested so far. It is this difference which probably underlies, at least in part, Roberts' and similar remarks that, "The enactments of the Qur'ān concerning the distribution of a deceased person's estate are, on the whole, equitable, and show a great advance upon the unjust, and indeed cruel customs which obtained among the Arabs in pre-Islāmic times." [9] The principle of difference will be our point of departure in this section since it seems more indicative of what is characteristic of the Islāmic system. This, of course, does not deny the similarities between the system and its predecessors. Such similarities did exist; but they, like the dissimilarities, have been exaggerated sometimes to the point of absurdity.[10]

The Islāmic law of inheritance did not mean a complete departure from the preceding traditions, any more than it did a total dependence on them. Rather, it blended custom with "revelation" and joined the old to the new. The emergent was something different, not only from the local Arabian practices, but also from the laws of the ancient Near East and Mediterranean regions. The difference was in some respects so fundamental that it caused resentment and dismay even among some Muslims.[11] In the following pages, various aspects of this difference will be briefly examined.

C. Basic Dimensions of the Law of Inheritance

1. The Grounds of Inheritance

The manifestations of the difference between the Islāmic system of inheritance and its predecessors are manifold and far-reaching. As we have noted, Greek-Roman law was determined by the domestic religion and thus excluded some immediate relatives, the daughters. The Hebrew system largely followed the patrilineal lines of descent and preferred some heirs to others. The pagan Arabian custom was arbitrary and basically determined by the so-called comradeship in arms. Hence it favored parental male descent, adoption, and sworn alliance or clientage. The Islāmic system, on the other hand, was founded on two bases: natural, "bilineal" relationship through paternal and/or maternal lines, and actual affinity through marriage and/or its "legitimate" variant "concubinage." In default of these two bases, a third was accepted by some law schools and may be called voluntary mutual patronage or *walā'*. This was a modified version of the pre-Islāmic practice of sworn alliance.[12]

These grounds of inheritance eliminated some traditionally eligible categories and included new classes of heirs. Those who formally succeeded to property on the bases of adoption, outright sworn alliance, and arbitrary will were no longer eligible under the new system of Islām. Adoption, in particular, was completely excluded from the grounds of inheritance. Outright sworn alliance was likewise eliminated, replaced, or so modified that it would be rarely applicable, and only in the opinion of some jurists. The right of will was reconsidered and held in check by certain measures. Every Muslim was urged by the Prophet to write his will as soon as possible and to have it certified by two qualified witnesses. The Muslim was forbidden to make wills in favor of any would-be heir, or to dispose by will of more than one-third of his net property without the future heirs' approval. The reason given by the Prophet for so restricting the right of will is that it is better to leave one's heirs comfortable than destitute.[13]

The added classes of heirs clearly outnumbered those who were excluded by the new law. That is, under Islām a larger number of heirs were accorded certain rights, which sometimes meant the division of the property into smaller shares. One's sex, age, or order of birth no longer constituted a total impediment to eligibility for inheritance. Women (mothers, wives, daughters, sisters), invalids, minors of both sexes, and parents were now entitled to fixed shares. Their inclusion became the prescribed rule rather than the benevolent or debatable exception. This marked a significant departure from the previous local as well as the surrounding systems of inheritance. For, in the Islāmic system no distinction was made between father and mother, first-born and last-born sons, children of free mothers and those of slave mothers, married and unmarried daughters. It was no longer a question of favorites or favors among heirs; it has become a wide, differentiated, but deemed equitable, distribution of the inherited property. Wherever there was a difference of degree between classes of heirs, it seems to have corresponded proportionately with differentiated obligations.[14] It may be pointed out that by prescribing fixed shares for the heirs mentioned in this context, Islām took a markedly different position. It "differed" from the Greek Roman system, which generally excluded the daughter; from the Hebrew and Mosaic system, which probably excluded the wife and certainly the daughter if there were surviving sons, and which granted the oldest son a double share; and the pre-Islāmic Arabian system, which excluded women, minors, and invalids.[15]

2. Bars to Inheritance; Complete and Partial

Just as Islām adopted different grounds of inheritance, it did with respect to exclusion from inheritance. Under this heading, three categories will be discussed: (a.) potential heirs who are completely debarred from inheritance because of something they have done or some attribute they possess; (b.) potential heirs who become totally excluded only because of the intermediacy of certain other recipients who are closer to the deceased; and (c.) potential heirs who are only partially excluded; their shares may be reduced on account of other beneficiaries.

a. The First Category; Categorical Impediments

This category consists of persons who are debarred because of certain acts and/or attributes which represent absolute bars to succession. These bars are basically the following:

(1) *Homicide.* A person who causes the death of another cannot inherit the property of the deceased, however formally close the relationship of the two may be, e.g., child-parent, husband-wife, etc. Homicide bars the murderer absolutely

from inheritance of the property of the murdered. Besides a
statement from the Prophet to this effect, the reason here is
that a potential heir may want to hasten the death of an innocent *praepositus* for the purpose of premature inheritance.
Part of the penalty is to deny him completely what he would
have received if he had not contemplated the unnatural death
of the *praepositus*. Moreover, inheritance among relatives is
based on mutual benevolence and solidarity, and it is designed to foster such familiar sentiments. Homicide is the
very antithesis of the whole idea of mutual inheritance among
relatives. The offender is, therefore, forbidden to make any
of his otherwise valid claims to the property of the deceased
victim.

2. *Difference of Religion.* It is held by all jurists that a non-
Muslim may not inherit a Muslim relative's property. The
basis of this doctrine is also a statement from the Prophet.
Since inheritance is a form of succession, an expression of
solidarity, and a medium of cooperation, (principles which do
not normally bind individuals of different religions), there is
little mutual basis of inheritance between Muslim and non-
Muslim relatives. As to the inheritance of a Muslim from a
non-Muslim relative, the same principle applies in the opinion
of all jurists except the Imāmī Shī'īs. The latter allowed the
Muslim party to inherit from the non-Muslim relatives, but not
vice versa. This position is based on a certain interpretation of
some Traditions and on the opinion of some leading Companions of the Prophet. However, the prohibition of mutual
inheritance between Muslim and non-Muslim relatives does
not exclude recourse to acts of testament. It is lawful, at least
for the Muslim party, to make wills in favor of his non-Muslim
spouse or close relatives within the one-third limit of his estate
or even beyond, but in this latter case with the other heirs'
consent.

3.) *Slavery.* A slave is not allowed to inherit from his free
deceased relative. The assumption is probably that there is no
likelihood of equal reciprocity between the two. The slave
owns practically nothing, and the chance of his leaving any

inheritable property to his free relative is virtually non-existent. However, if the deceased is survived only by a slave relative(s), some jurists held that the property should be sold and the proceeds applied to the emancipation of the slave. Other jurists maintained that the property or the proceeds therefrom should go to the Public Treasury.

4.) *Difference of Abode.* Some jurists are of the opinion that, in order to qualify, the heir must be the national and permanent resident of the same country, region, or locale. There can be no mutual inheritance between relatives who reside in different countries, especially if there are no binding pacts between them. Parenthetically, the assumption is that it is presumably impracticable to enforce the same law on people of different countries or regions and expect much solidarity or cooperation through inheritance. It is also possible that this provision might have been a result of the regional autonomy and/or conflict of the Muslim provinces comprising the Muslim Empire.[16]

b. *The Second Category; Complete Exclusion*

This category includes legitimate heirs who are excluded completely from inheritance because of the intermediacy of other relatives closer in lineal proximity to the deceased. The rule is apparently based on the principle of reciprocal priority of obligations and rights. Since mutual responsibility among relatives is distributed according to lineal proximity, it is probably felt that reciprocal benefits, e.g., inheritance rights, should be similarly treated. Thus a relative of the second grade, e.g., a grandparent of the deceased, does not inherit if there is among the survivors another relative of the first grade, such as a parent. Nor does a grandchild inherit with the son. If the deceased were in need during his life, relatives of the first grade, the child and the parent, would be called upon for support and enjoined to do so before those of the second grade, i.e., the grandchild and the grandparent. The distribution of the deceased person's property follows the same rule. The general principle here is that an heir, e.g., a brother, who relates to the deceased through another or who is remoter than another, e.g., a father or a son respectively, does not inherit if the latter are among the survivors.[17]

c. *The Third Category; Partial Exclusion*

This category consists of heirs whose shares may vary, but who are not entirely excluded. This may be called a partial exclusion, and its effect is a wider distribution of the property in smaller shares. For example, the husband's share depends on whether or not the deceased wife is survived by any children. If she leaves one child or more, the husband's share is reduced from one half to one fourth of the net property. It is inconsequential whether the children are also his or the deceased wife's only through another marriage. The same principle of reduction or partial exclusion is true of the shares of the wife, the daughters, sons, brothers, sisters, and so on. However, some partially excluded persons may become entirely excluded. For example, the sister of the deceased is excluded from the one-half share to the one-third if there is another sister to join her; but the sister will be entirely excluded if there is a son of the father of the deceased among the heirs. Yet certain heirs cannot be excluded completely; their right of inheritance is *primary*. It may be adjusted or reduced, but is never eliminated on account of any other heir. These primary heirs are the spouses (the husband and the wife), both parents, and the children (sons and daughters) of the deceased. No other person can entirely exclude any of these relatives from inheritance; their right is inalienable, although their shares may be reduced because of the presence of more beneficiaries.

The question of "representation" usually arises at this point. The formal position is that a fatherless grandchild, for instance, does not inherit from his grandfather if the latter is survived by other immediate children, who are the grandchild's uncles and/or aunts. Some jurists, however, maintain that the fatherless grandchild is entitled to what would have been his predeceased father's share had he survived. This is the so-called "mandatory testament," which must be executed within one third of the property.[18]

3. Classes of Heirs

In this section we shall consider briefly the various classes of heirs according to the grounds of their eligibility. It will not add much to our discussion to specify the shares of each member of every class and the detailed conditions implicated. Adequate charts, tables, and diagrams are given in the highly specialized sources.[19] Rather, the discussion will be broad, but with due emphasis upon differences and differentiations that may be helpful.

All the major Sunnī and Shī'ī schools of Islāmic law agree on the principles of inheritance being (a) ascriptive lineal relationship through marriage, (b) affinal relationship through marriage and (c) acquired patronage or walā' relationship. The heirs who are admitted on the basis of these principles are basically the same in all schools. The differences, on the whole, are of minor technical importance, although they may be sociologically interesting. However, the Hanafī scale of distribution will be taken here as generally representing the Sunnī interpretation of the law, the Ithnā 'Asharī scheme as generally representing the Shī'ī interpretation.

a. The Sunnī Scheme of Distribution

According to the Hanafī school, there are three principal classes of heirs.

1) THE QUR'ANIC PRIMARY HEIRS

The first class consists of the Qur'ānic heirs, the quota primary sharers, or the recipients of fixed shares as they are interchangeably called. These include four male and eight female subclasses. The male sharers are: the husband, the father, the so-called true grandfather how high soever, and the uterine brother. The female sharers are: the wife, the mother, the so-called true grandmother, the uterine sister, the daughter, the son's daughter, how low soever, the germane sister, and the "consanguine" sister (of the same father but not the same mother). The following simple chart may be useful.

The Sunnī (Hanafī) Scheme of Distribution of Inheritance:

THE SHARERS

MALE	SEX	FEMALE	Inexcludable M F	Excludable M F
Husband		Wife	X X	
Father		Mother	X X	
True Grandfather		True Grandmother		X X
Uterine Brother		Uterine Sister		X X
(Son)*		Daughter	X X	
		Son's Daughter		X
		Germane Sister		X
		Consanguine Sister (of same parents) X		

It should be pointed out that some of these sharers exclude others completely or partially, and that their shares may exhaust the property by reaching a unity. Sometimes, however, the fixed shares may add up to more than a unity as, for example, with a wife 1/8, two daughters 2/3, a father 1/6 and a mothter 1/6. This is called 'awl, and the fractional shares are proportionately reduced. Sometimes also the shares may not reach a unity, in which case the remainder will be divided among the heirs and the shares proportionately increased by way of radd or "returning," according to one legal interpretation, or the remainder will be transferred to the Public Treasury, according to another interpretation.

*Strictly speaking, the son is not among these sharers. But if there is a son he excludes all the excludable heirs and shares with the daughter(s) what is left, which will be at least a little over one half of the estate, i.e., 13/24. A son takes twice as much as the daughter.

2) *AGNATIC HEIRS*

The second principal class of heirs consists of the agnates or the so-called residuaries. An agnate is a male who relates to the deceased through another male or through a pair of one male and one female, e.g., a "consanguine" brother or a germane brother respectively. The agnates receive what is left, if any, after the sharers of the first principal class, the whole property in default of any sharer, and nothing if the sharers exhaust the entire property. An interesting subclass of agnates is that of the sons. The son is not one of the strictly Qur'ānic sharers; but he is a special agnate who cannot be excluded by any other heirs of any class, and who excludes other heirs, agnates or excludable sharers.

3) *NON-QUR'ANIC, NON-AGNATE HEIRS*

The third principal class consists of "uterine" heirs. A uterine heir is any relative who is neither a Qur'ānic sharer nor an agnate, e.g., the daughter's child. Uterine heirs inherit in default of Qur'ānic sharers and agnates, and in preference to mutual patrons and the State. The chief subclasses of these are: the daughter's children, the sister's children, the brother's daughter, the uterine brother's children, the mother's brothers and sisters, the paternal uncle's daughters, and the mother's father. This class of heirs has stimulated much discusion and legal controversy among the Sunni schools of law.[20]

The debate over the rights of the uterine heirs goes back in time to the days of the Companions and their early successors, some of whom interpreted the law sources as allowing these relatives to inherit. This interpretation was later adopted by the Hanafī jurists of al Kūfah, Iraq. Other jurists, including leaders of major Sunni schools, held that the uterine relatives do not inherit; whatever is left of the property, after the sharers and agnates, goes to the Public Treasury instead of the uterines. On each side of the debate were textual and analogical arguments produced to support the respective positions. Arguments seem to carry equal weight as far as internal consistency is concerned. The internal textual evidence is equivocal and thus lends itself to different interpretations. It would therefore be rather difficult to understand or explain the problem without reference to some external, extratheoretical factors in the social environment. Perhaps the 'Irāqī Hanafī jurists of al Kūfah adopted a position favorable to the uterine relatives because the society then was new and the population relatively heterogeneous, physically mobile, politically uncertain though central. The Muslim domain was expanding rapidly and growing complex administratively. The 'Irāqī environment, having become the official seat of political power, was to become also the official cultural center, into which poured various cultural channels of the East as well as of the West, sometimes harmoniously and sometimes disruptively. Under such conditions of cultural convergence and conflict, political uncertainty and centralization, departure from the familiar simple post and venture into the complex unknown, the family — the basic unit of society — may become subject to disturbing influences. Muslim jurists took and often played the role of religious leaders, social reformers, and unofficial guards of the religion and society. They must have been concerned about the welfare of society and the family. But in view of their limited or nonexistent political power over the official state of affairs, they probably sought to insure at least the family against disintegration. It is not unlikely that they believed one way to achieve this aim was to expand the sphere of reciprocity among the family members, to strengthen their sentiments of mutual obligations, and to foster their autonomy from the external official environment. Allowing the uterine relatives, instead of the patrons or the State, to inherit the residue of the property, would not only enhance kinship solidarity, but it would also make it unnecessary for the needy relatives to seek help from the State officials. The family members would become self-supporting and mutually committed to each other's aid, because with the right of inheritance in times of ease goes the corresponding obligation of support in times of need. It may be reiterated that it was the same 'Irāqī jurists who expanded the sphere of mutual responsibility of relatives and held the kindred of several grades responsible for one another's maintenance.

By contrast, the societies of al Madīnah and Makkah, where the counterposition developed, were not probably subject to the same kind and degree of influence. Nor was the family apparently threatened to the same extent. Here, too, the jurists who denied the uterine relatives the right to inherit were those who restricted the fixed mutual obligations of the kin to the most immediate family members.[21] It must be added, however, that these jurists supported their respective positions in the main by authentic, though equivocal, statements from the Qur'ān and the Prophet, which were interpreted differently in the light of the contemporary situation.

b. *The Shī'ī Scheme of Distribution*

According to the Shī'ī school of law, the grounds of inheritance are the same as those of the Sunnī, namely, ascriptive blood relationship, affinity through marriage, and patronage. The heirs by ascriptive consanguine relationship are divided into three classes, and each class is subdivided into two groups. The following simple chart may be helpful.

The Shī'ī Consanguineal Heirs

CLASS	SUBCLASS
CLASS I	Group (a) — Parents Group (b) — Children and lineal descendants, how low soever
CLASS II	Group (a) — Grandparents, how high soever Group (b) — Brothers and sisters and their descendants
CLASS III	Group (a) — Paternal, and Group (b) — maternal uncles and aunts of the deceased and of his parents and grandparents, how high soever, and their descendants, how low soever.

It should be pointed out that while Class I excludes Class II and Class II does Class III, heirs of the two groups in each class inherit jointly; they do not exclude each other.

The nonconsanguineal heirs are divided into two classes: (I) spouses, and (II) patrons. A spouse inherits from the deceased spouse and a patron does from his client. There are three types of patronage, but the patron inherits only in default of consanguineal and affinal heirs. The following chart may clarify the scheme.

The _Shī'ī_ Nonconsanguineal Heirs

CLASS	SUBCLASS
(I) MARITAL AFFINITY	a) Husband b) Wife
(II) PATRONAGE by a special cause or legal relationship (_walā'_)	a) _walā' 'itq,_ patronage of freedom between a freedman and his former master
	b) _walā' jarīrah,_ the right of obligations for delicts committed by the deceased
	c) _walā Imāmah,_ right by virtue of religious leadership, i.e., the Head Imām of the Sect inherits from the deceased who leaves no heirs, but the Imām transfers the property to the Treasury[22]

Both the Sunnī and the Shī'ī schemes agree on the major categories of heirs, i.e., the so-called Qur'ānic sharers, including the blood relations and spouses. Beyond that, there are some differences which are occasionally exaggerated by certain scholars and call for an explanation. For example, the Shī'īs, unlike the Sunnīs, do not allow the agnates as such to inherit. Nor do they distinguish between agnate and cognate relatives; all inherit equally, unless there is a clearly authentic provision to the contrary. They further recognize the right of succession of infidels, apostates, and murderers. The usual presentation, sometimes mistaken for an explanation, of these differences is that the Sunnīs, as represented by the Hanafī school, were interested in keeping intact the ancient tribal structure of society. For this reason, the agnate heirs "remained in the Hanafī scheme the *most* important heirs. This substratum of pre-Islāmic custom was not demolished. . . . [But the Shī'īs] destroyed this principle completely . . . Cognates and agnates are placed on a footing of equality." [23]

Both the Sunnī Hanafī and the Shī'ī systems altered the customary law in accordance with the Qur'ān. But the Hanafīs allowed a minimal change and interpreted the Qur'ān strictly, superimposing its provisions on the customary law. The Shī'īs, on the other hand, interpreted the Qur'ān in a wider sense as altering not simply the old principles, but also as giving rise to a new set of principles. The Hanafīs tended to *particularize* the provisions of the Qur'ān and thus remained within the customary frame of reference. The Shī'īs tended to *generalize* the Qur'ānic instances, apply them to new similar situations, and thus accepted change. One point of departure was to preserve as much of the old as possible; the other was to entertain as much change as possible. [24]

What is sometimes offered as an explanation is probably merely a statement of fact. A satisfactory explanation is yet to be sought. As Fayzee put it, "the real cause of the difference between the principles of the Sunnite [Sunnī] law of inheritance and its Shiite [Shī'ī] counterpart is one of the most important problems remaining unexplained by modern research . . ." [25] However, not all Sunnī jurists agreed with the Hanafī scheme as regards the agnate relatives. Nor are the agnates the most important heirs. They inherit, if and when they do, the residue of the fixed shares. The principal sharers, who are divided in the Sunnī scheme into twelve categories of four male and eight female subclasses, may well exhaust the entire property. These shares may even go beyond and exceed a unity, in which case the rule of 'awl applies. If the agnates exclude some uterine relatives, it is perhaps because the former beneficiaries would be the ones responsible for the *praepcsitus* in case of need. When certain uterine relatives are not among the eight female sharers and are excluded by some agnate residuaries, it is probably because they are "carefree," not responsible for the support of any needy relative from whom they would not be allowed to inherit. They are exempted from the duty of kin support, which is enjoined upon the agnates. What is being done here apparently is not giving the agnates and excluding or depriving the uterine cognates arbitrarily. Rather, it is giving what the recipient may have to spend on other needy relatives or even on the *praepositus* himself, if he were to need help. The excluded uterines are free from such responsibilities; but when they inherit, as they do in certain cases, they too will be required to contribute to the support of those needy relatives from whom they may be entitled to inherit. This seems closer to a correspondence of rights and duties than to interest in keeping intact the ancient tribal structure of society. It is very unlikely that the Sunnī Hanafīs of Iraq, the so-called "rationalists" and pioneers of the jurisprudential frontiers, were particularly interested in preserving the tribal structure of society, a structure which might have been well adapted to the Arabian inland, but hardly to the cultural "melting pot" of Iraq. Perhaps the Sunnī 'Irāqīs did not wish to accelerate social change any more than was necessary or already taking place. Perhaps they were politically "conservative" as they necessarily identified themselves with the established order of the majority and were thus unenthusiastic about change. On the other hand, the Shī'īs constituted a "radical" minority and developed their own political theory. They advocated abolition of the established order, and aspired to replace it. They throve on the idea of change. The Sunnī were probably more like a "church" than a "sect;" the Shī'īs were the opposite. All this may, and it probably did, have some bearings on the two positions. But it seems untenable to suggest that the urbane Hanafī jurists of Iraq were nostalgic about the pre-Islāmic customary law of inheritance or committed to the preservation of the ancient tribal structure of society.

4. *Further Comments on Certain Issues*

a. *A Note on the Female Share*

The foregoing discussion might have given the impression that in the Shī'ī scheme of inheritance the female's share is invariably equal to the male's, an impression which may add to the exaggeration of the differences between the two schemes. This impression is even sometimes stated positively.[26] But in fact this is not so. In both schemes the daughter and the germane sister receive half as much as the son and the germane brother, respectively. This distribution scale is enjoined by the Qur'ān and is therefore binding on both Sunnīs and Shī'īs alike. Beyond this, the male and the female recipients inherit equally according to the Shī'ī scheme.

On the other hand, a survey of the Sunnī and general "Islāmicist" literature may lead to the conclusion that the female invariably receives a half share as contrasted with the male's full share. The further conclusion is that the female is held inferior to the male; she is discriminated against because of her sex and in continuation of the old system, which Islām could not replace completely. This latter conclusion may be partly based on some contemporary behavioral manifestations in certain Muslim localities, where women are not allowed to inherit at all, or where the oldest son receives a double share, contrary to the prescriptions of the law.[27] However, it is inaccurate to say that the female invariably receives less than the male counterpart. Nor does the standard explanation of the sexually differentiated shares seem satisfactory. The female uterine sister inherits equally with her uterine brother, and so does the mother with the father of the deceased. It is the daughter and the germane or consanguine sister who receive only half as much as their male counterparts when they inherit jointly.[28]

The case of the wife is particularly interesting. Her share

is one half of what the husband would inherit from her were he the survivor. The full implication of this provision must be seen in the light of the fact that the husband and the wife hold their properties and possessions independently of each other; between them there is no mandatory community of property. It is an interestingly verifiable proposition that the Muslim husband usually owns more than his wife and is therefore likely to leave more behind than she would, if he were to survive her. If he survives her, which is less likely from a demographic standpoint, his arithmetically larger share of inheritance — the one-half of her independently held and owned property — may in fact be equal to or even less than her arithmetically smaller share, the one-fourth of his independently held and owned property. This is assuming that there are no children involved; otherwise, his one-half becomes one fourth and her one fourth an eighth. At any rate, the two shares are arithmetically different; one share is the double of the other. Yet the value of a larger share (the husband's) of a small estate (the wife's) may be equal to or perhaps even less than the value of a small share (the wife's) of a large estate (the husband's). The end result here would seem to be that, while the two shares are arithmetically different, they are not necessarily unequal in the final analysis. And even if they appear mathematically unequal, Muslims would most likely contend that they are morally equitable in view of the husband's varied financial duties, the demographic facts, and the noncommunity of property. The same contention may be extended to other female cases.

It seems unlikely, however, that what Islāmic law stipulated in this regard was categorically discriminatory against the female sex as such. It has been shown that, apart from the wife's interesting case, the female sharer inherits equally with her male counterpart in two out of the four basic instances. In the remaining two, she receives only a half share in contrast to his full share. But it is an open question whether this has much to do with the sharer's sex *per se*. The Qur'ān accords the daughter or the non-uterine sister as much as one half of the entire property when she inherits jointly with the father of the deceased, who is allocated only one sixth of the property. The fact is that in certain cases, not in all, the female sharers receive half the shares of their male counterparts of the same grade. This is sometimes explained by certain scholars as being the result of pre-Islāmic discrimination against women, the inferior sex, discrimination which was carried over, at least in part, into Islām. But such an explanation probably seems simplistic and unsatisfactory to Muslim scholars, who would suggest, instead, another explanation. It may be submitted that in the Islāmic scheme of society women are free from the usual economic responsibility. They are not legally required to provide for any person, not even for themselves. If they have no independent resources, they are to be fully maintained by their able male relatives. The female is always assured by law of adequate care. Even the wealthy wife is to be maintained by the husband, the needy sister by the brother, the mother by the son, the daughter by the father, etc. Every living person needs subsistence, and every able male is held responsible for his own and possibly for that of other dependents. But not every deceased person leaves property for inheritance. This may suggest that the male is more likely to be "liable" than "beneficiary." His obligations to relatives, male and female alike, may well exceed what he could possibly inherit from any of them. When he sometimes receives a larger share of inheritance, it is probably in recognition of his manifold obligation and in partial compensation therefor. The whole scheme seems so designed as to ensure equity. When a larger share of the property is allocated to the exclusively liable male, who may be responsible for an entire household or perhaps beyond, and a smaller share is allocated to the "carefree" and economically "nonresponsible" female, the allocation cannot be easily called discriminatory against women. It would be discriminatory, indeed, if men and women were given the same or equal financial responsibilities. Since they are not, the sociological concept of differentiation or the Islāmic term of equity characterizes the Islāmic system more accurately than discrimination.[29]

However, the Muslim woman, by receiving a smaller share of the property than the man's, is not in fact being denied the fruits of any effort on her part or the produce of any of her labor. It is not that she *earned* something which is being withheld or taken away from her. Whatever she takes of the property of the deceased relative is in return for nothing material she has done or contributed. She inherits out of compassion or kindness, so to speak, and not because she has discharged or will discharge any financial duty to any relative. Even the few jurists who held the woman with means responsible for the support of needy kin stipulated, in one interpretation, that her share of the burden will be only according to her share of inheritance. For example, if she joins a brother in the support of a needy father, she will bear one third of the cost, while he bears two thirds, just as if they were sharing the father's estate.[30]

b. *The Posthumous Relations of the Deceased to His Property*

A contemporary student of legal institutions, J. Kohler, has pointed out that, "Inheritance is based on the idea of the continuity of the individual property after the death of its owner, through a person who is connected with this owner in a definite way . . ."[31] The Muslim version of this view is that the rights and duties of the individual do not end with his death. This is probably illustrated by the rules of inheritance, which regulate what must be done after the death of the owner and before the final division of the property among the heirs. There are three hierarchical claims against the property that originate with the deceased and must be met before any heir may claim his share or receive it. First, all the normal expenses entailed in the funeral of the deceased, without superfluity or deficiency, must be paid out of the property. Next, the debts and liabilities of the deceased must be paid from the remaining effects. Then, his testaments and wills are to be executed out of what remains after paying the funeral expenses and the debts. Finally, the remainder of the property is to be distributed among the heirs, each according to his share and grade.[32]

This hierarchical order of claims against the property is based on the instructions as well as the practice of the Prophet, and also on the likening of the deceased person's need in his lifetime, e.g., food, to his need after death, e.g., funeral. But, according to the Zāhirī doctrine, the payment of debts comes before the funeral expenses. If debts exhaust the property, the funeral expenses shall be borne jointly by all those Muslims present at the time. In any case, should the debts exceed the assets of the deceased, all the property shall be applied to the debts. The prospective heirs receive nothing, nor are they required by law to pay from their own assets the outstanding debts of their deceased relative, another instance of difference between Islāmic and Roman law.[33]

c. *Recapitulation and Partial Conclusions*

It is obvious that the Islāmic law of inheritance differed from the pre-Islāmic Arabian and Hebrew systems, as well as from Greek and Roman law. This difference was particularly reflected in the grounds of inheritance, the criteria of inclusion and exclusion, the categories of heirs, the manner and the scale of distribution, and the restrictions on testaments or wills. What may be especially significant is the difference between the Islāmic law of inheritance and the pre-Islāmic Arabian practice, a difference which is variously characterized as modification, amendment, and reform. The basic aspects of this difference are briefly the following:

1) The husband or wife was made an heir(ess).

2) Females and cognates became qualified to inherit.

3) Parents and ascendants were accorded the right of inheritance even where there were male descendants.

4) The female's share was sometimes equal to and sometimes a half of the share of her male counterpart.

Certain general principles underline the actual application of the law. Among these were the following:

1) "No distinction is made . . . between movable or immovable property, joint or separate, . . . realty or personality . . ."

2) There is no recognition of a birth right. "Rights of inheritance arise only on the death of a certain person . . ." Nor is the principle of "representation" recognized, although it may be replaced by other measures, e.g., the so-called "mandatory testament."

3) Lines of succession cannot be invented. No potential *praepositus* may appoint, select, or arbitrarily choose his successors. If he does, his action is void and legally inconsequential.[34]

The implications of this difference have been interpreted as a design neither to sweep away the past practices nor to endorse them completely. The customs and usages of the tribes near Makkah and al Madīnah were adapted to the Muslim law of inheritance when they were not clearly altered or abrogated by the Qur'ānic rules and/or the Prophet's instructions. Such customs and usages had no force in themselves, but they became incorporated into the Islāmic law of inheritance by tacit approval of the Prophet. An illustration of this convergence or synthesis of the old and the new is the case of the agnates, *'asbāt',* who have been likened to the *agnati* of Roman law. Before Islām, they constituted the primary, almost the only, category of heirs. Under Islām, they were replaced by the Qur'ānic heirs and became residuaries.[35] However, the most significant effect of the Islāmic law of inheritance is probably what Coulson has called a transition "from a society based on blood relationship to one based on a common religion; and in this new society the individual family has replaced the tribe as the basic unit." [36]

Different from or similar to its predecessors, the Islāmic law of inheritance has certain interesting features which have provoked different reactions. One of these features is the principle of *'awl,* which is applied when the prescribed shares exceed a unity, in which case the fractional shares are proportionately reduced. Exceeding a unity can only happen because of the inclusion of heirs of several categories and the tendency to make as many beneficiaries as possible. In this way a wide circulation of the property can be fostered and the concentration of wealth checked. Among the underlying principles the following would seem noteworthy: (a) creating or fostering a social sentiment of sharing, cooperation, and solidarity; (b) regulating the exercise of personal freedoms and rights, (c) imparting the idea that everything in fact belongs to God and the owner himself is merely a transitory successor or executor, and (d) promoting kin solidarity without favoritism or prejudice.[37]

However, this orientation to a wide circulation of wealth in such small or almost atomic shares is sometimes viewed with considerable skepticism. For example, Goitein believes that, "This law of inheritance, which, in my opinion, was based on the model of the division of spoils in tribal warfare . . . is very impracticable for sedentary populations." [38] Goitein's remark only represents what has been voiced by many scholars. Yet something fundamental seems to be missing, namely, another distinct feature of the Islāmic system which is called takhāruj[39] which means one or more heirs may agree to a settlement in compensation for their prescribed shares. It is a negotiated exclusion, in full or in part, whereby an heir who may not be interested in realty can be compensated for his share. It also applies where the nature of the property does not make it profitable to divide it in rigorous conformity with the law. Applying the law strictly does encourage wide circulation of property to check the concentration of wealth. But the principle of takhāruj may be adopted to keep intact as much of the estate as practically necessary or economically advisable. Thus the law of inheritance may not be frozen or static. Rather, it may show a capacity for potential adaptability to new situations, a feature that may well be taken, with certain reservations, as characteristic of the family system in Islām and also of Islāmic law as a whole.

8   CONCLUSION AND GENERAL DISCUSSION

Earlier in the introduction to this study, three questions were suggested as the focal points of the discussion. They are:

A. What do the Islāmic provisions say about any given aspect of the family structure?

B. How did these provisions become what they are, and how were they conceived?

C. What was the relationship between these provisions and the social basis?[1]

With respect to the first question, the study has sought to present a general but relatively inclusive view of the various aspects of the family system in Islām. An attempt has been made to put together in a somewhat eclectic fashion the components of the Muslim family system and to systematize the scattered views contained in numerous sources of religion, law, history, and literature.

The presentation has tried to follow as closely as possible the procedure outlined in the introduction.[2] The various provisions of the Muslim family system were derived from the normative sources of Islām and related to their sociocultural bases whenever there was a likelihood of any clear connection between the ideological and the behavioral components of the system. For example, the discussion of the *mut'ah* union, adoption, certain aspects of mate selection and maintenance may serve as illustrations of the applicability of this sociological method. However, such suggested explanations may, for one reason or another, have fallen somewhat short of the rigorous sociological standards, in which case interpretative alternatives were proposed as provisional grounds for further consideration and research. Nothing more than this is claimed.

In regard to the second question, the discussion may have shown that Muslim jurists conceived of these provisions first and foremost as religious in nature and tried to formulate them in religious terms. Their first binding source of legislation and guidance was the Qur'ān and the authentic Sunnah of the Prophet. But this did not mean an automatic exclusion of custom, reason, or "foreign" elements. The presentation of the sources of Islāmic law and of the relationship between the primary and other sources of law may illustrate the point.[3] Muslim jurists had no doubt that the stipulations of the Qur'ān and the "legislative" Sunnah of the Prophet stood supreme and were taken as revelations of divine origin, far superior to any customary laws or local institutions. However, the relationship between the primary religious sources of law and the local customs was not always easy. On occasions there was tension, which often resulted in different interpretations of the same text or provision, and which caused some reluctance even on Muḥammad's part. This may be illustrated, for example, by his attitude to the problem of adoption and his hesitation to give any immediate definite answer to the woman who argued with him over the *ẓihār* divorce formula.[4]

The development of Islāmic family legislation is viewed from a different perspective by non-Muslim scholars. The general position may be summed up in the following propositions.

1. There seems to be at least an implicit recognition of the difficulty of establishing the exact nature of the relationship between the Islāmic provisions and the local customs or the neighboring cultures.[5]

2. It is also recognized that some of the Islāmic provisions are identical with those of neighboring systems and/or local customs, while others are entirely different.[6]

3. It is almost unanimously maintained that it is imperative to avoid any rash judgment about the "external" influences on the Islāmic provisions. It is suggested, for example, that the similarities between the Islāmic and other systems in this respect may be nothing more than parallel developments; or that they may be due to a general human nature expressed in styles of thought and that they may be due to the fact that the religious and moral exhortations of the Qur'ān are in

the main of such a very general nature that they could be paralleled in any literature of popular instruction.[7]

4. In spite of this appeal for caution and the differences between the Islāmic and other systems, many scholars are inclined to speak, in varying degrees, of the external influences on Islām's family provisions. Their views on the source and extent of this influence differ as the following summation may show.

a) The influence came basically from local and pre-Islāmic customs; very little was directly derived from the neighboring cultures.

b) It was more Christian than Jewish, according to some observers; more Jewish than Christian, according to others.

c) It took the form of what Obermann called "unmistakable borrowing," "faithful imitation," "explicit and solemn adherence to, and endorsement of, 'what had been revealed before.' " [8]

d) It took the form of limited adaptive borrowing, since Islām's main developments were in the context of a general human and cultural environment common to various peoples and cultures.[9]

e) It was not always in the positive direction; rather it took the form of a general debt, particularly to Judaism. In Rosenthal's words, "Islām is indebted to Judaism, be it by way of complete or partial acceptance, modification or outright rejection and opposition." [10]

f) However extensive, it was not always one-sided. As Goitein has put it, ". . . one is led to assume that the influence of Judaism on early Islām must have been considerable, if not decisive . . . [But] Islām amply repaid Judaism." [11]

These different views may be conveniently regarded as variations on the more general theme of acculturation and cultural change. Modern research has developed a large body of theory, to be sure, but it has not settled the lingering disputes between the diffusionists and the evolutionists, between those who incline to explain cultural similarities in terms of contact, conscious and explicit imitation or single occurrences

CONCLUSION AND GENERAL DISCUSSION

of cultural traits, and those who adhere to the idea of the independent growth or "rebirth" and change of cultures. Refinement and reconsideration of these theories have led some scholars to alternative modes of analysis, e.g., functionalism, linguistics, etc. But the fact still remains that the truth, as Linton has observed, lies somewhere between the polar extremes of diffusionism and evolutionism. There is no conclusive evidence in support of either. Certain findings seem to confirm diffusionism, while others substantiate evolutionism. The explanation probably lies in what Murdock calls "the principle of limited possibilities." Accordingly, "the various aspects of social organization admit of only a very few . . . alternative variations." [12]

In view of these factors, it would probably involve a long digression and yet hold little promise for us at this point to pursue the inquiry any further. Nevertheless, some general remarks may be helpful. It is reasonably well established that the provisions of the Islāmic family system did not bud and blossom in a wild desert or gush from nowhere. They did not come about as a result of some "immaculate conception" unrelated to any historical or social roots. Muslim scholars readily recognize, as we have shown, the role of custom in the development of Islāmic law and the strong affinities between Islām and its predecessors. They have gone so far as to declare laws based on previous revelations as an integral part of Islāmic law and thus binding on Muslims, unless there are clear instructions to the contrary. They believe that divine revelation is God's gift to mankind and not the exclusive monopoly of any single generation, group, or person. And if there were any conscious or deliberate borrowings from authentic Jewish or Christian sources, Muslims would most probably be the first to acknowledge the "debt," a debt which, in their idea system, is not owed so much to any given group as it is to a common universal source of guidance, namely God. In fact, such debts have been acknowledged. There is apparently no reason to do otherwise. The Qur'ān already speaks very highly and much more frequently of the previous

Messengers, particularly Moses and Jesus, than it does of Muḥammad. Their revelations are lauded as sources of light, guidance, and good news. Their followers are honorably called the People of the Book, the kind treatment of whom is enjoined upon Muslims. Islām itself was not so much a replacement or innovation as it was a restatement or continuity of the former revelations.[13] Such factors seem to cast doubt on any contention that Muslims borrowed from the neighboring systems without proper acknowledgement. They, together with the current theory of cultural change, may suggest new lines of research on the extent of the relationship between the Islāmic and other local or neighboring systems.

Considering the third question about the relationship between the Islāmic family provisions and their social basis, the discussion has probably shown that it was the interactive rather than the deterministic type. In numerous instances the new law endorsed the pre-existing principles and rules of marriage and divorce. In equally numerous instances it entirely abrogated or fundamentally modified many of the pre-existing patterns. The law was neither totally "passive" nor completely "active." Its provisions were sometimes received and implemented with enthusiasm, sometimes with astonishment and perhaps even resentment. Yet whatever it stipulated by way of either endorsement, modification, or fresh initiation took on religious characteristics and gradually commanded the allegiance of most Muslims most of the time.

Some observers, as Rosenthal, speculate that, although much of Islām's preaching ran counter to Arab ways of thought and life, basically it appealed to a contemporary religious longing among the Arabs. The social as well as the economic situation was no less favorable. But, "The genius of Mohammed has mixed the various ingredients in such a way that something new, something fresh, different from its sources, has emerged."[14] Certain Qur'ānic regulations "represent some of the most radical reforms of the Arabian customary law." Among these were the rules that the wife became the sole recipient of the dower and the socioeconomic implications thereof, the waiting period or *'iddah* for divorced and widowed women, the change of the honor criterion from lineage to piety, the relative expansion of incest boundaries, and so on. Yet these regulations, observes Coulson, "modify in certain particulars rather than supplant entirely the existing law." [15] It is, of course, a different question whether a total supplantation was intended, feasible, desirable, or necessary.

However, the most "radical reform" was probably the introduction into family life and social action in general of new religious elements that changed the moral character of the newly confirmed customs into sanctified precedents and brought about a new "definition of the situation." This was perhaps most manifest in the area of family stability. Stern has noted that the "outstanding feature" of the pre-Islāmic system "appears to be the looseness of marriage ties in general and the lack of any legal system for regulating procedure." But the situation changed after Islām and, according to the same source, one of the factors "which possibly introduced a further element of stability into the institution of marriage was that the origin of Muḥammad's ordinances on the subject was in divine revelation, which endowed them with a certain religious sanction hitherto unknown . . . [These ordinances] were applicable if not then, at a later date, to the whole community." [16] The same idea is reiterated by other scholars, who also attribute the relative stability of marriage in Islām to the fact that Muḥammad's own manner of living has become normative for Muslims, that there has never been a categorical distinction between religion and law, and that the law schools do subscribe to the same general system notwithstanding their innumerable differences on minor points.[17]

The discussion may have brought to light certain interesting facts which could conceivably reinforce the general thesis of interaction between the Islāmic normative system and its sociocultural basis. Islām had much in common with its predecessors, but it was also different from them in fundamental respects. Islāmic law was believed to be grounded in revelation, but it was also supplemented by various human sources, without consciously abandoning its basic religious characteristics. Its sources were found to be comprehensive, and its tributaries almost inexhaustible. It was extended to cover virtually every conceivable act of the body and the mind. This extensiveness inevitably raises extraordinary problems about the relation between law in action and law in conception, between law and religion, or law and morality. Some of these problems remain unsolved and are probably unsolvable; they are but reflections of the general condition of man the imperfect finite or "man the unknown." But one fact seems indisputable: divested of its religious and moral basis, the Islāmic family system is likely to appear meaningless, incomprehensible, inconsistent, and altogether impracticable. Given the assumed proper orientation and the expected moral conditions, the picture will reflect different colors. Whether this is a common fate of all legal codes or a unique case is another question.

Based on the main discussion, the Islāmic family law may be broadly characterized as an open system of alternatives, although these rest in the final analysis on some limited but general principles. These alternatives probably emerged first in response to the diversity of the pre-Islāmic Arabian mode of life, and, later, the heterogeneity of the societies into which Islām was introduced. However, being equally lawful or equally binding and applicable, such alternatives not only contain promising seeds of growth and carry great potentials, but they also can create problems of confusion, indecisiveness, and partisanship when alienated from their religious and moral foundations. Such an open system of various alternatives may leave the actor undecided or confused. When the situation is clearly structured and presents the actor with the only one fixed pattern to follow, it is relatively easy for him to conform or deviate, depending on his dispositions. But when the situation is open-ended or presents the actor with alternative choices, it may be difficult for him to choose the "right" course for the "right" occasion, unless he is richly endowed with judiciousness. Since most individuals are not so endowed, and since Islām recognizes no religious trusteeship over people, every individual is left with the task of choosing his course from among the alternatives available to him. Commoners may by accident or ascription subscribe to one particular alternative or pattern. They may adhere to it so closely that in time they come to believe theirs to be the only or most perfect pattern. The distance is very short between this and blind partisanship or intellectual barrenness. Thus what is originally or potentially a promising source of moral growth, constructive social change, and intellectual expansion may turn out at certain crossroads to be a cause of retardation and shrinking.

In this study there have been occasions on which an impasse was encountered because the internal or textual evidence was inconclusive. It could not support any given position more than it could its opposites. But when the problem was placed in the sociological realm, when the sociological principles and concepts were utilized, the problem became a little clearer and much better explained. This may suggest that the sociological perspective can be utilized at least as a complementary method to explain normative systems. To claim more or less may border on monism and thus become unwarranted.

Probably one of the most interesting and appreciable facts to come to light is what may be called "misplaced analogies" or "misguided contrasts." In their work, Muslim scholars almost invariably approach the Islāmic family system from an ideal, normative height. From such a standpoint, admiration, glorification, and even boasting may flow easily. In this quasi-ecstatic situation, comparisons or contrasts with other systems become particularly appealing and often take a wrong course. What is usually compared or contrasted is the ideal normative character of one system and the behavioral, often "deviant," representations of another. Even when reminded of the behavioral discrepancies within their own system, Muslim writers may merely hasten to condemn the

deviations and label them as untypical, unseemly aberrations
resulting from the lack of piety or weakness of character.
Little more than this is rarely attempted.

On the other hand, Western scholars approach the Muslim
family system almost entirely from a behavioral plane. In
their work they are more attracted to the discrepancies than
to the ideals or even the normalities. Here, too, comparisons
or contrasts are tempting, but they are usually made between such obvious deviations and the ideals of other systems, be they religious, moral, philosophical, legal, or even
personal. When such scholars do consider the ideal normative
elements of the Islāmic family system, they often call them
exceptions, particulars, short-lived transplantations or the
like. This seems to be the general characteristic of the
modern scene of Islāmic and Islāmicist scholarship.

The implications of this situation are clear enough and
need no further elaboration. It is now opportune for these
research strategies and approaches to be changed. For
scholarly as well as human reasons, comparisons and contrasts, if they are desired or relevant, should be attempted
on the same system level, that is, between the ideals only,
the actuals only, or, better yet, both the ideals and the actuals
of the respective systems. In this way, scholars will hope-
fully cease to talk past one another, sound fruitful scholarship
will develop, mutual human understanding and appreciation
will grow. Such goals are integral to the social scientific vocation.

This study has probably raised more questions than it has
sought to answer. Some of these pertain to the past, some
to the future course of the Muslim family. Such questions may
be formulated by every researcher according to his own purpose and interests. But in view of the rapid, unprecedented
rate of social change throughout the globe and the increasing
contact between the nations of the world, long-range pre-
dictions may be presumptuous on our part. Yet it can be
safely said that the ideological and behavioral differences
among peoples are narrowing. Acculturation is taking place

on a scale hitherto unknown. Ecumenism, pluralism, and similar terms are becoming commonplace in modern man's vocabulary. Traditional societies are adopting new ways and emulating modern social patterns. Modern industrialized societies themselves seem to some observers to have exhausted the possibilities of originality, and to be turning increasingly to what may be essentially traditional primitive ways. The claim is occasionally made, even by otherwise serious observers, that there is nothing "new" that has not been done or thought of by some one at some time in the remote or recent past.

Be that as it may, Islām is no longer the conquering faith or the dominant culture of the world. Muslim nations, intellectuals, leaders, and youth are becoming more and more active participants in world's affairs through international agencies, regional organizations, cultural contact, academic and intellectual cross-fertilization. They more or less partake of the new ecumenical world view of pluralism, accommodation, and co-existence. As a result, the contemporary Muslim family will most probably be forced by internal or external pressures of various kinds to change. The direction and extent of change will in all likelihood depend mainly on (1) how much use Muslim scholars can make of the resourceful foundations and alternatives of Islāmic law, and how much benefit they can draw from the vast experiences of mankind throughout the centuries; and (2) how strongly Muslim leaders and intellectuals are committed to the conservation and growth of the Islāmic ideology. The contemporary crisis of the family in the industrialized world is appealing to social reformers to seek remedies. If the true structure of the family in Islām is successfully brought to their attention, they may well discover how the classic solutions of Islām can help to solve their modern problems.

NOTES

CHAPTER ONE

1. In Nye, pp. 293 ff; cf. Fustel de Coulanges in Kocourek, 284-6; Davis (1), pp. 392 ff; Goode (3), p. vi; M. Levy (1),'pp. 30 ff.

2. Cf. Parsons (1), p. 21; Sorokin, pp. 14-17.

3. *Ibid.* p. 19. See also Bernard, p. 235; Buckley, p. 67 and *passim;* Christensen, pp. 24, 30, 253; M. Levy (1), pp. 6 f, 11 ff; Murdock, pp. 67 and *passim.*

4. See, for example, Catton, pp. 928 ff; Broom and Selznick, pp. 68 ff.

5. See, for example, Coulson (1), pp. 80 f; Faruki, pp. 20 ff.

6. See, for example, Arberry (1), pp. 1 ff.

7. Cf. J. 'Alī, vol. 6, pp. 6-7, 177 ff; Goitein, pp. 10 ff; Lewis, pp. 29 ff, 22 ff; Margoliouth (2), pp. 61-2; Rosenthal (3), pp. 5-6; Torrey, pp. 9-13, 17-8, 24 ff; Della Vida, pp. 26, 35, 54; Zaydān (1), pp. 17-23. For a general discussion of evolutionism see, for example, *American Sociological Review,* 29: 3 (June 1964); Davis (1), p. 515.

8. Lewis, pp. 21 ff; cf. S. A. Ali (2), p. LXIX; Della Vida, p. 35; Jeffery, p. 44; Hitti, pp. 14-23.

9. Lewis, pp. 30-1, 41; cf, J. 'Alī, vol. 8, 145 ff; al Alūsī, vol. I, 243; Fayzee, pp. 3, 6; Roberts, p. 3; Della Vida, pp. 41, 54-5; Watt (2), pp. 3, 16 ff and (4), pp. 10, 84 f, 154; Wolf, pp. 330 ff.

10. Lewis, p. 34; cf. Hitti, p. 23.

11. *Ibid.* pp. 25, 30, 35.

12. Arberry (1), p. 32; J. 'Alī, vol. 5, pp. 369-370; al Alūsī, vol. 2, pp. 194 ff; Bell (1), pp. 4, 9-11; *Ency. of Islām,* vol. 2, p. 258; Fayzee, pp. 10-11; Lewis, pp. 25 ff, 30, 39; Rosenthal (3), pp. 73, 139.

13. Lewis, p. 31; cf. al Dawālībī, pp. 57 *seqq.;* Gibb (3), pp. 1, 12, 24-5.

14. Smith (1), pp. 55-6.

15. Fayzee, pp. 4, 6.

16. This is the essence of a dialogue between an Arab notable and a Persian king as reproduced in Alūsī, vol. 1, p. 150; cf. Lewis, p. 30.

17. Cf. Roberts, pp. 3-6; Smith (1), pp. 22 *seqq.* and *passim;* Stern, pp. 24-5, 59-62, 67-70 and *passim;* Watt (2), pp. 19-20, 23-4, (4), pp. 10, 84-5, 154; Wolf, pp. 330 ff.

18. See, for example, Fayzee, pp. 5-7; R. Levy, pp. 53, 271-5; Smith, *loc. cit.* (note 17); Stern, *loc. cit.* (note 17); cf. Abū Zahrah (3), pp. 731 *seqq.;* al Alūsī, vol. 1, p. 243; al Hūfī (2), pp. 88 *seqq.;* Jum'ah. Gibb (2, p. 15), speaks of the Islāmic peoples as heirs of some of the

oldest societies which were in possession of "a highly developed social instinct," and which recognized that any enduring social structure "must rest upon a general will, not on enforced consent or on complex organization . . ."

19. Parsons (3), pp. 26 *seqq.,* p. 167 ff; Davis (1), p. 30.

20. Cf. Jum'ah, p. 9; 'Awwā, pp. 10 *seqq.*

21. Cf. Hitti, pp. 26-8; Lewis, pp. 29 ff; Watt (2), pp. 19, 72 ff.; Wolf, p. 335; Smith (1), pp. 1-3, 22-3 and *passim;* Roberts, pp. 3-4; R. Levy, pp. 53, 272 ff.

22. Smith (1), p. 22.

23. *Ibid.* p. 57; cf. pp. 160 ff.

24. Watt (2), p. 19; cf. pp. 72 *seqq.,* 152-3; Wolf, p. 335.

25. Smith (1), p. 41; cf. 44-5 and *passim;* Jum'ah; al Hūfī (2).

26. R. Levy, p. 272.

27. Wolf, pp. 335-6.

28. Fayzee, pp. 6-7; R. Levy, pp. 271 ff; Lewis, pp. 29-30.

29. Watt (2), pp. 20-24; cf. Farrūkh, p. 35; Wolf, p. 336.

30. Patai, p. 19; cf. al Hūfī (2), 230, 266-85, 294; MacDonald, p. 68.

31. See, for example, Smith (1); Jum'ah; Wāfī (3); al Hūfī (1 and 2); R. Levy; Roberts; Stern.

32. Goitein, esp. 6, 23, 25-7, 31, 89; J. 'Alī, vol. 6, pp. 6-8, 177-8, 283; Jum'ah, pp. 5 *seqq.;* Margoliouth (2), esp. 59-62, 70; Albright, 27; *The Times,* lit. supp., p. 943.

33. J. 'Alī, *loc. cit.* (note 32); Margoliouth, *loc. cit.* (note 32); Torrey, pp. 16-32.

34. For a general discussion of this complex problem see, for example, J. 'Alī, vol. 6, pp. 3-50, 177-8, 283; Bell (1), pp. 10-15; Della Vida, pp. 55-6; Geiger, pp. 4 ff; Goitein, pp. 10-12, 33ff, 49-50, 60-1; al Hūfī (1), pp. 137-142 and (2), pp. 22-30; Lewis, pp. 32-5; Margoliouth (2), pp. 1, 55-71, 81-2; Rosenthal (3), pp. xi-xii, 5 ff, 70 ff, 142; Torrey, pp. 3-8, 16-32; Watt (4), pp. 85 ff; Wolf, p. 329.

35. Della Vida, p. 54; cf. J. 'Alī, vol. 6, p. 68; Bell (2), p. 16 ff.

36. Bell (2), pp. 16-7; cf. 41 ff; Guillaume, p. 130; al Hūfī (1), p. 149 f.

37. Cf. Bell (1), 4, 10; Guillaume, *loc. cit.;* al Hūfī (1), 146-50 and (2), pp. 40-2; J. 'Alī, vol. 6, esp. pp. 51-9, 68, 89, 241, 280 f.

38. Von Grunebaum, pp. 2-3; cf. Fayzee, pp. 10-11; Watt (2), pp. 23-4, 152-3; Rosenthal (3), p. 4.

39. Lewis, p. 30; cf. p. 25; J. 'Alī, vol. 8, pp. 145 *seqq.;* Wolf, pp.

337 ff; al Alūsī, vol. 1, 243; Burton (1), p. 333.

40. Wolf, p. 329; cf. Gibb (3), pp. 1, 12, 24-5; Watt (2), pp. 23-4, 152-3.

41. Gibb (3), pp. 2-4. In view of the numerous and often inconsistent accounts of the rise of Islām, our summary review will be based mainly on Gibb's succinct survey; cf. R. Levy, pp. 1 ff; Watt (2), pp. 23-4, 152-3; Wolf, pp. 344 ff.

42. Ibid. pp. 5-7; cf. pp. 72-3 and (2), pp. 2-10.

43. Ibid. pp. 7-8.

44. Ibid. pp. 9-10.

45. Ibid. Coulson (1), pp. 97 seqq., takes a different view of the role of law in the unity of Islāmic society and its schools of legal thought. For a classical Muslim view, see al Tūsī vol. 2, pp. 251, 258, 276-81.

46. Ibid. pp. 11, 15-22. This survey covers the history of Islām up to the last two centuries. The reference cited here contains an annotated bibliography (pp. 192-3) of fourteen basic sources.

47. Shaltūt (2), p. 5 (this writer's translation).

48. Shorter Ency. of Islam, pp. 524 ff.

49. Ibid. p. 102.

50. Ibid. p. 524.

51. In connection with this discussion, see, for example, Madkūr (2), p. 11; Fayzee pp. 22 f.; Faruki, pp. 18 ff; Khallāf, p. 282; Coulson (1), p. 85; Schacht (2); Santillana, p. 290; Shorter Ency. of Islām, pp. 102-7, 524-9.

52. For a balanced view of this extremely controversial issue, see especially the following sources: al 'Anī; Coulson (1); Vesey-Fitzgerald; Ibn Taymiyyah; al Jaṣṣāṣ; Khadduri; Khallāf Madkūr; Maḥmaṣānī; Schacht (3); Shaltūt (2).

53. Gibb (1), p. 149; cf. pp. 146 ff; (2), p. 87, (3), pp. 88 ff, 99 seqq.; Khadduri, pp. 3-4; Coulson (1), pp. 11-4, 83; Schacht (2).

54. Gibb (3), pp. 33 ff; (1), pp. 150, 159 ff; cf. Abū Zahrah (3), p. 21; Coulson (1), p. 83; Khadduri, p. 22; MacDonald, pp. 86-7; Perelman, pp. viii-xi; Ibn Qudāmah, vol. 8, pp. 166 ff.

55. See, for example, Khallāf, pp. 112-132; Shorter Ency. of Islām, p. 526.

56. Cf. Justice Jackson, in Khaddouri et al., eds., p. vii; Gibb (3), pp. 99 ff; Coulson (1), pp. 83-4 Vesey-Fitzgerald, pp. 2, 7-8; Santillana, pp. 289-92, 305; Maḥmaṣānī (2), p. 106; al Qur'ān, 5:3; 21:107; 22:78.

57. Cf. Gibb (1), pp. 147, 164-5; (2), p. 88; (3), pp. 104 ff;

Coulson (1), pp. 25-6, 83-4; Khadduri, p. 22.

58. Cf. Gibb (1), p. 163. For a general discussion of the highly complex concept of justice and related issues, see Perelman. On the relationship between the differential effects of social norms, see, for example, Davis (1), ch. 3.

CHAPTER TWO

1. Murdock, p. 1.

2. *Ibid;* cf. pp. 41 ff; Bernard, pp. 221-2; Goode (1), p. 45; M. Levy (1), pp. 2-3, 102 *seqq.;* Zelditch (2), pp. 698-9.

3. The word "marital" is used in a general sense so as to include all legitimate sex relations, whether between free persons, slaves, or a combination of both.

4. Instead of the rather cumbersome phrase "mutual rights and obligations," "mutual obligations" will be used to denote the same.

5. Cf. Murdock, p. 1; Berelson and Steiner, p. 297.

6. The term "polygamy" denotes (a) polyandry (plurality of husbands only), (b) polygyny (plurality of wives only), and (c) group marriage (plurality of husbands and wives); cf. Murdock, pp. 24-5. Since (a) and (c) are absolutely forbidden in Islām, it would be more accurate to use the term polygyny instead of the equivocal term polygamy. This will be followed unless the word "polygamy" appears in quotations, in which case it is taken to mean polygyny. On the definition of the "extended," "polygamous" and other family types, see Murdock, pp. 1-2; 41 ff; Coser, p. xiv; Berelson and Steiner, p. 297; Bernard, pp. 221-4 Kirkpatrick, pp. 84-6; Christensen, pp. 3-5; Goode (1), p. 45.

7. On the definition of social position and related concepts, see, for example, Winch, pp. 391-2; Hill and Rodgers, pp. 176, 178-9, 203. For a kinship typology, see Murdock, pp. 41 ff.

8. This point will be elaborated in Chapter 5.

9. See, for example, *al Qur'ān,* 2:225-237; 3: 140; 4:1-35, 127-130, 176; 5:47-50.

10. To this effect there are many passages in the *Qur'ān* and the Traditions of the Prophet; cf. 2:177-182; 3:103-104; 4:34-37, 9:23-24; 17:23-24; 33:4-6; 49:10; 64:14-16.

11. Cf. *al Qur'ān,* 4:7-8, 36; 17:26; 30-38; Ibn al Qayyim (3), vol. 4, pp. 319 *seqq.*

12. Cf. *al Qur'ān,* 2:188; 4:11-12, 176; al Shāfi'ī (3), vol. 4, pp. 108, 112, 115, al Jaṣṣāṣ, vol. 2, pp. 119-22; Ibn al Kayyim (2), vol. 2, p. 310; Wāfī (2), 21 ff; Mūsā, pp. 86-7, 167 ff, 185-94; Jeffery, p. 70. See also *infra.* Chs. 5 and 7.

13. Cf. *al Qur'ān*, 33:4- 6.

14. *Ibid;* cf. al Zamakhsharī, vol. 3, pp. 519-22; Arberry (2), vol. 2, p. 121.

15. Smith (1), pp. 44-7; cf. R. Levy, p. 147.

16. On the fate of apostates see, for example, *Shorter Ency.*, pp. 413-4; Harb and Maẓhar, p. 12. The question is a highly controversial issue. As far as the Qur'ān stands, there is unanimity that the apostate is threatened with punishment in the next world only; nothing more could be inferred from the thirty-one references in the Qur'ān to apostasy (Cf. 3:86; 4:137; 5:54; 9:67; 16:106-7). The Traditions and other law sources contain equivocal provisions, the interpretation of which varies. In one interpretation, the apostate must be invited to repent and if he refuses he must be put to death. In another, even his repentance is unacceptable to God; only death is his lot. Still in another, Traditions report that the Prophet forgave apostates. Contemporary Muslim writers take the position that all the authentic sources of law and history insure the apostate's right to life, property, and freedom of conscience so long as he does not engage in subversive, disorderly activities to undermine the social fabric. To account for the death penalty cited in some Traditions and law books, these writers claim that it is the result of a confusion between the peaceful intellectual type of apostasy, which is, they maintain, tolerable in Islām, and the militant, aggressive type, which is punishable with death. Moreover, they contend that the ruling to kill apostates came to some Muslim jurists through the influence of Christian Byzantine traditions, according to which apostates were put to death (see the references cited above in this note).

17. In connection with this discussion, see, for example, *al Qur'ān*, 33:4-5, 36-7, 40; Watt (4), pp. 156-9; *Shorter Ency.*, p. 653; Haykal, pp. 315 *seqq.*

18. Cf. the references in note 14 of this chapter.

19. On the definition of "households," "secondary families," and related concepts, see Christensen, p. 5.

20. Cf. *al Qur'ān*, 3:103; 8:72-75; 9:22-23, 71; 33:3-6; 49:10; Wolf, pp. 344, 352; R. Levy, pp. 3, 55.

21. In connection with these illustrations, see, for example, *Shorter Ency.*, pp. 62, 500-01, 651; Hitti, pp. 106, 117, 259; R. Levy, pp. 425-6; Haykal, pp. 147-8, 330, 494, 514, 528; *al Tāj*, vol. 3, pp. 320-3.

22. Cf. *al Qur'ān*, 49:10-13; R. Levy, *loc. cit.* (note 20). A typical thirteenth century Muslim explanation is rendered by Levy (p. 55) as follows: "All are equal in this [being created by means of a father and

mother] and there is no reason therefore for boasting of one's lineage
. . . Through piety are souls brought to perfection and persons may
compete in excellence in it; and let him who desires honour seek it in
piety."

23. Cf. al Qur'ān, 2:184-185, 286; 6:119, 151-153; 17:8. Several
passages to this effect are also found in the Traditions of the Prophet.
While these passages were pronounced with reference to specific
events, the jurists, using the principle of analogy and guided by the
general spirit of Islām, have generalized them and derived universal
rules therefrom.

24. Cf. Murdock, pp. 26-7; M. Levy (1), p. 10.

25. Cf. al Qur'ān, 4:1-3, 127-30.

26. See, for example, Jeffery, pp. 58-9; Roberts, pp. 7 ff; Stern, pp.
78 seqq.; Merchant, p. 150; Wāfī (1), pp. 55 ff.

27. Cf. al Qur'ān, 2:170; 5:50; 6:4; 41:31-44; 46:7; 68:6-15;
81:21-27.

28. Ibid. 2:106.

29. Cf. Ibid. 5:24; Ibn al Qayyim (3), vol. 3, pp. 439 ff; al
Zamakhsharī, vol. 1, pp. 634-5.

30. It is a general rule of Islāmic law that duties are proportionate to
rights, or for every liability there is a corresponding gain. See, e.g.,
Maḥmaṣānī (1), pp. 342-3, (2), pp. 203 ff.

31. Cf. al Qur'ān, 4:36; 9:23-24; 17:22-29; 29:8; 31:15; 58:22,
64:14-16; Ibn al Qayyim (3), vol. 4, pp. 319 seqq.; also Ch. 5.

32. This permission is not granted to Muslim women for reasons
which will be discussed in Chapter 4.

33. Cf. al Qur'ān, 5:5; al Shāfi'ī (3), vol. 5, pp. 6-9; al Jaṣṣāṣ, vol. 1,
pp. 391 seqq.

34. al Shāfi'ī (3), vol. 4, pp. 73-4; 'Abd' Allāh, pp. 82-3. The same
rule is stated in many sources and is based on a Tradition attributed to
the Prophet as well as on the principle of analogy; cf. infra., Ch. 7.

35. Cf. al Qur'ān, 2:256; 10:99.

36. Cf. Ibid. 2:165-170; 19:41-48; 22:1-2; 23:101; 31:33; 33:65-
68; 40:47-48; 70:10-14; 80:34-37. It must be pointed out that there is
no way readily demonstrative of whether or not these suggested explanations were the actual reasons for Islām's position on these matters. What
is factual, however, is that there are textual passages and explicit provisions derived therefrom concerning individual responsibility, religious
freedom, mutual expectatons, and so on. But the interrelationship between these passages and the rationale behind these provisions is not

always so explicit or specific as they are. Nor do they seem to have been conceived in the same way as they are interpreted here. Perhaps, then, the most that can be claimed is this: if the historical situation were reconstructed in its entirety and the perspectives of social science applied to explain that interrelationship and rationale, the explanation would probably be very much similar to what is suggested here.

37. This recognition, together with its implications, is stated in several passages in the Qur'ān; cf. 6:35; 10:99; 11:117-118. See also the comment in the previous note.

38. Cf. al Qur'ān, 4:135; 5:8; 60:8.

39. Ibid. 17:22-29; 19:41-48; 29:5-8; 31:14-21; 46:15-19. All such references should be read in conjunction with the precautionary statement in note 36 above.

40. Cf. Murdock, p. 43; Bernard, pp. 223 f. A contemporary student of the family has observed that even the Anglo-Saxons were nearly like the Hebrews and Romans in stressing, among other things, the kinship group over the conjugal family; cf. Queen, p. 19. It is not clear, however, whether the kinship group was so stressed because it was considered more natural than other groups, or was considered more natural because it was so stressed. No matter which was the "cause" of which, the point is that the kinship group is more natural than any other grouping.

41. Cf. Murdock, pp. 5-9, 260-4; al Qur'ān, 23:1-7; 24:30-31; 70:22-35.

42. Cf. al Qur'ān, 2:225-236; 4:3, 13-14, 26-31; 56:1-7; Ibn al Qayyim (2), vol. 2, p. 52, vol. 3, p. 19.

43. Cf. al Qur'ān, 2:227-232, 236-237; 65:1-7.

44. Cf. Ibid. 4:19-22; 30:21. There are Traditions to this effect. See, for example, al Ṣāliḥ, pp. 447 seqq.; Ibnal Qayyim (2), vol. 3, pp. 153, 168; (3), vol. 2, pp. 433-6. Vesey-Fitzgerald (p. 35) summarizes the point as follows: "In spite of the ease of divorce, marriage is in intention a lifelong union."

45. Cf. Smith (1), pp. 68 ff; Fayzee, p. 112; Ency. of Islām, vol. 3, p. 774 ff; Farrukh, pp. 95-7; al Tūsī, vol, 2, pp. 394-5; Maghniyyah (1), pp. 128 ff; al Qur'ān, 4:29; Madkūr (2), p. 210 al Qayyim (3), vol. 2, pp. 433-6; al Shafi'ī (3), vol. 7, pp. 174-5; al Jaṣṣāṣ, vol. 2, pp. 177 ff. It is rather curious that many modern intellectuals, especially in the United States, have reacted to the relatively fixed religious code of sex and marriage of Western tradition by advocating "trial marriages" as a partial solution to the dilemma of sexual morality of modern so-

ieties. See, for example, *Time* (April 14, 1967), pp. 110, 112. Trial
marriage of one-year term was one of three types advocated after
W.W.I. The second type was *term marriage,* contracted for five years,
after which time the parties would be free to dissolve it or consummate
it permanently. The third type was *companionate marriage* or childless marriage with legalized birth control; Cf. Leslie, p. 126 (n.). For
a historical survey, see Westermarck (1), vol. 1, pp. 133 ff. More recently, some female state legislators have been trying to introduce bills
legalizing experimental marriage, especially for college students. De-
riding institutional marriage has become fashionable. The chaos in
contemporary sexual behavior almost defies description.

46. Cf. *al Qur'ān,* 23:5-7; 70:29-31; Smith (1), pp. 60 *seqq.* and
passim; Jum'ah, pp. 40-6; Stern, p. 74; al Alūsī, vol. 2, pp. 3 ff; 'Awwā,
pp. 17-23.

47. See, for example, Smith (1), pp. 68 ff, 82-3 and *passim;* Coulson
(1), pp. 14-5; R. Levy, p. 94; Roberts, pp. 1, 7-9; Jeffery, pp. 58-9;
Stern, pp. 81-2.

48. Cf. *al Qur'ān,* 2:187, 197, 221; 4:4, 15-6, 20-5; 23:5-7; 70: 29-
31; 'Abd al Bāqī (1), vol. 2, pp. 111 ff; Ibn al Qayyim (3), vol. 3, pp.
307 *seqq.;* Roberts, pp. 9, 18; Jeffery, pp. 58-9; notes 2-3 in Chapter
3 below.

49. Gordon, *Ency. Britannica,* vol. 20, p. 629 *seqq.;* cf. Finely, *International Ency. of the Social Sciences,* vol. 14, pp. 308 ff; Douglas (ed.),
pp. 1195. It may be noteworthy that this work makes extensive citations
of the relevant passages in the Bible and the Code of Hammurabi.

50. Quoted in Roberts, p. 53.

51. *al Qur'ān,* 2:177, 4:36; 9:60; 24:33; Roberts, pp. 56-60; Jeffery,
pp. 70-1; R. Levy, pp. 77, 221; Gordon, pp. 633-4; *al Tāj,* vol. 2, pp.
350 ff.

52. Cf. *al Qur'ān,* 2:177; 4:36, 92; 5:89; 9:60; 24-32-3; 47:4;
58:3. See also R. Levy, pp. 76, 80; Roberts, pp. 54 ff; Finely, p. 308;
Wāfī (3), pp. 92-8; *al Tāj,* vol. 2, pp. 246 *seqq.,* 322-3.

53. Cf. Jeffery, p. 59; R. Levy, pp. 79-80, 117-8, 136; Roberts, pp.
9-10, 16-7; Wāfī (1), pp. 59 ff.

54. Cf. the references cited in the previous note; also *al Tāj,* vol. 2,
pp. 284 ff; Jum'ah, pp. 33 *seqq.* The underlined conditional clause in
no way tolerates giving them to prostitution if they do not desire to
live in chastity. The structural peculiarities of Arabic render such a
phrase most reproachful of the masters and far more expressive of
the seriousness of the offense than any other clause. This translation

is adopted with slight modification from Arberry, vol. 1, pp. 100, 104 and vol. 2, p. 50; cf. al Zamakhsharī, vol. 3, p. 239, note 5.

55. See the references cited in the two previous notes.

56. In view of the common desire for children and the unpopularity of birth control techniques in those days, it was almost certain that cohabitation would result in pregnancy and birth. However, this is not the same thing as the often-cited "Law" that a slave population never reproduces itself, a law which Finely (p. 310), calls "certainly . . . fictitious." See also R. Levy, p. 234; al Tāj vol. 2, pp. 281 ff; Wāfī (1), pp. 61-2; Jeffery, p. 59; Jum'ah, p. 35.

57. Wāfī (1), pp. 61-2; cf. Roberts, p. 11; Jum'ah, p. 35; 'Abd al Bāqī (1), vol. 2, p. 107; Shorter Ency. of Islām, pp. 601 ff.

58. In Anshen (1), p. 59. (Emphasis is added to indicate how misleading the underlined words can be.)

59. Roberts, p. 10. The passage, from which the author quotes these verses, is worth quoting in full to show the background of the permission. It goes as follows:

Surely man was created fretful, when evil visits him, impatient, when good visits him, grudging, save those that pray and continue at their prayers, those in whose wealth is a right known for the begger and the outcast, who confirm the Day of Doom and go in fear of the chastisement of their Lord (from their Lord's chastisement none feels secure) and guard their private parts save from their wives and what their right hands own, then not being blameworthy (but who so seeks after more than that, they are the transgressors), and who preserve their trusts and their covenant, and perform their witnessings, and who observe their prayers. Those shall be in Gardens, high, honoured. (al Qur'ān, 70:20-34 as rendered by Arberry, vol. 2, pp. 300-1).

This is the religious context of cohabitation and such are the attributes of the people to whom the destiny of slaves is entrusted; cf. al Qur'ān, 23:1-10.

60. Ibid. p. 9.

61. Wāfī (1), pp. 62-3; Patai, p. 159. Wāfī draws in part from his doctoral work in French under Ali Abdel Wahed, Contribution a une Thérie Sociologique de l'Esclavage.

62. See, for example, Hitti, pp. 235, 341-3. He refers to several sources in Arabic giving "incredible" accounts of the numbers of, fascination by, and obsession with slaves, eunuchs, concubines, etc. For example, "The palace of al-Muqtadir (908-32), we are told, housed 11,000 Greek and Sudanese eunuchs. Al-Mutawakkil, accord-

ing to a report, had 4,000 concubines, all of whom shared his nuptial bed." (p. 342).

63. For a general survey of these basic developments see, for example, Hitti, parts II and III; Gibb (3), Chs. 1-2; Lewis, Chs. 2-6.

64. R. Levy, p. 67.

65. Gordon, pp. 633-4; cf. Roberts, p. 60; Douglas, pp. 1195 ff. The last two sources contain some interesting comparative material. Whether the practice of emasculation or castration reached the "institutional" level in a sociological sense is, of course, an open question which may be put to empirical investigation. But it would appear from the strong condemnations reported in the Traditions and from Islām's categorical disapproval of the practice that it must have existed long before Islām and persisted long thereafter to a considerable extent, at least among those who could afford to keep slaves for domestic purposes. For a general statement on the origin and development of the phenomenon, its social and economic impact, and the paradoxically prestigeous and privileged status of the eunuchs among Muslims, see Gray and Juynboll, *Ency. of Religion and Ethics,* vol. 5, pp. 579-84.

CHAPTER THREE

1. *Morals in Evolution,* p. 1.

2. Murdock, p. 260; cf. Wāfī (3), pp. 66 ff.

3. *Ibid.* pp. 260-1; cf. Westermarck (3), p. 7-11, 20.

4. Bardis, p. 451; cf. pp. 441 *seqq.;* Hobhouse, p. 213.

5. Ibn al Qayyim (3), vol. 3, pp. 307-8.

6. Patai, p. 159.

7. Berelson and Steiner, p. 298.

8. Cf. Bardis, pp. 450-1; Hobhouse, pp. 213-4; Wastermarck (2), vol. 1, pp. 654-5; vol 2, p. 392; Queen, p. 157, 164; Kirkpatrick, pp. 105-6. The proposition is simply that when there is systematic devaluation of sex, it is expected to find overemphasis on other-worldliness and so on. This is not a monistic causal relation, for it can be equally maintained that when there is systematic overemphasis on other-worldliness, devaluation of sex follows.

9. Cf. *al Qur'ān,* 4:29; 13:38; 24:32-33; Ibn al Qayyim (3), vol. 3, pp. 308-9; Jeffery, p. 42; Westermarck (3), p. 40; Stern, p. 94; Merchant, p. 127; 'Abd al Bāqī (2), p. 506.

10. Cf. Ibn Qudāmah, vol. 6, pp. 478-81; 'Awwā, pp. 43-5.

11. *al Qur'ān,* 4:29; 11:8, 24:32-33; Ibn al Qayyim (3), vol. 3, p. 308; Jeffery, p. 42. See also the discussion on concubinage and marriage alternatives, *supra.,* pp. 57 ff.

12. Cf. 'Awwā, pp. 150-2; Ibn Khaldūn, pp. 370 *seqq.; Shorter Ency. of Islām,* pp. 579 *seqq.;* Amīn (1), vol. 1, pp. 132-3; (3); vol. 2, pp. 56-63; vol. 4, p. 219.

13. This position has been taken by some zealous reformers who have been opposed to the Sūfīs as well as the power elites. The writer read this some time ago and heard it raised in various discussions. It is regrettable that the exact sources cannot be identified at this time. However, there are some suggestive remarks in Amīn (3), vol. 2, p. 61-2.

14. *Ibid.*

15. Cf. Ibn Khaldūn, pp. 370 *seqq.; Shorter Ency. of Islām,* pp. 579 *seqq.*

16. Cf. Pitts, pp. 67-8; Winch, p. 663; Murdock, pp. 5-8; M. M. Siddiqi, p. 40; al Alūsī, vol. 2, pp. 6-9; Ibn Qudāmah, vol. 6, p. 480; Queen, p. 169; Ibn al Qayyim (3), vol. 3, pp. 307 ff.

17. *al Qur'ān,* 2:226-237; 4:19-21, 34-36, 127-130; 65:1-7.

18. *Ibid.* 2:223; 4:1-3, 23; 30:20; Ibn Qudāmah, vol. 6,, p. 480; Ibn al Qayyim (3), vol. 3, p. 308 and vol. 4, pp. 61 ff; al Shafi'ī (3), vol. 5, pp. 86-7; cf. Gaudefroy-Demombynes (1), p. 132; Jeffery, pp. 55-6; Stern, p. 94; Westermarck (3), pp. 50 ff.

19. Hobhouse, p. 231; Westermarck (3), pp. 225-6.

20. See, for example, Bardis, pp. 433-40; Hobhouse, pp. 182-3; 206-10; al Hūfī (2), pp. 56-7, 61-5; Jum'ah, pp. 187-8; Zaydān (1), pp. 59-60.

21. Cf. Bardis, pp. 441 *seqq.;* Day, pp. 35-6; al Hūfī (2), pp. 30-2; Hobhouse, pp. 197-99; Sumner, *AJS,* Vol. 14, pp. 584-5; R. Brav, pp. 3 *seqq.*

22. Westermarck (3), p. 226; cf. Bardis, p. 420-21.

23. Cf. Warner, p. 70; Jessie Bernard, pp. 382-3; Bardis, pp. 444-5; Westermarck (2), vol. 1, pp. 654-5.

24. Westermarck (3), pp. 225.

25. *Ibid.* pp. 225-6; cf. Warner, pp. 66-72, 79-81; Bardis, p. 446; Hobhouse, pp. 222-4.

26. This point needs elaboration and will be discussed later (Ch. 5); cf. *al Qur'ān,* 3:195, 24:30-31; 33:35-36.

27. Prejudice against women in the Biblical tradition seems to rise mainly from the belief that Eve was responsible for the Fall as she weakened in face of the Satanic temptation. See, for example, Gen. 3:1-19; Douglas, p. 400; Bardis, p. 444-6; Warner, p. 70. The Qur'ān, on the other hand, does not reproach Eve any more than it does Adam.

In fact, he, not she, is depicted as more responsible for the whole affair. At any rate, both were responsible for whatever happened in the Garden of Eden. Both were equally subject to temptation, equally victimized and remorseful. More important is that they both prayed for God's forgiveness and were pardoned; cf. *al Qur'ān*, 2:35-37; 7:19-24; 20:117-122.

28. Cf. Ibn Qudāmah, vol. 7, pp. 13-6; Ibn al Qayyim (2), vol. 2, pp. 327-8; vol. 3, pp. 355-6; Fayzee, p. 85; Siddiqi, pp. 56-7; Farrūkh, pp. 84, 89-90; Maghniyyah (2), pp. 16-7.

29. Fayzee, p. 86; cf. *al Qur'ān*, 4:25; Merchant, p. 125; Vesey-Fitzgerald, pp. 34-5.

30. It will be remembered that a certain Shī'ī group permits marriage on a temporary basis; cf. Sarakhsī, vol. 5, p. 23.

31. Cf. Ibn Qudāmah, vol. 6, pp. 483-5; Maghniyyah (2), pp. 6-13; Farrūkh, pp. 78-81; 'Awwā, p. 40; *al Qur'ān*, 4:43; 33:50.

32. Jeffery, p. 50; Ibn Qudāmah, vol. 8, p. 3; 'Awwā, pp. 109-10; Shaltūt (1), p. 244; Westermarck (3), pp. 185-6; Ibn al Qayyim (2), vol. 3, pp. 153, 158; *al Tāj*, vol. 2, pp. 274-5.

33 Normally, this period is about one hundred and thirty days for the former and three months for the latter. It is enjoined to establish whether or not there is any pregnancy and, in the case of divorce, to give the couple a second chance to reconsider their positions and probably contemplate reconciliation; cf. *al Qur'ān*, 2:234-235; 65:1-7. As for the widow, the waiting period is perhaps a symbolic expression of respect for the memory of the deceased and of joint sympathy with his survivors. On the other hand, it is also probably a period of re-adjustments for the widow and preparation for another phase of her life.

34. *al Qur'ān*, 4:22-23; Stern, pp. 46 *seqq.;* Wāfī (3), pp. 44 *seqq.*

35. Some Shī'īs disagree with the rest of Muslim jurists. Some of them maintain that marriage to non-Muslim women is forbidden in accordance with a particular interpretation of the Qur'ān (2:221). Other Shī'īs hold that such marriages are lawful according to the Qur'ān (5:5) and in accord with the majority of jurists. There is yet a third position among the Shī'īs, taken by those who wish to reconcile the various opinions by holding a synthetic view, according to which such marriages are lawful if contracted on a temporary basis and unlawful as permanent unions; cf. Maghniyyah (2), pp. 32-3.

36. This issue centers on the interpretation of the verse (Q. 24:3). It seems to have been intended to penalize indulgent people by depriving them of the otherwise legitimate gratifications which they have hastened,

but only prematurely and irresponsibly. It may also have been meant
to warn against sexual violations which can be used as a means of
temptation or pressure to conclude a marriage that may not be normally
desirable or workable after the flare of passion dies away. Besides, a
woman who is conscious of her consent to premarital relationships in
a system opposed to such relationships may find her concession to be a
source of tension and a stigma on her character. Her co-offender
may not be the last one to remind her of it, nor is he himself completely
immune from such tension and guilt feelings; cf. Ibn al Qayyim (3),
vol. 4, p. 13; al Shafi'ī (3), vol. 5, p. 153; Ibn Qudāmah, vol. 7, pp.
39-40. Maghniyyah (2), pp. 27-8; Farrūkh, p. 80; al Zamakhsharī, vol.
9, pp. 211 ff.

37. The implications of this statement are highly problematic and
too complex to be discussed in a cursory footnote. They will be reconsidered later in the chapter.

38. al Qur'ān, 2:221; 4:22-24; 5:5; 24:31; Ibn Qudāmah, vol. 6, pp.
483-5; Maghniyyah (2), pp. 6-13, 32-7; 'Awwā, pp. 46, 50-53;
Farrūkh, pp. 78-81; Wāfī (3), pp. 29-31, 44 seqq.; Stern, pp. 96, 98,
103; Roberts, pp. 12 ff; Patai, pp. 156-7, 194; Smith (1), pp. 290-1.

39. Westermarck (3), pp. 156 ff, 166, 170; cf. Patai, p. 55; Smith
(1), p. 79.

40. Cf. Wāfī (3), pp. 105-14; Patai, pp. 60-1 (Gen. 29:18; 1 Sam.
17:25, 18:20, 25); al Qur'ān, 28:23-28; Westermarck (3), pp. 179-82.

41. Patai, p. 56; cf. Goode (1), p. 32; Bardis, pp. 411-2.

42. Patai, pp. 56-7.

43. Westermarck (3), p. 183.

44. Ibid. pp. 179-80, 182.

45. Bardis, p. 411.

46. Brav, p. 5.

47. Cf. al Qur'ān, 4:4, 19-20, 24-25, 34; 24:33; al Shāfi'ī (3), vol.
5, pp. 57 ff; Ibn al Qayyim (3), vol. 4, pp. 54-6; Merchant, p. 128;
Stern, p. 55.

48. Stern, pp. 33, 37, 45.

49. Cf. Ibid.; Smith (1), pp. 274-5.

50. Stern, p. 38.

51. Cf. al Qur'ān, 4:21; al Shafi'ī (3), vol. 5, pp. 57-60; Ibn al
Qayyim (3), vol. 4, pp. 54-6; Abū Zahrah (1), p. 141; Farrūkh, p. 91;
Maghniyyah (2), pp. 61-2. For this rough monetary equation, see
Webster's Third New International Dictionary, 1959, pp. 642, 1458.

52. Cf. al Qur'ān, 59:7-10.

53. Cf. Vesey-Fitzgerald, p. 34-5; Wāfī (3), pp. 106-7; *Shorter Ency, of Islām,* pp. 314-5.

54. This is reported through various reliable sources. The passage in question may be rendered as follows: "And if you desire to replace a wife with another, and you have given to one a hundredweight (a *qinṭār*), take of it nothing. What, will you take it by way of calumny and manifest sin? How you shall take it, when each of you has been privily with the other, and they have taken from you a solemn compact." (Adopted from Arberry, vol. 1, p. 103). The context in which this passage was revealed is interesting. It had been in practice that when a married man felt attracted to another woman, he exhibited hatred for his wife and accused her of infidelity, so that she would be forced to ransom herself by giving him back whatever he had given her. He would then use the "refund" to marry the woman he liked. The passage was revealed to condemn the practice and put an end to it; cf. al Zamakhsharī, vol. 1, p. 491.

55. See *supra,* pp. 62 ff.

56. Cf. *al Qur'ān,* 4:4; Ibn al Qayyim (3), vol. 4, p. 56; Vesey-Fitzgerald, p. 35.

57. Cf. M. M. Siddiqi, p. 59.

58. Cf. Westermarck (3), p. 180; (1) p. 493.

59. Cf. *al Hidāyah,* vol. 2, pp. 31-2; Wāfī (3), pp. 105-6; al Sarakhsī, vol. 5, pp. 62-94; *Shorter Ency. of Islām,* pp. 314-5.

60. Cf. *al Qur'ān,* 2:236; 4:4, 24-25; Wensinck (1), pp. 145-6, (2), pp. 509 f; al Shāfi'ī (3), vol. 5 pp. 57 *seqq.;* al *Hidāyah,* vol. 2, pp. 31 *seqq.*

61. Cf. *Shorter Ency. of Islām,* p. 447; Farrūkh, p. 113; Maghniyyah (2), p. 40.

62. On these requisites see, for example, Ibn Qudāmah, vol. 6, p. 500; Jeffery, p. 51; Fayzee, p. 200; R. Levy, p. 110.

63. Cf. Ibn Qudāmah, vol. 6, p. 481; al Jaṣṣāṣ, vol. 1, p. 474.

64. Maghniyyah (2), p. 42; Farrūkh, p. 113; Fayzee, pp. 199-200.

65. Cf. Ibn Qudāmah, vol. 6, pp. 482, 515-8. A contemporary observer has noted that guardianship was endorsed by Islām to satisfy the deep-seated pride of the Arabs and to avoid the insult to the tribe of a mésalliance. "It is, firstly, the kindred and, secondly, the woman herself, who must be protected from a mésalliance . . ." (Vesey-Fitzgerald, p. 54). This observation centers on one aspect, namely "equality" in marriage, which will be discussed later. But this is only one dimension of the general problem of guardianship. Besides, the

term guardian assumed its legal and technical significance after Muhammad's death and is found neither in the Qur'ān nor in pre-Islāmic poetry. It occurs in some passages of questionable authenticity which make no reference to pride. They state that the consent and presence of a guardian are required, and suggest that it is unseemly for a woman to act in her behalf on such matters as marriage. Moreover, legal principles and religious precepts apply to all Muslims, Arabs and non-Arabs alike; cf. Stern, p. 37; Mālīk Ibn Anas, vol. 2, p. 525; Ibn al Qayyim (3), vol. 4, p. 6.

66. Thes views are abstracted from several sources which must be consulted together. No single source contains a full or unequivocal presentation of the problem. See, for example, al Jaṣṣāṣ, vol. 1, pp. 473-6; Ibn Qudāmah, vol. 6, pp. 481-500; al Tūsī, vol. 2, pp. 357-9, 372 f, 394; Maghniyyah (2), pp. 40-2; Stern, pp. 39-42; Siddiqi, pp. 62-4; Fayzee, pp. 199-201; R. Levy, p. 51, 110-1; Vesey-Fitzgerald, pp. 54-55; Wāfī (2), pp. 54-5. It is reported that there were cases in which women refused to marry Caliphs and preferred unions with simple, ordinary people; cf. al Hūfī (2), pp. 187-8.

67. Cf. references cited in the previous note.

68. Cf. Ibn Qudāmah, vol. 6, p. 481; al Tūsī, vol. 2, p. 358; Maghniyyah (2), p. 41; *Shorter Ency. of Islām*, pp. 321, 447, 512-5.

69. Cf. R. Levy, p. 110; Vesey-Fitzgerald, p. 54.

70. Vesey-Fitzgerald, pp. 54-5.

71. Cf. Ibn Qudāmah, vol. 6, pp. 517-8; Fayzee, p. 200; R. Levy, p. 110.

72. Cf. Ibn al Qayyim (3), vol. 4, pp. 3 ff; Ibn Qudāmah, vol. 6, pp. 517-8; al Jaṣṣāṣ, vol. 1, p. 474; Maghniyyah (2), pp. 41-3; Vesey-Fitzgerald, p. 54. It should be noted that these provisions apply to majors, not to minors. The border between minority and majority is puberty. If there are no physical indications of puberty, the general view is that a person who has reached the age of fifteen is no longer a minor. Parenthetically, there are indications that minors were sometimes betrothed at an age as early as six, but final consummation took place years later; cf. M. F. 'Abd al Bāqī (1), vol. 2, p. 104.

73. Cf. Westermarck (3), p. 42; R. Levy, p. 106.

74. Westermarck (3), pp. 30, 42; cf. Pitts, p. 82; Margoliouth (2), p. 66; Brav, pp. 7, 11-12.

75. Cf. R. Levy, pp. 106-7.

76. Margoliouth (2), p. 66.

77. Westermarck (3), p. 40.

78. *Ibid.* pp. 46, 145; William Kephart, p. 945.
79. Cf. R. Levy, pp. 106-7; Farrūkh, pp. 119-20. On the definition of majority and minority, see note 72 above.
80. Cf. Westermarck (3), pp. 47, 235-6; Kephart, p. 945; Fayzee, pp. 199-200; Siddiqi, pp. 66-7; Farrūkh, p. 115; Wāfī (3), pp. 87-8; *Shorter Ency. of Islām,* pp. 255, 447; al Jaṣṣāṣ, vol. 2, pp. 60-1.
81. Cf. al Shāfi'ī (3), vol. 5, pp. 20-1; Farrūkh, pp. 114-15; al Hūfī (2), pp. 187-8.
82. Hobhouse, pp. 156-7. Cf. Winch, pp. 651-2; Coser, pp. xvii-iii; Goode (1), p. 32; Westermarck (3), pp. 135-6, 214-21; Patai, p. 49.
83. Cf. Westermarck (3), pp. 135-53.
84. Hobhouse, p. 157.
85. Abdur Rahim, p. 86; cf. Stern, p. 33.
86. Cf. al Hūfī (2), pp. 168 *seqq.;* (1) p. 221; R. Nicholson, p. 87.
87. Cf. al Hūfī (1), p. 221; (2) pp. 168-9, 172, 183-5; Patai, pp. 53-4; Westermarck (3), pp. 214 *seqq;* Mālik Ibn Anas, vol. 2, pp. 524-5; Zelditch (2), pp. 686-7.
88 Cf. Farrūkh, pp. 83-4.
89. Ibn Qudāmah, vol. 6, p. 516.
90. Cf. *Ibid.;* al Qur'ān, 65:4.
91. *Ibid,* pp. 516-7; Ibn al Qayyim (3), vol. 4, pp. 3 ff; al Tūsī, vol. 2, p. 360; Stern, pp. 32-4; cf. pp. 28-9.
92. Ibn Qudāmah, vol. 6, p. 517.
93 *Ibid.* pp. 520-1; cf. Ibn al Qayyim (3), vol. 4, p. 5.
94. *Ibid.* pp. 519-20.
95. *Ibid,* p. 518; cf. al Tūsī, vol. 2, p. 364.
96. See, for example, al Shāfi'ī (3), vol. 5, pp. 19-21; Mālik Ibn Anas, vol. 2, pp. 524-5; 'Abd al Bāqī (1), vol. 2, pp. 103-4; Ibn al Qayyim (3), vol. 4 pp. 3-6; Siddiqi, pp 62 *seqq.;* Patai, p. 47; Sayed Ameer Ali (1), vol. 2, pp. 235 ff; Stern, pp. 32-5; al Ghazalī, pp. 152-3; Fayzee, p. 199. It may be interesting to note that guardianship did not apparently mean coercing women to marry against their wishes. A daughter of Abū Bakr, the first Muslim Caliph (d. 634), refused to marry 'Umar I (d. 643). When her sister, 'A'ishah, wife of the Prophet, wondered why she had refused to marry 'Umar, the Commander of the believers, she said that she did not want to marry him because he was leading a life of austerity and was very strict with women. Similar instances took place where women declined to marry Caliphs and dignitaries, preferring, instead, common suitors to their liking (Cf. al Hūfī (2), p. 188). For comparative purposes, it may be useful

to note that, for practical reasons and due to the influence of various Christian leaders, a "marriage was often arranged." Some prelates preached that "no marriage was valid without the father's consent . . . In feudal times, marriages were also arranged by the overlord." (Bardis, p. 443). The case of the Hebrews had been much the same (*Ibid.* pp. 411-2); cf. Brav, pp. 7, 11.

97. The concept "equality in marriage" is rather ambiguous and interchangeable with terms such as suitability, compatibility, and so on. To avoid this ambiguity, we shall use the concept "social equality in marriage" to denote (1) that not all marriageable mates are socially equal or maritally accessible to one another, and (2) that if a suitor is to be socially eligible to marry a given woman, he must satisfy certain requirements that would place him on a social par with her. The scale of social equality includes elements like honor, lineage, fame, type of profession, etc. On the other hand, we shall introduce the concept of "religious equality in marriage." This denotes (1) that, according to the religion of Islām, all Muslims are brothers of one another and equal in the sight of God, (2) that the only recognizable criterion of ultimate distinction among them is piety or God-mindedness, and (3) that it is religious equality, not social equality, which is required in marriage. Any marriageable Muslim male of religious integrity is eligible to marry any marriageable woman, however high her social standing may be.

98. Haag, pp. 193-4; cf. Coser, pp. xvii f; Goode (1), pp. 32-5; Zelditch (2), p. 685. Leslie (p. 456) quotes Montaigne's "I see no marriages which sooner fail than those contracted on account of beauty and amorous desire."

99. Berelson and Steiner, pp. 305-8.

100. Burchinal, pp. 665-6; cf. Berelson and Steiner, *loc. cit.* (note 99).

101. Cf. Leslie, pp. 422 *seqq,* esp. 456.

102. Cf. al Hūfī (2), pp. 150-9; al Alūsī, vol. 2, pp. 9 ff, 13-4.

103. al Hūfī (2), pp. 168-82; cf. R. Levy, pp. 53 *seqq;* Wāfī (3), pp. 33-6.

104. Cf. Note 97 above; Ibn Qudāmah, vol. 6, pp. 509-10; al Tūsī, vol. 2, pp. 366 *seqq.;* 'Awwā, pp. 47-8, 108; Ziadeh (1), p. 508; *al Qur'ān,* 49:10-13; Ibn al Qayyim (3), vol. 4, pp. 41 ff.

105. Cf. Ibn al Qayyim (3), vol. 4, p. 42; 'Awwā, pp. 47-8; al Ṣāliḥ, pp. 79-80, 468-9. For more information on the hardships of, and threats to, the early Muslim community, see *Shorter Ency. of Islām,*

pp. 391 *seqq.*

106. Cf. Ibn al Qayyim, *loc. cit.* (Note 105). It is interesting that this interpretation was still echoed by jurists of as late as the fourteenth century, in which the author cited here flourished.

107. *Ibid.;* cf. al Tūsī, vol. 2. pp. 366 *seqq.;* Ibn Qudāmah, vol. 6, pp. 509-10; Maghniyyah (2), pp 45-6; 'Awwā, pp. 47-8.

108. For more biographical information, see, for example, *Shorter Ency. of Islām,* pp. 9-10, 20-1, 512-5, 534 *seqq;* Ziadeh (1), pp. 504-9.

109. Cf. *Shorter Ency. of Islām,* pp. 534 *seqq.;* Wāfī (3), p. 30; al Shībī, esp. pp. 15 *seqq.* Some of these facts are still observable today.

110. It is sometimes suggested that the Shī'īs may have adopted this egalitarian position because "the prevalence of *mut'ah* (temporary) marriage [of pleasure] among them was not favorable for the maintenance of an esteemed position for women which is necessary to the doctrine of kafā'ah [social equality in marriage]." (Ziadeh (1), pp. 507-8). But this is unlikely because it is not certain how prevalent *mut'ah* marriage has been among them; they insist that it has been neither commendable nor popular. In addition, there are jurists who do not allow *mut'ah* marriage yet take the same position on equality as the Shī'īs. Moreover, the belief that the doctrine of social equality means an esteemed position for women is only one among other points of view. Some observers interpret it to mean primarily protection of the marriage guardian's interests (cf. Coulson (1), p. 94). Furthermore, it is sometimes considered as a right of the woman and the guardian (cf. Ibn al Qayyim (3), vol. 4, p. 43). Some advocates of social equality explain their position in terms having little to do with esteem for women, as will be seen in the following pages.

111. Cf. al Tūsī, vol. 2, pp. 366-7; Ibn Qudāmah, vol. 6, pp. 509-10; 'Awwā, pp. 47 ff; Farrūkh, pp. 82-3; al Shāfi'ī (3), vol. 5, p. 15; Ibn al Qayyim (3), vol. 4, pp. 41 ff.

112. Fayzee, p. 105; cf. R. Levy, pp. 53 ff.

113. Ibn al Qayyim (3), vol. 4, pp. 41 ff; Coulson (1), p. 94; Abū Zahrah (1), p. 140; al Sharabāsī, p. 53; Ziadeh (1), 505 ff. See also the two previous notes.

114. For the historical background, see Gibb (3), chs. 1 and 2; R. Levy, Introduction and Chapter 1; al Ṣāliḥ, pp. 19 *seqq.;* Ziadeh (1), pp. 506-7; Coulson (1), p. 49; Westermarck (3), p. 61.

115. Gibb (3), pp. 5 ff.

116. Cf. Ibn Qudāmah, vol. 6, pp. 509-10; al Sarakhsī, vol. 5, pp.

23-4; al Tūsī, vol. 2, pp. 366-7; Farrūkh, pp. 82-3; Abū Zahrah (1),
p. 140.

117. For more factual information see, for example, Ibn Qudāmah,
vol. 6, p. 509; al Shaybānī (1), p. 78; al Sarakhsī, vol. 5, pp. 22-3;
'Awwā, pp. 47-8.

118. See the references cited in the previous note; cf. Ibn al Qayyim
(3), vol. 4, p. 41 ff.

119. Fayzee, pp. 104-5; cf. Farrūkh, p. 83.

120. Cf. Ibn Qudāmah, vol. 6, pp. 510-1.

121. Cf. Ibid. p. 515; Maghniyyah (2), p. 45. For more relevant
theoretical suggestions, see Davis (2), pp. 106, 114 seqq.; Merton (1),
p. 371 seqq.; Goode (1), pp. 82-3; Zelditch (2), pp. 688 seqq.

122. Stern, pp. 28, 33.

CHAPTER FOUR

1. Davis (1), p. 417.

2. Cf. Westermarck (2), vol. p. 392, (3), pp. 7-9; Day, pp. 38,
41-2, 78, 128 ff; al Hūfī (2), pp. 235-8; Brav, pp. 3 seqq; Jum'ah, pp.
68-73; Wāfī (1), pp. 21 ff.

3. Cf. Merchant, p. 150; Stern, p. 77; Wāfī, loc. cit. (note 2).

4. See, for example, Patai, pp. 39-40, 42; Murdock, pp. 26-7, 36 ff;
M. Levy (1); p. 10; Pitts, p. 71; Linton pp. 27 ff; Bernard, p. 226;
Goitein pp. 184-5; Westermarck (1), pp. 442, 450, 483 seqq.; (2), vol.
2, p. 399; al Hūfī (2), pp. 234-5; Jum'ah, p. 74.

5. Ibn Qudāmah, vol. 7, pp. 13-4; Wāfī (1), pp. 33 ff; Maghniyyah
(2), pp. 16-7.

6. Cf. Smith (1), pp. 122-39; Pitts, p. 71; Bernard, pp. 226-7;
Westermarck (1), pp. 472 ff; (2), vol. 2, p. 387; Thomas, pp. 532 ff.;
Jum'ah, pp. 14 seqq.; Wāfī (3), pp. 66 seqq.; Murdock, pp. 36-7.

7. See the references cited in the previous note; cf. al Alūsī, vol. 3,
pp. 43-4; Roberts, pp. 94-5; Wāfī (3), pp. 117-8.

8. See, for example, al Alūsī, vol. 2, p. 4; Wāfī (3), p. 78; 'Awwā,
pp. 17-8.

9. It is generally believed that pre-Islāmic Arabs, men and women,
were possessed by the desire for good progeny. So much was this
the case that a childless husband might ask his wife to cohabit with
another man of some notable quality, e.g., bravery, nobility, etc., in
the hope that she would conceive. The offspring, if any, would be
regarded as belonging to the husband, not to the natural father. This
was known as *Istibḍā'* cohabitation. (See for example, Stern, p. 74;

Wāfi (3), p. 78; al Alūsī, vol. 2, p. 4). If a married woman could consent to this kind of arrangement, the inducement might have been due to her feeling that she would be honored to cohabit with men of distinction, and more honored if she conceived and had the liberty to choose her child's father. Such women could not have been of the common type; if they were, nothing would have compelled the male partners to respond to their calls and abide by their arbitrary choice. (cf. n. 12 in this chapter).

10. Cf. al Alūsī, vol. 2, pp. 4-5; Wāfī (3), pp. 72-3, 78; Smith (1), p. 286; *al Qur'ān*, 24:33; 60-12; al Zamakhsharī, vol. 3, pp. 239-40; vol. 4, p. 520.

11. This term is adopted from Jum'ah, a student of Semitic languages and institutions (cf. p. 54).

12. See Smith (1), pp. 74-6, 80-7, 91; Westermarck (3), p. 157; Patai, pp. 98-103; Stern, p. 74; Wāfī (3), pp. 78, 83-4, 88; al Hūfī (2), pp. 247-8; Jum'ah, pp. 40-67; al Alūsī, vol. 2, pp. 4-5; *al Qur'ān*, 4:19, 22, 25; 27:20-28; al Zamakhsharī, vol. 1, p. 490. It is important to note that these sources are complementary; that some of the cited forms of marriage and cohabitation were more common and perpetuated longer than others; and that not all of them were sexually motivated. See, for example, Patai, pp. 39-42, 101 ff; Jum'ah, pp. 59-64, 73-4; Smith, *loc. cit.* For a historical review of the trial, experimental cohabitation throughout the ages, see, for example, Westermarck (1), vol. 1, pp. 126 *seqq.* On concubinage in the Greco-Roman traditions, see, for example, Leslie, p. 169. It may be interesting to note that because of the militaristic ideology of Sparta, "Husbands were encouraged to promote the production of physically superior children by lending their wives to men healthier than themselves." (Bardis, p. 429).

13. Cf. *supra.* chs. 2-3.

14. Smith (1), pp. 68 ff.

15. See, for example, al Tūsī, vol. 2, pp. 394-5; Maghniyyah (1), pp. 128 ff; *Shorter Ency. of Islam,* pp. 418 ff.

16. Cf. *al Qur'ān,* 22:5-7; 70:29-31; 'Abd al Bāqī (4), vol. 2, p. 542; al Shāfi'ī (3), vol. 5, pp. 79-80; al Sarakhsī, vol. 5, pp. 152-3; Ibn al Qayyim (2), vol. 3, pp. 153-68; vol. 4, pp. 11-12; Ibn Qudāmah, vol. 7, p. 16.

17. Cf. al Tūsī, vol. 2, pp. 394-5; Maghniyyah (1), p. 130. Both authors are Shī'īs.

18. Cf. Fayzee, p. 112.

19. Ibn al Qayyim (3), vol. 4, pp. 11-2.

20. Cf. Fayzee, p. 112; Coulson (1), pp. 115 ff.

21. On the many innovations introduced by 'Umar I in the various sectors of public and official life, see *Shorter Ency. of Islām,* pp. 139, 600 f. One of such innovations was the adoption of the event of the flight (Hijrah) of Muslims to al Madīnah in the year 622 to mark the beginning of the Muslim era. However, there is no evidence that the Shī'īs opposed this. Nor did they reject other innovations just because they questioned 'Umar's political credentials. Coulson (1), has pointed out that the political factor was not the reason for the Shī'ī position on the *mut'ah* marriage. They derived their doctrine from a particular interpretation of some Qur'ānic verses through certain juristic methods (cf. pp. 110, 115 ff). But this leaves much to be desired and raises more questions than it answers. It may be asked: why did they choose that particular interpretation or apply those certain juristic methods? What led them to disagree with the majority of Muslims? It must have been something other than juristic methodology or textual interpretation. We shall look into that in the main text.

22. Cf. al Shībī, esp. ch. 1; al Ṣāliḥ, pp. 95-125; Vesey-Fitzgerald, p. 19.

23. Cf. Maghniyyah (1), pp. 128 ff; Farrūkh, pp. 95-7; Coulson (1), p. 110; Smith (1), pp. 68 ff.

24. See *supra,* pp. 9 ff.

25. Linton, p. 27; cf. Pitts, pp. 58, 71; Westermarck (1), p. 483, (2), vol. 2, pp. 387-8. It should be pointed out that the discussion makes use of these sources but follows an independent logical order of presentation. It is interesting that a Muslim scholar of the classical tradition has noted that, contrary to popular belief, women's sexual needs are actually less pressing than men's. Because women are usually secluded and, as compared with men, they generally lead an indolent, leisurely life, their physical energies are below capacity and their sexual passions somewhat lukewarm. It is true that their relative freedom from mundane preoccupations and anxieties may seem to intensify whatever passions they have and make them appear more fervent than they actually are. To illustrate the point, he noted that a man can have a sexual intercourse and remain capable or even desirous of more with the same or with another woman. That is not true of a woman who has just had an intercourse (Ibn al Qayyim (2), vol, 2, pp. 85 ff).

26. Cf. Patai, p. 39; Linton, p. 28; Westermarck (1), pp. 485-8; (2), vol. 2, p. 388; Bardis, pp. 414-5; Hitti, pp. 332-3.

27. Linton, pp. 28-9; cf. Patai, pp. 39-40; Pitts, p. 71; Murdock, p. 30; Bardis, p. 414; *Gen.* 29:31; 30:15; *al Qur'ān,* 66:1-5.

28. Linton, p. 27; Westermarck (1), pp. 493 *seqq.*; (2), vol. 2 p. 399; Murdock, pp. 36-7.

29. Westermarck (1), pp. 442, 450.

30. M. Levy (1), p. 10. (Emphasis is implied in the original by the fact that the two underlined words are italicized in the preceding sentence in the same context). See also Linton, p. 27; Patai, p. 39; Bardis, p. 414.

31. Cf. Westermarck (3), pp. 232-5; Bardis, pp. 433, 440; al Hūfī (2), pp. 234 ff; Roberts, pp. 7-9; Leslie, pp. 169 ff.

32. Cf. Patai, pp. 19, 41-2, 78; Day, pp. 38, 128-9; Bardis, pp. 413 ff, 420; Brav, p. 8; Westermarck (3), p. 233; al Hūfī (2), p. 236; Hobhouse, pp. 197-8; Sumner (1), p. 584; Roberts, pp. 8-9.

33. Day, p. 38.

34. Cf. Westermarck (3), p. 233. Goitein (pp. 184-5) has recently pointed out that, "The impact of Muslim religion and society was certainly substantial with regard to the position of the Jewish woman in Eastern countries. Polygyny was prohibited by the Jewish rabbis in Europe, but remained legal in the countries of Islam . . . and in a thorough Arab country like Yemen it has been in vogue well into our own time. A number of immigrants from Yemen to Israel arrived in the company of two or even three wives, quite a problem to the housing authorities . . . Although the law of the State of Israel permits a man to keep the wives he has brought from abroad, many have separated since their arrival."

This explanation does not seem to account sufficiently for the known facts. Neither Islām nor Muslim authorities can be said to have directly interfered with the "personal laws" of other groups; this is an area which Islām has respected (see n. 29 in ch. 2). If the Jews living in Muslim countries had actually wanted to prohibit polygyny or abandon the practice completely, like their European co-religionists, no Muslim could have prevented them. The Christians of the same general environment have kept their monogamous traditions unhindered. And if there had been such an impact, as the observation states, it would probably have affected the Christian minorities in Muslim countries in a similar fashion. Jews and Christians share with the Muslims around them many social and environmental conditions, but the Jews and the Muslims react to these conditions differently, as do the Christians. The reason for the survival of polygyny among the Muslims and

some Jews living in Muslim countries probably lies in the long tradition
and religious sanction of the practice, not in the impact of one party
upon the other. Had the Bible, the Talmud, or the Eastern Rabbis
forbidden polygyny categorically, the Jews of Muslim countries would
most likely have been unaffected by what the Muslims do or do not
do in this regard.

35. Cf. Westermarck (1), 434, (3), pp. 235-6, 249-50; Linton,
p. 29; Wāfī (1), pp. 29, 56-7; al Ṣāliḥ, pp. 456 ff; Roberts, pp. 8-9;
al Hūfī (2), p. 237. A reaction which is by no means typical or
statistically normal was voiced in *The Edmonton Journal* (Edmonton,
Alberta, Canada) of August 19, 1963. It had a report on p. 1 under
the title "Bishop Backs Honest Polygamy [polygyny]." In the issue
of August 24 of the same journal, a housewife wrote to the editor
under "Polygamy", expressing her agreement with Bishop Odutola
of West Africa, who had stated that "the African practice of having
three or more wives was more honest than Western marriage and
divorce, then marriage again... I whole-heartedly agree with him.
I have always felt this way and I believe that Bishop Emrich is
mistaken when he says that the only sexual relationship which gives
dignity to women is monogamy." The housewife went on contending
that "if polygamy were legalized in the Western world, men would
no longer have to cheat on the sly and wives could still have dignity
... without having to hide their heads in the sand . . ." She went on
to identify herself as a housewife with a small child, who would rather
see her husband bring the other woman into the home and be honest
about it than lie or cheat.

36. Westermarck (3), p. 235.

37. Westermarck (2), vol. 2, p. 392.

38. Cf. Hobhouse, p. 213; Westermarck (2), vol. 1, p. 654-5, vol.
2, p. 392, (3), p. 235; Sumner (1), p. 584; Warner, pp. 70 ff; Bardis,
pp. 444-6; Bernard, p. 382.

39. Some writers are inclined to impute to the Bible the ideal of
monogamy on the basis of similar indications. See, for example, Bardis,
p. 413; *Gen.* 2:24. The Qur'ān implies that Adam, Noah, Moses, and
other prominent figures were monogamous; cf. 2:35; 4:1; 7:187;
28:27-29; 66:10.

40. Cf. *al Qur'ān*, 4:1-6, 6:152-155; Shaltūt (2), pp. 168 *seqq.*
esp. 175-6; Wāfī (1), pp. 46-8; Jeffery, p. 59.

41. *al Qur'ān* 4:3 (Adopted modified from Arberry, vol. 1, p.
100.) The verse in 4:2, which preceded this one, came to affirm that

it is a heinous crime to devour the property of the orphans or take advantage of their dependency. Guardians used to marry their orphan wards or marry them off to their own children to incorporate the wards' property into their own. When they were told that it was forbidden to do so they became apprehensive and hesitated to assume responsibility for the orphans, lest it might involve injustice. Then they were told again (4:3) that they should assume their responsibility as guardians, and they even could marry their orphan wards or give them in marriage to their children if it did not entail injustice to the orphans involved. But if they feared injustice to them, the guardians should not marry them; they were offered alternatives as they were allowed to take two, three or four wives, so that they would not be tempted to marry their orphan wards and slip into the forbidden act of injustice.

It is also reported that some men who feared injustice to the orphans were keeping ten, eight, or six wives without equity among them. This was plain inconsistency, and the Qur'ān reminded them of it; it told them, in effect, that if they feared injustice to the orphans, they should likewise fear injustice to their wives and reduce their number to the limit within which justice is attainable. Another interpretation suggests that guardians were not so perturbed by illicit sexuality as they were by the fear of injustice to the orphans. So the Qur'ān told them that they should be equally alarmed by illicit sexuality and restrict their sexual relationship to their lawful wives; a man might take two, three, or even four wives, and yet that would still be more wholesome than injustice to the orphans or engagement in illicit relationships; cf. the references cited in n. 43 esp. al Zamakhsharī.

42. *al Qur'ān*, 4:129 (adopted from Arberry vol. 1, p. 119).

43. See, for example, al Shāfi'ī (3), vol. 5, pp. 190-2; Ibn al Qayyim (3), vol. 4, pp. 36 ff; al Zamakhsharī, vol. 1, pp. 572-3; Shaltūt (2), pp. 172-7; (3) pp. 188-90; Wāfī (1), pp. 21 ff.

44. Ibn al Qayyim (2), vol. 3, pp. 149-71. The author cites ninety-nine cases in confirmation of this principle and makes extensive reference to the Qur'ān, the Sunnah, and the rulings of leading jurists.

45. Cf. Ibn Qudāmah, vol. 7, pp. 13 ff; Maghniyyah (2), pp. 16-7; Coulson (1), p. 207; Wāfī (1), pp. 33 ff; Farrūkh, p. 84; Burton, p. 327. The fact that the Qur'ān allows a man to keep *four* wives has been the subject of some curious comments. Stern (p. 81) has observed that this suggestion of four wives was probably based on the fact that Muḥammad himself had four wives when the rule was first made; he found that he could satisfactorily maintain them. When he felt

later that he could act with equity toward a greater number of unfortunate women who had lost their husbands fighting for or against his cause, he accepted the responsibility for taking them as wives. Stern's suggestion is very unlikely to have been the specific reason for setting the maximum of polygyny at four. This doubt emanates from theological as well as social sources. First, Stern's explanation implies that it was Muḥammad who composed the Qur'ān and arbitrarily made the rules of polygyny. Such implications raise more questions than they provide answers. Secondly, the principle of *consultation* with his companion is enjoined by the Qur'ān upon Muḥammad himself and is portrayed among the virtues of Muslims (Q. 3:159; 42:38). In fact, Chapter 42 of the Qur'ān is named "Counsel." It is very unlikely, therefore, that Muḥammad would have acted so arbitrarily on such a matter as this. Thirdly, the Qur'ān on several occasions presents the Muslims as having questioned Muḥammad and even argued with him on problems pertaining to the family legislation (cf. 2:222; 4:127-130, 176; 58:1). Chapter 58 is called "The Dispute", signifying the famous exchange between a grieved woman and Muḥammad over a question of repudiation, which was finally settled by a divine rule. Fourthly, in some instances Muḥammad made decisions without the guidance of explicit divine instructions. These decisions were sometimes verified and sometimes criticized by the Qur'ān (8:67; 66:12). This would indicate that he did not claim any authority to legislate on his own, and his decisions were checked not only by his opponents, but also by the divine source. Finally, Muḥammad is the ideal model of conduct for his followers (Q. 33:21). If his particular polygynous status had been the basis of this rule, he probably would have urged his followers to do likewise; or they, on their own initiative, would have attempted to emulate him in this regard to approximate his status. But none of these happened. On the other hand, Roberts, following Sale, has suggested (pp. 8-9), that in restricting polygyny to four wives, Muḥammad was perhaps "influenced by the decision of the Jewish doctors, who, by the way of counsel, limit the number of wives to four, though their law confines them not to any certain number." But this is also unlikely to have been the sole or even the main reason, because Islām made this limit a binding law, not only a piece of advice or bit of conventional wisdom (cf. Jeffery, p. 58; Roberts, p. 8). It is probable, however that the general conditions that had led the Jewish doctors to give their counsel were also common to or active upon the Arabian environment and were thus taken into consideration by the Maker of Islāmic law.

At any rate, a classical interpretation maintains that the maximum was set at four because with a greater number the probability of injustice is much higher, and the risk of failing to provide for them adequately is greater, which may lead to some forbidden acts. Moreover, the maximum was set at four because some men are overwhelmed by passionate needs and may not find legitimate or adequate satisfaction with less. Besides, since every year has four seasons and every man has four [unspecified] dispositions, it is reasonable to set at four the maximum of wives that a man may keep at a given time. Furthermore, in Arabic, the language of the Qur'ān, the minimum of a plural is three, not two. It is thought, therefore, that equity and considerateness require the minimization of a wive's anxiety over her husband's absence and deprivation of his companionship. Thus, if there is to be a plurality of wives, and if this is to entail relatively minimal anxiety and deprivation for the wife, it should be set at the absolute minimum of plurality. If we take the day as a time unit, this means that in a polygynous state no wife should be deprived of her husband's companionship longer than the absolute minimum of time, three days. This is possible only if the number of wives remains within four. If the husband divides his days equally among them, each will have her share on the fourth day, thus restricting the period of separation to three days. [This is a simplified summary of a vague, complicated discussion in Ibn al Qayyim (2) vol. 2, pp. 84-5, vol. 3, p. 153.]

46. Reported in Farrūkh, p. 89; cf. Shaltūt (2), p. 177.

47. See, for example, Stern, pp. 78-9; Merchant, p. 130; Jeffery, pp. 58-9; Burton (1), p. 327; Roberts, pp. 8-9.

48. Stern, p. 81.

49. On the principles of economic solidity, religious tax, and the administration of public revenues, see, for example, al Qur'ān, 2:177; 8:41; 9:60. A symbolic account is often cited about 'Umar, the second Caliph, who succeeded Abū Bakr only two years after Muḥammad's death. A certain provincial governor asked 'Umar what to do with the surplus funds at his disposal. 'Umar instructed him to distribute them among the poor and needy. When he was informed that the poor (Muslims, Christians, and Jews, alike) were so well taken care of that none in the territory were eligible for any more public assistance, 'Umar then instructed his deputy to transfer the surplus

funds to the Central Treasury to meet the other needs of the state. Whether the account is fully authentic or somewhat exaggerated is immaterial here; the story is symbolic enough to show the level of economic solidarity and also of social cohesiveness attained at the time. See Arberry (1), pp. 12 ff; Hitti, pp. 136 ff, 169 *seqq.*

50. Ibn al Qayyim (2), vol. 3, pp. 153, 158; *al Qur'ān,* 2:230; 17:32; 24:2-20; cf. R. Levy, p. 234. On marriage guardianship and the *mut'ah* see *supra.* pp. 70 ff, 103 ff. The difference of opinion on the details of these matters should be remembered.

51. Stern, p. 82.

52. Roberts, p. 9.

53. Jeffery, p. 58.

54. Ibn al Qayyim (2), vol. 2, pp. 85-7; cf. n. 25 in this chapter.

55. Merton (1), pp. 361-2.

56. Brav, p. 5; Patai, pp. 32, 35; Wāfī (3), pp. 31 *seqq.*; Westermarck (3), pp. 57-8, 61.

57. See, for example, Smith (1), pp. 60, 184-5; Patai, pp. 24-5; Roberts, p. 12; Wāfī (3), pp. 45-6. R. Levy (p. 102) claims that marriage among paternal cousins "prevailed amongst a majority of the Arabian tribes."

58. Cf. R. Levy, p. 104.

59. *Ibid*; al Hūfī (1), p. 221; Smith (1), p. 60; cf. Murdock, p. 290. The statement attributed to the Prophet contains an equivocal word which can designate weakness, shrinking in size and/or strength, slenderness, etc.

60. Smith (1), pp. 60-1.

61. Wāfī (3), pp. 33-4.

62. Aḥmad Amīn (2), p. 6; Stern, pp. 24-5, 57 *seqq*; Watt (4), pp. 10, 84 *seqq.*

63. On the distinction between items (1) and (2) in this category see n. 67 in this chapter.

64. See *al Qur'ān,* 2:233; 4:22-23; 24:31; 46:15; Patai, pp. 193-4; Wāfī (3), pp. 44 *seqq*; Stern, p. 96, 103; Smith (1), pp. 290-1; Maghniyyah (2), pp. 35-7. It should be remembered that these incest rules are not the only reasons for prohibition; any marriageable person who does not fall within these forbidden degrees must satisfy, in addition, certain conditions other than the incest regulations.

65. Cf. Murdock, pp. 284 *seqq*; Leslie, pp. 55-60; Wāfī (3), pp. 48 *seqq*; Zelditch (2), pp. 712 *seqq.*

66. Murdock, p. 298.

67. Stern, p. 103; cf. n. 45 in this chapter. Smith also has attempted
to explain in similar fashion (a) why it is forbidden for a man to
marry the mother of his "spouse", even if his marriage to her daughter
is not actually consummated due to death or divorce; and (b) why it
is forbidden to marry the daughter of a spouse only if his marriage
to her mother has been consummated. "The point here," according
to Smith, "seems to be that the daughter of a wife to whom you have
come in is a sort of adopted daughter; which certainly is consistent
with the doctrine that adoption makes no real blood, and therefore
cannot be the source of an impediment to marriage. But this view
was given out only to legitimize Mohammed's own marriage with
the wife of his adopted son . . . so that one cannot expect consistency."
(p. 290 n.); cf. *supra.* pp. 20 *seqq.*

This explanation seems inadequate. If the spouse's daughter is
regarded as "a sort of adopted daughter", and if "adoption makes no
real blood," then the daughter should be lawful or unlawful to her
mother's husband, whether or not he 'has come in' to the mother.
But that is not the rule. On the other hand, if it were a matter of
adoption, the rule would apply equally to the mother and the daughter.
But that is not the case either. What, then, is the meaning of this
articulate distinction? Why is the mother forbidden to the man who
has contracted marriage with her daughter, whether or not the contract
is executed and the marriage actually consummated? And why is the
daughter forbidden to him only if his contract with the mother has
been fully executed, and he 'has come in' to her? It seems that a
contract with the daughter almost surely leads to the final consummation of the marriage; her life expectancy is normally longer than her
mother's; her youth qualities are more conducive to the execution
of the contract; and her future productivity has greater appeal. Besides,
if the contract with the daughter does not forbid the mother to the
daughter's prospective husband, it is not inconceivable that a situation
may arise in which minds are changed, and mother-daughter rivalry
or conflict results. To avoid such a situation and enhance the execution
of an initial contract, which is already surrounded by most favorable
conditions, is probably the reason for the exclusion of a mother from
the field of eligibles of a man who has contracted marriage with her
daughter, even if the contract is not yet fully executed. In contrast,
consummation of a marital contract with the mother of a marriageable daughter is much less certain, if only because of the age factor.

Besides, the prospective mate of the mother would hardly be desirable by the daughter as a partner. Hence, the rise of rivalry or conflict is unlikely. But it may happen that, prior to and after a contract which is not actually executed, the contractants invest money, emotions, and intimacy with their respective family members. If the marriage does not consummate, there may yet be another chance for a workable, economical union between the same male contractant and a daughter of the principal contracting woman, if the parties so desire. This is not a prescription; it is merely one legitimate alternative, a permissible choice that may serve to perpetuate the initial interfamily relationships and prove economical. It must be pointed out, however, that most of the discussion here is academic or hypothetical. It is undertaken to show the difficulty of trying to explain the Islāmic rules in terms of the personality factors of Muḥammad, instead of searching for the sociological explanations. Moreover, the most likely case where a daughter may accept to replace her mother in an unfinished marriage is when the mother dies in the process. If the mother is divorced before the consummation of the marriage contract, it is most unlikely that her daughter would wish to take her place, notwithstanding the jurists' academic interest in the logical possibility thereof.

68. Patai, p. 193.

69. Stern, p. 96.

70. Cf. Haykal, pp. 103, 109-10; Watt (4), p. 7; al Tāj, vol. 2, p. 284. This explanation is developed independently; but some factual hints can be found here and there. The present writer, once again, draws on some readings of years past, yet regrets the inaccessibility of the exact sources at this time.

71. Cf. Patai, pp. 24-7, 92 seqq; Roberts, pp. 12 ff.

72. R. Levy, p. 102; cf. Murdock, p. 84. For a typology of cross-cousin marriages, see Zelditch (1), pp. 472-3.

73. See supra, pp. 127 ff.

74. R. Levy, p. 102.

75. Stern, p. 60.

76. Patai, pp. 32, 35; Wāfī (3), pp. 29 ff; Westermarck (3), pp. 57-8.

77. In addition, see 'Abd al Bāqī (4), vol. 2, p. 540; Maghniyyah (2), pp. 32-3; Roberts, pp. 14-5; Shaltūt (1), pp. 251 ff.

78. Roberts, p. 15; cf. supra. pp. 33 ff.

79. Cf. Shaltūt (1), p. 253.

80. A thin thread of explanation may be found in A. Yūsuf 'Alī's commentary on *al Qur'ān* (5:6), vol. 1, p.241, n. 700. The rest is suggested independently.

81. This explanation is guided by some broad principles and derives from certain bare facts stated in the Qur'ān. Foremost among these are the following: (a) The Muslims believe in what is revealed to them in the Qur'ān and what has been revealed to the previous messengers of God, among whom the Muslims make no discrimination (2:136; 3:84; 43:13). (b) There should be no compulsion or coercion in religion; the truth is clear and every one must make his own religious choice (2:256; 18:29). (c) God accepts none other than the true religion of Islām (3:19, 85). (d) It is lawful to intermarry with the chaste women of the People of the Book (5:5). (e) Men are the guardians and protectors of women (4:34). If the prohibition of intermarriage between Muslim women and non-Muslim men is to be explained in the light of these principles and facts, in accordance with role differentiation, the explanation will probably follow the line suggested in the text of the discussion.

The concepts "equal" and "identical" are introduced here to differentiate sex roles. Such differentiation in Islām does not mean inequality, even though it may preclude identicalness. The rights and obligations attached to a woman's role, when taken an item for an item, do not identically correspond with those specified by a man's role. But when allowing for the sex role differentials, weighing the overall constituents of each role, and adjusting the scale of the respective rights and obligations, it will become clear that (a) the rights and obligations of any member of a given sex balance one another in the final analysis, and (b) the role constituents of the male "equal" those of the female's (also in the final analysis). For example, in certain cases of inheritance a woman's share is one half a man's. On the surface this is an injustice, or inequality, but in reality it is not necessarily the case. What is seen here is that the two specific shares are not identical, i.e., not the same. Yet this does not necessarily mean inequality or inequity. Considering that the woman is not denied the fruits of anything she has earned or worked for, and that she is practically carefree (since all her basic financial needs are met by some male in her family of orientation or procreation), and realizing, on the other hand, the man's position as the party responsible for the financial needs of his immediate family and possibly beyond, it becomes evident that the distribution of shares is based on differential needs and responsibilities. Where the man's obligations outweigh those of the woman, he is compensated for that by additional allowances drawn from such funds as the property of a deceased relative. This extra-allowance is not based on discrimination or inequality; rather, it is in return for his additional burdens. If we take the situation in its totality, weighing the respective rights and obligations of both men and women, the end result would seem to be an equal, though not identical, distribution.

82. See *supra*. pp. 50 ff.

83. *Ibid*. pp. 61 ff; Shaltūt (1), pp. 142-3.

CHAPTER FIVE

1. Adopted with some modification from a summary in Fayzee, p. 111. On dowry, the difference of religion, and the additional stipulations in the contract, see *supra,* pp. 33 ff, 38 ff.

2. See, for example, al Jaṣṣāṣ, vol. 1, pp. 442, ff; Ibn Qudāmah, vol. 7, pp. 223 *seqq*; Hobhouse, pp. 201-2; Demombynes (1), pp. 132-3; Jeffery, p. 54 ff; Vesey-Fitzgerald, pp. 43 ff. An example of the jurists' intricate elaboration of the legal formalities is their discussion of the "when," the "where," the "how," and the "why" a wife is entitled to be maintained by her husband; cf. al Kāsānī, vol. 4, pp. 15-6; *al Hidayah,* vol. 2, pp. 30 ff: al Shāfi'ī (3), vol. 5, p. 87.

3. The concept of role is used here to designate a *"pattern of behavior associated with a distinctive social position* ... Most roles specify the rights and duties belonging to a social position; they tell the individual what he ought to do in his role ... to whom he has obligations, and upon whom he has a rightful claim." (Broom and Selznick, p. 18).

4. See, in addition, *al Tāj,* vol. 2, pp. 286 ff; Ibn Qudāmah, vol. 7, pp. 223 ff; al Jaṣṣāṣ, vol. 1, pp. 442-3; Shaltūt (2), pp. 143 ff.

5. Cf. the references cited in the previous note. The terms *reproach* and *injury* seem the closest translation of the Arabic terms, *mann* and *adhā,* meaning in this context that men should not feel that by providing for women they are doing them favors. Nor should men cause their dependent women injury or grief by way of boasting or arrogance.

6. *al Qur'ān,* 2:233; 65:6-7; al Kāsānī, vol. 4, pp. 15-6; *al Hidāyah,* vol. 2, pp. 30 ff; al Shāfi'ī (3), vol. 5, p. 87.

7. See, for example, *al Qur'ān,* 2:233; 65:1-7; al Jaṣṣāṣ, vol. 1,

pp. 444 f; Jeffery, p. 54; Murdock, pp. 17-21, 203-6; al Shāfiʿī (3), vol. 5, p. 87; Vesey-Fitzgerald, p. 43; Wāfī (1), p. 5.

8. The legal discussion is summarized in Maghniyyah (2), p. 126; cf. Vesey-Fitzgerald, p. 44.

9. See, for example, Jeffery, p. 55; Vesey-Fitzgerald, p. 43; Maghniyyah (2), p. 113.

10. al Hidayah, vol. 2, pp. 30 ff; al Subkī, pp. 136 ff; ʿAbd Allāh, pp. 250 ff; Maghniyyah (2), p. 116; al Kāsānī, vol. 4, pp. 15 f.

11. See supra. pp. 15 ff.

12. Cf. the references cited in note 10 above.

13. Ibn Taymiyyah, al Fatāwā, p. 454. The denial of maintenance to a sick wife does not mean that she will be left to exposure or starvation. If she has any property she must maintain herself of her own assets. Otherwise, the responsibility will be discharged by the nearest consanguine male who can afford it; if not, it becomes a community or state responsibility; see al Qur'ān, 16:90; 17:26; ʿAbd Allāh, pp. 250, 446; Wāfī (2), pp. 48 ff.

14. See, for example, Maghniyyah (2), pp. 124-5; Abū Zahrah (3), pp. 335 ff; ʿAbd Allāh, p. 250.

15. For some suggestive historical remarks, see Hitti, esp. pp. 333 seqq., 485; R. Levy, esp. ch. IX; Leslie, p. 169.

16. Remmling, p. 4.

17. Cf. Ibn al Qayyim (3), vol. 4, pp. 319 f.

18. Farrūkh, p. 137; al Hidayah vol. 2, p. 30; Maghniyyah, (2), p. 115; al Subkī, pp. 136 ff.

19. Cf. al Qur'ān, 4:34, 128; Abū Zahrah (3), pp. 66, 332 f; Vesey-Fitzgerald, p. 43; Jeffery, p. 55.

20. Cf. al Qur'ān, 4:35, 128; Abū Zahrah (3), p.\66.

21. Abū Zahrah, (1), pp. 144-5.

22. Ibid; cf. al Hidayah, vol. 2, pp. 30-1; Ibn al Humām, vol. 3, p. 329; Ibn al Qayyim (3), vol. 4, p. 297; al Shāfiʿī (3), vol. 5, p. 91; al Subkī, p. 145.

23. See the references cited in the previous note, esp. Ibn al Qayyim; al Qur'ān, 2:280-281; 65:7.

24. For a general historical view, see, for example, Hitti, chs. 23, 26, 34; Durant, chs. 11-4; Lewis, chs. 5, 7; Shāfiʿī (3), vol. 5, p. 105; Taymūr, pp. 1-6, 12-28; al Sharabāṣī, pp. 98-101.

25. Cf. the historical sources cited in the previous note.

26. This discussion is guided by some thin threads of facts. It cannot be claimed that the explanation offered here is actually suggested

by, or found in, the law schools. The juristic views are taken as a mirror reflecting certain social undercurrents which we have tried to reconstruct. There is no way to confirm or deny the correlation between these views and the suggested reconstructions. What is proposed here is that, if a given jurist were to restate his position in some sociological fashion, he very likely would follow a theme similar to the one presented in this discussion. The significance of this attempt is twofold. First, it tries to illustrate the advantages of a sociological explanation of doctrines that are usually presented as strictly religious. Secondly, it tries to show how interdependent and mutually enlightening are the religious context of a doctrine and the social setting of that doctrine.

27. See *supra*. pp. 62 ff; *al Qur'ān;* 4:40, 20; al Jaṣṣāṣ, vol. 1, p. 442; Hobhouse, p. 201; Vesey-Fitzgerald, p. 44.

28. Demombynes (1), p. 132; cf. Jeffery, p. 56.

29. Lichtenstadter, p. 122.

30. See note 28 above. The whole question of subjection will be examined later in this chapter.

31. As far as it was possible to check the writings of the school founders, no definite statement on the point was found. In fact, the only available source of the factual information is Vesey-Fitzgerald (p. 44), who undoubtedly draws from other sources. This seems to indicate that the Mālikī writers who specified the husband's rights over the wife's property were probably of later generations. It is possible that such an articulate focalization of these rights may be the work of Western scholarship. The present writer, though reasonably familiar with Islāmic law, was somewhat suprised to find, for the first time, the point presented in a summary of Islāmic law by a Western scholar.

32. Jeffery, p. 70; Mūsā, pp. 105, 168 ff; Wāfī (2), p. 23.

33. See notes 30 and 31 above.

34. Cf. *al Qur'ān*, 2:187; 30:21; 49:10.

35. Cf. *Ibid*. 2:229, 231-2; 4:129; *al Taj*, vol. 2, pp. 288 f.

36. *Ibid*. 25:74. See also Jeffery, p. 55; 'Awwā, pp. 110-1.

37. Cf. *al Qur'ān*, 4:34; al Jaṣṣāṣ, vol. 1, p. 443; Jeffery, p. 56; Vesey-Fitzgerald, p. 43.

38. Ibn Qudāmah, vol. 7, pp. 225-6; Vesey-Fitzgerald, p. 43; also note 22 in this chapter.

39. Ibn Qudāmah, vol. 7, pp. 223-5, 228 ff. Cf., *al Qur'ān*, 2:187, 228; Vesey-Fitzgerald, pp. 42-3; Jeffery, p. 54; Murdock, p. 3 and *passim*; Zelditch (2), p. 681.

40. al Jaṣṣāṣ, vol. 1, p. 443.
41. Cf. *al Qur'ān,* 6:74; 17:28; 19:41-48; 31:15; 66:11.
42. Ibn Qudāmah, vol. 7, p. 223.
43. See, for example, the Prophet's statement quoted in Jeffery, p. 55 and in Hobhouse, p. 200.
44. Jeffery, pp. 55-6.
45. Demombynes (1), p. 132.
46. Ibn Qudāmah, vol. 7, pp. 225 f; al Jaṣṣāṣ, vol. 1, pp. 444-5; Jeffery, p. 56; Hobhouse, pp. 201 f; Vesey-Fitzgerald, p. 43; 'Awwā, pp. 111 f; Wāfī (1), pp. 96-7; *al Taj,* vol. 2, pp. 286 ff.
47. Quoted in Bernard, p. 420.
48. *Ibid.* pp. 426 f.
49. Berelson and Steiner, p. 314; cf. Pitts, p. 75.
50. Pitts, pp. 63, 72; cf. Zelditch (2), p. 699, 703.
51. See, for example, Demombynes (1), p. 132.
52. Cf. al 'Aqqād, p. 68; n. 82 in ch. 4; also ch. 7 *infra.;* Shaltūt (2), p. 202 *seqq.*
53. al Ghazālī, pp. 132 ff; Wāfī (2), pp. 48 ff; *Kitāb al Fiqh,* vol. 1, pp. 122, 128, 430.
54. For some further factual information see, for example, al Ghazālī, p. 152; Wāfī (2), p. 108; Shaltūt (2), pp. 211 ff.
55. See "The Basis of Obedience," *supra.* pp. 173 ff; cf. al 'Aqqād, p. 114; 'Awn, p. 61-4; al Ghazālī, pp. 132 ff; Wāfī (2), pp. 52.
56. See, for example, Ibn Qudāmah, vol. 7, pp. 223 ff; Demombynes (1), p. 132; Jeffery, p. 55.
57. Wāfī (2), pp. 52-6; cf. Shaltūt (2), pp. 146 ff.
58. 'Awn, pp. 61-4; cf. *ibid.*
59. Shaltūt (5), pp. 57 f.
60. *al Qur'ān,* e.g., 6:127; 140, 151; 17:31; also the child's right to life, *infra.* pp. 184 ff.
61. Cf. *al Qur'ān,* 3:14; 8:28; 9:69; 18:46; 23:55, 34:35; 57:20; 64:15; 68:14.
62. *Ibid.* 9:55, 85; 18:46; 64:15.
63. *Ibid.* 310, 116; 4:11; 9:24; 11:45-57; 26:88; 31:33; 34:37; 58:17; 60:3; 63:9; 64:14; 71:21; *supra.* pp. 22 ff.
64. Jeffery, pp. 63 f; cf. Roberts, pp. 41 ff; R. Levy, pp. 135-49.
65. Patai, p. 135; cf. pp. 127 ff; also Westermarck (2), vol. 1, pp. 401-7.
66. Bardis, pp. 415 f.
67. *Ibid.* pp. 446-7; cf. Hobhouse, p. 218.

68. See, for example, *al Qur'ān,* 6:151; 17:31; 'Awn, pp. 20 f.

69. Cf. al Alūsī, vol. 3, p. 42; al Hūfī (1), pp. 226 ff; (2), pp. 298 ff; Wāfī (3), pp. 117 ff; Zaydān (1), p. 64.

70. Roberts, pp. 96-7. (Emphasis is not in the original.) In the same vein, Jeffery (p. 43) has observed that, "far too much has been made of the Prophet's injunction prohibiting female infanticide. The practice . . . must have been of limited incidence . . . The women, indeed, were a very important factor in the life of ancient Arabia . . . All the world knows about the Queen of Sheba . . . and about Zenobia of Palmyra who led a spirited resistance against the Roman Legions But these women were not exceptional . . ."

71. Bell (1), pp. 6-7; cf. Smith (1), pp. 171-2.

72. See, for example, Wāfī (3), p. 118.

73. Cf, al Alūsī, vol. 3, p. 46; al Hūfī (1), p. 226.

74. Cf. Roberts, pp. 94-5; Smith (1), pp. 129-30, 282 f; al Alūsī, vol. 3, pp. 43 f; Zaydān (1), p. 64.

75. al Alūsī, vol. 3, pp. 43-4; al Hūfī (1), p. 225.

76. Cf. Smith (1), p. 281; Bell (1), p. 8; al Alūsī, vol. 3, pp. 50 ff; al Hūfī (1), pp. 226 f.

77. Wāfī (3), pp. 118 ff.

78. Smith (1), p. 279.

79. For a description of the economic activities of Arabian women, see 'Awn, pp. 21 ff; al Hūfī (2), pp. 398 ff.

80. Smith (1), p. 281.

81. Cf. *al Qur'ān,* 16:56-62; 42:49-50; 43:15-19. On the question of equal treatment, see, for example, Shaltūt (1), pp. 310 ff; *al Taj,* vol. 2, pp. 228 f; vol. 3, pp. 97 f; vol. 5, pp. 7-8, 246 ff.

82. Coser, p. xvi.

83. Smith (1), pp. 64-5, 172 ff and *passim;* Jum'ah, pp. 75 ff, cf. pp. 10 ff; Patai, pp. 223 f.

84. al Hūfī (2), pp. 105-12. It is noteworthy that the author made a most extensive study of pre-Islāmic poetry in which numerous illustrations of these points are cited. It is also interesting that the strong son-mother relationship produced a special kind of fealty between sons and their maternal uncles. This fealty continued into Islām and manifested itself in several crucial moments of political rivalry. For example, the Kalbīs of al Yaman supported Mu'āwiyah against 'Alī because the former was related to, and had avenged the death of, Caliph 'Uthmān who had been married to a Yamanī woman. The Persians supported their maternal nephew al Ma'mūn against his rival

brother al Amīn in their bids for the Caliphate. Moreover, the Abbāsī Caliph al Mu'taṣim favored the Turks over the Persians because his mother was a Turk; cf. pp. 132 ff.

85. Cf. Wāfī (3), p. 10; Farrūkh, p. 35; Jeffery, p. 63.

86. Jeffery, p. 63; *al Tāj*, vol. 2, pp. 320 f.

87. Jeffery, p. 63. R. Levy (pp. 135 ff) presents an interesting summary of the legal views as expressed in the law books. See also Roberts, pp. 49 ff; Farrūkh, pp. 98 ff; *al Qur'ān*, 24:6-9; 33:4-5; *al Tāj*, vol. 2, pp. 248 f, 317 *seqq*. The implications of the one-sided legitimacy and the unknown descent will become clear as the discussion proceeds.

88. Reported in *al Tāj*, vol. 2, pp. 319 f.

89. Queen, p. 10.

90. Cf. note 88 in this chapter.

91. Cf. the immediately preceding two paragraphs and three notes.

92. Cf. *al Tāj*, vol. 2, pp. 238 f.

93. *al Qur'ān*, 3:135; 4:32; 7:149; 14:48; 35:18; 41:46; 49:13; 53:31-42; 63:6.

94. Cf. *ibid*. 49:10-13; *al Tāj*, vol. 2, p. 239.

95. *al Qur'ān*, e.g., 4:36-42; 17:32; 24:2-3; 33:4-6; 35:18. See also Shaltūt (2), pp. 364 *seqq.*; al Madanī, pp. 98 ff.

96. Cf. *al Qur'ān*, 4:1, 29-33; 8:75; 17-26; 30:38; 33:6; 47:22.

97. *Ibid*. 4:36-42; 6:74-90; 17:23-26; 31:13-15. The following letter is not necessarily typical, but it is suggestive of what may happen as a result of legal or social adoption.

Dear Abby: I am 17 years old and am like walking around in a fog. I just found out that my 'mother' is really my aunt, and my 'aunt' is my real mother.

My mother wasn't married at the time, so she gave me to her married sister to raise. Later, my real mother got married and had children. That means my brothers and sisters are really my cousins, and the kids I always thought were my cousins are really my half-sisters and brothers. I feel terrible to think almost everybody in the family has known this all along and I had to find it out from a stranger.

There is nothing I can do about it because I feel toward the aunt who raised me just like any kid would feel toward his own mother. And I don't honestly feel anything extra special for my real mother who I thought was just another aunt.

I guess what I want to say is this: Please tell people if they have a secret like this in their family, it's best to tell the kids before they hear it from strangers.

Hurt and In A Fog
(*The Observer-Dispatch,* Daily, Utica, N. Y., 7-30-70).

Such experiences may raise some interesting questions with respect to the comparative effects of of adoption and nonadoption systems upon personality and society. For example, it may be submitted that even with such confusions and uncertainties, adoption is still a more adaptive social policy than some other alternatives, e.g., nonadoption at all.

98. Cf. *al Qur'ān,* 24:2-3; *al Tāj,* vol. 2, pp. 319 ff.

99. For some factual information see Shaltūt (1), pp. 293, ff; *al Tāj,* vol. 2, pp. 325 ff; Jeffery, pp. 63 f; Roberts, pp. 43 ff.

100. See, for example, Roberts, pp. 49 ff; Haykal, pp. 322 ff.

101. The discussion of this problem is based primarily on the summary statement in Shaltūt (1), pp. 290-6. See also *al Qur'ān,* 5:2, 35; 8:75; 33:4-5; 37; 76:8; 89:17-18; 107:1-3. It should be pointed out that these Qur'ānic statements deal with the duties of Muslims toward the orphans, the foundlings, etc. These numerous references may suggest how insecure and exploited the orphans were, and also how entrenched the Arabian kinship was. To shake loose this system and reorganize it, such strong religio-moral injunctions were needed; cf. Roberts, pp. 41 ff.

102. See the references cited in the previous note.

103. See *al Tāj,* vol. 3, pp. 97-8; vol. 5, pp. 7-8, 246 ff; cf. Jeffery, pp. 63-4; *al Mukhtasar,* p. 193.

104. See, for example, *al Qur'ān,* 2:233; 65:6-7; Jeffery, p. 64; Farrūkh, pp. 105 ff; Fāyid, pp. 73 f.

105. Cf. *al Qur'ān* 2:256; 18:29; 82; 19:28; 41:46; *al Tāj,* vol. 5, pp. 66 ff.

106. See, for example, *al Hidāyah,* vol. 2, pp. 34 ff; Abū Zahrah (1), pp. 157 ff; Maghniyyah (2), pp. 135 f; *al Mudawwanah,* vol. 2, p. 247.

107. Cf. *al Tāj,* vol. 2, p. 325; Shaltūt (1), p. 251 ff.

108. *al Tāj,* vol. 2, p. 325.

109. Cited in *ibid.*

110. Cf. *ibid.* pp. 326 f; Roberts, pp. 32, 41 ff; Stern, pp. 144 f; Farrūkh, pp. 104 ff; Maghniyyah (2), pp. 105 ff.

111. Cf. *al Tāj,* vol. 2, pp. 326 f; Maghniyyah (2), pp. 111 f.

112. *al Qur'ān,* 2:177; 4:36-39; 107:1-3; *al Tāj,* vol. 5, pp. 7 ff;

Roberts, pp. 41 ff; Shaltūt (2), pp. 362 ff; al Madanī, pp. 98 ff, 343 ff, also the references cited in note 101 in this chapter.

113. Cf. *al Qur'ān,* 4:7, 11; 17:22; *al Tāj,* vol. 5, pp. 4 ff.

114. Cf. *al Qur'ān,* 11:42-48; 12:8; 19:43-45; 46:17.

115. *Ibid.* 2:170; 5:104; 7:28; 10:78; 21:53; 26:74; 31:21; 43:22-23.

116. *Ibid.* See also 4:135; 9:23-24; 28:22; 31:33.

117. Cf. *ibid.* 4:36; 17:22; 31:14.

118. *Ibid.* 2:83, 180, 215; 4:36; 6:151; 14:41; 17:22; 19:32; 27:19; 29:8; 31:14; 46:10; 71:28; also *al Tāj,* vol. 5, pp. 4 ff; Roberts, pp. 46 ff.

119. Cf. *al Qur'ān;* 4:59; 18:28; 26:151; 29:8; 31:15; 68:8-10; also *al Tāj,* vol. 5, pp. 4 ff. pp. 262.

120. Cf. al Kāsānī, vol. 4, pp. 30 f; Abū Zahrah (1), p. 159; Ibn 'Abidīn, vol. 2, pp. 933 ff; *al Mudawwanah,* vol. 2, pp. 248 ff.

121. *al Hidāyah,* vol. 2, pp. 34 ff; Ibn 'Abidīn, vol. 2, pp. 933 ff; Maghniyyah (2), pp. 131 ff; Abū Zahrah (1), pp. 157 ff; *al Mudawwanah,* vol. 2, pp. 247 f; Ibn Taymiyyah, *al Fatāwā,* p. 453.

122. Ibn al Qayyim (3), vol. 4. pp. 319 ff.

123. Patai, pp. 214 ff. It is interesting to note that this author cites numerous Biblical references.

124. *al Qur'ān,* 2:178; 3:103; 9:11; 12:69; 19:53; 20:30; 25:35; 28:34-35; 49:10-12; 59:10.

125. al Hūfī (2), pp. 315 ff.

126. See the references cited in note 124 in this chapter; cf. *al Qur'ān,* 9:24; 23:9; 58:22; 80:34.

127. See *supra,* pp. 304 ff; also *al Qur'ān,* 4:7, 11, 170.

128. Cf. Ibn Taymiyyah, *al Fatāwā,* p. 453; Ibn al Qayyim (3), vol. 4, pp. 319 ff; al Subkī, pp. 148-9; Abū Zahrah (1), p. 159.

129. Cf. *al Qur'ān,* 2:83, 177, 180, 215; 3:6; 4:1, 7-8, 32, 36, 135; 6:152; 8:75; 9:113; 16:90; 17:26; 24:22; 30:38; 33:6; 35:18; 60:3; *al Tāj,* vol. 5, pp. 8 ff.

130. Cf. Abū Zahrah (1), p. 159; al Subkī, pp. 148 f; Ibn al Qayyim (3), vol. 4, pp. 319 ff; *al Hidāyah,* vol. 2, pp. 35 f; al Shāfai'ī (3), vol. 5, p. 90; al Tabarī, vol. 2, pp. 308 ff, 374; Sha'bān, pp. 240 ff. It is interesting to note that these various positions on the mainte- nance rights of relatives are based on different interpretations of one and the same verse in the Qur'ān (2:233). It is also interesting that the Hanbalī doctrine is regarded as more conducive to social solidarity. Thus, it was recommended by the Conference on Social Studies held

in Damascus in 1952 to adopt this position (cf. al Sharabāṣī, p. 209). On the other hand, Ibn al Qayyim, a Hanbalī himself, regarded the Hanafī position the closest to the spirit of the Qur'ān and Traditions (cf. Ibn al Qayyim (3), vol. 4. p. 323).

131. Shaltūt (1), pp. 263-5; cf. Kirk, p. 575.
132. *Ibid.* pp. 266-70.
133. Kirk, pp. 567-8.
134. *Ibid.* pp. 569-71.
135. *Ibid.* pp. 574-5.
136. For further historical information, see Taymūr, pp. 15 ff and *passim;* R. Levy, pp. 166 ff; al Sharabāṣī, pp. 52 *seqq.*
137. For more factual background data, see Amīn (2), pp. 175 ff; Coulson (1), p. 97; Farrūkh, p. 112.

CHAPTER SIX

1. Pitts, p. 76.
2. Berelson and Steiner, p. 310.
8. See, for example, Bardis, pp. 418-9, 447; al Hūfī (1), pp. 222-3, pp. 259 ff; Patai, pp. 113 *seqq; Roberts,* pp. 24 ff; Siddiqi, p. 76; Westermarck (1), pp. 517 ff; Winch, pp. 690 ff.
4. Winch, p. 693.
5. Cf. *ibid.* pp. 691 ff.
6. Bardis, p. 447.
7. Quoted in Siddiqi, p. 77.
8. See, for example, Bardis, pp. 418--9, 447; al Hūfī (1), pp. 222-3, (2), pp. 259 ff; Patai, pp. 113 ff; Westermarck (1), pp. 518 ff.
9. Quoted in Roberts, p. 123.
10. Berelson and Steiner, pp. 311-2.
11. See, for example, al Qur'ān, 2:233, 286.
12. Cf. *al Tāj,* vol. 2, pp. 308 ff; Ibn Qudāmah, vol. 7, pp. 296-7; 'Awn, p. 94 ff; Roberts, pp. 18-9; Siddiqi, p. 81; Abū Zahrah (3), pp. 70-1, 684; Wāfī (1), pp. 65 ff.
13. *al Qur'ān,* 2:143 (with A. Yūsuf 'Alī's translation and commentary); 42:40-3; *al Tāj,* vol. 2, pp. 308 ff.
14. See, for example, Wāfī (1), pp. 65-7; Siddiqi, p. 76.
15. Jeffery, p. 60 (emphasis added). The same idea has been expressed by R. Levy (p. 121) and Roberts (p. 19) with almost identical words. Roberts, in particular, (pp. 19-20; cf. pp. 22-3) remarks that the Arabs, and indeed Eastern peoples in general, have a greater need for divorce, "since their social relations are so very different from ours.

The need arises especially from the seperation of the sexes, and . . . the practice among women of wearing the veil . . . The great facility with which a man may divorce his wife . . . naturally weakens the marital bond, and reduces a woman to the most degrading position in the social scale."

16. See, for example, *al Tāj*, vol. 2, pp. 310-1 with the commentary; Wāfī (1), pp. 66-7; 'Awn, pp. 103-4. Parenthetically, this was the case because marriages then were costly affairs for men. An irrevocable triple divorce must have meant a great deal of concern for the man who carelessly pronounced it.

17. Cf. Abū Zahrah (3), pp. 683-4; 'Awn, pp. 103-4. It is noteworthy that many of these considerations are being re-examined by contemporary Muslim authorities in their search for the spirit and equity of the law. It is also interesting that what some observers, as Jeffery, have called unjustifiable facilities of divorce in Islām were in fact instituted as disciplinary or punitive measures against irresponsible parties. For example, a divorce pronouncement by an intoxicated, jesting, or thoughtless man is considered by some jurists as valid. The idea here is not so much to certify a divorce formula as to discipline an irresponsible, heedless person and alert him to the serious nature of his action. See also *al Tāj*, vol. 2, p. 309; Wāfī (1), pp. 76-7.

18. Roberts, pp. 19-20.

19. Cf. al 'Aqqād, pp. 63 ff; Jeffery, pp. 56-7; *al Qur'ān* 24:27-8; 33:53-5, 58-9.

20. Cf. *al Tāj*, vol. 2, pp. 259 ff; al Ghazālī, pp. 69 ff.

21. Berelson and Steiner, p. 312 (emphasis added).

22. See *infra*. pp. 231 ff.

23. Cf. *al Qur'ān*, 2:227-38; 4:19-21, 127-30; 65:1-4; *al Tāj*, vol. 2, pp. 308 ff. Perhaps man's behavior does not justify Islām's confidence in human integrity. Or, perhaps Islām saw little good in setting explicit formal rules since man could violate them overtly or covertly. At any rate, Islām seems to entrust a great deal in this regard to the individual's conscience and his sense of religious morality. But if any abuse is detected, it becomes a God-enjoined duty of the men in authority, as well as common Muslims, to seek the full implementation of the spirit of the law. This is what the Qur'ān commands. See, e.g., *al Qur'ān*, 3:104; the examples of 'Umar and Ibn Taymiyyah, *supra*. pp. 220 ff.

24. Cf. Abū Zahrah (3), p. 71; al Ghazālī, pp. 72 ff.

25. See Abū Zahrah, *op. cit.* p. 122.

26. Cf. *supra*, pp. 39 :; 99 ff; 'Awwā, p. 62; Siddiqi, p. 82; Wāfī (1), pp. 65 ff.

27   Cf. *al Qur'ān*, 2:229.

28. Cf. *ibid.* 2:130; Abū Zahrah (3), pp. 70-2.

29. Cf. *al Tāj*, vol. 2. 299-300, 327; Ibn Qudāmah, vol. 7, pp. 109 ff; Jeffery, p. 60; Maghniyyah (2), pp. 47 ff, 176; Farrūkh, p. 149 ff; R. Levy, p. 123; Stern, p. 150.

30. Cf. *al Qur'ān*, 2:228-32, 237; 65:1-4; *al Tāj*, vol. 2, pp. 237-8; Haykal, p. 490.

31. The legal views are summarized in Maghniyyah (2), pp. 140-8. The Shī'īs and the Zāhirīs require certain additional conditions for the validity of a divorce, e.g., the presence of two qualified witnesses, the use of one of three specific formulas, etc. Perhaps the Shī'īs took this position because they allowed the "temporary" *mut'ah* marriage, a measure which could release much of the ordinary pressure on full-fledged marriages and therefore reduce the need for their dissolution. In any case, it is noteworthy that many of these additional conditions are being adopted by contemporary Muslim societies. See also *al Qur'ān*, 65:1-6; *al Tāj*, vol. 2, pp. 309 ff; al Ghazālī, pp. 175 ff.

32. Cf. 'Awn, pp. 95 ff; al Ghazālī, pp. 175 ff; Siddiqi, p. 94; *al Qur'ān*, 2:222; *al Tāj*, vol. 2, p. 312.

33. In connection with this discussion, see, for example, *al Qur'ān*, 4:21; 30:21; *al Taj*, vol. 2, pp. 257-9, 287-8; Abū Zahrah (3), pp. 70-1; 'Awwā, p. 62; al Ghazālī, pp. 169 *seqq;* Siddiqi, p. 82; Wāfī (1), pp. 65 ff.

34. Cf. *supra*, pp. 225 ff. See also *Qur'ān*, 2:216 ,226-7; 4:19-21, 34-6, 127-30; 'Awn, pp. 91 ff; Abū Zahrah (3), pp. 70-1; Farrūkh, pp. 149 ff; al Ghazālī, pp. 169 ff; Wāfī (1), pp. 68-70. It is interesting to note that the idea of arbitration can facilitate reconciliation or make divorce less inconvenient. Perhaps this is best illustrated by the experiment of a certain Justice Paul W. Alexander of Toledo, Ohio, and his Family Court plan. It was based on the premise, that "it is important to try to restore congeniality where possible . . . [and] the further premise that where it seems improbable that congeniality can be restored, it is desirable to allow the couple to part by means of a legal divorce without the sort of perjurous degradation required by the adversary procedure. Basic to this view is the proposition that congeniality is a characteristic of a couple rather than of an individual; hence the effort to establish the guilt of one of the parties becomes an irrelevance and a legal fiction." (Winch, p. 694).

35. *al Qur'ān,* 2:229; 65:1-7; Abū Zahrah (3), p. 71; 'Awn, pp. 94 ff; Farrukh, pp. 149 ff; al Ghazālī, pp. 165 ff; Siddiqi, pp. 82 ff; Wāfī (1) pp. 71 ff.

36. See the references cited in the previous note and *al Qur'ān,* 2:230; cf. the immediately following note and the related discussion.

37. Cf. *al Qur'ān,* 2:230; *al Tāj,* vol. 2, p. 313; Abū Zahrah (3), pp. 73-4, 107; 'Awn, pp. 96 ff; Merchant, p. 152; Roberts, p. 26; Siddiqi, p. 84; Ibn Qudāmah, vol. 7, pp. 105-6, 153-4. These are only the highlights of an involved discussion with many intricate details and arguments, which do not particularly interest us here. This form of *tahlil* marriage is a basic source of many humorous tales in folkloric literatuure. However, this abnormal behavior is perhaps no more typical than the following incidence (as syndicated in the Utica Observer-Dispatch, 8-13-1975): Dear Abby: Joe, a guy I bowl with, told me that he just came back from Las Vegas where he had been the best man at three weddings. (I'll call the bridegroom "Paul.")

Joe said that Paul first married a girl who was visibly pregnant just to give her baby a name. Immediately after they were married, Paul divorced her.

Then Paul went back to the chapel and married Girl No. 2 for the same reason. As soon as they were married, Paul divorced her, too.

Paul said the divorces had been set up in advance.

Then, Paul and Joe went back to the chapel, and Paul married the girl he was really in love with. (Joe said the third one didn't look pregnant.)

How about blood tests and waiting periods? Personally, I think this so-called "best man" is full of baloney, but he swears this actually happened.

Is this possible?—Doubting Thomas.

Dear Tom: It's possible. Blood tests and waiting periods are not required in Nevada. I am informed that divorces are final when granted and the parties are free to marry immediately.

38. See also Merchant, p. 149; *Shorter Enc. of Islām,* pp. 565 ff; 'Awn, pp. 97 ff; Wāfī (1), p. 75.

39. Cf. Abū Zahrah (3), pp. 71-2; 'Awn, pp. 103-4; Farrūkh, pp. 141-2; 154 ff; al Ghazālī, pp. 163 ff; Wāfī (1), pp. 76-7.

40. See *infra.* pp. 224 f; and *supra.* pp. 229 f.

41. See *supra,* pp. 232 ff.

42. Cf. *al Qur'ān,* 2:226; al Alūsī, vol. 2, pp. 49-50; *al Tāj,* vol. 2, pp. 316-7; 'Awwā, pp. 64-5.

326 **THE FAMILY STRUCTURE IN ISLAM**

43. Cf. *al Qur'ān,* 58:1-5; *al Tāj,* vol. 2, pp. 322-3; *Shorter Ency. of Islām,* p. 570; Stern, pp. 127 ff; Smith (1), p. 289.

44. *al Qur'ān,* 24:6-9; *al Tāj,* vol. 2, pp. 317 ff; Ibn Qudāmah, vol. 8, p. 3; Merchant, pp. 152-3. Patai (pp. 66-7, 70) and Roberts (pp. 35-6) mention some interesting contrasts. For example, the Qur'ān requires four witnesses to prove adultery; the Old Testament (Deut. 17, 6) requires two or three. Also, where there is no proof one way or the other, the Islāmic form of double testimony ends in the dissolution of marriage, because it would probably be unwarranted to assume arbitrarily the guilt or innocence of either party. The Old Testament and the Code of Hammurabi seem to take as given the man's guilt and the wife's innocence; unless she is caught or proven guilty, she remains his wife all his days, in spite of him and of their double swearing; cf. Deut. 17, 6; 22; 19-20, 29.

45. *al Qur'ān,* 2:229; *al Tāj,* vol 2, p. 308; 'Awn, pp. 101-2; al Ghazālī, pp. 174 ff; Siddiqi, pp. 89-90; Stern, pp. 129 ff; Tūsī, vol. 2, p. 428.

46. Cf. Farrūkh, pp. 157 ff; Stern, pp. 134-5; Wāfī (1), pp. 80 ff.

47. Cf. *supra,* pp. 231 ff.

48. *Ibid.* pp. 232 *seqq.*

49. Cf. *al Tāj,* vol. 2, p. 310; Farrūkh, pp. 141 ff.

50. See for example 'Awn, p. 103; al Ghazālī, pp. 178 ff; Wāfī (1), pp. 76-7; Jeffery, pp. 60-1; R. Levy, p. 123; Roberts, pp. 25 ff.

51. Cf. R. Levy, p. 121; Jeffery, p. 60; Merchant, p. 149; Roberts, pp. 19, 23.

52. Cf. Fayzee, pp. 142 ff; Farrūkh, p. 148.

53. See *supra.* pp. 223 ff.

54. Cf. *al Tāj,* vol. 2, p. 257; Abū Zahrah (1), p. 147; (3), p. 70; al 'Aqqād, pp. 97 ff; Merchant, pp. 149, 156-7; Berelson and Steiner, p. 312.

55. Cf. *supra,* pp. 223 ff, 224 ff; Farrūkh, p. 148.

56. Cf. Abū Zahrah (1), p. 147; 'Awwā, p. 75; Fayzee, pp. 142 ff; Farrūkh, p. 148; Siddiqi, p. 90; Wāfī (1), pp. 14-5. The woman's right of "delegated" and "suspended" divorce may sound peculiar. Probably equally peculiar is the man's right of *'ilā* and *zihār.*

57. Cf. Fayzee, pp. 142 ff; *Supra.* pp. 239 ff.

58. See the references cited in the last three notes; cf. R. Levy, p. 123; Jeffery, pp. 60-1; Siddiqi, pp. 85 ff; Wāfī (2), pp. 88-9.

59. Cf. *al Qur'ān,* 2:228-32, 236, 241; 'Awn, p. 102; Farrūkh, pp. 157 ff; Maghniyyah (2), pp. 177-8.

60. Cf. *al Qur'ān,* 2:228, 231; 65:1-5; 'Awn, pp. 94 ff; Farrūkh, pp. 154 ff; Roberts, pp. 28 ff; Siddiqi, pp. 83-4; Stern, p. 140; Wāfī (1), pp. 70 ff.

61. Cf. *al Qur'ān,* 65:1-6; 'Awn, pp. 99 ff; al Ghazālī, pp. 147 ff; Wāfī (1), pp. 70 ff.

62. Cf. *al Qur'ān,* 2:233, 65:4-7; Wāfī (1), pp. 70-1; *Supra.* pp. 198 ff.

63. Cf. *al Qur'ān* 33:49; 'Awn, p. 102; Farrūkh, pp. 157 ff; Roberts, pp. 28 ff; Wāfī (1), p. 70.

64. Cf. *al Qur'ān,* 2:230; 'Awn, p. 97; Roberts, p. 31; Wāfī (1), pp. 73 ff.

CHAPTER SEVEN

1. De Coulanges, p. 542; cf. Kohler, p. 537.

2. Patai, p. 219; cf. Goitein, pp. 40-1; Bardis, p. 419.

3. Aziz Ahmad, pp. 507-8; Coulson (1), pp. 15-6; Demombynes (1), p. 139; Roberts, pp. 62-3; Smith (1), p. 264; Tyabji, p. 821.

4. This situation created a tension between the religious prescription which forbade inheritance and the fatherly sentiment which favored it. In some cases a reconciliation was legislated, whereby it was decided that the daughter should marry the heir. But this, in turn, created further complications. If the daughter was already married, she was to abandon her husband to marry her heir; if the heir was married, he was to divorce his wife, in order for him to marry his relative who would inherit from her father (cf. De Coulanges, pp. 543 ff).

5. See Bardis, p. 419; Goitein, pp. 40-1; Mūsā, pp. 38-9; Patai, pp. 219 ff. The assumption here is that family members who did not inherit, e.g., the daughters, younger sons, or wives, were cared for by those who did.

6. Cf. Kohler, pp. 539-40. What seems to be implied here is that where both sexes inherit, and where the members of either sex inherit equally, it may be said that a strong sense of individualism obtains. Otherwise, the individual's interest may be sacrificed for the group's sake.

7. With primogeniture, younger brothers either had to stay celibates with the main household or move to emerging industrial centers where new opportunities were made available. But when all sons divided the property among themselves, each one set up his household on his own separate piece of land, which frequently was inadequate for subsistence. Consequently, the landowner had to look for work to

supplement his income. But rather than leave the land in search for better opportunities, he would instead try to find work in local small enterprise (cf. Coser, p. xxvi).

8. Cf. al Qur'ān, 59:7-9; Mūsā, pp. 185-6, 194; Wāfī (2), pp. 21 ff.

9. Roberts, p. 62; cf. Wāfī (2), pp. 21 ff; Infra. pp. 267 ff.

10. Cf. Goitein, pp. 40-1; Roberts, pp. 65 ff.

11. See, for example, Coulson (1), pp. 16-7; Fayzee, pp. 380-1; Tyabji, pp. 820, 825; Amīn (2), pp. 232-3.

12. See Mūsā, pp. 147-8; al Tāj, vol. 2, pp. 228 ff; cf. notes 1, 2 & 5 in this chapter. Voluntary patronage (walā may be between a freedman and his former master. According to one interpretation, the latter inherits from the former in default of other heirs. Another interpretation holds the right of succession to be reciprocal; whoever survives of the patrons, inherits from the heirless deceased. At any rate, this was regarded as a valid agreement between private persons and was accepted by all Muslim groups except the Khārijī sect of the Ibāḍīs. Patronage may also obtain between common associates and ordinary friends. This would be similar to the pre-Islāmic form of sworn alliance or clientage, and it was acceptable only to the Hanafī school. A variant of this type was accepted by the Shī'īs whereby a man would agree to bear another's delicts and inherit from him in default of primary heirs. Finally, the Shī'ī Imāmīs adopted the so-called Imāmah patronage, according to which the Head Imām of the Sect would inherit from all those who have no survivors and transfer the estate to public services. This is the same as the Sunnī doctrine, except the latter does not specify the Head of State as an intermediary between the deceased and the Public Treasury; cf. al Tāj, vol. 2, pp. 237-8; the references cited in this note.

13. Cf. Demombynes (1), p. 142; Fayzee, p. 367; Jeffery, p. 70; Merchant, p. 179; Mūsā, pp. 63 ff; Roberts, p. 62; al Tāj, vol. 2, pp. 241-4. The Shī'īs allowed testaments in favor of the heirs; cf. al Mukhtaṣar, p. 163. It may be interesting to note that, "The legal philosophical significance of the will lies in the increased importance of the individual, as opposed to the family, and in the insistent claims of the members of the family to the property left." A correspondence obtains between the popularity of the right of will and the predominance of individualism, human progress, the spirit of acquisition, devotion to work, and similar characteristics (Kohler, p. 541). It may also be interesting that the right to dispose of one's property by will

was freely exercised by the Hebrews and the pre-Islāmic Arabians (cf. Fayzee, pp. 9-10; Mūsā, pp. 24-5, 63-4; Vesey-Fitzgerald, p. 167). In contrast, the restrictions by Islām on the right of will are interpreted so as to deny the idea of absolute rights, to stress the principle of inter-dependence or provisionality in the exercise of one's rights, and to attest the social nature and shared circulation of the property, as well as the continued considerateness of the kindred (cf. Mūsā, pp. 186 ff; al Tāj, vol. 2, pp. 241-4; Wāfī (2), pp. 21 ff).

14. Cf. Fayzee, pp. 382 ff; Mūsā, pp. 63 ff, 186 ff; Roberts, pp. 65-6; Stern, pp. 158 ff; al Qur'ān, 4:11-3, 176.

15. See the references cited in notes 1-3 in this chapter.

16. Cf. Mūsā, pp. 161 seqq.; Fayzee, pp. 387-8; 'Abd Allāh, p. 73; Abū Zahrah (1), p. 165, Roberts, pp. 66-7; al Tāj, vol. 2, pp. 229-30. There are many intricate details which do not add much to the discussion here. Our interest is in the basic doctrines and the common characteristics of the system.

17. Cf. Fayzee, pp. 386-7; Aziz Ahmad, pp. 602, 618.

18. Cf. the references cited in the previous note; also, Merchant, pp. 179-80; al Mukhtaṣar, p. 163; Ahmad, p. 508.

19. Cf. Ahmad, chs. XX-I; Fayzee, ch. XXI.

20. 'Abd Allāh, pp. 99 ff; Coulson (1), p. 24; Fayzee, pp. 389 seqq; Ibn Qudāmah, vol. 6, pp. 281-3; al Tāj, vol. 2, 230 seqq. Other remote heirs will be subsidiary classes. They are entitled in default of principal heirs and on the grounds of patronage, testament, or escheat; cf. Fayzee loc. cit. The most fundamental difference between the Sunnī schools of law is probably the one concerning the right of the uterine relatives.

21. See supra. pp. 209-11. It is interesting to note that Coulson (1) has made an attempt to explain sociologically some aspects of this problem. He pointed out (pp. 48-9) that nonagnate relatives (the uterines) were never allowed to inherit in al Madīnah, which was a natural result of the patrilineal system of that society. It was the Kūfī jurists of Iraq, the Hanafīs, who allowed the uterines to inherit, which was also a natural result of "a higher estimation" for women in the cosmopolitan society of al Kūfah.

These remarks are interestingly suggestive. If al Madīnah society was patrilineal, it was also sustained mainly by an agricultural economy. With these two variables, parilineality and agriculture, one would ex-pect the kinship tie to be exceptionally strong and extensive. But the legal doctrines of al Madīnah suggest the opposite. Mālik Ibn Anas (d.

795), the leading Madanī jurist, after whom one of the four major schools of Sunnī law was named, adopted the narrowest view of kin's mutual obligations. For example, a person is obliged to support only his most near children and parents, not grandchildren and grandparents. (cf. Ibn al Qayyim (3), vol. 4, pp. 319-20). Such needy relatives are entrusted to the community as a whole, which, through the Public Treasury, inherits the residue of the property and excludes the nonsharers (cf. the discussion related to the previous note, i.e., 20). On the other hand, allowing the uterine relatives to inherit, as the Kūfī jurists held, does not seem particularly indicative of any higher estimation for women. Cosmopolitan environments are hardly conducive to such an estimation. Also, the Kūfī jurists held that a divorce pronouncement made under pressure was valid (cf. *supra.* p. 227 and the related note). It is questionable whether this is consistent with a higher estimation for women. If Coulson's remarks are meant to imply that Islām was the root of this estimation, it is not clear why other Muslim jurists did not adopt a similar position. But if he means to suggest external influences from Persian and/or neo-Hellenistic sources, his suggestion would be more problematic than in fact explanatory. The treatment of women in those ancient societies hardly bespeaks such estimation. In any case, his remarks seem untenable; cf. Bardis, pp. 416, 432, 440, 443; Day, pp. 35-6; al Hūfī (2), pp. 56 *seqq.,* 550 ff; Leslie, ch. 6.

22. Cf. Fayzee, pp. 434 *seqq.*

23. *Ibid.* pp. 456-7. Emphasis is added to illustrate the exaggeration of the issue. The author himself is a contemporary Shīʿī lawyer; cf. Demombynes (1), pp. 139, 142; Tyabji, pp. 825-6.

24. Cf. *Ibid;* Abū Zahrah (3), pp. 341-3; Vesey-Fitzgerald, p. 145.

25. Fayzee, p. 459.

26. See, for example, Demombynes (1), p. 141.

27. Cf. *ibid.* p. 139; ʿAwwā, pp. 157 ff; Patai, pp. 224-5.

28. Cf. *al Qur'ān,* 4:11-3, 176.

29. In connection with this point, see, for example, al Ghazālī, pp. 132 ff; Wāfī (2), pp. 50-1. These two authors represent other contemporary Muslim scholars. However, their version of the explanation is only partial. The main part of the argument is developed by this writer independently as probably the closest approximation to the Muslim mind.

30. See note 121 in ch. 5; *al Qur'ān,* 4:12, 176; *al Tāj,* vol. 2, pp. 233-6. The fewer jurists among these few, who would distribute the

responsibility for a needy relative equally between able male and female heirs but divide the property differentially, do seem to have a flaw in their position. The only likely way for them to explain their view is probably this: there is no precedent, nor is it normally expected, that the female would be called upon to support a needy male relative; it is unmanly, and neither men nor women would be comfortable about it. The provision of equal responsibility of the male and the female for needy relatives is therefore unlikely to be rigorously enacted or insisted upon. In any case, the inconsistency remains, in spite of this suggested explanation.

31. Kohler, p. 536.
32. Cf. Farrūkh, p. 172; Fayzee, p. 367; Mūsā, pp. 105-6.
33. Cf. Mūsā, pp. 86-7, 106.
34. Cf. Fayzee, pp. 382 ff; Tyabji, p. 829; Ahmad, pp. 507-8; Demombynes (1), pp. 139 ff; al Jaṣṣāṣ, vol. 2, pp. 90 ff; Smith (1), p. 264.
35. Cf. Demombynes (1), p. 139; Tyabji, p. 820; Coulson (1), p. 22.
36. Coulson (1), p. 16; cf. pp. 22-3.
37. Cf. Mūsā, pp. 186 seqq; Coulson (1), p. 24; Wāfī (2), pp. 21 ff; al Qur'ān 57:7.
38. Goitein, p. 41. The author's remark leaves much to be desired. It may be asked: when did women, children, minors, invalids, etc. share in the spoils of tribal warfares? How were their shares in Islām modeled on the pre-Islāmic system of distribution which excluded them? How would this interpretation be reconciled with the generally accepted view that Islām was urban, starting in the commercial city of Makkah and growing in the agricultural environment of al Madīnah?
39. Cf. Amin (2), p. 372 ff, also p. 202; Farrūkh, p. 182.

CONCLUSION AND GENERAL DISCUSSION

1. Cf. Gibb (3), pp. 37-8; Torrey, pp. 6-7, 148 ff; Watt (2), p. 81.
2. Cf. Geiger, pp. 158 ff; Rosenthal (3), p. 21 ff; Patai, pp. 88-91; Guillaume, pp. 163-6; Bell (1), pp. 169-70.
3. Cf. Obermann, pp. 58-60; Geiger, pp. vi, 25 ff; Roberts, pp. 2 ff; Torrey, pp. 6-7; Rosenthal (3), p. 29.
4. Obermann, pp. 59-60; cf. Torrey, pp. 3-7, 148 ff; Geiger, pp. vi,

25 ff; 70; Rosenthal (3), pp. 21 ff; Roberts, pp. 2 ff; Margoliouth (1), pp. 64 ff.

5. Cf. Bell (1), pp. 168 ff; Gibb (3), pp. 46-7; Roberts, pp. 2-3; Watt (2), pp. 29 ff, (4), pp. 41 *seqq.*, esp. 55.

6. Rosenthal (3), pp. 28-9.

7. Goitein, pp. 60-1; cf. ch. 7.

8. Murdock, pp. 192 *seqq.*, esp. p. 200; cf. Linton, pp. 368-9.

9. Cf. *al Qur'ān*, 2:136; 3:3; 5:44-6; 7:157; 9:111; 42:12; 60:8.

10. Rosenthal (3), pp. 3-4, 40.

11. Coulson (1), pp. 14-5; cf. R. Levy, pp. 55, 106, 122; al Alūsī, vol. 2, pp. 52 ff.

12. Stern, pp. 70 ff, 104, 107.

13. Cf. Gibb (2), pp. 89-90; Jeffery, pp. 40-2; Rosenthal (3), pp. 3-4.

BIBLIOGRAPHY

This bibliography is more selective than inclusive. Many of the sources used contain excellent and comprehensive bibliographies as partially indicated here.

'Abd Allāh, 'Umar. *Aḥkām al Sharī'ah* . . . Alexandria: Dār al Ma'ārif, 1956.

'Abd al Bāqī, M.F.

1. comp. & ed. *al Lu'lu' wa al Marjān,* being a selection of the most authentic Traditions originally compiled by al Bukhārī and Muslim. Cairo: al Halabī and Co., 3 vols., 1949.

2. Trans. *Miftāḥ Kunūz al Sunnah,* Cairo: Maṭba'at Mīṣr, 1933. (See Wensinck, A. J.)

3. *al Mu'jam al Mufahras.* Cairo: Dār al Sha'b, 7 vols. 1959.

4. ed. *al Muwaṭṭa'.* Cairo: al Halabī and Co., 2 vols., 1951.

'Abd al Laṭīf, 'Abd al Wahhāb, ed. *Muwaṭṭa'* . . . Cairo: The Supreme Council of Islāmic Affairs, 1967.

'Abd al Wahhāb, Salāh al Dīn (a.k.a. Abdel-Wahab, Salah El-Din). *An Introduction to Islāmic Law.* Cairo: al Azhar Press, 1963.

Abdur Rahim, M. A. *The Principles of Muhammadan Jurisprudence.* Lahore: The All-Pakistan Legal Decisions, 1958.

Abū al Faraj al Iṣfahānī, 'Alī Ibn Hasan. *al Aghānī.* Cairo: Dār al Taḥrīr, 1963-6.

Abū Zahrah, Muḥammad.

1. "Family Law." In Khaddouri, M. *et. al.,* eds. *Law in the Middle East.* Washington: The Middle East Institute, 1955, pp. 132-78.

2. *al Shāfi'ī.* Cairo: Dār al Fikr al 'Arabī, 2nd ed., 1948.

3. ed. *Usbū' al Fiqh al Islāmī.* Cairo: al Majlis al A'lā li Ri'āyat al Funūn, 1963.

al Afghānī Sa'īd. *al Islām wa al Mar'ah,* Damascus: Dār al Fikr, 1964.

Ahmad, Aziz. *Islāmic Law in Theory and Practice.* Lahore: The All-Pakistan Legal Decisions, 1956.

Albright, William Foxwell. (See L. Finkelstein, ed., *The Jewish People: Past and Present*).

Ali, Abdullah Yūsuf, trans, and comm. *The Holy Qur'ān.* New York: Hafner Publishing Co., 2 vols. 1946. (See *al Qur'ān.*)

'Alī, Jawwād. *Tārīkh al 'Arab Qaby al Islām.* Baghdad: al Majma' al 'Ilmī, 8 vols. vol. 5, 1956; vol. 6, 1957; vol. 8, 1959.

Ali, Syed Ameer.

1. *Mahommedan Law,* Calcutta: Thacker, Spink & Co., vol. II, 5th ed., 1929.

2. *The Spirit of Islam.* London: Christophers, 6th impression, 1952.

Allport, Floyd H. "The Nature of Institutions." *Social Forces,* 6:167-179, 1927.

al Alūsī, al Sayyid Maḥmūd Shukrī. *Bulū al Arab . . .,* ed. M. B. al Atharī. Cairo: Dār al Kitāb al 'Arabī, 3rd ed., 3 vols., 1342 (A. H.) 1922.

'Amīr, 'Abd al Azīz. *Khāwatir Hawl Qānūn al Usrah fi al Islām.* Beirut: The Arab University Lectures for the academic year 1961-1962.

al 'Anī, M. Sh., *al Fiqh al Islāmī.* Cairo: Ma'had al Dirāsāt al 'Arabiyyah (League of the Arab States), 1965.

Anshen, Ruth Nanda, ed.

1. *The Family: Its Future and Destiny.* New York, Harper and Brothers, 1949.

2. ed. *Moral Principles of Action: Man's Ethical Imperative.* New York, Harper and Brothers, 1952.

al 'Aqqād, 'Abbās Maḥmūd. *al Mar'ah fi al Qur'ān.* Cairo: Dār al Hilāl, 1962.

Arberry, A. J.

1. *Aspects of Islāmic Civilization.* New York: A. S. Barnes and Co., Inc. 1964.

2. Trans., *The Koran Interpreted.* New York: The Macmillan Co., 2 vols., 1955.

Aries, Phillippe. *Centuries of Childhood: A Social History of Family*

Life, translated from the French by Robert Baldick. New York: Alfred A. Knopf, 1962.

Arnold, Sir Thomas, and Guillaume, Alfred, eds. *The Legacy of Islam.* London: Oxford University Press, 1947.

'Awn, Kamāl Aḥmad. *al Mar'ah fi al Islām.* Tanṭa (Egypt): Sha'rāwī Press, 1374 A.H., 1955.

'Awwā, Bashīr, *al Usrah bayn al Jāhiliyyah wa al-Islām.* Damascus: Dār al Fikr al Islāmī, 1967.

Baldick, Robert, trans. *Centuries of Childhood,* by Phillippe Aries. New York: Alfred A. Knopf, 1962.

Bardis, Panos D. "Family Forms and Variations Historically Considered." In Christensen, Harold T., ed., pp. 403-61.

al Baydāwī . . . *Anwār al Tanzīl* . . . Cairo: al Maktabah al Tijāriyyah, 197, 4 vols. in 2.

Bayer, Alan E. "The Psychoanalytic Frame of Reference in Family Study." In Nye, F. I., and Berardo, eds., pp. 152-75. (See Nye.)

Becker, Howard, and Hill, Reuben, eds. *Family, Marriage, and Parenthood.* Boston: D. C. Heath and Co., 1948.

——. "Interpreting Family Life in Context." In Becker, Howard, and Hill, Reuben, eds., p. 1-49.

Bell, Richard.

1. *Introduction to the Qur'ān.* Edinburgh: The University Press, 1953.

2. *The Origin of Islām in Its Christian Environment.* London: Macmillan and Co., Ltd., 1926.

Berardo, Felix M., and Nye, F. I., eds.

1. *Emerging Conceptual Frameworks in Family Analysis.* New York: The Macmillan Co., 1966.

2. "The Anthropological Approach to the Study of the Family." In Nye, F. Ivan and Berardo, Felix M., eds.

Berelson, Bernard, *et. al.,* eds. *Family Planning and Population Programs.* Chicago: The University of Chicago Press, 1966.

Berelson, Bernard, and Steiner, Gary A., eds. *Human Behavior: An Inventory of Scientific Findings.* New York Baltimore: Harcourt, Brace and World, Inc., 1964.

Bernard, Jessie. *American Family Behavior.* New York: Harper and Brothers, 1942.

Bevan, Edwyn R., and Singer, Charles, eds. *The Legacy of Israel.* Oxford: The Clarendon Press, 1928.

The Holy Bible, Revised Standard Version. New York: Thomas Nelson and Sons, 1952.

Bint al S̲h̲āṭi. *Nisā' al Nabī.* Cairo: Dār al Hilāl, 1961.

Brav, Stanley R. *Jewish Family Solidarity: Myth or Fact?* Vicksburg (Mississippi): Nogales Press, 1942.

Briffault, R. *The Mothers: The Matriarchal Theory of Social Origins.* New York: Macmillan Co., 3 vols. 1927.

Broom, Leonard, and Selznick, Philip. *Sociology.* New York; Harper and Row, 4th ed., 1968.

Brown, William D. "A Social Psychological Conceptual Framework of the Family." In Nye, F. I. and Berardo, Felix M., eds. pp. 176-97.

Buckley, Walter. *Sociology and Modern Systems Theory.* Englewood Cliffs (N.J.): Prentice-Hall, 1967.

Burchinal, Lee G. "The Premarital Dyad and Love Involvement." In Christensen, Harold T., ed. pp. 623-74.

Burton, Sir Richard F.

1. *The Jew, The Gypsy and El Islām,* edited, with a preface and brief notes by W. H. Wilkins. Chicago and New York: Herbert S. Stone and Co., 1898.

2. *Love, War and Fancy,* edited and introduced by Kenneth Walker. London: William Kember, 1964.

Catton, William R., Jr. "The Development of Sociological Thought" In Faris, Robert E. L., ed. pp. 912-50.

Cavan, Ruth Shanle. "Subcultural Variations and Mobility." In Christensen, Harold T., ed. pp. 535-81.

Christensen, Harold T., ed.

1. *Handbook of Marriage and the Family.* Chicago: Rand McNally and Co., 1964.

2. "The Development of the Family Field of Study." In Christensen, Harold T., ed., pp. 3-32.

Coser, Rose Laub, ed. *The Family: Its Structure and Functions.* New York: St. Martin's Press, 1964.

de Coulanges Fustel (See Kocourek and Wigmore, below)

Coulson, N. J.

1. *A History of Islāmic Law.* Edinburgh: The University Press, 1964

2. *Succession in Islāmic Law.* Cambridge: The University Press, 1971.

Cross, Earle B. *The Hebrew Family:* A Study in Historical Sociology. Chicago: University of Chicago Press, 1927.

Davis, Kingsley.

1. *Human Society*. New York: The Macmillan Co., 1949.

2. "Intermarriage in Caste Societies." In Coser, Rose L., ed. *The Family*, pp. 105-27.

3. The same article appeared in *American Anthropologist*. 43:376-95, 1941.

al Dawālībī, Muḥammad M. *al Madkhal 'ila Usūl al Fiqh*. Beirut: Dār al 'Ilm . . ., 15th ed., 1965.

Day, Edward. *The Social Life of the Hebrew*. New York: Charles Scribner's Sons, 1901.

Dean, K. Imogene, and Kargman, M. W. "Is there a Legal Conceptual Framework for the Study of the American Family?" In Nye, F.I., and Berardo, F.N., eds., pp. 269-92.

Della Vida, Giorgio Levi. "Pre-Islāmic Arabia." In Faris, N.A., ed. *The Arab Heritage*. Princeton: Princeton University Press, 3rd printing, 1946, pp. 25-57.

Demombynes (See Gaudefroy-Demombynes).

Diamond, A.S. *Primitive Law*. London: Longman's Green and Co., 1935.

Dickson, H. R. P. *The Arab of the Desert*. London: George Allen and Unwin Ltd., 2nd ed., 1951.

Douglas, J. D., ed. *The New Bible Dictionary*. Grand Rapids (Mich.): Wm. B. Eerdmans Publishing Co., 1962.

Durant, W. *The Story of Civilization,* (vol. 1), *Our Oriental Heritage*. New York: Simon and Schuster, 1935.

Eisenstadt, S. N. "Institutionalization and Change." *American Sociological Review,* 29:235-47, 1964.

Epstein, Louis M. *Marriage Laws in the Bible and the Talmud*. Cambridge: Harvard University Press, 1942.

Evans-Pritchard, E. E. *Social Anthropology and Other Essays*. New York: The Free Press of Glencoe, 1964.

Farber, Bernard. *Family: Organization and Institution*. San Francisco: Chandler Publishing Co., 1964.

Faris, Nabih Amin, ed. *The Arab Heritage*. Princeton (N.J.): Princeton University Press, 3rd printing, 1946.

Faris, Robert E. L., ed. *Handbook of Modern Sociology*. Chicago: Rand McNally & Co., 1964.

Farrūkh, 'Umar, *al Usrah fi al Shar' al Islāmī*. Beirut: Maṭba'at al Maktabah al Islāmiyyah, 1951.

Faruki, Kemal A. *Islāmic Jurisprudence*. Karachi: Pakistan Publishing House, 1962.

Fāyid, M. A., ed. *Marāqī al Falāḥ*. Cairo: Ṣubayḥ & Sons, 1950.

Fayzee, Asaf A. A. *Outlines of Muhammadan Law*. London: Oxford University Press, 3rd ed., 1964.

Feucht, O. E., ed. *Sex and the Church*. St. Louis: Concordia, 1961.

Fish, T. "Law and Religion in Babylonia and Assyria." In Rosenthal, E. I. J., ed. *Judaism and Christianity*. (vol. III);: *Law and Religion*. London: The Sheldon Press, 1938, pp. 29-44.

Fitzgerald, S. V. "The Alleged Debt of Islāmic to Roman Law." *Law Quarterly Review*, 67:81-102, 1951.

Gaudefroy-Demombynes, Maurice.

1. *Muslim Institutions*, translated from the French by MacGregor, John P. London: George Allen and Unwin Ltd., 1950.

2. al *Nuẓum al Islāmīyah*, translated from the French by al Sāmir, Fayṣal, and al S̲h̲ammā', Sālih. Beirut: Dār al Nashr . . ., 1961.

Geiger, Abraham, *Judaism and Islām: A Prize Essay*, translated from the German by Young, F. M. Madras (India): The M.D.C.S.P.C.K. Press, 1898.

al Ghazālī, Muḥammad. *Huqūq al Insān* . . . Cairo: al Makatabah al Tijāriyyah, 1963.

Gibb, H. A. R.

1. "Law and Religion in Islām." In Rosenthal, E. I. J., ed. *Judaism and Christianity* (vol. III): *Law and Religion*, pp. 145-69.

2. *Modern Trends in Islām*. Chicago: The University of Chicago Press, 1947.

3. *Mohammedanism: An Historical Survey*. London: Oxford University Press, 1949. Gibb has access to the original sources and makes good use of some of the basic references.

Glubb, Sir John. *The Empire of the Arabs*. Englewood Cliffs (N.J.): Prentice-Hall, Inc., 1965.

Goitein, S. D. *Jews and Arabs: Their Contacts Through the Ages*. New York: Schocken Books, 1964.

Goldschmidt, Walter. "Ethics and the Structure of Society: An Ethnological Contribution to the Sociology of Knowledge." *American Anthropologist* 53:506-24, 1952.

Goldziher, Ignaz. *Mohammed and Islām*, translated from the German by Kate Chambers Seelye. New Haven: Yale University Press, 1917.

Goode, William J.

1. *The Family*. Englewood Cliffs (N.J.): Prentice-Hall, 1964.

2. *Religion Among the Primitives*. Glencoe, Ill.: The Free Press, 1951.

3. *World Revolution and Family Patterns.* Glencoe: The Free Press, 1963.

Goodman, Philip, and Hanna. *The Jewish Marriage Anthology.* Philadelphia: The Jewish Publication Society of America, 1965.

Goodsell, Willystine. *A History of Marriage and the Family.* New York: The Macmillan Co., 1934.

Gray, Louis H. "Eunuch." *Ency. of Religion and Ethics,* 5:579-84, 1912.

von Grunebaum, G. E. *Islām: Essays in the Nature and Growth of a Cultural Tradition.* The American Anthropological Association, vol. 57, No. 2, Part 2, Memoir No. 81, April 1955.

Guillaume, Alfred. "The Influence of Judaism on Islām." In Bevan, Edwyn R., and Singer, Charles, eds. *The Legacy of Israel.* Oxford: The Clarendon Press, 1928, pp. 129-71.

Gurvitch, Georges. *Sociology of Law,* with a preface by Roscoe Pound. London: Kegan Paul, Trench, Trubner and Co., Ltd., 1947.

Haag, Ernest van den. "Love or Marriage." In Coser, Rose L., ed. *The Family.* pp. 192-202.

Hamīdullāh, Muḥammad. *The Muslim Conduct of State.* Lahore (Pakistan): Sh. M. Ashraf, revised 3rd ed., 1953.

Hammūdah, 'Abd al Wahhāb, ed. al Mukhtār *min Kitāb al Itqān . . .* Cairo: Ministry of National Guidance, 1960.

Harb, Muḥammad al Ghazālī, and Maẓhar, Ismā'īl. "Tasāmuḥ al Islām . . ." *al Akhbār,* The Daily . . . Cairo: Dār Akhbār al Yawm. (1-12-1962).

Hastings, James, ed. *Dictionary of the Bible.* New York: *Charles* Scribner's Sons, 1909.

Haykal, Muḥmmad Husayn. *Hayāt Muḥammad.* Cairo: Dār al Qalam, 7th ed., 1960.

al Hidāyah (See al-Marghīnānī)
Hill, Reuben, and Rodgers, Roy H.
1. "The Developmental Approach." In Christensen, Harold T., ed. *Handbook of Marriage and the Family,* pp. 171-211.
2. and Becker, Howard, eds. *Family, Marriage and Parenthood.* Boston: D. C. Heath and Co., 1948.
3. and Hansen, D. "The Identification of Conceptual Frameworks Utilized in Family Study. *"Marriage and Family Living,* 22 (Nov. 1960), pp. 299-311.
al Hillī, Abū al Qāsim Ja'far Ibn al Hasan. *al Mukhtaṣar . . .* Cairo: Dār al Kitāb al 'Arabī 1376 (1957).

Hitti, Philip K. *History of the Arabs.* London: Macmillan & Co., Ltd., 8th ed., 1963. This work makes constant reference to the original historical and literary sources.

Hobhouse, L. T. *Morals in Evolution: A Study of Comparative Ethics,* with a new introduction by Morris Ginsberg. London: Chapman and Hall, 1951.

Hoebel, E. Adamson. *The Law of Primitive Man:* A Study in Comparative Legal Dynamics. Cambridge: Harvard University Press, 1954.

Hourani, A. H., and Stern, S. M., eds. *The Islāmic City: A Colloquium.* Philadelphia: The University of Pennsylvania Press, 1970.

al Hūfī, Aḥmad.

1. *al Hayāh al 'Arabīyah min al Shi'r al Jāhilī.* Cairo: Naḥdat Miṣr 4th ed., 1962.

2. *al Mar'ah fi al Shi'r al Jāhilī.* Cairo: Dār al Fikr al 'Arabī, 2nd ed., 1963.

Hughes, E. C. "The Study of Institutions." *Social Forces,* 20:307-10, 1942.

Ibn 'Abd Rabbuh, *al 'Iqd al Farīd,* ed. M. Y. Zāyid. Beirut: Khayyāṭ, 1967.

Ibn 'Abidin, Muḥammad Amīn. *Hāshiyat Ibn 'Abidīn.* Cairo: Dār al Sh'ādah, 1905, 5 vols.

Ibn al Athīr. *al Kāmil fi al Tārīkh,* Beirut: Dār Ṣādir, 1965.

Ibn Baṭṭūṭah. *Rihlat* . . . Cairo: al Maktabah al Tijāriyyah, 1964.

Ibn Hazm, 'Alī Ibn Aḥmad. *al Muḥallā,* ed. Harrās, M. Kh. Cairo: al Imām Press, 1962.

Ibn Hishām. *Tahdhīb Sīrat* . . ., ed. Hārūn, A. S. Cairo: Dār Sa'd Miṣr, 2 vols., 1955.

Ibn al Humām al Sīwāsī, Muḥammad Ibn 'Abd al Wāḥid. *Fatḥ al Qadīr.* Cairo: 1938.

Ibn al 'Imād, 'Abd al Hàyy ibn Aḥmad. *Shadharāt al Dhahab* . . . Beirut: al Maktab al Tijārī, 1966.

Ibn Khaldūn.

1. *al Muqaddimah.* Cairo: Maṭba'at al Taqaddum, 1904.

2. *Muqaddimat Ibn Khaldūn,* edited with an introduction and commentary by 'Alī 'Abd al Wāḥid Wāfī. Cairo: Lajnat al Bayān al 'Arabī, 2nd ed., 4 vols., 1965.

Ibn Khallikān. *Wafayāt al A'yān* . . . , ed. 'Abd al Hamīd, M. M. D. Cairo: Maktabat al Nahḍah, 6 vols., 1948.

Ibn Qayyim al Jawaziyyah. (also Ibn al Qayyim).

1. *I'lām al Muwaqqi'īn,* ed. 'Abd al Hamīd, M. M. D. Cairo: al Maktabah al Tijāriyyah, 4 vols., 1955.

2. *Kitāb Ahkbār al Nisā.* Cairo: Maṭba'at al Taqaddum, 1900.

3. *Zād al Ma'ād,* ed. al Fiqī, M. H. Cairo: Maṭba'at al Sunnah al Muḥammadiyyah, 4 vols., 1953.

Ibn Qudāmah, Muwaffaq al Dīn 'Abd Allāh . . . *al Mughnī,* ed. Marrās, M. Kh. Cairo: al Imām Press, 10 vols., 1964-66.

Ibn Qutaybah. *al Ma'ārif,* ed. Ukāshah, Tharwat. Cairo. Dār al Kutub, 1960.

Ibn Taymiyyah, Aḥmad . . .

1. *Mukhtaṣar al Fatāwā* . . . Cairo: M. Ibn 'Alī al Ba'lī, 1949.

2. *Ṣīḥḥat Usūl Madhhab Ahl al Madīnah,* ed. Yūsuf, Z. A. Cairo: al Imām Press, n.d.

al Jaṣṣāṣ, al Rāzī, Aḥmad Ibn Alī. *Aḥkām al Qur'ān.* Cairo: 'Abd al Raḥmān Muḥammad, 3 vols. 1347 (A.H.), 1927.

Jeffery, Arthur. "The Family in Islām." In Anshen, Ruth Nanda, ed. *The Family: Its Future and Destiny.* pp. 39-72.

The Jewish People: Past and Present, ed. L. Finklestein. New York: Central Yidish Culture Organization (CYCO), vol. 1, 1946. (See Albright, William Foxwell.)

Jum'ah. M. M. *al Nuẓum al Ijtimā'īyah wa al Siyāsīyah 'Ind Qudamā al 'Arab.* Cairo: al Sa'ādah Press, 1949. This work contains a good number of rare and original sources in Arabic, English, and French.

Juynboll, Th. W. "Eunuch (Muslim)." *Ency. of Religion and Ethics.* 5:584-5, 1912.

al Kāsānī, Abū Bakr Ibn Mas'ūd. *Badā'a' al Ṣanā'i'* . . . Cairo: Z. A. Yūsuf, 1909-10, 5 vols.

Kennett, R. H. *Ancient Hebrew Social Life and Custom.* London: Oxford University Press, 1933.

Khaddouri, M., *et. al.,* eds. (See Khadduri, M.)

Khadduri, Majid, trans.

1. *Islāmic Jurisprudence: Shāfi'ī's Risāla,* with an introduction, notes, and appendices. Baltimore: The Johns Hopkins Press, 1961.

2. *Law in the Middle East,* ed. Khaddouri, M. Washington, D. C.: The Midle East Institute, 1955. (See Khaddouri, M.)

Khallāf, 'Abd al Wahhāb. *'Ilm Usūl al Fiqh* . . . Cairo: Maṭba'at al Naṣr, 7th printing, 1956.

al Khashshāb, Muṣṭafā. *Dirāsāt fi al Ijtimā'al 'A'ilī.* Cairo: Lajnat al Bayān al 'Arabī Press, 1957.

al-Khūlī, Amin. *Mālik: Tajārib Hayāḥ.* Cairo: al Mu'assasah al Miṣrīyyah li al Ta'līf, 1967.

Kirk, Dudley. "Factors Affecting Moslem Natality." In Berelson, Bernard *et. al.,* eds. *Family Planning and Population Programs.* Chicago: The University of Chicago Press, 1966, p. 561-81.

Kirkpatrick, Clifford. *The Family as Process and Institution.* New York: The Ronald Press Co., 2nd ed., 1963.

Kitāb al Fiqh . . . Cairo: Ministry of Awqāf, 5th ed., 1950.

Kocourek, Albert, and Wigmore, John H., compilers. *Primitive and Ancient Legal Institutions.* Boston: Little, Brown, and Co., 1915.

Koenig, Daniel J., and Bayer, Allen E. "The Institutional Frame of Reference in Family Study." In Nye, F. I., and Berardo, F. M., eds. pp. 78-96.

Kritzeck, James. *Sons of Abraham; Jews Christians and Moslems.* Baltimore: Helican Press, Inc., 1965.

Leslie, Gerald R. *The Family in Social Context.* New York: Oxford University Press, 1967.

Levi-Straus, Claude. "Reciprocity, The Essence of Social Life." In Coser, Rose L., ed. *The Family,* pp. 36-48.

Levy, Marion J., Jr. *et al.*
1. *Aspects of the Analysis of Family Structure.* Princeton (N.J.): Princeton Press, 1965.
2. *The Family Revolution in Modern China.* Cambridge (Mass.): Harvard University Press, 1949.

Levy, Reuben. *The Social Structure of Islām.* Cambridge: Cambridge University Press, 1957. This work makes extensive use of the literary and folk tale sources.

Lewis, Bernard. *The Arabs in History.* New York: Harper and Row, 1960.

Libby, Roger W. and Whitehurst, Robert N., eds. *Renovating Marriage.* Danville, California: Consensus Publishing Inc., 1973.

Lichtenstadter, Ilse. *Islām and the Modern Age.* New York: Bookman Associates, 1958.

Linton, Ralph. *The Study of Man.* New York: D. Appleton-Century Inc. 1936.

Loewe, H., ed. *Judaism and Christianity* (vol. II). London: The Sheldon Press, 1937.

Lowie, Robert H. *Primitive Society.* New York: Boni and Liveright, 1925.

MacDonald, Duncan B. *Development of Muslim Theology, Juris-*

prudence and Constitutional Theory. New York: Charles Scribner's Sons, 1903.

al Madanī, M. M. *al Mujtama' al Islāmī* . . . Cairo: Mukhaymar Press, 1957.

Madkūr, M. S.

1. *al Ibāḥah* . . . Cairo: Dār al Nahdah, 1963.

2. *Madkhal al Fiqh al Islāmī.* Cairo: al Dār al Qawmiyyah, 1964.

Maghnīyah, Muḥammad J.

1. *Ma'a al Shī'ah al Imāmiyyah.* Beirut: Maktabat al Andalus, 2nd ed., 1956.

2. *al Zawāj wa al Talāq 'alā al Madhāhib al Khamsah.* Beirut: Dār al 'Ilm, 1960.

Mahmaṣānī Ṣubḥī.

1. *Falsafat al Tashrī' fī al Islām.* Beirut: Dār al- 'Ilm, 3rd ed., 1961.

2. *The Philosophy of Jurisprudence in Islām* trans. Ziadeh, Farhat J. (See Ziadeh).

Mālik Ibn Anas. *al Muwaṭṭa',* ed. M. F. 'Abd al Bāqī. Cairo: al Halabī and Co., 2 vols., 1951.

Mandelbaum, Maurice. *The Problem of Historical Knowledge: An Answer to Relativism.* New York: Liveright Publishing Corp., 1938.

al Marghīnānī, 'Alī Ibn Abū Bakr. *al Hidāyah.* Cairo: Ṣubayḥ, 1936.

Margoliouth, D. S.

1. *The Early Development of Mohammedanism.* London: Constable and Co., Ltd., 1926.

2. *The Relations Between Arabs and Israelites Prior to the Rise of Islām.* London: Oxford University Press, 1924.

McIntyre, Jennie. "The Structure—Functional Approach to Family Study." In Nye, F. I., and Berardo, F. M., eds. pp. 52-77.

McIver, R. M., and Page, Charles. *Society.* New York: Rinehart and Co., Inc., 2nd ed., 1949.

Merton, Robert K.

1. "Intermarriage and Social Structure." *Psychiatry,* 4:361-74, 1941.

2. In Coser, Rose L., ed. *The Family,* pp. 128-52.

Middleton, Russel. "A Deviant Case: Brother-Sister and Father-Daughter Marriage in Ancient Egypt." In Coser, Rose L., ed. *The Family,* pp. 74-89.

al Mubarrad, Muḥammad Ibn Yazīd. *al Kāmil.* Cairo: Maktabat Nahaḍat Miṣr, 1956.

al Mudawwanah al Kubrā (See al- 'Utāqī).

al Mukhṭaṣar (See al-Hillī, A. Q. J.).

Murdock, George Peter. *Social Structure*. New York: The Free Press, 1965.

Murphy, J. "Primitive Origins of Law in Relation to Religion." In Rosenthal, E. I. J., ed. *Judaism and Christianity* (vol. III), *Law and Religion,* pp. 3-26.

Mūsā, Muḥammad Yūsuf. *al Tarikah wa al Mīrāth fi al Islām.* Cairo: Dār al Kitāb al 'Arabī, 1960.

Nicholson, R. A. *A Literary History of the Arabs.* London. Unwin, 1907.

Nye, F. Ivan, and Berardo, Felix M., eds. *Emerging Conceptual Frameworks in Family Analysis.* New York: The Macmillan Co., 1966.

Obermann, Julian. "Islāmic Origins: A Study in Background and Foundation." In Faris, N. A., ed. *The Arab Heritage.* Princeton (N.J.): Princeton University Press, 3rd printing, 1946, pp. 58-120.

Ossowska, Maria. *Social Determinants of Moral Ideas.* Philadelphia: The University of Pennsylvannia Press, 1970.

Parsons, Talcott.

1. *Essays in Sociological Theory, rev. ed.* New York: The Free Press, 1966. et. al.

2. *Family, Socialization and Interaction Process.* Glencoe (Ill.): The Free Press, 1955.

3. *The Social System.* New York. The Free Press, 2nd Printing 1965.

Patai, Raphael. *Sex and Family in the Bible and the Middle East.* New York: Doubleday and Co., Inc., 1959.

Perelman, C. *The Idea of Justice and the Problem of Argument.* translated from the French by Petrie, John. New York: The Humanities Press, 1963.

Petrie, John, trans. *The Idea of Justice and the Problem of Argument,* by Perelman, C.

Pitts, Jesse R. "The Structural-Functional." In Christensen, Harold T., ed. pp. 51-124.

al Qādī, M. M. *al Ra'y fi al Fiqh al Islāmī.* Cairo: Cairo University, 1949.

Queen, Stuart A., and Adams, John B. *The Family in Various Cultures.* Chicago. J. B. Lippincott, 1952, 1967.

al Qur'ān: Arabic text.

al Qur'ān (See Arberry)

The Holy Qur'ān, Text, Translation and commentary by Ali, A. Yūsuf. New York: Hafner Publishing Co., 2 vols., 1946.

al Qurṭubī, Muḥammad Ibn Ahmad. *al Jāmi' li Aḥkām al Qur'ān.* Cairo: Dār al Kitāb al 'Arabī, 20 vols., 1967.

Rallings, E. M. "A Conceptual Framework for Studying the Family: The Situational Approach." In Nye, F. I., and Berardo, F. M., eds. pp. 130-51.

Ramadan, Said. *Islamic Law: Its Scope and Equity.* London: P. R. Macmillan, Ltd., 1961.

Reiber, Stanley R. "Western Christian Conceptual Framework for Viewing the Family." In Nye, F. I., and Berardo, F. M., eds. pp. 293-316.

Remmling, Gunter W. *Road to Suspicion . . .* New York: Appleton-Century-Crofts, 1967.

Rice, Ann Smith. "An Economic Framework for Viewing the Family." In Nye, F. I., and Berardo, F. M., eds. pp. 223-268.

Rifā'ī. Aḥmad Farīd, ed. *Mu'jam al Udabā'.* (See Yāqūt . . .)

Roberts, Robert. *The Social Laws of the Qoran.* London: Williams and Norgate, Ltd., 1925.

Robertson, Edward. "Law and Religion Amongst the Samaritans." In Rosenthal, E. I. J., ed. *Judaism and Christianity* (vol. III), *Law and Religion,* pp. 69-88.

Robinson, H. Wheeler. "Law and Religion in Israel." In Rosenthal, E. I. J., ed. *Judaism and Christianity* (vol. III) *Law and Religion,* pp. 47-66.

Rosenthal, E. I. J.
1. "Islam," in Loewe, H., ed. *Judaism and Christianity* (vol. II). London: The Sheldon Press, 1937. pp. 147-85.
2. ed. *Judaism and Christianity* (vol. III), *Law and Religion.* London: The Sheldon Press, 1938.
3. *Judaism and Islam.* London: Thomas Yoseloff, 1961.

Rowe, George P. "The Developmental Conceptual Framework of the Study of the Family." In Nye, F. I., and Berardo, F. M., eds. pp. 198-222.

al Ṣāliḥ, Ṣubḥī. *al Nuẓum al Islāmīyah.* Beirut: Dār al 'Ilm, 1965.

DeSantillana, David. "Law and Society." In Arnold, Sir Thomas, ed. *The Legacy of Islam.* London: Oxford University Press, 1947, pp. 284-310.

al Sarakhsī, . . . Abū Bakr Muḥammad, *al Mabsūṭ.* Cairo: 1906-13, 30 vols. in 15.

Shacht, J.

1. "Foreign Elements in Islāmic Law." *Journal of Comparative Legislation and International Law,* 32:9-17, 1950.

2. *Introduction to Islāmic Law.* Oxford: Clarendon Press, 1964.

3. *The Origins of Muhammadan Jurisprudence.* Oxford: Clarendon Press, 1950.

Schvaneveldt, Jay. "The Interactional Framework in the Study of the Family." In Nye, F. I., and Berardo, F. M., eds. pp. 97-129.

Selznick, Philip, and Broom, Leonard. *Sociology.* New York: Harper and Row, 4th ed., 1968.

al Shāfiʻī, Muḥammad Ibn Idrīs.

1. *Aḥkām al Qur'ān.* Cairo: al Sayyid 'Izzat al 'Aṭṭār al Husaynī, 2 vols., 1952.

2. *al Risālah,* trans. Khadduri, M. (See Khadduri).

3. *al Umm,* ed. al Naggār, M. Z. Cairo: Maktabat al Kulliyāt al Azhariyyah, 8 vols., 1961.

Shaltūt, Maḥmūd.

1. *al Fatāwa.* Cairo. al Azhar Press, 1959.

2. *al Islām* . . . Cairo: al Azhar Press, 1959.

3. *Min Tawjīhāt al Islām.* Cairo: al-Azhar Press, 1959.

4. *Tafsīr al Qur'ān al Karīm.* Cairo: Dār al Qalam, 1960.

5. *Yas'alūn.* Cairo: al Halabī and Co., 1957.

al Sharabāṣī, Aḥmad. *Al A'immah al Arabaʻah* . . . Cairo: Dār al Hilāl, 1964.

al Shaybānī, Muḥammad Ibn al Hasan.

1. *Juz' min al Amālī.* Haidarabad: Da'irat al Maʻārif al 'Uthmāniyyah, 1941.

2. *Kitāb al Athar.* Lucknow (India), 1883?

al Shībī, Kāmil Muṣṭafā. *al Fikr al Shīʻī* . . . Baghdad: al Nahḍah, 1966.

Shorter Encyclopedia of Islām, eds., Gibb, H. A. R., and Kramer, J. H. Leiden: E. J. Brill, 1953.

al Sibāʻī, Muṣṭafā.

1. *al Mar'ah bayn al Fiqh wa al Qānūn.* Damascus: The University Press, 1962.

2. *al Sunnah wa Makānatuhā.* Cairo: Dār al 'Urūbah, 1961.

Siddiqi, Muhammad Mazheruddin, *Women in Islām.* Lahore (Pakistan): The Institute of Islāmic Culture, 1952.

Sirjamaki, John. "The Institutional Approach." In Christensen, Harold T., ed. pp. 33-50.

346   THE FAMILY STRUCTURE IN ISLAM

Slater, P. E. "Parental Role Differentiation." *American Journal of Sociology,* 67:296-308, 1961.

Smith, W. Robertson.

1. *Kinship and Marriage in Early Arabia.* Cambridge: The University Press, 1885.

2. *Lectures on the Religion of the Semites.* London: Black, 3rd ed., 1927.

Soares, T. G. *The Social Institutions and Ideals of the Bible.* New York: Abingdon Press, 1915.

Sorokin, Pitirim A. *Sociological Theories of Today.* New York: Harper, 1966.

Stark, Werner. *The Sociology of Knowledge.* New York: Humanities, 1958.

Steiner, Gary A., and Berelson, Bernard, eds. *Human Behavior . . .* New York/Baltimore: Harcourt, Brace and World, Inc., 1964.

Stern, Gertrude H. *Marriage in Early Islām.* London: The Royal Asiatic Society, 1939.

Streib, Gordon S. ed. *The Changing Family: Adaptation and Diversity.* Reading, Mass.: Addison-Wesley Publishing Company, 1973.

Summer, William Graham.

1. "The Family and Social Change." *American Journal of Sociology,* 14:577-591, 1909.

2. *Folkways.* Boston: Ginn and Co., rev. ed., 1910.

3. "Religion and Mores." *American Journal of Sociology,* 15:577-591, 1910.

al Suyūṭī, Jalāl al Dīn 'Abd al Raḥmān . . .

1. *Asbāb al Nuzūl.* Cairo: Dār al Taḥrīr, 1963.

2. ————. . . *al Itqān.* . . , ed. by Hammūdah, 'Abd al Wahhāb. Cairo: Ministry of National Guidance, 1960.

al Tabarī, Muḥammad ibn Jarīr.

1. *Tafsīr al Qur'ān,* eds., S̲h̲ākir, M. M., and S̲h̲ākir, A. M. Cairo: Dār al Ma'ārif, 1957, 16 vols.

2. *Tārīkh al Rusul* . . . Cairo: Dār al Ma'ārif, 1960, vols. 1-10.

3. *Tārīkh al Umam* . . . Cairo: 1939, 8 vols.

al Tāj, being a comprehensive selection of the most authentic Traditions of the Prophet, comp., ed. and comm., Nāṣif, Manṣūr 'Alī. Cairo: al Halabī and Co., 5 vols., 1932.

Taylor, Stanley, *Conceptions of Institutions and the Theory of Knowledge.* New York: Bookman Associates, 1956.

Taymūr. Aḥmad (Pasha). *Naẓrah Tārīkhīyyah Fi Hudūth al*

Madhāhib . . . Cairo: Dār al Kitāb al 'Arabī, 1965.

Thomas, W. I. *Source Book for Social Origins.* Boston: The Gorham Press, 1909.

The Times, literary supplementary, October 13, 1966.

Torrey, Charles Cutler. *The Jewish Foundation of Islām.* New York: Jewish Institute of Religion Press, 1933.

Tozzer, Alfred Marston. *Social Origins and Social Continuities.* New York: The Macmillan Co., 1925.

al Tūsī, Abū Ja'far Muḥammad Ibn al Hasan. *Kitāb al Khilāf.* Tehran: Sharikat Dār al Ma'ārif al Islāmiyyah, 1370 A.H. (1950).

Tyabji, Faiz Badruddin. *Muhammadan Law.* Bombay: M. M. Tripathi and Co., 3rd ed., 1940.

Tyler, Edward B. "On a Method of Investigating the Development of Institutions; Applied to Laws of Marriage and Descent." *The Journal of the Royal Anthropological Institute* XVIII:245-72, 1889.

al 'Utāqī, 'Abd al Raḥmān Ibn al Qāsim, *al Mudawwanah al Kubrā . . .* Cairo: 1905.

Vesey-Fitzgerald, Seymour. *Muhammadan Law: An Abridgement.* London: Oxford University Press, 1931.

Wāfī 'Alī A. W.

1. *Bayt al Tā'ah.* Cairo: Mu'assasat al Maṭmū'aṭ al Hadīthah, 1960.

2. *Huqūq al Insān fī al Islām.* Cairo: Maktabat Nahḍat Miṣr, 1957?

3. *al Usrah wa al Mujtama'.* Cairo: al Halabī and Co., 1948.

Warner, W. Lloyd. *The Family of God: A Symbolic Study of Christian Life in America.* New Haven: Yale University Press, 1961.

Watt, W. Montgomery.

1. *Islām and the Integration of Society.* London: Routledge, 1961.

2. *Muhammad at Mecca.* Oxford: The Clarendon Press, 1953.

3. *Muhammad at Medina.* Oxford: The Clarendon Press, 1956.

4. *Muhammad, Prophet and Statesman.* London: Oxford University Press, 1964.

Wensink, A. J.

1. *A Handbook of Early Muhammadan Tradition.* Leiden: Brill, Ltd., 1927.

2. *Miftah Kunuz al-Sunnah,* trans. M. F. Abd al-Baqi, M. F. (See Abd al-Baqi).

Westermarck, Edvard Alexander.

1. *The History of Human Marriage.* New York: The Allerton Book Co., 5th ed., 3 vols., 1922.

2. *The Origin and Development of the Moral Ideas*. 2nd ed. London: Macmillan and Co., 2 vols., 1917-24.

3. *A Short History of Marriage*. New York: The Macmillan Co., 1926.

Winch, Robert F. *The Modern Family*. New York: Holt, Rinehart and Winston, Inc., rev. ed., 1963.

Wolf, Eric. "The Social Organization of Mecca and the Origins of Islām." *Southwestern Journal of Anthropology*, 329-56, 1951.

Yaqūt Ibn 'Abd Allāh al Hamawī. *Mu'jam al Buldān*. Beirut: 5 vols., 1955-57.

————. *Mu 'jam al Udaba*, ed. Aḥmad Farīd Rifā'ī. Cairo: 20 vols., 1936-38.

Yinger, J. M. ed., *Religion, Society and the Individual*. New York: The Macmillan Co., 1957.

al Zamakhsharī, Muḥammad ibn 'Umar. *al Kashshāf*, with four commentaries. Beirut: Dār al Kitāb al 'Arabī, 4 vols., 1947.

Zaydān, Jurjī.
1. *al 'Arab Qabl al Islām*, edited with an introduction by Mu'nis, Husayn, Ph.D. Cairo: Dār al Hilāl, 1965.
2. *Tārīkh al Tamaddun al Islāmī*. Cairo: Dār al Hilāl, 5 vols., 1958.

Zelditch, Morris, Jr.
1. "Cross-cultural Analysis of Family Structure." In Christensen, Harold, T., ed. pp. 462-500.
2. "Family, Marriage, and Kinship." In Faris, Robert E. L. *Handbook of Modern Sociology*, pp. 680-733.
3. "Role Differentiation in the Nuclear Family: A Comparative Study." In Parsons, Talcott, *et. al., Family, Socialization and Interaction Process*. Glencoe (Ill.): The Free Press, 1955, pp. 307-51.

Ziadeh, Farhat J.
1. "Equality (Kaf'ah) in the Muslim Law of Marriage." *The American Journal of Comparative Law*, 6:503-17, 1957.
2. Trans. *Falsafat al-Tashrī' fi al-Islām: The Philosophy of Jurisprudence in Islām*. Leiden: Brill, 1961. (See Maḥmaṣānī.)
3. "'Urf and Law in Islām." In Kritzeck, James, and Winder, R. Bayly, eds. *The World of Islām*, studies in honour of Philip K. Hitti. London: Macmillan and Co., Ltd., 1959, pp. 60-67.

al Zurqānī Muḥammad ibn 'Abd al Bāqī. *Sharḥ Muwaṭṭa' al Imām Mālik*, ed. 'Awaḍ, I. A. Cairo: al Halabī and Co. (See Mālik ibn Anas.)

INDEX

Tozzer, Alfred Marston, 346
al Tūsī, Abū Jafar Muḥammad
　Ibn al Hasan, 286 *n.*45,
　290 *n.*45, 298 *n.*66, 299 *n.*91,
　*n.*95; 300 *n.*104; 301 *n.*107,
　*n.*111; 302 *n.*116, 303 *n.*15,
　*n.*17; 326 *n.*45, 346
Tyabji, Faiz Badruddin, 327 *n.*3,
　*n.*11; 330 *n.*23, 331 *n.*34, *n.*35;
　346
Tyler, Edward B., 346

'Umar (the Caliph), 67, 104-6,
　130, 134, 221, 227, 236, 237,
　238, 299 *n.*96, 304 *n.*21
Usāmah, 30
al Utāqī, 'Abd al Raḥmān Ibn al
　Qāsim, 342, 346-7

Vesey-Fitzgerald, Seymour,
　286 *n.*52, *n.*56, 290 *n.*44,
　295 *n.*29, 297 *n.*53, *n.*65;
　298 *n.*66, *n.*69, *n.*70; 304 *n.*22,
　314 *n.*2, *n.*7, *n.*8; 315 *n.*9,
　*n.*19; 316 *n.*27, *n.*31, *n.*37,
　*n.*38, *n.*39; 317 *n.*46, 328 *n.*13,
　330 *n.*24, 336, 347
Wāfī, 'Alī A. W., 186,285 *n.*31,
　287 *n.*12, 289 *n.*26, 291 *n.*52,
　*n.*53; 292 *n.*56, *n.*57, *n.*61;
　293 *n.*2, 295 *n.*34, 296 *n.*38,
　297 *n.*59, 298 *n.*66, 299 *n.*80,
　300 *n.*103, *n.*109; 302 *n.*2, *n.*3,
　*n.*5, *n.*6, *n.*7, *n.*8, *n.*9; 303 *n.*10,
　*n.*12; 306 *n.*35, *n.*40;
　307 *n.*43, *n.*45; 310 *n.*56, *n.*57,
　*n.*61, *n.*64, *n.*65; 312 *n.*76,
　314 *n.*7, 315 *n.*13, 316 *n.*32,
　317 *n.*46, *n.*53, *n.*54, *n.*55,
　*n.*57, *n.*69; 318 *n.*72, *n.*77,

*n.*85; 322 *n.*12, *n.*14, *n.*16;
　323 *n.* 17, *n.*26; 324 *n.*33,
　*n.*34, *n.*35; 325 *n.*38, *n.*39;
　326 *n.*46, *n.*50, *n.*56, *n.*58,
　*n.*60, *n.*61, *n.*62, *n.*63;
　327 *n.*64, *n.*8; 328 *n.*13,
　330 *n.*29, 331 *n.*37, 347
Walker, Kenneth, 335
Warner, W. Lloyd, 294 *n.*23,
　*n.*25, *n.*27; 306 *n.*38, 347
Watt, W. Montgomery, 284 *n.*9,
　*n.*17; 285 *n.*21, *n.*24, *n.*29,
　*n.*38; 286 *n.*40, *n.*41, *n.*42;
　288 *n.*17, 310 *n.*62, 312 *n.*70,
　331 *n.*1, *n.*5; 347
Weber, 155
Wensinck, A. J., 297 *n.*60, 347
Westermarck, Edvard Alexander,
　68, 115, 291 *n.*45, 293 *n.*3,
　*n.*8, *n.*9; 294 *n.*18, *n.*19, *n.*22,
　*n.*23, *n.*24; 295 *n.*32, 296 *n.*39,
　*n.*40, *n.*43; 297 *n.*58, 299 *n.*73,
　*n.*74; 301 *n.*114, 302 *n.*2, *n.*4,
　*n.*6; 303 *n.*12, 304 *n.*25, *n.*26;
　305 *n.*28, *n.*29, *n.*31, *n.*32,
　*n.*34; 306 *n.*35, *n.*36, *n.*37,
　*n.*38; 310 *n.*56, 312 *n.*76,
　317 *n.*65, 322 *n.*3, *n.*8; 347
Whitehurst, Robert N., 341
Wigmore, John H., 340
Winch, Robert F., 287 *n.*7,
　294 *n.*16, 299 *n.*82, 322 *n.*3,
　*n.*4, *n.*5; 324 *n.*34, 347
Winder, R. Bayly, 348
Wilkins, W. H., 335
Wolf, Eric, 284 *n.* 17, 285 *n.*21,
　*n.*24, *n.*27, *n.*29, *n.*34, *n.*39;
　286 *n.*41, 288 *n.*20, 347
Yaqūt Ibn 'Abd Allāh al
　Hamawī, 347